On the Plurality of Worlds

On the Plurality of Worlds

DAVID LEWIS

© 1986 by David Lewis

BLACKWELL PUBLISHING
350 Main Street, Malden, MA 02148-5020, USA
9600 Garsington Road, Oxford OX4 2DQ, UK
550 Swanston Street, Carlton, Victoria 3053, Australia

First published 1986
Reissued 2001

Library of Congress Cataloging in Publication Data

Lewis, David K., 1941-
     On the plurality of worlds / David Lewis.
          p. cm.
     First published: 1986.
     ISBN 978-0-6312-2496-9 (hbk. : alk. paper) — ISBN 978-0-6312-2426-6 (pbk. : alk. paper)
     1. Plurality of worlds. 2. Modality (Theory of Knowledge) 3. Realism. I. Title.
     BD655 .L48 2000
     111—dc21

                                                                          00-059900

A catalogue record for this title is available from the British Library.

Printed in the UK

For further information on
Blackwell Publishing, visit our website:
www.blackwellpublishing.com

Contents

Preface

This book defends modal realism: the thesis that the world we are part of is but one of a plurality of worlds, and that we who inhabit this world are only a few out of all the inhabitants of all the worlds.

I begin the first chapter by reviewing the many ways in which systematic philosophy goes more easily if we may presuppose modal realism in our analyses. I take this to be a good reason to think that modal realism is true, just as the utility of set theory in mathematics is a good reason to believe that there are sets. Then I state some tenets of the kind of modal realism I favour.

In the second chapter, I reply to numerous objections. First I consider arguments that modal realism leads to contradiction; and I reply by rejecting some premises that are needed to produce the paradoxes. Then I turn to arguments that modal realism leads to consistent but unwelcome views: inductive scepticism, a disregard for prudence and morality, or a loss of the brute arbitrariness of our world; and again I reply by finding premises to reject. Finally I consider the sheer implausibility of a theory so much at variance with commonsensical ideas about what there is; I take this to be a fair and serious objection, but outweighed by the systematic benefits that acceptance of modal realism brings.

In the third chapter, I consider the prospect that a more credible ontology might yield the same benefits: the programme of ersatz modal realism, in which other worlds are to be replaced by 'abstract' representations thereof. I advance objections against several versions of this programme. I urge that we must distinguish the different versions, since they are subject to different objections; it will not do to dodge trouble by favouring abstract ersatz worlds in the abstract, without giving any definite account of them.

In the fourth and final chapter, I consider the so-called 'problem of trans-world identity'. I divide it into several questions, some of them good and some of them confused, and I compare my counterpart-theoretic approach with some alternatives.

Nowhere in this book will you find an argument that you must accept the position I favour because there is no alternative. I believe that philosophers who offer such arguments are almost never successful, and philosophers who demand them are misguided. I give some reasons that favour my position over some of its close alternatives. But I do not think that these reasons are conclusive; I may well have overlooked some close alternatives; and I do not discuss more distant alternatives at all. For instance, I do not make any case against a hard-line actualism that rejects any sort of quantification over possibilities. You will find it easy enough to guess why I would not favour that view; I have nothing new, and nothing conclusive, to say against it; so it would serve no purpose to discuss it.

It may come as a surprise that this book on possible worlds also contains no discussion of the views of Leibniz. Is it that I consider him unworthy of serious attention? – Not at all. But when I read what serious historians of philosophy have to say, I am persuaded that it is no easy matter to know what his views were. It would be nice to have the right sort of talent and training to join in the work of exegesis, but it is very clear to me that I do not. Anything I might say about Leibniz would be amateurish, undeserving of others' attention, and better left unsaid.

About twelve years ago, I gave my thesis a bad name. I called it 'modal realism'. Had I foreseen present-day discussions of what 'realism' really is, I would certainly have called it something else. As it is, I think it best to stick with the old name. But I must insist that my modal realism is simply the thesis that there are other worlds, and individuals inhabiting these worlds; and that these are of a certain nature, and suited to play certain theoretical roles. It is an existential claim, not unlike the claim I would be making if I said that there were Loch Ness monsters, or Red moles in the CIA, or counterexamples to Fermat's conjecture, or seraphim. It is *not* a thesis about our semantic competence, or about the nature of truth, or about bivalence, or about the limits of our knowledge. For me, the question is of the existence of objects – not the objectivity of a subject matter.

At many points, I am greatly indebted to friends who have helped me by discussion or correspondence about topics covered in this book: especially Robert M. Adams, D. M. Armstrong, John G. Bennett, John Bigelow, Phillip Bricker, M. J. Cresswell, Peter Forrest, Allen Hazen, Mark Johnston, David Kaplan, Saul Kripke, Robert Stalnaker, Pavel Tichý and Peter van Inwagen.

Part of this book was delivered as the John Locke Lectures at the University of Oxford in Trinity Term, 1984. I am most honoured by Oxford's invitation; and I am most grateful to Oxford for providing me with the occasion to write on modal realism more fully than I had done before, and also with a much-needed deadline. I am grateful to Princeton University for sabbatical leave, and to the National Endowment for the Humanities for financial assistance, during the year in which most of this book was written.

1

A Philosophers' Paradise

1.1 The Thesis of Plurality of Worlds

The world we live in is a very inclusive thing. Every stick and every stone you have ever seen is part of it. And so are you and I. And so are the planet Earth, the solar system, the entire Milky Way, the remote galaxies we see through telescopes, and (if there are such things) all the bits of empty space between the stars and galaxies. There is nothing so far away from us as not to be part of our world. Anything at any distance at all is to be included. Likewise the world is inclusive in time. No long-gone ancient Romans, no long-gone pterodactyls, no long-gone primordial clouds of plasma are too far in the past, nor are the dead dark stars too far in the future, to be part of this same world. Maybe, as I myself think, the world is a big physical object; or maybe some parts of it are entelechies or spirits or auras or deities or other things unknown to physics. But nothing is so alien in kind as not to be part of our world, provided only that it does exist at some distance and direction from here, or at some time before or after or simultaneous with now.

The way things are, at its most inclusive, means the way this entire world is. But things might have been different, in ever so many ways. This book of mine might have been finished on schedule. Or, had I not been such a commonsensical chap, I might be defending not only a plurality of possible worlds, but also a plurality of impossible worlds, whereof you speak truly by contradicting yourself. Or I might not have existed at all – neither I myself, nor any counterpart of me. Or there might never have been any people. Or the physical constants might have had somewhat different values, incompatible with the emergence of life. Or there might have been altogether different laws of nature; and instead of electrons and quarks, there might have been alien particles, without charge or mass or spin but with alien physical properties that nothing

1

in this world shares. There are ever so many ways that a world might be; and one of these many ways is the way that this world is.

Are there other worlds that are other ways? I say there are. I advocate a thesis of plurality of worlds, or *modal realism*,[1] which holds that our world is but one world among many. There are countless other worlds, other very inclusive things. Our world consists of us and all our surroundings, however remote in time and space; just as it is one big thing having lesser things as parts, so likewise do other worlds have lesser other-worldly things as parts. The worlds are something like remote planets; except that most of them are much bigger than mere planets, and they are not remote. Neither are they nearby. They are not at any spatial distance whatever from here. They are not far in the past or future, nor for that matter near; they are not at any temporal distance whatever from now. They are isolated: there are no spatiotemporal relations at all between things that belong to different worlds. Nor does anything that happens at one world cause anything to happen at another. Nor do they overlap; they have no parts in common, with the exception, perhaps, of immanent universals exercising their characteristic privilege of repeated occurrence.

The worlds are many and varied. There are enough of them to afford worlds where (roughly speaking) I finish on schedule, or I write on behalf of *impossibilia*, or I do not exist, or there are no people at all, or the physical constants do not permit life, or totally different laws govern the doings of alien particles with alien properties. There are so many other worlds, in fact, that absolutely *every* way that a world could possibly be is a way that some world *is*. And as with worlds, so it is with parts of worlds. There are ever so many ways that a part of a world could be; and so many and so varied are the other worlds that absolutely every way that a part of a world could possibly be is a way that some part of some world is.

The other worlds are of a kind with this world of ours. To be sure, there are differences of kind between things that are parts of different worlds – one world has electrons and another has none, one has spirits and another has none – but these differences of kind are no more than sometimes arise between things that are parts of one single world, for instance in a world where electrons coexist with spirits. The difference between this and the other worlds is not a categorial difference.

Nor does this world differ from the others in its manner of existing. I do not have the slightest idea what a difference in manner of existing is supposed to be. Some things exist here on earth, other things exist extraterrestrially, perhaps some exist no place in particular; but that is no difference in manner of existing, merely a difference in location or

[1]Or 'extreme' modal realism, as Stalnaker calls it – but in what dimension does its extremity lie?

lack of it between things that exist. Likewise some things exist here at our world, others exist at other worlds; again, I take this to be a difference between things that exist, not a difference in their existing. You might say that strictly speaking, only this-worldly things *really* exist; and I am ready enough to agree; but on my view this 'strict' speaking is *restricted* speaking, on a par with saying that all the beer is in the fridge and ignoring most of all the beer there is. When we quantify over less than all there is, we leave out things that (unrestrictedly speaking) exist *simpliciter*. If I am right, other-worldly things exist *simpliciter*, though often it is very sensible to ignore them and quantify restrictedly over our worldmates. And if I am wrong, other-worldly things fail *simpliciter* to exist. They exist, as the Russell set does, only according to a false theory. That is not to exist in some inferior manner – what exists only according to some false theory just does not exist at all.

The worlds are not of our own making. It may happen that one part of a world makes other parts, as we do; and as other-worldly gods and demiurges do on a grander scale. But if worlds are causally isolated, nothing outside a world ever makes a world; and nothing inside makes the whole of a world, for that would be an impossible kind of self-causation. We make languages and concepts and descriptions and imaginary representations that apply to worlds. We make stipulations that select some worlds rather than others for our attention. Some of us even make assertions to the effect that other worlds exist. But none of these things we make are the worlds themselves.

Why believe in a plurality of worlds? – Because the hypothesis is serviceable, and that is a reason to think that it is true. The familiar analysis of necessity as truth at all possible worlds was only the beginning. In the last two decades, philosophers have offered a great many more analyses that make reference to possible worlds, or to possible individuals that inhabit possible worlds. I find that record most impressive. I think it is clear that talk of *possibilia* has clarified questions in many parts of the philosophy of logic, of mind, of language, and of science – not to mention metaphysics itself. Even those who officially scoff often cannot resist the temptation to help themselves abashedly to this useful way of speaking.

Hilbert called the set-theoretical universe a paradise for mathematicians. And he was right (though perhaps it was not he who should have said it). We have only to believe in the vast hierarchy of sets, and there we find entities suited to meet the needs of all the branches of mathematics;[2] and we find that the very meagre primitive vocabulary of set theory, definitionally extended, suffices to meet our needs for mathematical

---

[2]With the alleged exception of category theory – but here I wonder if the unmet needs have more to do with the motivational talk than with the real mathematics.

predicates; and we find that the meagre axioms of set theory are first principles enough to yield the theorems that are the content of the subject. Set theory offers the mathematician great economy of primitives and premises, in return for accepting rather a lot of entities unknown to *Homo javanensis*. It offers an improvement in what Quine calls ideology, paid for in the coin of ontology. It's an offer you can't refuse. The price is right; the benefits in theoretical unity and economy are well worth the entities. Philosophers might like to see the subject reconstructed or reconstrued; but working mathematicians insist on pursuing their subject in paradise, and will not be driven out. Their thesis of plurality of sets is fruitful; that gives them good reason to believe that it is true.

Good reason; I do not say it is conclusive. Maybe the price is higher than it seems because set theory has unacceptable hidden implications – maybe the next round of set-theoretical paradoxes will soon be upon us. Maybe the very idea of accepting controversial ontology for the sake of theoretical benefits is misguided – so a sceptical epistemologist might say, to which I reply that mathematics is better known than any premise of sceptical epistemology. Or perhaps some better paradise might be found. Some say that mathematics might be pursued in a paradise of *possibilia*, full of unactualised idealisations of things around us, or of things we do – if so, the parallel with mathematics serves my purpose better than ever! Conceivably we might find some way to accept set theory, just as is and just as nice a home for mathematics, without any ontological commitment to sets. But even if such hopes come true, my point remains. It has been the judgement of mathematicians, which modest philosophers ought to respect, that *if* that is indeed the choice before us, then it is worth believing in vast realms of controversial entities for the sake of enough benefit in unity and economy of theory.

As the realm of sets is for mathematicians, so logical space is a paradise for philosophers. We have only to believe in the vast realm of *possibilia*, and there we find what we need to advance our endeavours. We find the wherewithal to reduce the diversity of notions we must accept as primitive, and thereby to improve the unity and economy of the theory that is our professional concern – total theory, the whole of what we take to be true. What price paradise? If we want the theoretical benefits that talk of *possibilia* brings, the most straightforward way to gain honest title to them is to accept such talk as the literal truth. It is my view that the price is right, if less spectacularly so than in the mathematical parallel. The benefits are worth their ontological cost. Modal realism is fruitful; that gives us good reason to believe that it is true.

Good reason; I do not say it is conclusive. Maybe the theoretical benefits to be gained are illusory, because the analyses that use *possibilia* do not succeed on their own terms. Maybe the price is higher than it seems, because modal realism has unacceptable hidden implications. Maybe the price is *not* right; even if I am right about what theoretical benefits can be had for what ontological cost, maybe those benefits just are not worth those costs. Maybe the very idea of accepting controversial ontology for the sake of theoretical benefits is misguided. Maybe – and this is the doubt that most interests me – the benefits are not worth the cost, because they can be had more cheaply elsewhere. Some of these doubts are too complicated to address here, or too simple to address at all; others will come in for discussion in the course of this book.

1.2 Modal Realism at Work: Modality

In the next four sections, I consider what possible worlds and individuals are good for. Even a long discussion might be too short to convince all readers that the applications I have in mind are workable at all, still less that approaches employing *possibilia* are superior to all conceivable rivals. (Still less that *possibilia* are absolutely indispensable, something I don't believe myself.) Each application could have a book of its own. Here I shall settle for less.

The best known application is to modality. Presumably, whatever it may mean to call a world actual (see section 1.9), it had better turn out that the world we are part of is the actual world. What actually is the case, as we say, is what goes on here. That is one possible way for a world to be. Other worlds are other, that is *un*actualised, possibilities. If there are many worlds, and every way that a world could possibly be is a way that some world is, then whenever such-and-such might be the case, there is some world where such-and-such is the case. Conversely, since it is safe to say that no world is any way that a world could not possibly be, whenever there is some world at which such-and-such is the case, then it might be that such-and-such is the case. So modality turns into quantification: possibly there are blue swans iff, for some world W, at W there are blue swans.

But not just quantification: there is also the phrase 'at W' which appears within the scope of the quantifier, and which needs explaining. It works mainly by restricting the domains of quantifiers in its scope, in much the same way that the restricting modifier 'in Australia' does. In Australia, all swans are black – all swans are indeed black, if we ignore everything not in Australia; quantifying only over things in Australia, all swans are black. At some strange world W, all swans are blue – all swans are indeed blue, if we ignore everything not part of the world W; quantifying only over things that are part of W, all swans are blue.

Such modifiers have various other effects. For one thing, they influence the interpretation of expressions that are not explicitly quantificational, but that reveal implicit quantification under analysis: definite descriptions and singular terms definable by them, class abstracts and plurals, superlatives, etc. An example: it is the case at world W that nine numbers the solar planets iff nine numbers those solar planets that are part of W. Another example: words like 'invent' and 'discover' are implicitly superlative, hence implicitly quantificational; they imply doing something *first*, before *anyone* else did. So the inventor of bifocals at W is the one who is part of W and thought of bifocals before anyone else who is part of W did. For another thing, besides restricting explicit or implicit quantifiers, our modifiers can restrict proper names. In Australia, and likewise at a possible world where the counterparts of British cities are strangely rearranged, Cardiff is a suburb of Newcastle – there are various places of those names, and we banish ambiguity by restricting our attention to the proper domain. Here I am supposing that the way we bestow names attaches them not only to this-worldly things, but also to other-worldly counterparts thereof. That is how the other-worldly Cardiffs and Newcastles bear those names in our this-worldly language. In the same way, the solar planets at W are those that orbit the star Sol of the world W, a counterpart of the Sol of this world. Natural language being complex, doubtless I have not listed all the effects of our modifiers. But I believe the principle will always stay the same: whatever they do, they do it by instructing us, within limits, to take account only of things that are part of a limited domain – the domain of things in Australia, or the domain of parts of a certain world.

Two qualifications concerning our restrictive modifiers. (1) I do not suppose that they must restrict all quantifiers in their scope, without exception. 'In Australia, there is a yacht faster than any other' would mean less than it does if the modifier restricted both quantifiers rather than just the first. 'Nowadays there are rulers more dangerous than any ancient Roman' would be trivialised if we ignored those ancient Romans who are not alive nowadays. 'At some small worlds, there is a natural number too big to measure any class of individuals' can be true even if the large number that makes it true is no part of the small world. (2) Of course there will usually be other restrictions as well; doubtless we are already ignoring various immigrant swans and their descendants, and also whatever freak or painted swans there may be in Australia or among the parts of world W, so our modifier 'in Australia' or 'at W' adds more restrictions to the ones already in force. In short, while our modifiers tend to impose restrictions on quantifiers, names, etc., a lot is left up to the pragmatic rule that what is said should be interpreted so as to be sensible. If that means adding extra tacit restrictions, or waiving some of the restrictions imposed by our modifiers, then – within limits – so be it.[3]

As possibility amounts to existential quantification over the worlds, with restricting modifiers inside the quantifiers, so necessity amounts to universal quantification. Necessarily all swans are birds iff, for any world W, quantifying only over parts of W, all swans are birds. More simply: iff all swans, no matter what world they are part of, are birds. The other modalities follow suit. What is impossible is the case at no worlds; what is contingent is the case at some but not at others.

More often than not, modality is *restricted* quantification; and restricted from the standpoint of a given world, perhaps ours, by means of so-called 'accessibility' relations. Thus it is nomologically necessary, though not unrestrictedly necessary, that friction produces heat: at every world that obeys the laws of our world, friction produces heat. It is contingent which world is ours; hence what are the laws of our world; hence which worlds are nomologically 'accessible' from ours; hence what is true throughout these worlds, i.e. what is nomologically necessary.

Likewise it is historically necessary, now as I write these words, that my book is at least partly written: at every world that perfectly matches ours up to now, and diverges only later if ever, the book is at least partly written.

---

[3]This discussion of restricting modifiers enables me to say why I have no use for impossible worlds, on a par with the possible worlds. For comparison, suppose travellers told of a place in this world – a marvellous mountain, far away in the bush – where contradictions are true. Allegedly we have truths of the form 'On the mountain both P and not P'. But if 'on the mountain' is a restricting modifier, which works by limiting domains of implicit and explicit quantification to a certain part of all that there is, then it has no effect on the truth-functional connectives. Then the order of modifier and connectives makes no difference. So 'On the mountain both P and Q' is equivalent to 'On the mountain P, and on the mountain Q'; likewise 'On the mountain not P' is equivalent to 'Not: on the mountain P'; putting these together, the alleged truth 'On the mountain both P and not P' is equivalent to the overt contradiction 'On the mountain P, and not: on the mountain P'. That is, there is no difference between a contradiction within the scope of the modifier and a plain contradiction that has the modifier within it. So to tell the alleged truth about the marvellously contradictory things that happen on the mountain is no different from contradicting yourself. But there is no subject matter, however marvellous, about which you can tell the truth by contradicting yourself. Therefore there is no mountain where contradictions are true. An impossible world where contradictions are true would be no better. The alleged truth about its contradictory goings-on would itself be contradictory. At least, that is so if I am right that 'at so-and-so world' is a restricting modifier. Other modifiers are another story. 'According to the Bible' or 'Fred says that' are *not* restricting modifiers; they do not pass through the truth-functional connectives. 'Fred says that not P' and 'Not: Fred says that P' are independent: both, either, or neither might be true. If worlds were like stories or story-tellers, there would indeed be room for worlds according to which contradictions are true. The sad truth about the prevarications of these worlds would not itself be contradictory. But worlds, as I understand them, are *not* like stories or story-tellers. They are like this world; and this world is no story, not even a true story. Nor should worlds be replaced by their stories, for reasons discussed in section 3.2.

Putting together nomological and historical accessibility restrictions, we get the proper treatment of predetermination – a definition free of red herrings about what can in principle be known and computed, or about the analysis of causation. It was predetermined at his creation that Adam would sin iff he does so at every world that both obeys the laws of our world and perfectly matches the history of our world up through the moment of Adam's creation.

As other worlds are alternative possibilities for an entire world, so the parts of other worlds are alternative possibilities for lesser individuals. Modality *de re*, the potentiality and essence of things, is quantification over possible individuals. As quantification over possible worlds is commonly restricted by accessibility relations, so quantification over possible individuals is commonly restricted by counterpart relations. In both cases, the restrictive relations usually involve similarity. A nomologically or historically accessible world is similar to our world in the laws it obeys, or in its history up to some time. Likewise a counterpart of Oxford is similar to Oxford in its origins, or in its location *vis-à-vis* (counterparts of) other places, or in the arrangement and nature of its parts, or in the role it plays in the life of a nation or a discipline. Thus Oxford might be noted more for the manufacture of locomotives than of motor cars, or might have been a famous centre for the study of paraconsistent hermeneutics, iff some other-worldly counterpart of our Oxford, under some suitable counterpart relation, enjoys these distinctions.

Sometimes one hears a short list of the restricted modalities: nomological, historical, epistemic, deontic, maybe one or two more. And sometimes one is expected to take a position, once and for all, about what is or isn't possible *de re* for an individual. I would suggest instead that the restricting of modalities by accessibility or counterpart relations, like the restricting of quantifiers generally, is a very fluid sort of affair: inconstant, somewhat indeterminate, and subject to instant change in response to contextual pressures. Not anything goes, but a great deal does. And to a substantial extent, saying so makes it so: if you say what would only be true under certain restrictions, and your conversational partners acquiesce, straightway those restrictions come into force.[4]

The standard language of modal logic provides just two modal expressions: the diamond, read as 'possibly', and the box, read as 'necessarily'. Both are sentential operators: they attach to sentences to make sentences, or

---

[4]See section 4.5; Kratzer, 'What "Must" and "Can" Must and Can Mean'; and my 'Scorekeeping in a Language Game'.

to open formulas to make open formulas. So a modal logician will write

$\Diamond$ for some x, x is a swan and x is blue

to mean that possibly some swan is blue, i.e. that there might be a blue swan; or

$\Box$ for all x, if x is a swan then x is a bird

to mean that necessarily all swans are birds. Likewise

$\Diamond$ x is blue

is a formula satisfied by anything that could possibly be blue, and

$\Box$ x is a bird

is a formula satisfied by anything that must necessarily be a bird. When they attach to sentences we can take the diamond and the box as quantifiers, often restricted, over possible worlds. How to take them when they attach to open formulas – sentential expressions with unbound variables – is more questionable.

A simple account would be that in that case also they are just quantifiers over worlds. But that raises a question. Start with something that is part of this world: Hubert Humphrey, say. He might have won the presidency but didn't, so he satisfies the modal formula 'possibly x wins' but not the formula 'x wins'. Taking the diamond 'possibly' as a quantifier over worlds, (perhaps restricted, but let me ignore that), that means that there is some world W such that, at W, he satisfies 'x wins'. But how does he do that if he isn't even part of W?

You might reply that he *is* part of W as well as part of this world. If this means that the whole of him is part of W, I reject that for reasons to be given in section 4.2; if it means that part of him is part of W, I reject that for reasons to be given in section 4.3. Then to save the simple account, we have to say that Humphrey needn't be part of a world to satisfy formulas there; there is a world where somehow he satisfies 'x wins' *in absentia*.

We might prefer a more complex account of how modal operators work.[5] We might say that when 'possibly' is attached to open formulas, it is a quantifier not just over worlds but also over other-worldly counterparts of this-worldly individuals; so that Humphrey satisfies

---

[5]This is essentially the account I gave in 'Counterpart Theory and Quantified Modal Logic'.

'possibly x wins' iff, for some world W, for some counterpart of Humphrey in W, that counterpart satisfies 'x wins' at W. The satisfaction of 'x wins' by the counterpart is unproblematic. Now we need no satisfaction *in absentia*.

The simple and complex accounts are not in competition. Both do equally well, because there is a counterpart-theoretic account of satisfaction *in absentia* that makes them come out equivalent. Satisfaction *in absentia* is vicarious satisfaction: Humphrey satisfies 'x wins' vicariously at any world where he has a winning counterpart. Then according to both accounts alike, he satisfies 'possibly x wins' iff at some world he has a counterpart who wins. -

The box and diamond are interdefinable: 'necessarily' means 'not possibly not'. So what I have said for one carries over to the other. According to the simple account, Humphrey satisfies the modal formula 'necessarily x is human' iff it is not the case that there is some world W such that, at W, he satisfies 'x is not human'; that is, iff at no world does he satisfy – *in absentia* or otherwise – x is not human'. According to the complex account, Humphrey satisfies 'necessarily x is human' iff it is not the case that for some world W, for some counterpart of Humphrey in W, that counterpart satisfies 'x is not human' at W; that is, iff there is no counterpart in any world of Humphrey who satisfies 'x is not human'. Taking satisfaction *in absentia* to be vicarious satisfaction through a counterpart, the simple and complex accounts again agree: Humphrey satisfies 'necessarily x is human' iff he has no non-human counterpart at any world.

(It is plausible enough that Humphrey has no non-human counterpart. Or, if I am right to say that counterpart relations are an inconstant and indeterminate affair, at any rate it is plausible enough that there is *some* reasonable counterpart relation under which Humphrey has no non-human counterpart – so let's fix on such a counterpart relation for the sake of the example.)

The alert or informed reader will know that if what I've said about how Humphrey satisfies modal formulas sounds right, that is only because I took care to pick the right examples. A famous problem arises if instead we consider whether Humphrey satisfies modal formulas having to do with the contingency of his existence. According to what I've said, be it in the simple or the complex formulation, Humphrey satisfies 'necessarily x exists' and fails to satisfy 'possibly x does not exist' iff he has no counterpart at any world W who does not exist at W. But what can it mean to say that the counterpart is 'at W' if not that, at W, the counterpart exists?[6] So it seems that Humphrey *does* satisfy 'necessarily

[6]We might just *say* it, and not mean anything by it. That is Forbes's solution to our present difficulty, in his so-called 'canonical counterpart theory' – my own version is

x exists' and *doesn't* satisfy 'possibly x does not exist'. That is wrong. For all his virtues, still it really will not do to elevate Humphrey to the ranks of the Necessary Beings.

What I want to say, of course, is that Humphrey exists necessarily iff at every world he has some counterpart, which he doesn't; he has the possibility of not existing iff at some world he lacks a counterpart, which he does. It's all very well to say this; but the problem is to square it with my general account of the satisfaction of modal formulas.

So shall we give a revised account of the satisfaction of modal formulas? Should we say that Humphrey satisfies 'necessarily ϕx' iff at every world he has some counterpart who satisfies 'ϕx'? Then, by the interdefinability of box and diamond, Humphrey satisfies 'possibly x is a cat' iff it is not the case that at every world he has some counterpart who satisfies 'not x is a cat'; and indeed that is not the case, since at some worlds he has no counterparts at all; so it seems that he *does* satisfy 'possibly x is a cat' even if he has not a single cat among his counterparts! This is no improvement. What next?

Shall we dump the method of counterparts? – That wouldn't help, because we can recreate the problem in a far more neutral framework. Let us suppose only this much. (1) We want to treat the modal operators simply as quantifiers over worlds. (2) We want to grant that Humphrey somehow satisfies various formulas at various other worlds, never mind how he does it. (3) We want it to come out that he satisfies the modal formula 'necessarily x is human', since that seems to be the way to say something true, namely that he is essentially human. (4) We want it to come out that he satisfies the modal formula 'possibly x does not exist', since that seems to be the way to say something else true, namely that he might not have existed. (5) We want it to come out that he does *not* satisfy the model formula 'possibly x is human and x does not exist' since that seems to be the way to say something false, namely that he might have been human without even existing. So he satisfies 'x is human' at all worlds and 'x does not exist' at some worlds; so he satisfies both of them at some worlds; yet though he satisfies both conjuncts he doesn't satisfy their conjunction! How can that be?

---

hereby named 'official standard counterpart theory' – in which, if Humphrey has no ordinary counterpart among the things which exist at W, he does nevertheless have a counterpart at W. This extraordinary counterpart is none other than Humphrey himself – he then gets in as a sort of associate member of W's population, belonging to its 'outer domain' but not to the 'inner domain' of things that exist there fair and square. This isn't explained, but really it needn't be. It amounts to a stipulation that there are two different ways that Humphrey – he himself, safe at home in this world – can satisfy formulas *in absentia*. Where he has proper counterparts, he does it one way, namely the ordinary vicarious way. Where he doesn't, he does it another way – just by not being there he satisfies 'x does not exist'.

There might be a fallacy of equivocation. Maybe what it means for Humphrey to satisfy a formula *in absentia* is different in the case of different kinds of formulas, or in the case of different kinds of worlds. Maybe, for instance, he can satisfy 'x does not exist' at a world by not having a counterpart there; but to satisfy 'x is human' at a world he has to have a counterpart there who is human, and to satisfy 'x is human and x does not exist' he would have to have one who was human and yet did not exist. Or maybe the language is uniformly ambiguous, and different cases invite different disambiguations. Either way, that would disappoint anyone who hopes that the language of quantified modal logic will be a well-behaved formal language, free of ambiguity and free of devious semantic rules that work different ways in different cases.

Or maybe the satisfying of modal formulas does not always mean what we would intuitively take it to mean after we learn how to pronounce the box and diamond. Maybe, for instance, saying that Humphrey satisfies 'necessarily x is human' is *not* the right way to say that he is essentially human. That would disappoint anyone who hopes that the language of boxes and diamonds affords a good regimentation of our ordinary modal thought.

Whichever it is, the friend of boxes and diamonds is in for a disappointment. He can pick his disappointment to suit himself. He can lay down uniform and unambiguous semantic rules for a regimented formal language – and re-educate his intuitions about how to translate between that language and ordinary modal talk. He can discipline himself, for instance, never to say 'necessarily human' when he means 'essentially human'; but instead, always to say 'necessarily such that it is human if it exists'. Alternatively, he can build his language more on the pattern of what we ordinarily say – and equip it either with outright ambiguities, or else with devious rules that look at what a formula says before they know what it means to satisfy it.[7]

What is the correct counterpart-theoretic interpretation of the modal formulas of the standard language of quantified modal logic? – Who cares? We can make them mean whatever we like. We are their master. We needn't be faithful to the meanings we learned at mother's knee – because we didn't. If this language of boxes and diamonds proves to be a clumsy instrument for talking about matters of essence and potentiality,

[7]If he likes, he can give himself more than one of these disappointments. As I noted, Forbes's talk of non-existent counterparts in outer domains amounts to a stipulation that satisfaction *in absentia* works different ways in different cases; so I find it strange that he offers it in rejoinder to a proposal of Hunter and Seager that modal formulas of parallel form needn't always be given parallel counterpart-theoretic translations. But this divided treatment does not pay off by making the modal formulas mean what we would offhand expect them to – it is exactly the non-existent counterparts in the outer domains that keep Humphrey from satisfying 'necessarily x is human' even if he is essentially human.

let it go hang. Use the resources of modal realism *directly* to say what it would mean for Humphrey to be essentially human, or to exist contingently.

In any case, modality is not all diamonds and boxes. Ordinary language has modal idioms that outrun the resources of standard modal logic, though of course you will be able to propose extensions. Allen Hazen mentions several examples of this in his 'Expressive Completeness in Modal Languages'. But let me mention some more.

There is what I take to be numerical quantification: it might happen in three different ways that a donkey talks iff three possible individuals, very different from one another, are donkeys that talk. It scarcely seems possible to cover the entire infinite family of numerical modalities unless we resort to the pre-existing apparatus of numerical quantification. Then we need some entities to be the 'ways' that we quantify over. My candidates are the possible worlds and individuals themselves, or else sets of these.

There are modalised comparatives: a red thing could resemble an orange thing more closely than a red thing could resemble a blue thing. I analyse that as a quantified statement of comparative resemblance involving coloured things which may be parts of different worlds.

For some x and y (x is red and y is orange and
   for all u and v (if u is red and v is blue, then
     x resembles y more than u resembles v))

Try saying that in standard modal logic. The problem is that formulas get evaluated relative to a world, which leaves no room for cross-world comparisons.

Maybe you can solve the problem if you replace the original comparative relation '. . . resembles . . . more than . . . resembles . . .' by some fancy analysis of it, say in terms of numerical measures of degrees of resemblance and numerical inequalities of these degrees. After that, you might be able to do the rest with boxes and diamonds. The fancy analysis might be correct. But still, I suggest that your solution is no fair. For that's not how the English does it. The English does not introduce degrees of resemblance. It sticks with the original comparative relation, and modalises it with the auxiliary 'could'. But this 'could' does not behave like the standard sentence-modifying diamond, making a sentence which is true if the modified sentence could be true. *I* think its effect is to unrestrict quantifiers which would normally range over this-worldly things. The moral for me is that we'd better have other-worldly things to quantify over. I suppose the moral for a friend of primitive modality is that he has more on his plate than he thinks he has: other primitive modal idioms than just his boxes and diamonds.

Another modal notion which is badly served by diamonds and boxes is supervenience. The idea is simple and easy: we have supervenience when there could be no difference of one sort without differences of another sort. At least, this *seems* simple and easy enough; and yet in recent discussions[8] we get an unlovely proliferation of non-equivalent definitions. Some stick close to the original idea but seem too weak; others seem strong enough but out of touch with the original idea. A useful notion threatens to fade away into confusion. I offer this diagnosis of the trouble. There really *is* just one simple, easy, useful idea. However, it is unavailable to those who assume that all modality must come packaged in boxes and diamonds. Therefore we get a plethora of unsatisfactory approximations and substitutes.

To see why there is a problem about formulating supervenience theses, we need a few examples. First, a fairly uncontroversial one. A dot-matrix picture has global properties – it is symmetrical, it is cluttered, and whatnot – and yet all there is to the picture is dots and non-dots at each point of the matrix. The global properties are nothing but patterns in the dots. They supervene: no two pictures could differ in their global properties without differing, somewhere, in whether there is or isn't a dot.

A second example is more controversial and interesting. The world has its laws of nature, its chances and causal relationships; and yet – perhaps! – all there is to the world is its point-by-point distribution of local qualitative character. We have a spatiotemporal arrangement of points. At each point various local intrinsic properties may be present, instantiated perhaps by the point itself or perhaps by point-sized bits of matter or of fields that are located there. There may be properties of mass, charge, quark colour and flavour, field strength, and the like; and maybe others besides, if physics as we know it is inadequate to its descriptive task. Is that all? Are the laws, chances, and causal relationships nothing but patterns which supervene on this point-by-point distribution of properties? Could two worlds differ in their laws without differing, somehow, somewhere, in local qualitative character? (I discuss this question of 'Humean supervenience', inconclusively, in the Introduction to my *Philosophical Papers*, volume II.)

A third example. A person has a mental life of attitudes and experiences and yet – perhaps! – all there is to him is an arrangement of physical particles, interacting in accordance with physical laws. Does the mental supervene on the physical? We can distinguish two questions. (1) *Narrow* psychophysical supervenience: could two people differ mentally without

8Surveyed in Teller, 'A Poor Man's Guide to Supervenience and Determination'.

also themselves differing physically? (2) *Broad* psychophysical super-venience: could two people differ mentally without there being a physical difference somewhere, whether in the people themselves or somewhere in their surroundings? We can also distinguish questions in another way, cross-cutting the distinction of narrow and broad, depending on how restricted a range of possibilities we consider. If we restrict ourselves to worlds that obey the actual laws of nature, then even a dualist might accept some kind of psychophysical supervenience, if he believes in strict laws of psychophysical correlation. If we impose no restriction at all, then even a staunch materialist might reject all kinds of psychophysical supervenience, if he takes materialism to be a contingent truth. If we want to define materialism in terms of psychophysical supervenience, we will have to steer between these extremes.[9]

Supervenience means that there *could* be no difference of the one sort without difference of the other sort. Clearly, this 'could' indicates modality. Without the modality we have nothing of interest. No two dot-for-dot duplicate pictures differ in symmetry; they could not, and that is why symmetry is nothing but a pattern in the arrangement of dots. Maybe also it happens that no two dot-for-dot duplicate pictures differ in their origins. But if so, that just means that a certain sort of coincidence happens not to have occurred; it doesn't mean that the origin of a picture is nothing but a pattern in the arrangement of dots. Dot-for-dot duplicates perfectly well could come from different origins, whether or not they ever actually do.

So we might read the 'could' as a diamond – a modal operator 'possibly' which modifies sentences. 'There could be no difference of the one sort without difference of the other sort' – read this to mean that it is not the case that, possibly, there are two things which have a difference of the one sort without any difference of the other sort. That is: it is not the case that there is some world W such that, at W, two things have a difference of the one sort but not the other. That is, taking 'at W' as usual as a restricting modifier: there is no world wherein two things have a difference of the one sort but not the other. Is this an adequate way to formulate supervenience?

Sometimes it is. It will do well enough to state our supervenience theses about dot-matrix pictures. Symmetry (or whatnot) supervenes on the arrangement of the dots iff there is no world wherein two pictures differ in symmetry without differing in their arrangement of dots. It will do also to state narrow psychophysical supervenience: that thesis says that there is no world (or, none within a certain restriction) wherein two people differ mentally without themselves differing physically. So far, so good.

[9]See Kim, 'Psychophysical Supervenience', and my 'New Work for a Theory of Universals'.

But sometimes the formulation with a diamond is not adequate. We start to hit trouble with the thesis of broad psychophysical supervenience. The idea is that the mental supervenes on the physical; however, the physical pattern that is relevant to a given person's mental life might extend indefinitely far outside that person and into his surroundings. Then the thesis we want says that there could be no mental difference between two people without there being some physical difference, whether intrinsic or extrinsic, between them. Reading the 'could' as a diamond, the thesis becomes this: there is no world (or, none within a certain restriction) wherein two people differ mentally without there being some physical difference, intrinsic or extrinsic, between them. That is not quite right. We have gratuitously limited our attention to physical differences between two people in the same world, and that means ignoring those extrinsic physical differences that only ever arise between people in different worlds. For instance, we ignore the difference there is between two people if one inhabits a Riemannian and the other a Lobachevskian spacetime. So what we have said is not quite what we meant to say, but rather this: there could be no mental differences without some physical difference *of the sort that could arise between people in the same world*. The italicised part is a gratuitous addition. Perhaps it scarcely matters here. For it doesn't seem that the sort of very extrinsic physical difference that could never arise between people in the same world would make much difference to mental life. Nevertheless, insistence on reading the 'could' as a diamond has distorted the intended meaning.

For a case where the distortion is much more serious, take my second example: the supervenience of laws. We wanted to ask whether two worlds could differ in their laws without differing in their distribution of local qualitative character. But if we read the 'could' as a diamond, the thesis in question turns into this: it is not the case that, possibly, two worlds differ in their laws without differing in their distribution of local qualitative character. In other words: there is no world wherein two worlds differ in their laws without differing in their distribution of local qualitative character. That's trivial – there is no world wherein two worlds do anything. At any one world W, there is only the one single world W. The sentential modal operator disastrously restricts the quantification over worlds that lies within its scope. Better to leave it off. But we need *something* modal – the thesis is not just that the one actual world, with its one distribution of local qualitative character, has its one system of laws![10]

[10]One more example of the same sort of distortion. Let *naturalism* be the thesis that whether one's conduct is right supervenes on natural facts, so that one person could do right and another do wrong only if there were some difference in natural facts between the two – as it might be, a difference in their behaviour or their circumstances. Consider the theory that, necessarily, right conduct is conduct that conforms to divinely

What we want is modality, but not the sentential modal operator. The original simple statement of supervenience is the right one; in all cases: there *could* be no difference of the one sort without difference of the other sort. What got us into trouble was to insist on reading 'could' as a diamond. Just as in the case of modalised comparatives, the real effect of the 'could' seems to be to *un*restrict quantifiers which would normally range over this-worldly things. Among all the worlds, or among all the things in all the worlds (or less than all, in case there is some restriction), there is no difference of the one sort without difference of the other sort. Whether the things that differ are part of the same world is neither here nor there. Again the moral is that we'd better have other-worldly things to quantify over – not just a primitive modal modifier of sentences.

When I say that possible worlds help with the analysis of modality, I do not mean that they help with the metalogical 'semantical analysis of modal logic'. Recent interest in possible worlds began there, to be sure. But wrongly. For that job, we need no possible worlds. We need sets of entities which, for heuristic guidance, 'may be regarded as' possible worlds, but which in truth may be anything you please. We are doing mathematics, not metaphysics. Where we need possible worlds, rather, is in applying the results of these metalogical investigations. Metalogical results, by themselves, answer no questions about the logic of modality. They give us conditional answers only: if modal operators can be correctly analysed in so-and-so way, then they obey so-and-so system of modal logic. We must consider whether they may indeed be so analysed; and then we are doing metaphysics, not mathematics.

Once upon a time, there were a number of formal systems of sentential modal logic. (Also of quantified modal logic, but I shall not discuss those further.) Their modal operators, box and diamond, were said to mean 'necessarily' and 'possibly', but were not interpreted as quantifiers over

---

willed universal maxims. Suppose it is contingent what, if anything, is divinely willed. And suppose that facts about what is divinely willed are supernatural, not natural, facts. You might well expect that this divine-will theory of rightness would contradict naturalism; for if two people are alike so far as natural facts are concerned, but one of them lives in a world where prayer is divinely willed and the other lives in a world where blasphemy is divinely willed, then what is right for the first is not right for the second. But if we read the 'could' as a diamond, we get an unexpected answer. A difference in what universal maxims are divinely willed never could be a difference between two people in the same world. Within a single world, the only differences relevant to rightness are natural differences, such as the difference between one who prays and one who blasphemes. So indeed there is no world wherein one person does right and another does wrong without any difference in natural facts between the two. So either this divine-will theory of rightness is naturalistic after all; or else – more likely – something has gone amiss with our understanding of supervenience.

worlds. These systems differed from one another mostly by including or excluding various controversial axioms about iterated modality, most prominently these:

(B)   If P, then necessarily possibly P.

(4)   If necessarily P, then necessarily necessarily P.

(E)   If possibly P, then necessarily possibly P.

It was possible to investigate the deductive interrelations and consequences of various modal principles. For instance, given the plausible further axiom

(T)   If P, then possibly P.

and a fairly minimal (but not entirely uncontroversial) basic system K,[11] it turns out that (E) can be deduced from (B) and (4) together, and conversely. But what was not possible was to intuit clearly which of these principles were to be accepted, and why; or even to command a clear view of what was at issue.

At this point it was discovered, by several people at about the same time, that if you interpret the box and diamond as restricted quantifiers over a set of entities 'regarded as possible worlds', then (B), (4), (E), and (T) turn out to correspond to simple conditions on the relation whereby the box and diamond are restricted.[12] We spell this out as follows. A (*relational*) *frame* consists of a non-empty set – call it the set of *indices* – and a binary relation R on the indices. A *valuation* for the language of a

---

[11]K is given by rules of truth-functional implication; the rule that any substitution instance of a theorem is a theorem; the rule of interchange of equivalents, which says that if 'ϕ_1 iff ϕ_2' is a theorem, and $-\phi_2-$ comes from $-\phi_1-$ by substituting ϕ_2 for ϕ_1 at one or more places, then '$-\phi_1-$ iff $-\phi_2-$' is a theorem; and three axioms:

Possibly P iff not necessarily not P.

Necessarily (P and Q) iff (necessarily P and necessarily Q).

Necessarily (P iff P).

When a new system is made by adding further axioms to K, it is understood that the word 'theorem' in the rules of substitution and interchange applies to all theorems of the new system.

[12]The first discussions of this, some much more developed than others, are Hintikka, 'Quantifiers in Deontic Logic'; Kanger, *Provability in Logic*; Kripke, 'A Completeness Theorem in Modal Logic'; and Montague, 'Logical Necessity, Physical Necessity, Ethics, and Quantifiers'. There is also unpublished work of C. A. Meredith, reported in Prior, *Past, Present and Future*, page 42. A well known early discussion is Kripke, 'Semantical Considerations on Modal Logic'.

system of modal logic over a frame specifies a truth value for every sentence of the language at every index, and does so in conformity to the standard rules for the truth-functional connectives together with the following rules for modal operators:

'Necessarily ϕ' is true at i iff ϕ is true at all j such that iRj.

'Possibly ϕ' is true at i iff ϕ is true at some j such that iRj.

(Here is where we treat the modal operators as restricted quantifiers.) A frame *validates* a sentence iff every valuation over that frame makes that sentence true at every index; and validates a system of modal logic iff it validates every theorem of that system. Given the following correspondence between our axioms and conditions on frames –

(B) corresponds to being symmetric: if iRj, then jRi

(4) corresponds to being transitive: if iRj and jRk, then iRk

(E) corresponds to being 'euclidean': if iRj and iRk, then jRk

(T) corresponds to being reflexive: iRi

it is easy to see that by adding any combination of zero or more axioms to the basic system K, we get a system that is validated by all frames that satisfy the corresponding combination of conditions. Further, every such system is *complete* in the sense that if any sentence is validated by all frames that validate the system, then that sentence already is a theorem of the system. The same is true for a very much longer list of corresponding axioms and conditions. The results can be extended to quantified modal logic, and related results are available for systems weaker than K.

These metalogical investigations seemed to cast light on the status of the controversial axioms. Maybe we didn't yet know whether the axioms were to be accepted, but at least we now knew what was at issue. Old questions could give way to new. Instead of asking the baffling question whether whatever is actual is necessarily possible, we could try asking: is the relation R symmetric?

But in truth the metalogical results, just by themselves, cast no light at all. *If* the modal operators can be correctly interpreted as quantifiers over the indices of some or other frame, restricted by the relation of that frame, *then* we have found out where to look for illumination about controversial axioms. If not, not. To apply the results, you have to incur a commitment to some substantive analysis of modality. To be sure, you might not have to be a genuine modal realist like me. You might prefer an analysis on which the modal operators are quantifiers over some sort of abstract ersatz worlds – linguistic descriptions, maybe. (If you meant that as a fully general analysis of modality, I would raise several objections; see section 3.2. If you meant it to apply only in certain limited cases, for instance to modal talk about how a chess game might have gone, I would not object at all.) But if the metalogical results are to be at all relevant to modality, *some* quantificational analysis has to be correct. If modal operators were quantifiers over towns restricted by the relation of being connected by rail, that would validate some system or other of modal logic. – So what, since modal operators are nothing of the sort? What good is it to know which *mis*interpretations would validate a system?

I myself, of course, do think that modal operators are quantifiers over possible worlds; that very often they are restricted; and that the applicable restriction may be different from the standpoint of different worlds, and so may be given by a relation of 'accessibility'. Therefore I do not just think that the indices of frames 'may be regarded as' possible worlds. I think that among all the frames, there are some whose indices *are* the possible worlds; and that among such frames there are some whose relations *do* give the correct restrictions on modal operators (correct for appropriate contexts). So for me, the metalogical results are applicable, because I believe that there exist frames which afford correct interpretations of the modal operators.

Return to an example I mentioned before: it is nomologically necessary that friction produces heat because at every world nomologically accessible from ours – every world that obeys the laws of ours – friction produces heat. Then, indeed, puzzling questions about the logic of iterated nomological necessity turn into more tractable questions about the relation of nomological accessibility. Is it symmetric? Transitive? Euclidean? Reflexive? In other words, is it so that whenever world W_1 obeys the laws of W_0, then also W_0 obeys the laws of W_1? Is it so that whenever W_2 obeys the laws of W_1 which in turn obeys the laws of W_0, then W_2 obeys the laws of W_0? Is it so that whenever W_1 and W_2 both obey the laws of W_0, then they obey each other's laws? Is it so that every world obeys its own laws? – A theory of lawhood can be expected to answer these questions, and we can see how different theories would answer them differently. (For instance, my own views on lawhood answer all but the last in the negative.) This transformation of questions is helpful indeed. But the help comes from a substantive theory of what nomological necessity is – not from metalogical investigations that keep silent about which frames, if any, afford correct interpretations. It is the substantive theory, not the metalogic, for which we need possible worlds.

1.3 Modal Realism at Work: Closeness

A counterfactual (or 'subjunctive') conditional is an invitation to consider what goes on in a selected 'counterfactual situation'; which is to say, at some other possible world. Partly, the world in question is specified explicitly by the antecedent of the conditional: 'If kangaroos had no tails . . . .' Partly, it is specified by a permanent understanding that there is to be no gratuitous departure from the background of fact: ignore worlds where the kangaroos float around like balloons, since the kangaroos of our world are much too heavy for that. Partly, it is specified by temporary contextual influences that indicate what sorts of departures would be especially gratuitous; for instance, facts just mentioned may have a special claim to be held fixed.

Partly, it is not specified at all: no telling whether the kangaroos have stumps where the tails should be. So it is an idealisation to think that we have to do with a single world, rather than an ill-defined class. Under that idealisation, we can say that a counterfactual conditional 'If it were that A, then it would be that C' is true iff C is true at the selected A-world. More generally, the conditional is true at a world W iff C is true at the A-world selected from the standpoint of W.[13]

Within the approach to counterfactuals just sketched, there is room for debate on a number of questions.

(1) How might we best deal with the idealisation just noted? Should we write the analysis of conditionals so that it tolerates ties in the similarity relation? So that it tolerates incomparabilities? So that it tolerates a (somewhat far-fetched) situation in which there are no A-worlds *most* similar to W, but only more and more similar ones *ad infinitum*? How much should be done by complicating the analysis of counterfactuals, how much by joining a simple analysis of counterfactuals with a general treatment for phenomena of semantic indeterminacy?

(2) If one A-world is selected and another A-world is not, from the standpoint of W, that establishes a sense in which we may say that the first is *closer* to W. What are the formal properties of this 'closeness' ordering? Is it a well-ordering? Does it admit ties? Does it admit incomparabilities?

(3) Is it useful to describe it as a *similarity* ordering, saying that the selected A-worlds are the A-worlds most similar to W? We could mean too little or too much by that: too little if we meant only that the ordering had certain formal properties, too much if we meant that our immediate 'intuitions' of similarity could be relied on to follow the ordering. Is there an intermediate meaning that would be more satisfactory? To say that counterfactuals work by similarity is the skeleton of a theory. To flesh it out, we must say which are the important respects of comparison. How far can we answer that question once and for all? How far must we answer it differently for different sorts of counterfactuals in different sorts of contexts?

[13]See my *Counterfactuals* and Stalnaker, 'A Theory of Conditionals'.

(4) How do we connect the 'would' counterfactual with 'might' counterfactuals and probabilistic counterfactuals? Should we have a family of related connectives? Or should we have a single conditional connective, and apply modal or probabilistic modifiers either to the consequent or to the entire conditional?

(5) Is the indicative conditional something else altogether? Is it, for instance, the truth-functional conditional plus conventional or conversational implicatures? Or does it also work by truth of the consequent at a selected antecedent-world, with the difference between indicative and subjunctive being simply a difference in the principles of selection?

These questions have been much discussed, and I do not want to pursue them here.[14] I do want to point out that they are all within the family. They do nothing to threaten the core idea that counterfactuals have to do with what goes on at possible worlds given jointly by the antecedent, factual background, and contextual influences.

A challenge which goes deeper, and which does question the utility of bringing possible worlds into the story, goes as follows. Here is our world, which has a certain qualitative character. (In as broad a sense of 'qualitative' as may be required – include irreducible causal relations, laws, chances, and whatnot if you believe in them.) There are all the various A-worlds, with their various characters. Some of them are closer to our world than others. If some (A-and-C)-world is closer to our world than any (A-and-not-C)-world is, that's what makes the counterfactual true at our world. Now, whether or not this closeness ought to be called similarity, still somehow it's a matter of the character of the worlds in question. It's the character of our world that makes some A-worlds be closer to it than others. So, after all, it's the character of our world that makes the counterfactual true – in which case why bring the other worlds into the story at all?

To which I reply that is indeed the character of our world that makes the counterfactual true. But it is only by bringing the other worlds into the story that we can say in any concise way what character it takes to make what counterfactuals true. The other worlds provide a frame of reference whereby we can characterise our world. By placing our world within this frame, we can say just as much about its character as is relevant to the truth of a counterfactual: our world is such as to make an (A-and-C)-world closer to it than any (A-and-not-C)-world is.

If counterfactuals were no good for anything but idle fantasies about unfortunate kangaroos, then it might be faint praise to say that possible

---

[14]As well as the works cited in the previous footnote, see my 'Ordering Semantics and Premise Semantics for Counterfactuals'; my *Philosophical Papers*, volume II, chapter 17; and Stalnaker, *Inquiry*, chapters 6–8.

worlds can help us with counterfactuals. But, in fact, counterfactuals are by no means peripheral or dispensable to our serious thought. They are as central as causation itself. As I touch these keys, luminous green letters appear before my eyes, and afterward black printed letters will appear before yours; and if I had touched different keys – a counterfactual supposition – then correspondingly different letters would have appeared. That is how the letters depend causally upon the keystrokes, and that is how the keystrokes cause letters to appear.

Suppose that two wholly distinct events occur, C and E; and if C had not occurred, E would not have occurred either. I say that if one event depends counterfactually on another in this way (and if it's the right sort of counterfactual, governed by the right sort of closeness of worlds) then E depends causally on C, and C is a cause of E. To be sure, this is only the beginning of a counterfactual analysis of causation. Not all counterfactuals are of the right sort, and it is a good question how to distinguish the ones that are from the ones that aren't. We need an account of eventhood, and of distinctness of events. And not all effects depend counterfactually on their causes; for instance, we may have causation by a chain of stepwise dependence, in which E depends on D which depends on C, and thereby C causes E, yet E does not depend directly on C because of some alternate cause waiting in reserve.[15] You may or may not share my optimism about an analysis of causation in terms of counterfactual dependence of events. But even if you give up hope for an analysis, still you can scarcely deny that counterfactuals and causation are well and truly entangled.

Causal theories of this, that, and the other have been deservedly popular in recent years. These theories are motivated by imagining cases where normal patterns of counterfactual dependence fail. Normally, my perceptual experience depends on what is going on around me, in such a way as to make its content largely correct. Normally, my movements depend on my beliefs and desires, in such a way that they tend to serve my beliefs according to my desires. Normally, the way I am depends on the way I was just before, in such a way as to keep change gradual. What if these normal dependences were absent? If my perceptual experience would be the same no matter what was going on around me, I would not be perceiving the world. If the movements of my body would be the same no matter what I believed and desired, those movements would not be my actions. If the man who will wake up in my bed tomorrow would be exactly the same regardless of what befell me today, he would be an impostor.

If possible worlds help with counterfactuals, then, they help with many parts of our thought that we could scarcely imagine being without.

---

[15] I discuss these issues in my *Philosophical Papers*, volume II, part 6.

Closeness of worlds can also help us to say what it means for a false theory of nature to be close to the truth. False is false – and it takes only a trace of error to make a theory false – but false theories are not all on a par. We may reasonably think that present-day scientific theories, if not entirely free of error, are at any rate closer to the truth than previous theories were. We may hope that future theories will be closer still. How can we explain this?

Risto Hilpinen has proposed that we might explain this closeness to the truth (or 'truthlikeness' or 'verisimilitude') in terms of closeness of possible worlds. As in the case of counterfactuals, this closeness is a matter of some sort of similarity. A theory is close to the truth to the extent that our world resembles some world where that theory is exactly true. A true theory is closest to the truth, because our world *is* a world where the theory is true. As for false theories, the ones that can come true in ways that involve little dissimilarity to the world as it really is are thereby closer to the truth than those that cannot.

For instance, we have the simple, approximate gas laws; and then we have correction terms. But if the correction terms were all zero, things wouldn't be too different. (You couldn't tell the difference unless either the circumstances were extraordinary or you made a very careful measurement.) The closest of the approximate-gas-law worlds are pretty close to ours. That is why the approximate gas laws are close to the truth. Suppose we improve the gas laws by putting in the most important of the corrections. Then we get a theory that holds in some worlds that imitate ours still better, so the improved theory is still closer to the truth.

Just as in the case of counterfactuals, what we have here is the mere skeleton of an analysis. To put flesh on the bones, we need to say something about what an appropriate similarity ordering of worlds might be – what sort of respects of comparison are the ones that count. (It seems unlikely that we could use the same similarity ordering both for verisimilitude and for counterfactuals.) But even a skeleton is well worth having. It tells us what sort of flesh to look for – to explain what we mean by verisimilitude, pick out the appropriate respects of comparison of worlds.

Whether we must settle for a messy business of comparative similarity depends on whether we can hope for something cleaner. It would be nice to give equal weight to all agreements and disagreements between a theory and the truth, and never fuss about which ones matter most to verisimilitude. But the problem is harder than it may seem, and there seems to be little hope that egalitarian methods can ever deliver non-trivial comparisons of verisimilitude. Suppose we subject two rival theories to a true–false quiz covering all sentences in the appropriate language. When a theory declines to answer, that is better than a wrong answer and worse than a right answer. How do we translate the question-by-question performance of rival theories into an overall comparison? Counting fails: all false theories alike give equal infinite numbers of right and wrong answers. Dominance fails: it cannot happen that one of two false theories sometimes does better than the other and never does worse.[16] If the quiz were better made, if questions were selected for their importance, if redundancy were avoided, and if there were less opportunity for errors to cancel out, then numerical score or dominance on the quiz could mean more. Of course, a selective quiz – unlike a quiz that includes all possible questions – calls for judgement on the part of the examiner. It is open to challenge by those who disagree about what are the most important things for a theory to get right. So what? *Any* standard for preferring one theory to another is open to challenge – if, *per impossibile*, the method of dominance had succeeded in ranking some false theories above others, it could still have been challenged by those who care little about truth. But there is a more serious difficulty with the selective quiz: our original problem returns for every question. When theories give the wrong answer to a question on the quiz, false is false – however, some mistakes are farther off the mark than others. Does anything go faster than light?' – 'No' says the truth (let us suppose). 'Yes' says the better theory, according to which a very few very rare particles do. 'Yes' says the worse theory, according to which most planes and some birds do. If the quiz were unselective, the difference between the better and worse theories would show up on some follow-up question. But if the quiz is selective, as it must be to give a meaningful comparison, maybe sometimes the revealing follow-up question will have been left out.

I don't deny that verisimilitude might be explained in terms of performance on a suitably selective quiz. However, the choice of which questions to include and how to weight them will be just as problematic, and will raise just the same issues about what it is important to get right, as the choice of a similarity relation of worlds on Hilpinen's proposal. In fact, I suggest that the best intuitive guide to what makes a quiz suitable is exactly that we want score on it to be a good measure of how closely our world resembles any of the worlds that conform to the theory under test. If so, there is no way to get out of judging which respects of comparison are the important ones – not unless, with absurd disdain for what we understand outside the philosophy room, we junk the very idea of closeness to the truth.

[16]*Ex hypothesi* both theories are false; so let F be the disjunction of a falsehood affirmed by one and a falsehood affirmed by the other; then F is a falsehood affirmed by both. Suppose one theory does better on one question: is it so that A? Then the other theory does better on another question: is it so that A iff F? Then neither theory dominates the other. The conjecture that dominance would give useful comparisons of verisimilitude is due to Popper, *Conjectures and Refutations*, page 233; the refutation is due to Miller and Tichý.

A merit of Hilpinen's proposal is that it distinguishes aspects of verisimilitude which comparison by means of quizzes tends to run together. A theory T defines a region in the space of possible worlds: namely, the class of all T-worlds. The whole truth defines another region: the unit class of our world. There are three relevant ways to compare these regions in terms of similarity distance. (1) Size: the smaller the region of T-worlds is, the more it resembles the point-sized region defined by the truth. (2) Shape: the more compact the region of T-worlds is, the less it consists of far-flung and scattered parts, the more it resembles the point-shaped truth.[17] (3) Separation: the distance, at closest approach, between the region of T-worlds and our world. It is the separation which most clearly deserves the name 'closeness to the truth'. But small size and compact shape also are merits of theories, and might be considered as aspects of verisimilitude or 'truthlikeness' in a broader sense. All three aspects are involved if we consider not only separation at closest approach, but also further questions of separation: how distant at most are the T-worlds from our world? How distant are they on average (with respect to some sort of measure)? As can be seen from the spatial analogy, these comparisons have to do with size and shape as well as separation at closest approach.

Verisimilitude, as such, has been discussed mostly in connection with scientific progress. We can credit the false theories of former times with some degree of closeness to the truth; and even those sceptics who are quite certain that science will never rid itself of all error may hope at least to approach the truth ever more closely.

But the verisimilitude of false theories is not limited to theories that are at some time accepted as true. It applies equally to deliberate falsifications: the theory of the frictionless plane, the massless test particle, the ideally rational belief system, and suchlike useful idealisations. These theories never were meant to be any better than truthlike. When we disregard friction in saying how things slide on a plane, that is fiction, truthlike but false. When we go on to say that the fiction about the frictionless plane is close to the truth about what really happens on slick black ice, *that* is physics and true. One handy way to tell the truth about complicated phenomena is to say how they resemble simpler idealisations. Maybe the same truth could in principle be told directly – it is hard to see why not – but there is no doubt that we do find it much easier to tell the truth if we sometimes drag in the truthlike fiction.[18]

---

[17]The variety – that is, dissimilarity – within a region reflects both its size and shape, just as a spatial region including points separated by at most 14 miles might be a long thin strip with very little area or might be a circular region of about 154 square miles. Bennett, in 'Killing and Letting Die', and Bigelow, in 'Possible Worlds Foundations for Probability', have discussed methods for disentangling variety due to size from variety due to shape.

When we do, we traffic in possible worlds. Idealisations are unactualised things to which it is useful to compare actual things. An idealised theory is a theory known to be false at our world, but true at worlds thought to be close to ours. The frictionless planes, the ideal gases, the ideally rational belief systems – one and all, these are things that exist as parts of other worlds than our own.[19] The scientific utility of talking of idealisations is among the theoretical benefits to be found in the paradise of *possibilia*.

1.4 Modal Realism at Work: Content

An inventory of the varieties of modality may include *epistemic* and *doxastic* necessity and possibility. Like other modalities, these may be explained as restricted quantification over possible worlds. To do so, we may use possible worlds to characterise the content of thought. The content of someone's knowledge of the world is given by his class of *epistemically accessible* worlds. These are the worlds that might, for all he knows, be his world; world W is one of them iff he knows nothing, either explicitly or implicitly, to rule out the hypothesis that W is the world where he lives. Likewise the content of someone's system of belief about the world (encompassing both belief that qualifies as knowledge and belief that fails to qualify) is given by his class of *doxastically accessible* worlds. World W is one of those iff he believes nothing, either explicitly or implicitly, to rule out the hypothesis that W is the world where he lives.

Whatever is true at some epistemically or doxastically accessible world is epistemically or doxastically possible for him. It might be true, for all he knows or for all he believes. He does not know or believe it to be false. Whatever is true throughout the epistemically or doxastically accessible worlds is epistemically or doxastically necessary; which is to say that he knows or believes it, perhaps explicitly or perhaps only implicitly.

Since only truths can be known, the knower's own world always must be among his epistemically accessible worlds. Not so for doxastic accessibility. If he is mistaken about anything, that is enough to prevent his own world from conforming perfectly to his system of belief.[20]

---

[18]See Scriven on the recognised inaccuracy – idealisation – of some so-called laws. See Glymour on the way we often credit superseded physical theories with being right in a limiting case. This connects our two applications: the verisimilitude of a superseded theory rests on the verisimilitude of an idealisation.

[19]Then it won't be much use trying to do without possible worlds and replacing them with ideally rational belief systems, as Ellis has proposed; for the ideal belief systems themselves are other-worldly. *I* can believe in Ellis's replacement for possible worlds. Can he?

[20]See Hintikka, *Knowledge and Belief*, and his subsequent discussions of knowledge and belief in *Models for Modalities* and *The Intentions of Intentionality*.

No matter how we might originally characterise the content of knowledge or belief, it ought to be possible afterward to introduce the distinction between worlds that do and worlds that do not conform to that content. That done, we could go on to introduce the epistemic and doxastic modalities. For instance if we began with a notion of belief as some sort of acceptance of interpreted sentences – perhaps of our language, perhaps of some public language the believer speaks, or perhaps of the believer's hypothetical 'language of thought' – then we could say that a doxastically accessible world is one where all the accepted sentences are true. I am quite sceptical about this order of proceeding, for reasons that need not be reviewed here.[21] A more promising plan, I think, is to characterise the content of knowledge or belief from the outset in terms of something rather like the epistemically or doxastically accessible worlds. (Let me concentrate simply on belief, passing over the added complications that arise when we distinguish someone's knowledge from the rest of his system of belief.) The class of doxastically accessible worlds is roughly what we want, but it isn't exactly right; some changes must be made.

For one thing, I said that the doxastically accessible worlds give the content of one's system of belief *about the world*; but not all belief is about the world. Some of it is egocentric belief; or, as I have called it elsewhere, 'irreducibly *de se*'.[22] Imagine someone who is completely opinionated, down to the last detail, about what sort of world he lives in and what goes on there. He lacks no belief about the world. For him, only one world is doxastically accessible. (Or, at most, one class of indiscernible worlds – let me ignore this complication.) And yet there may be questions on which he has no opinion. For instance he may think he lives in a world of one-way eternal recurrence, with a beginning but no end, with a certain course of history repeated exactly in every epoch; and he may have no idea which epoch he himself lives in. Every epoch of the world he takes to be his contains someone who might, for all he believes, be himself. He has no idea which one of them he is. If he did, for instance if he somehow became persuaded that he lived in the seventeenth epoch, he would believe more than he does. But he would not believe more about the world. The added belief would be not about the world, but about his own place therein.

So if we want to capture the entire content of someone's system of belief, we must include the egocentric part. We should characterise the content not by a class of possible worlds, but by a class of possible individuals – call them the believer's *doxastic alternatives* – who might,

[21]See Stalnaker, *Inquiry*, chapters 1 and 2.

[22]See my 'Attitudes *De Dicto* and *De Se*' and 'Individuation by Acquaintance and by Stipulation'; and see Chisholm, *The First Person*, for a parallel theory in a somewhat different framework.

for all he believes, be himself. Individual X is one of them iff nothing that the believer believes, either explicitly or implicitly, rules out the hypothesis that he himself is X. These individuals are the believer's doxastic possibilities. But they are not different possible ways for the world to be; rather, they are different possible ways for an individual to be, and many of them may coexist within a single world. (For further discussion of individual possibilities, in other words possible individuals, see section 4.4). Suppose that all of someone's doxastic alternatives have a certain property; then he believes, explicitly or implicitly, that he himself has that property.

One property that an inhabitant of a world may have is the property of inhabiting a world where a certain proposition holds. (Or, of inhabiting a world that falls in a certain set of worlds. In the next section, I shall suggest that these come to the same thing.) So if all of someone's doxastic alternatives inhabit worlds where a certain proposition A holds, then he believes that he himself inhabits an A-world. In other words, he believes that A holds at his world, whichever world that may be. We may say, simply, that he believes the proposition A. So belief about the world comes out as a special case of egocentric belief. And the original treatment of belief about the world in terms of doxastically accessible worlds still works, within its limits. The doxastic alternatives determine the doxastically accessible worlds, though not conversely: a world is accessible iff at least one of the alternatives inhabits it. If each alternative inhabits an A-world, then A holds at every accessible world, so it is doxastically necessary according to the original treatment that A holds.

The same person can have different systems of belief at different times. Suppose it is true, as I think it is, that a person persists through time by consisting of many different momentary stages located at different times. (This is a controversial view; for some discussion of it, see section 4.2.) Then we can say first that the various stages have various systems of belief; and then that the continuing person has a system of belief at a time by having a stage at that time which has that system of belief.

By treating the subjects of belief as momentary, we can subsume belief about what time it is as a special case of egocentric belief. You may last threescore years and ten; but the stage that does your believing at a given moment is a momentary stage. If that stage has as its doxastic alternatives various person-stages all of which are located at about noon on 11 March 1985, that is how you at that moment have a belief about what time it is. (On what it means to compare times across worlds, see section 1.6.) If, on the other hand, that stage has as its alternatives various stages on various hours of various days, that is how you, at that moment, are uncertain what time it is. Note that you can lose track of the time no matter how certain you are about what sort of world you live in, and about which continuing person in that world you are.

(Knowledge, as well as belief, may be egocentric: besides knowing what sort of world you live in, you can also know who in the world you are and what time it is. So again we don't get a complete characterisation of knowledge by taking a class of epistemically accessible worlds; rather, we need a class of possible individuals within worlds as the subject's *epistemic alternatives*. What the subject knows in the first place is that he is some or another one of these possible individuals. So if all of them have some property in common, then he knows that he has that property; and if all of them live in worlds where some proposition holds, then he knows that proposition.)

Besides providing for egocentric belief by switching from accessible worlds to alternative individuals, we must also provide for partial belief. Being a doxastic alternative is not an all-or-nothing matter, rather it must admit of degree. The simplest picture, idealised to be sure, replaces the sharp-edged class of doxastic alternatives by a subjective probability distribution. Thus you may give 90 per cent of your credence to the hypothesis that you are one or another of the possible individuals in *this* class, but reserve the remaining 10 per cent for the hypothesis that you are one of the members of *that* class instead. We can say that a doxastic alternative *simpliciter* is a possible individual who gets a non-zero (though perhaps infinitesimal) share of probability, but the non-zero shares are not all equal.

Precise numerical degrees of belief look artificial, so we might favour a coarser-grained system with some small number of distinct grades of belief. But whatever small number of grades we took, it is likely that our scale would seem sometimes too coarse to capture real distinctions and sometimes too fine to be realistic. A better response is to continue to treat a belief system as a precise numerical probability distribution, but then to say that normally there is no fully determinate fact of the matter about exactly which belief system someone has. There are a range of belief systems that fit him equally well, thought it may be that none fits perfectly; and there is no saying that his real belief system is one rather than another within this range. Then whatever coarse-graining is appropriate comes out as a spread of exact numerical values within the systems in the range. There may be more spread and there may be less; we needn't try to settle once and for all how coarse the grain should be.

We have another reason also to acknowledge that someone may have a multiplicity of belief systems. To a greater or lesser extent, we are all doublethinkers: we are disposed to think differently depending on what question is put, what choice comes before us, what topics we have been attending to. Belief is compartmentalised and fragmented.[23] Sometimes a doublethinking believer acts in a way that best fits one belief system,

[23]See Stalnaker, *Inquiry*, chapter 5; and my 'Logic for Equivocators'.

sometimes in a way that best fits another. And it should not be said just that his belief system changes rapidly; because, throughout, he remains simultaneously disposed toward both systems. In this way also, both systems may fit him equally well even if neither fits perfectly.

In such a case, there are two methods we might follow in saying what someone believes. There is no need to choose between the two once and for all, but it is useful to distinguish them. We might take an intersection, and concentrate on what is common to his many belief systems. Or we might instead take a union, and throw together the different things he believes under different systems.

To illustrate, suppose that hypochondria and good cheer are at war within you. You are simultaneously disposed toward both. Sometimes one is manifest, controlling your thought and conduct; sometimes the other. You have one belief system, the hypochondriac one, under which all your doxastic alternatives are in the early, invisible stages of a dread disease. You have another belief system, the cheery one, under which all your alternatives are healthy. Thus you have entirely different alternatives under the two systems. (Other cases of doublethink would be less extreme, and involve some overlap.) But though the two lots of alternatives differ in respect of health, they have much in common: for instance, all of them live in worlds where the disease in question is incurable. Under the method of intersection, you believe neither that you are diseased nor that you are healthy. Under the method of union, you believe that you are diseased (under one system) and also you believe that you are healthy (under the other). But though you believe that you are diseased and you believe that you are healthy, you do not believe that you are both diseased and healthy; because none of your alternatives under either system, and indeed no possible individual whatever, is both diseased and healthy.

In your state of doublethink, you have no whole-hearted belief about whether you are healthy; you are half-heartedly certain that you are diseased, half-heartedly certain that you are healthy. The two half-hearted certainties are not at all the same thing as partial belief. Your condition is not one of whole-hearted uncertainty about whether you are diseased or healthy, characterised by one unified belief system under which some of your alternatives are diseased, some are healthy, and your subjective probability is divided more or less evenly between the two subclasses. If you had the opportunity to bet on whether or not you were diseased, the difference between the two states would be plain. If you are whole-heartedly uncertain, you hedge your bets. If you are half-heartedly certain each way, you plunge one way or the other – but which way you go depends on exactly how the question is put to you, and on how you're feeling at the time. Indeed, in a more complicated case, belief could be both half-hearted and uncertain: you have one belief system in which your subjective probability is divided evenly between diseased and healthy alternatives, another where it goes mostly or entirely to diseased alternatives, and still another where it goes mostly or entirely to healthy alternatives.

If content is given by a class of doxastic alternatives (or by a probability distribution), what is characterised is one whole system of belief, not several beliefs – the relevant notion of belief is singular, not plural. This built-in holism is one way in which the present approach contrasts with strategies in which there is a different belief for every different sentence of the languge of thought that is written in the 'belief box'. There is no sensible question whether something is one of your beliefs in its own right, or whether it is merely a consequence of some of your other beliefs. There is no sensible question whether your belief that you are hirsute is or isn't the same belief as your belief that you are hairy; your doxastic alternatives are all hairy, in other words they are all hirsute; and that's that. What is written in your 'belief box', if anything, or what word if any you might use to express yourself, is beside the point.

Of course, we can introduce a derivative notion whereby one belief system brings with it many different beliefs. We could do so in various ways. For instance we could say that each property common to all the believer's doxastic alternatives is one of his beliefs, namely his belief that he has that property. (As a special case, each proposition common to all his belief worlds is one of his beliefs, namely his belief that he inhabits a world where that proposition holds.)

A different way would be to say that he has one belief for every ordinary language belief-ascribing sentence (for short: belief sentence) that is true of him. That would be quite a different thing; because the connection between doxastic alternatives and the truth of belief sentences is far from uniform or straightforward. There are various ways for a system of belief to make a belief sentence true. I cannot propose any unified formula to cover all cases.

One way involves the doxastically accessible worlds. Each of Fred's doxastic alternatives inhabits a world where all things decay; and that is what makes it true to say that Fred believes that all things decay.

A second way involves not the worlds, but the doxastic alternatives themselves. Each of René's alternatives is immaterial; and that is what makes it true to say that René believes that he himself is immaterial. It isn't so, however, that each of René's alternatives inhabits a world where René is immaterial; for we may suppose that René is essentially material – he has no immaterial counterparts – in which case there are no such worlds. This means that René's alternatives are not among his counterparts.[24]

---

[24]At least, not under any ordinary counterpart relation. We could introduce a special 'counterpart-by-acquaintance' relation on which René's alternatives would be among his counterparts; see my 'Individuation by Acquaintance and by Stipulation'. This just moves the disunification. We get somewhat less variety of ways to make a belief sentence true in return for somewhat more variety of ways to have counterparts.

A third way involves the ascription of properties to things other than oneself via relations of acquaintance. Each of Ralph's doxastic alternatives is watching a spy at work, sneaking through the shadows; Ralph himself is watching Bernard, though he doesn't recognise him; thereby Ralph ascribes spyhood to Bernard; and that is how Ralph believes that Bernard is a spy.[25] It isn't so, however, that each of Ralph's alternatives inhabits a world where Bernard is a spy; for we may suppose that none of the other-worldly spies whom Ralph's alternatives watch is a counterpart of Bernard. Bernard gets into the act not through his other-worldly counterparts, but because he is the one Ralph is actually watching.

A relation of acquaintance needn't be so very direct and perceptual. Other relations will do, so long as they afford channels for the flow of information. For instance there is the relation which obtains when one has heard of something by name. Let us say that one is '*Londres*' – acquainted with something when one has heard of it under the name '*Londres*'. Each of Pierre's doxastic alternatives is '*Londres*'-acquainted with a pretty city; Pierre himself in *Londres*-acquainted with London; thereby Pierre ascribes prettiness to London; and that is how he believes that London is pretty. (See Kripke, 'A Puzzle About Belief'.) Likewise each of Fred's alternatives is 'arthritis'-acquainted with a disease that he has in his thigh; Fred himself is 'arthritis'-acquainted with arthritis; and that is how he believes that he has arthritis in his thigh. (See Burge, 'Individualism and the Mental'.) It isn't so, however, that each of Fred's alternatives has arthritis in his thigh; because arthritis is a disease of the joints which no possible individual has in his thigh. For the same reason, it isn't so that Fred has arthritis in his thigh at his doxastically accessible worlds.

A fourth way involves the acceptance of sentences. Each of Peter's doxastic alternatives is in a position to say truly 'Santa brings presents'; what is more, Peter and his alternatives more or less understand what this sentence means; and that is how Peter believes that Santa brings presents. It isn't so that Peter ascribes present-bringing to Santa under any relation of acquaintance, since there is no Santa for him to be related

---

[25] The so called belief sentence 'Ralph believes that Bernard is a spy' has a mixed subject matter. It is not entirely about Ralph's system of belief. It is made true partly by Ralph's psychological state, and partly by his relationship to his surroundings. It is a matter of psychology that his system of belief has content given by a certain class of doxastic alternatives, all of whom watch spies. It is not a matter of psychology that the one he is in fact watching is none other than Bernard.

You might protest that belief is, by definition, that which belief sentences report; and psychology, by definition, covers such phenomena as belief; so if it turns out that relationships of the believer to external things get into the subject matter of belief sentences, then those relationships are *ipso facto* psychological! This may seem far-fetched; but after all it is a mere terminological proposal, and as such is harmless. However, it would compel us to introduce some new name for what hitherto has been called 'psychology', and there seems to be no good reason why we should have to do so.

to. Each of Peter's alternatives is 'Santa'-acquainted with a present-bringer, to be sure, but Peter himself is not 'Santa'-acquainted with anyone. Nor is it so, anyway not clearly, that each of Peter's alternatives inhabits a world where Santa brings presents. To be sure, each of them inhabits a world where someone with a red suit and a belly like jelly and so forth brings presents – but as any reader of *Naming and Necessity* should know, it is one thing to fit the Santa-stereotype, another thing to be Santa.

Four ways, so far, for a system of belief to make a belief sentence true; they cover a lot of the ground, but perhaps not quite all. Here is one further case. Each of Pierre's doxastic alternatives is '*Père Noel*'-acquainted with a present-bringer, although Pierre himself is not '*Père Noel*'-acquainted with anyone. Each of them is in a position to say truly '*Père Noel* brings presents'. (Pierre and his alternatives know English, and are not averse to mixing languages in their speech.) So Pierre believes that *Père Noel* brings presents. So far, it's just like the case of Peter. But also, Pierre believes that Father Christmas brings presents. Why so? Not because Pierre's doxastic alternatives are in a position to say truly 'Father Christmas brings presents' – we may suppose that they are not. Pierre has never heard the name 'Father Christmas', nor has it ever occurred to him to translate the name '*Père Noel*' into English. Presumably it's crucial that the two denotationless names '*Père Noel*' and 'Father Christmas' emerge from one tradition common to speakers of English and French. If there had been two fortuitously similar stories and if Pierre had been out of touch with the English story, then it would have been false to say that Pierre believes that Father Christmas brings presents. But how to work that fact into a general analysis of belief sentences? – Never mind; I have made my point that the connection of belief sentences with belief as characterised by doxastic alternatives is complicated and multifarious.

The use of classes of *possibilia* to specify content is supposed to be discredited by the way it imputes logical omniscience. Not so. We have seen several ways for someone to fall into inconsistency, either by holding impossible beliefs or by holding possible beliefs that conflict with one another.

(1) There is doublethink, as when our hypochondriac believes that he is healthy and also believes, but in a different compartment, that he is diseased. That is an extreme case. Often the walls of the compartments will be weaker and more temporary, due more to momentary inattention than to underlying confusion, and yet sufficient to produce lapses from logical perfection. Consider an everyday failure to draw a conclusion from several premises that one believes. Stalnaker (*Inquiry*, chapter 5) has shown how this can be explained as a case of compartmentalised thinking. Take the simplest way to believe something: a proposition holds throughout

your doxastically accessible worlds. Suppose that you believe that P, also you believe that Q, and P and Q jointly imply R in the sense that every world that is both a P-world and a Q-world is also an R-world; nevertheless, we may suppose that you fail to believe R. We may even suppose that *none* of your doxastically accessible worlds is an R-world. How can this be? – The answer is that you may be thinking double, with P and Q in different compartments. You believe that P by believing it in one system; that one gives you doxastically accessible worlds where P holds but Q and R do not. You believe that Q by believing it in the other system; that one gives you doxastically accessible worlds where Q holds but P and R do not. Thus you believe P and you believe Q, though in both cases half-heartedly; but you whole-heartedly disbelieve the conjunction of P and Q, and you whole-heartedly disbelieve R. You fail to believe the consequence of your two premises taken together so long as you fail to take them together.

(2) When René, an essentially material thinking thing, believes that he himself is immaterial, he self-ascribes a property contrary to his essence, and thereby believes the impossible. Likewise someone might ascribe to something else, via some relation of acquaintance, a property contrary to its essence.

(3) Someone might ascribe conflicting properties to the same thing via two different relations of acquaintance.[26] Pierre is both '*Londres*'-acquainted and 'London'-acquainted with London: each of his doxastic alternatives is '*Londres*'-acquainted with a pretty city and 'London'-acquainted with an ugly one; and that is how Pierre has inconsistent beliefs, believing that London is pretty and also believing that London is ugly. Of course none of his alternatives is in any way acquainted with anything that is both pretty and ugly, because there are no such things in any world to be acquainted with. It would not, I think, be true to say that Pierre believes that London is both pretty and ugly. (But if that were true, it would just go to show that belief sentences work in even more miscellaneous ways than I have given them discredit for – it would not be an objection to what I am saying.) This failure of beliefs to conjoin may suggest a case of doublethink; but it is not the same thing. I don't know whether leading philosophers and logicians like Pierre are less prone to doublethink than the rest of us, but at any rate Pierre is a paragon of mental unity. Far from keeping his '*Londres*'-thoughts and his 'London'-thoughts in separate compartments, he constantly bemoans his fate: 'Would that I had fetched up in *la belle Londres* instead of this dump London!' There is nothing in the least contradictory or impossible about

---

[26]Cresswell and von Stechow show how to account for arithmetical error along the lines of (2) and (3), provided that there is something akin to a relation of acquaintance that we can bear to numbers.

Pierre's alternatives or the worlds they are part of. Of course, that is because the alternatives – unlike Pierre himself, who is not one of them – are never '*Londres*'-acquainted and 'London'-acquainted with the same city.

(4) Someone could believe that a sentence is true when in fact it is subtly contradictory. Thus we may suppose that each of Duntz's doxastic alternatives is in a position to say truly 'There is a barber who shaves all and only those who do not shave themselves'; and that is how Duntz believes there is such a barber, and thereby believes the impossible. Of course, nobody could be in a position to say it truly and mean by it *exactly* what we (or Duntz) would mean; so none of the doxastic alternatives has the meaning exactly right. Note well that this is not the sort of case where Duntz has no idea what the sentence means, and only thinks that it means something or other true; in that case it would be wrong to describe his belief by indirect quotation. No; the indirect quotation is legitimate because he has a pretty good idea what the sentence means, even if his understanding is not quite good enough to enable him to notice the contradiction.[27] In summary: if we characterise content by means of *possibilia* we need not ignore the phenomenon of inconsistent belief. On the contrary, we are in a position to distinguish several varieties of it. *All* the varieties? – That question, no doubt, remains open.

If the content of belief, as given in terms of the subject's doxastic alternatives, is not tied in any uniform and straightforward way to the truth of ordinary language ascriptions of belief, and also is not tied to the subject's acceptance of inner sentences, how is it tied down at all? I would say that it is tied down mainly by belief–desire psychology. We suppose that people tend to behave in a way that serves their desires according their beliefs. We should take this principle of instrumental rationality to be neither descriptive nor normative but *constitutive* of belief. It enters into the implicit definition of what it is for someone to have a certain system of belief.

That is a rough approximation, and there is more to be said. The first thing is that what fits behaviour is not a system of belief alone but rather a combined system of belief and desire. Not only are the possible individuals divided into those which are and are not doxastic alternatives for the subject; also, there are some which he would rather be than others. In general, both belief and desire will admit of degree. Saying what it

[27]We may ask how it is that Duntz fails to notice the contradiction. He knows enough: we may suppose that he believes each of several premises, having to do with various aspects of the syntactic structure of the sentence and the meanings of the words, and from these premises taken together it follows that the sentence is contradictory. Then how can he fail to draw the conclusion? – We have addressed this question already. Duntz is no doubt a doublethinker, and never puts together all the things he knows. The different ways of falling into inconsistency interact, and Duntz combines our cases (1) and (4). See Stalnaker, *Inquiry*, chapters 4 and 5.

means for behaviour to fit a system of degrees of belief and desire is the business of decision theory. But here it will suffice to look at an absurdly simplified case, devoid of degrees or gradations: all black or white, no shades of grey. On the side of belief, some possible individuals are doxastic alternatives for the subject and others are not. On the side of desire, some individuals belong to the class in which the subject would prefer to be and others do not. (It is not assumed that the subject's preferences are selfish; maybe the preferred class consists of those individuals who inhabit possible worlds where mankind generally flourishes.) Now suppose that there is a certain bodily movement, which the subject is able to perform at will; and which is maximally specific with respect to his ability, so that he would not be able at will to perform it in one more specific way rather than another. Let it be waving the left hand in a certain way (for short: waving). Suppose further that each of the subject's doxastic alternatives is such that, if he were to wave, he would be in the preferred class. We understand this in terms of closeness of worlds and in terms of counterparts: each alternative is such that the closest world to his where his counterpart waves is one where his counterpart belongs to the preferred class. (We want the kind of closeness of worlds that's right for causal counterfactuals. We ignore complications about what happens if there are several counterparts in one world, or if several among the worlds where counterparts wave are tied for closest.) Then waving is a piece of behaviour that serves the subject's desires according to his beliefs. If he does wave, then to that extent the system of belief and desire in question is a system that fits his behaviour.

Besides the fit of belief and desire to behaviour at a moment, there is also fit over time. One way to think of this would be as fit between a succession of systems of belief and a stream of evidence: the changes in belief are as they should be, given the evidence. But it is easier to think of it as fit between the momentary system of belief and desire and present dispositions to follow contingency plans whereby future behaviour depends on what happens meanwhile. That way we can continue to concentrate on the present system of belief and desire of the momentary subject. Return to our simple case, all black and white, and elaborate it further. Suppose the rest of us are in a car parked near a restaurant; the subject is supposed to walk over and wave to us if the restaurant turns out to be open and not too crowded. What serves the subject's desires according to his beliefs is not waving now, and not waving unconditionally later, but rather following a certain contingency plan to wave or not depending on what he sees. He is able to follow this contingency plan at will, and it is maximally specific with respect to his ability. Each of the subject's doxastic alternatives is such that, if he were to follow the plan, he would be in the preferred class. That is, each of them is such that the closest world to his where his counterpart follows the plan is one where his counterpart belongs to the preferred class. Then if the subject is now disposed to follow the plan in whatever way turns out to be right when he gets to the restaurant, to that extent the system of belief and desire in question is a system that fits his present behavioural dispositions.

(How does a momentary stage follow a plan that covers a period of time? – By being the first of a succession of suitably interrelated stages which together follow the plan. What makes a momentary stage able, in this sense, to follow a plan? – The fact that belief changes under the impact of evidence in such a way that, whatever may be observed, continuing to follow the plan will be the behaviour that fits the sytem of belief and desire of each subsequent stage. So the epistemic rationality of belief change has not, after all, been passed by; it is still there within the supposition that the subject is able to follow the contingency plan.)

What makes an assignment of a system of belief and desire to a subject correct cannot just be that his behaviour and behavioural dispositions fit it by serving the assigned desires according to the assigned beliefs. The problem is that fit is too easy. The same behaviour that fits a decent, reasonable system of belief and desire also will serve countless very peculiar systems. Start with a reasonable system, the one that is in fact correct; twist the system of belief so that the subject's alleged class of doxastic alternatives is some gruesome gerrymander; twist the system of desire in a countervailing way; and the subject's behaviour will fit the perverse and incorrect assignment exactly as well as it fits the reasonable and correct one.[28] Thus constitutive principles of fit which impute a measure of instrumental rationality leave the content of belief radically underdetermined.

However, instrumental rationality, though it is the department of rationality that has proved most tractable to systematic theory, remains only one department among others. We think that some sorts of belief and desire (or, of dispositions to believe and desire in response to evidence) would be unreasonable in a strong sense – not just unduly sceptical or rash or inequitable or dogmatic or wicked or one-sided or short-sighted, but utterly unintelligible and nonsensical. Think of the man who, for no special reason, expects unexamined emeralds to be grue. Think of Anscombe's example (in *Intention*, section 37) of someone with a basic desire for a saucer of mud. These beliefs and desires are unreasonable; though if twisted desire is combined with correspondingly twisted belief, then it may be that the failing lies entirely outside the purview of the department of instrumental rationality. So I say that other departments of rationality also may have a constitutive role. What makes the perversely twisted assignment of content incorrect, however well it fits the subject's behaviour, is exactly that it assigns ineligible, unreasonable content when

---

[28]I have shown how this can happen in my 'New Work for a Theory of Universals', pages 374–5, though only for a very simplified case.

a more eligible assignment would have fit behaviour equally well. The theory that implicitly defines the functional role of belief and desire, and so specifies *inter alia* what it is for a possible individual to be one of the subject's doxastic alternatives, is the constitutive theory not just of instrumental rationality but of rationality generally.[29]

I have objected to the radical indeterminacy, especially the indeterminacy between reasonable and perverse systems of belief and desire, that would result if we tried to get by with instrumental rationality as the only constitutive constraint. But I do not object at all to milder forms of indeterminacy. Far from being something forced upon us by the requirements of some theory, it seems independently plausible that there might be no straightforward and determinate fact of the matter about what a doublethinker does or doesn't believe. I said before that in cases of doublethink, or less remarkably in cases where the exact degrees of belief are indeterminate, someone might have multiple belief systems; none would fit him perfectly, all would fit him about equally well, and well enough. Now I have said what sort of fit I had in mind.

There is one further complication; doubtless not the last, but the last that I wish to consider here. I have been speaking as if the assignment of content were an assignment directly to a given subject. But I would rather say that the content belongs to some state – a brain state, perhaps – that recurs in many subjects. It recurs in many subjects in many worlds, the worlds being sufficiently similar in the anatomy of their inhabitants and in the relevant laws of nature; and it recurs in many subjects even in the same world, for instance if it is a world of eternal recurrence or if it is a world where the inhabitants' brains have a lot of hard-wiring in common. The recurrent state would tend to dispose anyone who had it to behaviour fitting a certain reasonable assignment of content. Therefore we can say that the state *is* a system of belief and desire with that content, and when a subject has that state he thereby has the content that belongs to the state. The reason why I prefer to attach content to the state, rather than directly to the subject, is that it leaves room for exceptional cases in which, despite the constitutive role of principles of fit, the subject's behaviour somehow fails to fit his system of belief and desire. I said that the state *tends* to dispose anyone who has it to behave in a certain way; but such a tendency might be defeated. Compare a state of a pocket calculator: that state tends, throughout all the calculators built to a certain plan, to cause '137' to be displayed when the 'recall' key is pressed, and so on; wherefore we call it the state of having the number 137 stored in memory. But there are a few calculators with defective 'recall' keys; they get into the very same state, but you press the key and nothing happens.

---

[29]See section 2.3; my 'New Work for a Theory of Universals', pages 373–7; and Grandy, 'Reference, Meaning and Belief', on 'principles of humanity'.

We can say of them along with the rest, by courtesy, that they have 137 stored in memory; and this is defined in terms of what the state tends to cause; but in the defective calculators the tendency is defeated. The state of the memory gets its numerical content in virtue of what it would generally, but not invariably, tend to cause; and so it might be, also, with a brain state which is assigned content as a system of belief and desire.[30]

Possible worlds and individuals are useful not only in connection with thought but also for the analysis of language. Suppose we want a systematic grammar, covering not only syntax but semantics, for a natural language or some reasonable imitation or fragment thereof. Such a grammar is meant to plug into an account of the social practice of using language. It encapsulates the part of the account that is different for different linguistic communities who are party to different conventions of language. What makes the grammar correct for a given population is that, when plugged into its socket, what results is a correct description of their linguistic practice – of the way they suit their words to their attitudes, of the way they suit their attitudes to others' words, and of their mutual expectations concerning these matters.

A principal way we use language is in conveying needed information. You know whereof you speak, and you want me to know something; so you tell me something true; I rely on you to know whereof you speak and be truthful; and that is how I come to have the knowledge you wanted me to have. But when you tell me the truth, and when I rely on you to be truthful, your words will not be true *simpliciter*. They will be true under some semantic interpretations and false under others. The right interpretation, for us, is the one that specifies truth conditions under which we are indeed truthful and do indeed rely on one another's truthfulness. So if a grammar is to plug into its socket in an account of the use of language, it has to specify truth conditions for (many or all) sentences of the language.

These may well depend on the circumstances of utterance. A sentence is said by some particular speaker, at some particular time, at some particular world. Further, it is said at a certain place; to a certain audience; accompanied perhaps by certain gestures of ostension; in the presence of certain conspicuous things; and in the context of previous discourse which influences what is to be presupposed, implicit restrictions of quantifiers, prevailing resolution of vagueness, and much more. All these things may be relevant to whether that sentence can be said truly. But speaker, time, and world determine the rest: the place is the place where that speaker is at that time, audience consists of those present whom the speaker intends to address, and so on.

---

[30]See my *Philosophical Papers*, volume I, pages 119–21.

I might even say that the *speaker* determines the rest. The appropriate world is the world that he is part of. As for time, of course it is not to be denied that we persist through time and speak at different times. But we do so by being composed of different temporal stages. The stages also may be called speakers; and if it is the momentary speaker we mean, then the appropriate time is the time at which the speaker is.

So the speaker, at a definite world and time, is one of those momentary subjects of attitudes just considered. His knowledge and belief are given by his epistemic and doxastic alternatives – those possible momentary individuals who might, for all he knows or believes, be himself. He can speak truly by luck if the sentence he says is true for him; but to exhibit the sort of truthfulness that members of a linguistic community expect from one another, the things he says will have to be true not only for him but also for all his alternatives. When language is used to convey information between truthful and trusting partners, the communication may take place all in this world; but nevertheless the truth conditions must involve other-worldly individuals. To plug into its socket in an account of the use of language, a semantically interpreted grammar has to specify which speakers at which times at which worlds are in a position to utter which sentences truly.

Then it must accomplish an infinite specification by finite means. Here is a way that can be done. First list a finite vocabulary of basic expressions – words, near enough – and assign each of them some sort of syntactic category and semantic value. Then list rules for building expressions from other expressions; and within each rule, specify the syntactic category and semantic value of the new expression as a function of the categories and values of the old expressions whence it was built. One syntactic category will be the sentences. Then specify truth conditions for sentences in terms of their semantic values.

The semantic values have two jobs. They are there to generate other semantic values; and they are there to generate truth conditions of sentences. The second job is what the whole system of semantic values is for; the first job is what gives us a whole system of semantic values.

I have said all this in a skeletal fashion, intending to say something that will be neutral between many conceptions of what the system of vocabulary, rules, categories, and semantic values might look like. For the same reason, I have chosen the colourless term 'semantic values' instead of some more familiar term that would convey some more definite idea of what the values might be and how they might do their job. The object is not that we should find entities capable of deserving names from the established jargon of semantics, but that we should find entities capable of doing the pair of jobs.[31]

---

[31]For instance, I don't think we should say that an ordinary proper name *refers* to a

We have a choice of strategies. What we want from our system of semantic values is a specification of which sentences are true for which of all the (momentary) speakers scattered through the worlds. We might put context-dependence outside the semantic values – call this the *external* strategy – by making the entire assignment of semantic values, from the words on up, be speaker-relative. Since different speakers are part of different worlds, this initial speaker-relativity brings *possibilia* into the picture, no matter what the semantic values themselves might look like. For a given speaker and sentence, we have first the semantic values for that speaker of each word of the sentence. In accordance with the rules of the grammar, these generate the semantic values for that speaker of expressions built up from these words. Among those expressions is the sentence itself; and the semantic value of the sentence for the speaker somehow determines whether it is true for him. We want a semantic value for a sentence, relative to a speaker, to deliver a truth value. We might even hope that it could just *be* a truth value – call this the *extreme* external strategy.

At the opposite extreme, we could assign semantic values once and for all, and put all the context-dependence inside them – call this the *internal* strategy. In that case *possibilia* may enter into the construction of the semantic values themselves. Else it will be hard for the fixed semantic value of a sentence to determine which of the speakers scattered over the worlds that sentence is true for.

In between, we might of course mix the two methods. We could put some of the context-dependence inside the semantic values, and some of it outside in the speaker-relativity of semantic values – call this the *moderate* external strategy.[32]

To illustrate this difference of strategies, and to illustrate various other choices and problems that arise, it will help to look at a miniature language. We shall have one kind of modification, namely modification of sentences; but that will do to illustrate phenomena that could take place also for modification of common nouns, verbs, quantifiers, and modifiers themselves in a more elaborate language. Our little language will have a categorial grammar with three categories altogether, one basic and two derived: *sentence, modifier, connective*. There are basic expressions in

---

bundle of properties. My name, for instance, refers to me – and I am not a bundle of properties. Property bundles might nevertheless be serviceable semantic values for proper names, along with other noun phrases. (See my 'General Semantics', section VII; and Montague, *Formal Philosophy*, chapter 8.) If so, it would be unwise to use 'refer' as our word for having a semantic value. There is, of course, no reason not to say both that my name has me as its referent and also that it has a certain property bundle as its semantic value.

[32]An example of a pure internal strategy is my treatment in 'General Semantics'. Moderate external strategies are to be found in Montague's papers on natural language in *Formal Philosophy*, and in Cresswell, *Logics and Languages*.

all three categories. What the semantic values for sentences are remains to be seen; a semantic value for a modifier is a function from semantic values for sentences to semantic values for sentences; a semantic value for a connective is a function from pairs of semantic values for sentences to semantic values for sentences. There are two grammatical rules.

Rule for Modifiers. If S is a sentence with semantic value s, and M is a modifier with semantic value m, then MS is a sentence with semantic value m(s).

Rule for Connectives. If S_1 and S_2 are sentences with semantic values s_1 and s_2 respectively, and C is a connective with semantic value c, then CS_1S_2 is a sentence with semantic value $c(s_1, s_2)$.

Given this much, all else depends on the basic expressions and their semantic values.

First let's try treating the language in an extreme external fashion: semantic values are assigned relative to a speaker, semantic values for sentences are mere truth values, semantic values for modifiers and connectives are made to fit and therefore are functions from and to truth values. For a little while all goes well. We have two basic sentences. They exhibit two kinds of context-dependence, both handled externally.

'Rains' is a basic sentence; its semantic value for any speaker is *truth* iff, at the world and time and the vicinity of the place where that speaker is, it is raining.

'Cold' is a basic sentence; its semantic value for any speaker is *truth* iff, at the world and time and the vicinity of the place where that speaker is, the temperature is below a certain level. This level is somewhat flexible, and depends on the previous course of the conversation in which the speaker is participating. If someone says something that requires a shift of the border to make it true for him, thereby the border shifts.

We also have one modifier and one connective, both truth-functional.

'Not' is a basic modifier; its semantic value for any speaker is the function that maps either truth value to the other.

'Iff' is a basic connective; its semantic value for any speaker is the function that maps a pair of truth values to *truth* iff both truth values in the pair are the same, and to *falsity* otherwise.

(We could have had a context-dependent modifier or connective; for some speakers its semantic value would be one truth-function, for others another. I omit an example.)

So far, so good. But suppose our little language also includes the modifier 'possibly'; and suppose that a sentence 'Possibly φ' is to be true for a speaker iff φ is true under some shift of world. (Let us postpone the important question of what happens to the speaker, and his time and place and so forth, when we shift worlds.) That frustrates the extreme external strategy. If semantic values for sentences are just truth values, there is, of course, no way we can derive the semantic value for a given speaker of 'Possibly φ' from the semantic values for that speaker of 'possibly' and of φ. The trouble is that we've discarded information about the truth value of φ for other worlds than the speaker's own. It would do us no good to reconstruct the grammatical rule for modifiers, abandon the function-and-argument method of generating semantic values for modified sentences, and devise some fancy semantic value for 'possibly'. Once the needed information is gone, we can't bring it back.

(But if the rule said that the semantic value of 'Possibly φ' for *this* speaker depends on the semantic value of φ for *other* speakers, then couldn't the semantic values be truth values? – There is a question, still postponed, of what happens if the world-shift takes us to a world with no speakers. But even setting that aside, the proposal rests on a misunderstanding. To be a semantic value is to be a big enough package of information. A semantic value worthy of the name must carry all the information that will be needed to generate other semantic values. Anything that we need to bundle together many of to get a big enough package is *ipso facto* not an adequate semantic value.)

Since the extreme external treatment fails, we have a choice between a moderate external and an internal treatment. The moderate external alternative could go as follows. Let our new semantic values for sentences be functions from worlds to truth values; then we get our truth conditions by saying that a sentence is true for a speaker iff its semantic value, for that speaker, assigns truth to that speaker's world. The rest gets adjusted to fit. Our new semantic values for modifiers and connectives are functions to and from the new semantic values for sentences. The rules for modifiers and connectives have the same form as before. As for the basic expressions:

'Rains' is a basic sentence; its semantic value for any speaker is the function that assigns *truth* to all and only those worlds W such that, for some counterpart X in W of the speaker, it is raining at W at the time and the vicinity of the place where X is. ('Cold' is similar.)

'Not' is a basic modifier; its semantic value for any speaker is the function that maps f to g iff both are functions from worlds to truth values and g(W) is *truth* when and only when f(W) is *falsity*.

'Iff' is a basic connective; its semantic value for any speaker is the function that maps e and f to g iff all three are functions from worlds to truth values and g(W) is *truth* when and only when e(W) and f(W) are the same.

'Possibly' is a basic modifier; its semantic value for any speaker is the function that maps f to g iff both are functions from worlds to truth values and either g(W) is *truth* for all worlds and f(W) is *truth* for some world or else g(W) and f(W) both are *falsity* for all worlds.

Now we have accommodated the modifier 'possibly', thanks to the world-dependence within the semantic values. But there is still external context dependence; the semantic value for me of the basic sentence 'Rains' has to do with rain in the vicinity of my counterparts, the semantic value for you of 'Rains' has to do with rain in the vicinity of your counterparts.

I still haven't put in a context-dependent modifier or connective, but a true-to-life example could be now given: 'possibly' with accessibility restrictions, where the appropriate restrictions are somewhat flexible and depend, for a given speaker, on the previous course of the conversation in which the speaker is participating. Similarly, inconstancy in the counterpart relation (see section 4.5) could create another dimension of context-dependence, besides the sort already noted, in the semantic value of 'Rains'.

The present semantic values for sentences might look little different from the truth conditions that the whole system of semantic values is built to deliver. However, suppose our language turns out to contain another basic sentence.

'Am' is a basic sentence; its semantic value for any speaker is the function that assigns *truth* to all and only those worlds that contain counterparts of that speaker.

'Am' has quite a simple truth condition: it is true for any speaker whatever. (Assuming, as I do, that anything is one of its own counterparts.) But its semantic values, for various speakers, are not so simple. In general, they will assign *truth* to the world where the speaker in question is and to some but not all other worlds. That's how 'Possibly not am' can come out true for a speaker, as, of course, it should. Call 'Am' a case of the 'contingent *a priori*' if you like – though it seems doubtful that there is any *one* thing to which both adjectives apply.

Given a speaker, his world is given; but when we shift worlds in connection with 'possibly', we don't necessarily shift speakers. What happens to the speaker when we shift worlds (our postponed question) may be that he completely disappears. We may shift to a world where there is no counterpart of a given speaker; that is how 'Possibly not am' comes out true. We might even shift to a world where there are no speakers at all. Worlds started out fixed to speakers, but now they are varying independently.

So far, our moderate external strategy is working nicely; but now suppose it turns out that our little language contains some modifiers we haven't yet taken into account. Suppose there is 'past', and a sentence 'Past ϕ' is to be true for a (momentary) speaker iff ϕ is true, not with respect to the time when the speaker is, but with respect to some earlier time. Now we have to start over once more, taking semantic values for sentences as functions from world-time pairs (such that the time exists at the world) to truth values, and adjusting the rest to fit. Then we can say, for instance:

> 'Past' is a basic modifier; its semantic value for any speaker is the function that maps f to g iff both are functions from world-time pairs to truth values and g(W,t) is *truth* when and only when f(W,t') is *truth* for some time t' that exists at world W and is earlier than t.

> 'Rains' is a basic sentence; its semantic value for a given speaker is the function f from world-time pairs to truth values that assigns *truth* to all and only those pairs of a world W and time t such that, for some counterpart X in W of the speaker, it is raining at W at t in the vicinity of the place where X is.

As with worlds and 'possibly', so with times and 'past'. Given a speaker, his time is given; but when we shift times in connection with 'past', we never shift speakers. (For a speaker is momentary, and if present at one time he will never be found at an earlier time.) So when we speak of rain at t in the vicinity of the place where X is, that will not be his place at t – he has none – but his place when he exists.

And next suppose there is 'sorta', and a sentence 'Sorta ϕ' is to be true for a speaker iff ϕ is true for him under an adjustment of context-dependent flexible borders – such as the border for what counts as cold – that makes it easier for ϕ to be true. So 'Sorta cold' is true when it isn't quite cold enough to make 'Cold' true; 'Sorta not cold' is true when it isn't quite warm enough to make 'Not cold' true; 'Sorta sorta cold' is true when it isn't quite cold enough to make 'Sorta cold' true; and so on. We could make yet another new start, taking semantic values for sentences now as functions from world-time-border triples to truth values, and adjusting the rest yet again.

Is there no end to this? Maybe, maybe not. I'm making up the story of this little language as I go along, so let me make an end to it. Here is a conceivable phenomenon that turns out *not* to happen. There *isn't* a modifier 'reversedly' such that a sentence 'Reversedly ϕ' is true for a speaker iff ϕ is true for some hearer he is addressing. If there had been, we would have had to go back and take semantic values for sentences as functions from world-time-border-speaker quadruples; since it doesn't happen (just as no such thing happens in English) perhaps we needn't. We can leave the speaker-relativity external to the semantic values.

By now the moderate external strategy has come to look cumbersome, and so we might wish we'd tried the internal alternative instead. The simplest method would be to say that a semantic value for a sentence, assigned once and for all, is a function from speakers to truth values. Again the semantic values for modifiers can be made to suit, and the rule for modifiers can prescribe a function-and-argument method of generating the semantic value of a modified sentence; and likewise for connectives. We read the truth conditions of a sentence directly off the semantic value.

Life cannot be that easy. Consider two sentences: 'Am' and 'Iff rains rains'. Both have the same truth condition: true for any speaker whatever. But they can't both have the same semantic value; because when we apply two more modifiers we get sentences 'Possibly not am' and 'Possibly not iff rains rains' which cannot have the same semantic value because they do not have the same truth conditions. The second is false for any speaker whatever; not so for the first.

So a better internal strategy would be to say that a semantic value for a sentence, assigned once and for all, is a function from speaker-world pairs to truth values. Adjust the rest to fit. A sentence is true for a speaker iff its semantic value assigns *truth* to the pair of that speaker and his own world. Now we can handle our problem about the two sentences, as follows.

'Rains' is a basic sentence; its semantic value is the function that assigns *truth* to all and only those pairs of a speaker Y and world W such that, for some counterpart X in W of Y, it is raining at W at the time and the vicinity of the place where X is.

'Am' is a basic sentence; its semantic value is the function that assigns *truth* to all and only those pairs of a speaker Y and world W such that W contains a counterpart of Y.

'Not' is a basic modifier; its semantic value is the function that maps f to g iff both are functions from speaker-world pairs to truth values and g(Y,W) is *truth* when and only when f(Y,W) is *falsity*.

'Iff' is a basic connective; its semantic value is the function that maps e and f to g iff all three are functions from speaker-world pairs to truth values and g(Y,W) is *truth* when and only when e(Y,W) and f(Y,W) are the same.

'Possibly' is a basic modifier; its semantic value is the function that maps f to g iff both are functions from speaker-world pairs to truth values and, for any Y, either g(Y,W) is *truth* for all worlds and f(Y,W) is *truth* for some world or else g(Y,W) and f(Y,W) both are *falsity* for all worlds.

Now we can check that, because the embedded sentences 'Am' and 'Iff rains rains' have different semantic values despite their sameness of truth conditions, the sentences 'Possibly not am' and 'Possibly not iff rains rains' differ not only in semantic values but in truth conditions. As we would expect, the first is true for any speaker unless he has counterparts at all the worlds; the second is true for no speaker.

This is very like what we saw before under a moderate external strategy in considering the behaviour of 'possibly' and 'Am'. We needed to let world vary independently of speaker, despite the fact that a world is originally given as the world of a speaker. Taking speaker-world pairs is just another way to get independent variation. The pair delivers worlds twice over, not necessarily the same world both times, because there is the world of the speaker who is the first term of the pair and there is the world that is the second term of the pair.[33]

If we go on to consider the modifier 'past' under the internal strategy, we will find ourselves forced to say that the semantic values for sentences, assigned once and for all, are functions from speaker-world-time triples to truth values. And if we next consider 'sorta', we will have to say instead that they are functions from speaker-world-time-border quadruples. This begins to seem cumbersome. It's good luck that 'reversedly' is absent from the language, so that we may be spared functions from speaker-world-time-border-speaker quintuples. – Plainly, we are covering the same ground twice. There is no great divide between the moderate external and the internal strategies. There is a trivial translation between a speaker-relative assignment of semantic values that are functions from world-time-border triples and an assignment, once and for all, of semantic values that are functions from speaker-world-time-border quadruples. If pursued satisfactorily, the two strategies come to the same thing.[34]

It is clear from our little language that sameness of truth conditions – in the sense I gave to that phrase – does not imply sameness of meaning. Else 'Am' would mean the same as 'Iff rains rains', which surely it doesn't. It is less clear whether we should say that sameness of semantic values implies sameness of meaning. The semantic values are the same for 'Rains' and 'Not not rains'; or for 'Iff rains rains' and 'Iff am am'. Do these sentences mean the same or not?

---

[33]Either way, we have a form of 'double indexing'. See van Fraassen, 'The Only Necessity is Verbal Necessity', for discussion of the uses and origins of this device.

[34]For further discussion of this point, see my 'Index, Context, and Content'.

I think this is not a real question. Is there really anything in our theoretical or everyday use of the term 'mean' to suggest that we have settled the matter – settled it unequivocally, settled it the same way each time someone undertook to settle it? No, it is just a question of what to mean by 'mean'. Given a superfluity of more or less interchangeable semantic jargon, none of it very precisely pinned down, perhaps it might be convenient to reserve 'meaning' for the fine-grained notion of something that differs when – as in the examples just noted – we generate the same semantic value by different routes.

If this is what we want 'meanings' to be, we can let them encode the way a semantic value is generated. In view of the artificial simplicity of our illustrative language, it is an easy matter to let the generation of meanings go piggyback on the generation of semantic values, as follows. (For simplicity let's follow the internal strategy; if we preferred the external strategy, we could let meanings be speaker-relative along with the semantic values.) (1) The meaning of any basic expression is its semantic value. (2) If S is a sentence and M is a modifier, then the meaning of the sentence MS is the sequence of the meaning of M and the meaning of S. (3) If S_1 and S_2 are sentences and C is a connective, then the meaning of the sentence CS_1S_2 is the sequence of the meaning of C, the meaning of S_1, and the meaning of S_2. So a meaning amounts to a parsed expression with semantic values of words put in where the words themselves should be. Meanings determine semantic values; but not conversely, as witness the different meanings of 'Rains' and 'Not not rains' or the different meanings of 'Iff rains rains' and 'Iff am am'.[35]

Because meanings carry more information that semantic values (anyway, the semantic values so far considered) we can use them to make distinctions which would not show up in semantic values. Consider differences of triviality. Suppose that for every speaker, there is some world where he lacks a counterpart; that is a non-contingent matter, but it is far from trivial. It depends on just what the other worlds are like, on what sort of thing exactly can qualify as a 'speaker', and on the counterpart relation. If so, the semantic value of 'Possibly not am' is a constant function that always takes the value *truth*. So the sentence is a necessary truth, but it is not trivially so. The semantic value of 'Iff rains rains' is exactly the same; this sentence too is a necessary truth, but this time trivially so. This difference in triviality is captured by a difference of meanings; but not by a difference of semantic values, for there is no difference of semantic values.

---

[35]For further discussion of meanings, see my 'General Semantics'; for background, see Carnap on 'intensional isomorphism', *Meaning and Necessity*, section 14; and C. I. Lewis on 'analytic meaning' in 'The Modes of Meaning'.

(This raises a difficult problem.[36] Suppose it turns out that we have the modifier 'trivially' *within* our little language, and it works as we might expect. Then 'Trivially possibly not am' should be false for every speaker, but 'Trivially iff rains rains' should be true. This suggests that what we have been calling the 'semantic values' are not really quite big enough packages of information to do their jobs and deserve their names; and what we have been calling the 'meanings' are the things that really can do the job of the semantic values and deserve to be so called. Maybe something of the sort could and should be permitted, but it is not at all easy. The trouble comes when we ask what is the semantic value of 'trivially' itself? Our previous practice would lead us to think that it is a function which takes as argument the semantic value – hitherto called 'meaning' – of a sentence ϕ, and yields as value something whence we can retrieve the truth condition of 'Trivially ϕ'. Now let ϕ be the sentence 'Trivially iff rains rains'; and we have an argument of a function outranking the function itself in the set-theoretic hierarchy, which is impossible. What to do? Resort to queer set theory? Claim that it was illicit to stipulate that our little language contains the sentence 'Trivially trivially iff rains rains'? Allow the sentence, but insist that it can have no truth condition? Require the first 'trivially' and the second in the sentence to be homonymous words with different semantic values? No solution seems very nice.)

1.5 Modal Realism at Work: Properties

We have frequent need, in one connection or other, to quantify over properties. If we believe in possible worlds and individuals, and if we believe in set-theoretic constructions out of things we believe in, then we have entities suited to play the role of properties.

The simplest plan is to take a property just as the set of all its instances – *all* of them, this- and other-worldly alike. Thus the property of being a donkey comes out as the set of all donkeys, the donkeys of other worlds along with the donkeys of ours.[37]

[36]For discussion of it see Cresswell, 'Hyperintensional Logic', and Bigelow, 'Believing in Semantics'.

[37]I say 'set' not 'class'. The reason is that I do not want to restrict myself to properties of individuals alone; properties themselves have properties. Properties must therefore be sets so that they may be members of other sets.

When I use the term 'set' and 'class' in this book, the reader would not go far wrong to suppose that I am following the standard usage: 'class' is the more general term, and covers not only sets but also 'proper' classes. Those are supposed to be set-like things which, by reason of the boundless rank of their members, are somehow disqualified from membership in any class or set. But in fact I use the terms to mark a somewhat different distinction, as follows. It is sometimes suggested that

The usual objection to taking properties as sets is that different properties may happen to be coextensive. All and only the creatures with hearts are creatures with kidneys; all and only the talking donkeys are flying pigs, since there are none of either. But the property of having a heart is different from the property of having a kidney, since there could have been an animal with a heart but no kidneys. Likewise the property of being a talking donkey is different from the property of being a flying pig. If we take properties as sets, so it is said, there is no distinguishing different but accidentally coextensive properties.

But according to modal realism, these 'accidentally coextensive' properties are not coextensive at all. They only appear so when we ignore their other-worldly instances. If we consider all the instances, then it never can happen that two properties are coextensive but might not have been. It is contingent whether two properties have the same this-worldly instances. But it is not contingent whether they have the same instances *simpliciter*.

It is a mistake to say that if a property were a set, then it would have its instances – its members – essentially, and therefore it never could be contingent whether something has or lacks it. Consider the property of being a talking donkey, which I say is the set of all talking donkeys throughout the worlds. The full membership of this set does not vary from world to world. What does vary from world to world is the subset we get by restricting ourselves to the world in question. That is how the number of instances is contingent; for instance, it is contingently true that the property has no instances. Further, it is a contingent matter whether any particular individual has the property. Take Brownie, an

---

there is an irreducibly plural way of referring to things, or quantifying over them. I say 'There are some critics such that they admire only one another' or 'There are all the non-self-members, and they do not comprise any sort of set or class', and I am not quantifying in the ordinary way over any set or class of critics or of non-self-members; rather I am quantifying over nothing but critics or non-self-members themselves, however I am quantifying over them in an irreducibly plural way. See Black; Stenius; Armstrong, *Universals and Scientific Realism*, volume I, pages 32–4; and especially Boolos. I find it very plausible that there is indeed such a thing as ontologically innocent plural quantification, and that it can indeed replace quantification over sets – sometimes. It would be delightful (except when I want to cite belief in sets as a precedent for my modal realism) if plural quantification could be iterated up the hierarchy, so that some fancy kind of plurally plural quantification over individuals could replace *all* quantification over sets or classes. But I think this project has very little hope of success. So I consider some apparent quantification over sets or classes of whatnots to carry genuine ontological commitment not only to the whatnots, but also to sets or classes of them; and then I use the word 'set'. But sometimes I think my quantification could be read as, or replaced by, innocent plural quantification that carries no commitment except to the whatnots themselves; and then I use the word 'class'.

An exception: since the phrase 'equivalence class' is standard, I use it whether or not I take there to be genuine ontological commitment.

other-worldly talking donkey. Brownie himself is, once and for all, a member of the set; hence, once and for all, an instance of the property. But it is contingent whether Brownie talks; Brownie has counterparts who do and counterparts who don't. In just the same way, it is contingent whether Brownie belongs to the set: Brownie has counterparts who do and counterparts who don't. That is how it is contingent whether Brownie has the property.

As it is for properties, so it is for relations. An instance of a dyadic relation is an ordered pair of related things; then we may take the relation again to be the set of its instances – all of them, this- and other-worldly alike. Again, it is no problem that different relations may happen to be coextensive; for this is only to say that the this-worldly parts of the sets are the same, and there is more to a set than its this-worldly part. Again, a pair may stand in a relation contingently, if it has counterpart pairs that do and counterpart pairs that don't.[38] In the same way, a triadic relation can be taken as a set of ordered triples, and so on. Also we can include relations of variable degree, since there is no reason why pairs and triples, for instance, cannot both belong to a single set.[39]

Often it is said that things have some of their properties relative to this or that. Thirst is not a property you have or lack *simpliciter*; you have it at some times and lack it at others. The road has different properties in different places; here it is surfaced, there it is mud. Nine has the property of numbering the planets at our world, but not at a possible world where a planet takes the place of our asteroid belt. (I mean the solar planets at present; and I mean to take another world where there are clear counterparts of the solar system and the present time.) Relative to Ted, Fred has the property of being a father, but relative to Ed, he has the property of being a son. Relative to the number 18, the number 6 has the property of being a divisor; but not relative to 17.

A property that is instantiated in this relative way could not be the set of its instances. For when something has it relative to this but not to

---

[38]Not just any pair of counterparts should count as a counterpart pair; it may be that pair ⟨X, Y⟩ counts as a counterpart of pair ⟨V, W⟩ partly because the relations between X and Y resemble those between V and W. See Hazen, 'Counterpart-Theoretic Semantics for Modal Logic'; my *Philosophical Papers*, volume I, pages 44–5; and the discussion of joint possibilities in section 4.4.

[39]There is a choice between various set-theoretic constructions of ordered pairs, triples, etc. I shall leave the choice unmade, since making it would serve no useful purpose. (At one point in section 4.4 I shall take them as sequences, consisting of terms indexed by numbers, because that makes it easy to leave gaps in them. But even that won't settle the matter. To make sequences by pairing the terms with their index numbers presupposes some different, prior construction of the term-index pairs, and I shall leave it open what that is to be.) So all that I say of pairs, triples, . . ., and relations is systematically ambiguous. No harm, unless I said something that would have different truth values on different disambiguations; which I have no intention of doing.

that, is the thing to be included in the set or not? Therefore we often see philosophers go to great lengths to provide for relative instantiation when they construct 'properties' in terms of possible worlds and individuals. A property is taken as a function from worlds to sets of things, giving for each world the things that have the property relative to that world. Or it is a function from world–time pairs to things, thus providing also for temporary properties like thirst. In the same way we could take the property of being surfaced as a function that assigns to each place the set of things surfaced there; or the property of being a son as a function that assigns to each person a set of sons; or the property of being a divisor as a function that assigns to each number the set of its divisors.

I find such constructions misguided: what is had by one thing relative to another might better be called a *relation*, not a *property*.[40] It may indeed turn out that one thing stands in a relation because another thing has a property, as when the part of the road that is at a certain place has the property of being surfaced, and that is how the whole road bears the 'surfaced at' relation to that place. Likewise it is by having temporal parts which are thirsty that a person is thirsty at various times. Of course, a disbeliever in temporal parts cannot agree; *he* thinks thirst is irreducibly relational. That is a central feature of his view and, for better or worse, it ought to be unhidden. That is why I do not approve of the terminology of 'properties' instantiated relative to this or that – it obfuscates and belittles the distinction between relations and genuine properties, and so puts us off guard against those theories that try to tell us that there are only relations where we might have thought there were genuine properties. (See section 4.2.) And that is why I offer a treatment of properties that requires things to have or to lack them *simpliciter*, together with a separate but parallel treatment of relations.

Likewise I have made no place for properties that admit of degree, so that things may have more or less of the same property. Instead, there are families of plain properties: the various lengths, the various masses. And there are relations to numbers, such as the mass-in-grams relation that (a recent temporal part of) Bruce bears to a number close to 4,500.

I identify propositions with certain properties – namely, with those that are instantiated only by entire possible worlds. Then if properties generally are the sets of their instances, a proposition is a set of possible worlds. A proposition is said to *hold* at a world, or to be *true at* a world. The proposition is the same thing as the property of being a world where that proposition holds; and that is the same thing as the set of worlds

---

[40]More precisely, what is had by X relative to Y is not a property of X. It *is* a property of the pair ⟨X, Y⟩ – on my account, any relation is a property of the pairs (or triples, or whatnot) that instantiate it.

where that propositions holds. A proposition holds at just those worlds that are members of it.[41]

Just as it is sometimes said that properties are had relative to this or that, so it is sometimes said that propositions hold relative to this or that. No harm in their holding at worlds, of course; but other relative holding requires a switch in what we mean by 'propositions'. For instance a *tensed* proposition, which is said to hold at some times but not others, can be taken as a set of world–time pairs; in other words a relation of worlds and times. If as I think (see section 1.6) no time is identically a common part of two different worlds, then this can be simplified: we can say that the tensed proposition is simply a property, that is a set, of times.

Likewise an *egocentric* proposition, which holds for some people but not others, could be taken as a property, that is a set, of people. And if we generalise, and countenance also egocentric propositions which hold for things other than people – such as the proposition that one is a poached egg – then we should say that the egocentric proposition is a property, that is a set, of possible individuals. But if we can already call it a 'property', what's the sense of also calling the same thing an 'egocentric proposition'?

There might be a good reason. The conception we associate with the word 'proposition' may be something of a jumble of conflicting *desiderata*. Part of the idea is that propositions are supposed to be true or false *simpliciter*. Or at any rate, their truth or falsity is not supposed to be relative to anything except the world – unlike a sentence, a proposition is not supposed to be true on one interpretation but false on another, true on one resolution of vagueness but false on another, true in Melbourne but false in Adelaide, true yesterday but false today, true for

---

[41]Distinguish my proposal from a different way of unifying propositions, properties, and relations. The idea is that relations properly speaking are two-place, three-place, and on up; properties are one-place relations; and propositions are zero-place relations. See, for instance Montague, *Formal Philosophy*, pages 122–3. This strikes me as misguided elegance. How can we make sense of it? – Only by giving *everything* one more place than meets the eye. The so-called n-place relations are instantiated not *simpliciter* but relative to a world. (Or for Montague, relative to an index that might or might not be a world.) I say that means they all have an extra, hidden place to them. Thus a proposition is supposed to be a zero-place relation, but it turns out to be a one-place relation – that is, a set of one-tuples of worlds. A so-called property is supposed to be a one-place relation, but it turns out to be a two-place relation of things to worlds; what is supposed to be a two-place relation turns out to be three-place; and so on up. The treatment of propositions is the only satisfactory part. If we identified a one-tuple of a world with the world itself, as we might but needn't, it is exactly my own treatment; if not, still sets of worlds and sets of their one-tuples would correspond so closely that we needn't care which ones get called the propositions. The rest of the unified treatment is not satisfactory because it relies on the obfuscatory notion of relative instantiation. Therefore the whole idea is best abandoned.

me but false for you. But another part of the idea is that propositions are supposed to be the objects of thought. They are supposed to be capable of giving the content of what we know, believe, and desire. But it is clear that some thought is egocentric, irreducibly *de se*, and then its content cannot be given by the propositions whose truth is relative to nothing but worlds; for those propositions do not discriminate between inhabitants of the same world. If you insist that propositions, rightly so called, must be true or false relative to worlds and nothing else, then you had better say that the objects of at least some thought turn out not to be propositions. Whereas if you insist that propositions, rightly so called, are the things that serve as objects of all thought, then you had better admit that some propositions are egocentric. The point is the same whichever way you say it: the objects of thought in general are not sets of possible worlds; they sometimes must be, and always can be, taken instead as sets of possible individuals.

Everyone agrees that it won't do to take a property as the sets of its this-worldly instances, because then two properties will be taken to be identical if they happen to be coextensive. Some will say that it is just as bad to take a property as the set of all its instances throughout the worlds, because then two properties will be taken to be identical if they are necessarily coextensive. The stock example concerns the properties of triangularity and of trilaterality. Necessarily, a planar figure bounded by line segments has the same number of angles as sides. So, throughout the worlds, all and only triangles are trilaterals. Yet don't we want to say that these are two different properties?

Sometimes we do, sometimes we don't. I don't see it as a matter for dispute. Here there is a rift in our talk of properties, and we simply have two different conceptions. It's not as if we have fixed once and for all, in some perfectly definite and unequivocal way, on the things we call 'the properties', so that now we are ready to enter into debate about such questions as, for instance, whether two of them ever are necessarily coextensive. Rather, we have the word 'property', introduced by way of a varied repertory of ordinary and philosophical uses. The word has thereby become associated with a role in our commonsensical thought and in a variety of philosophical theories. To deserve the name of 'property' is to be suited to play the right theoretical role; or better, to be one of a class of entities which together are suited to play the right role collectively. But it is wrong to speak of *the* role associated with the word 'property', as if it were fully and uncontroversially settled. The conception is in considerable disarray. It comes in many versions, differing in a number of ways. The question worth asking is: which entities, if any, among those we should believe in, can occupy which versions of the property role? My answer is, in part, that sets of *possibilia* are entities we should believe in which are just right for *one* version of the property role.

There's no point in insisting that this one is the only rightful conception of the properties. Another version of the property role ties the properties more closely to the meanings of their standard names, and to the meanings of the predicates whereby they may be ascribed to things. 'Triangular' means having three angles, 'trilateral' means having three sides. These meanings differ. (Or do they? The conception of 'meaning' also is in disarray!) So on this conception of properties, we want to distinguish triangularity from trilaterality, though we never can distinguish their instances. We can put the distinction to use, for instance, in saying that one of the two properties is trivially coextensive with triangularity, whereas the other is non-trivially coextensive with triangularity.

This conception demands that properties should be *structured*. If we want to match up properties with the meanings of linguistic expressions that have syntactic structure, then we want to give the properties themselves some kind of quasi-syntactic structure. We can construct structured properties on the model of the structured 'meanings' considered in the previous section. We needn't build them from scratch; we can begin with the unstructured properties and relations we have already, the sets of this- and other-worldly instances. So these structured properties will require *possibilia* just as much as the unstructured ones did. We will need not only properties and relations of individuals; also we will make use of a higher-order unstructured relation that holds between properties and relations of individuals. It is a relation all the same – a set of pairs – and it is constructed out of *possibilia* just as much as first-order properties and relations of individuals are.

Let A be the relation of being an angle of; let S be the relation of being a side of. Suppose for simplicity that these can be left as unstructured relations; we could go to a deeper level of analysis if we like, but that would complicate the construction without showing anything new. Let T be the higher-order unstructured relation which holds between an unstructured property F of individuals and an unstructured relation G of individuals iff F is the property of being something which exactly three things bear relation G to. A certain unstructured property is the unique thing which bears T to A, and therefore it is the (unstructured) property of triangularity; it also is the unique thing which bears T to S, and therefore it is the (unstructured) property of trilaterality. Therefore let us take the structured property of triangularity as the pair ⟨T, A⟩, and the structured property of trilaterality as the pair ⟨T, S⟩. Since S and A differ, we have the desired difference between the two pairs that we took to be our two structured properties.

Likewise we can construct structured relations. And if at some deeper level of analysis, we had structured versions of the relation of being an angle of and the relation of being a side – these might be pairs $\langle A_1, A_2 \rangle$ and $\langle S_1, S_2 \rangle$ respectively, or something still more complicated – then we could build these instead of the original A and S into our structured properties, getting structured triangularity as $\langle T, \langle A_1, A_2 \rangle \rangle$ and structured trilaterality as $\langle T, \langle S_1, S_2 \rangle \rangle$.

Likewise for propositions. If it is central to the role you associate with 'proposition' that there should be some sort of quasi-syntactic structure, so that it makes sense to speak of subject–predicate propositions or negative or conjunctive or quantified propositions, then sets of worlds will not do. But more complicated set-theoretic constructions out of *possibilia* can serve instead. In some cases, these might closely resemble the 'meanings' for sentences of our little language in the previous section. For instance we could associate the modifier 'not' with the unstructured relation N that holds between any unstructured proposition and its negation, that being the set of all worlds where the original proposition does not hold. Then a negative structured proposition could take the form $\langle N, P \rangle$, where P is a (structured or unstructured) proposition. Taking propositions as sets of worlds, it is nonsense to distinguish a proposition P from its double negation; the double negation of a proposition is the original proposition all over again. But the structured propositions P and $\langle N, \langle N, P \rangle \rangle$ do indeed differ; although they are equivalent, having the same truth value at every world.

Another kind of structured proposition corresponds to meanings we would have had if our illustrative language had been equipped for predication and if it had used individuals and properties as the semantic values, respectively, for individual constants and monadic predicates. Corresponding to an atomic predication in which the subject and predicate have as semantic values an individual A and a property P, we have as meaning the pair $\langle A, P \rangle$. This is a structured subject–predicate proposition; we might also call it a *singular* proposition or a *de re* proposition. It is true iff the individual A has the property P, otherwise false.

(Two elaborations. First, the properties so used might or might not themselves be structured. Second, we could just as well have a relation and several individuals: $\langle R, A, B \rangle$, a structured proposition which is true iff A and B stand in the relation R. It could be the meaning of a dyadic atomic predication in which R is the semantic value of the predicate, and A and B the semantic values of two individual constants that appear as arguments.)

These singular propositions have been much discussed, under a variety of names, but mostly in connection with inappropriate questions. Should we believe that they exist? – Of course we should. We *must*, if we believe in properties and we believe in individuals and we believe in ordered pairs of things we believe in. You don't even have to believe in the sets of *possibilia* that I call properties, just in entities suited to occupy some or other version of the property role.

Are they, rightly speaking, *propositions*? – Certainly they (and their more complicated relatives) occupy a version of the proposition role. They do not occupy the one and only rightful version, because nothing in our tangled and variable usage suffices to settle which version that would be.

Are they objects of thought? – This much is true: somehow, by our thought, we do ascribe properties to individuals. (Not by thought *alone*, of course, special cases aside; rather, by thought plus the relations of subject to environment.) Whenever you ascribe a property to an individual, there is the pair of that property and that individual. So your accomplishments in property ascribing can be characterised in terms of property-individual pairs, in other words in terms of the singular propositions that are true according to your ascribing. That much ought to be uncontroversial, and that much is enough to provide a good sense in which we can say that singular propositions are objects of thought.

Are they *the* objects of thought? That is, are they the entities that serve best for characterising the subject? – Surely that cannot be answered once and for all. It all depends on what purpose the characterisation is meant to serve.

When it is meant to serve a narrowly psychological purpose, revealing how the subject's actions serve his desire according to his belief and how his belief evolves under the impact of his experience, then the use of singular propositions to characterise his thought will be rather unsatisfactory. It will tend to suppress relevant information about how exactly the subject does his ascribing; it will drag in psychologically irrelevant information about which individuals exactly stand at the far end of the various relationships that connect him to other parts of his world.

(To illustrate, remember Pierre. Let us present him with an unlimited bus pass, and take him to an international bus station. First he comes to an English bus with its destination shown in English, and he shuns it. Why? Because he believes it goes to London; that is, because he ascribes the relation of *going to* to the pair of the bus and London; that is, because the singular proposition ⟨*going to*, the bus, London⟩ is, in the appropriate sense, an object of his belief. Next he comes to another bus, a French bus with its destination shown in French, and he hops on with glee. Why? Because he believes it goes to London, that is, because the singular proposition ⟨*going to*, the other bus, London⟩ is an object of his belief. Evidently something relevant has been left out. I don't say that we *cannot* tell the whole story if we insist on characterising Pierre's thought by means of singular propositions. We could, for instance, mention the singular propositions which pair the two buses with the two properties of *going to an ugly city* and *going to a pretty city*. The characterisation by means of singular propositions is badly matched to the needs of belief–desire psychology, but I don't deny that with sufficient effort we can overcome the mismatch and pull out all the information we need.)

But when we are interested less in the subject's psychology, and more in his dealings with the things around him, as happens if we are interested in him as a partner in cooperative work and as a link in channels for information, then it is otherwise. The more he and we ascribe the same properties to the same individuals, the better we fare in trying to coordinate our efforts to influence those individuals. We learn from him by trying to ascribe the same properties to the same things that he does. We teach him by trying to get him to ascribe the same properties to things that we do. What matters is *agreement* about how things are; and we agree not when we think alike, but when we ascribe the same properties to the same things. To characterise him and ourselves in the sense that is relevant to our agreement, singular propositions are just right. When the same singular propositions are true according to him and according to us, that is when we ascribe the same properties to the same things.

In short, there is no contest between structured and unstructured versions of the properties, relations and propositions. Given the combined resources of set theory and modal realism, we have both versions. (That is: we have suitable candidates to fill both versions of the roles associated with the terms 'property', 'relation', and 'proposition'.) Both versions require *possibilia*. We needn't worry about which versions better deserve the names, since previous use of the names has not been uniform enough to settle the matter. I shall reserve the names 'property', 'relation', and 'proposition', when used without an adjective, for the unstructured versions: the sets of instances, or of worlds. Likewise I shall reserve them for properties and relations of the kind that do not admit of degree and that are instantiated *simpliciter*, not relative to anything, and for propositions of the kind that hold or not relative only to a world. But all this is terminology, not doctrine.[42]

There is another great rift in our talk of properties. Sometimes we conceive of properties as *abundant*, sometimes as *sparse*. The abundant properties may be as extrinsic, as gruesomely gerrymandered, as miscellaneously disjunctive, as you please. They pay no heed to the qualitative joints, but carve things up every which way. Sharing of them has nothing to do with similarity. Perfect duplicates share countless properties and fail to share countless others; things as different as can be imagined do exactly the same. The abundant properties far outrun the predicates of any language we could possibly possess. There is one of them for any condition we could write down, even if we could write at infinite length and even if we could name all those things that must remain nameless because they

---

[42]But sometimes, especially when considering alternatives to modal realism in chapter 3, I shall use the names 'property', 'relation', and 'proposition' in a vague and neutral way, to apply to whatever the most satisfactory occupants of the appropriate roles might be.

fall outside our acquaintance. In fact, the properties are as abundant as the sets themselves, because for any set whatever, there is the property of belonging to that set. It is these abundant properties, of course, that I have identified with the sets.

The sparse properties are another story. Sharing of them makes for qualitative similarity, they carve at the joints, they are intrinsic, they are highly specific, the sets of their instances are *ipso facto* not entirely miscellaneous, there are only just enough of them to characterise things completely and without redundancy.

Physics has its short list of 'fundamental physical properties': the charges and masses of particles, also their so-called 'spins' and 'colours' and 'flavours', and maybe a few more that have yet to be discovered. In other worlds where physics is different, there will be instances of different fundamental physical properties, alien to this world. (See section 3.2, where these alien properties get in the way of the project of building ersatz possible worlds out of this-worldly constituents.) And in unphysicalistic worlds, the distribution of fundamental physical properties won't give a complete qualitative characterisation of things, because some of the 'fundamental' properties of things will not be in any sense physical. What physics has undertaken, whether or not ours is a world where the undertaking will succeed, is an inventory of the *sparse* properties of this-worldly things. Else the project makes no sense. It would be quixotic to take inventory of the *abundant* properties – the list would not be short, nor would we discover it by experimental and theoretical investigation.

I would not recommend that we enter into debate over whether the properties really are abundant or whether they really are sparse. We needn't choose up sides. Rather we should acknowledge that we have both conceptions, and an adequate account of what there is ought to accommodate both.[43]

If we have the abundant properties (as we do, given set theory and *possibilia*) then we have one of them for each of the sparse properties. So we may as well say that the sparse properties are just some – a very small minority – of the abundant properties. We need no other entities, just an inegalitarian distinction among the ones we've already got. When a property belongs to the small minority, I call it a *natural* property.[44]

---

[43]Here I am in partial agreement with Bealer, who advocates a twofold scheme of abundant 'concepts' and sparse 'qualities'. However, he brings the abundant-versus-sparse division into line with the structured-versus-unstructured division, whereas I take the two divisions as cutting across each other.

[44]The name is borrowed from the familiar term 'natural kind'; the contrast is meant to be with unnatural, gerrymandered, gruesome properties. The name has proved to have a drawback: it suggests to some people that it is supposed to be *nature* that distinguishes the natural properties from the rest; and therefore that the distinction is a contingent matter,

Probably it would be best to say that the distinction between natural properties and others admits of degree. Some few properties are *perfectly* natural. Others, even though they may be somewhat disjunctive or extrinsic, are at least somewhat natural in a derivative way, to the extent that they can be reached by not-too-complicated chains of definability from the perfectly natural properties. The colours, as we now know, are inferior in naturalness to such perfectly natural properties as mass or charge; grue and bleen are inferior to the colours; yet even grue does not plumb the real depths of gruesomeness. If it did, we would not have been able to name it.

Relations, like properties, can be conceived as abundant or as sparse: a relation for any set of pairs (or triples, or . . .) whatever, or else a minimum basis of relations sufficient to characterise the relational aspects of likeness and difference. Again we may say that some relations are natural, or that some are more natural than others; and that the natural relations are the same sort of thing as other relations, just a distinguished minority among the sets of pairs, triples, and so on. Also propositions can be conceived as abundant or sparse, and sets of worlds may accordingly be divided into the more and less natural. This is automatic, given the division of properties plus the identification of propositions with properties of worlds.

In systematic philosophy we constantly need the distinction between the more and the less natural properties. It is out of the question to be without it. I have discussed some of its uses in 'New Work for a Theory of Universals' and in 'Putnam's Paradox'. Here I shall mention only one.

We distinguish *intrinsic* properties, which things have in virtue of the way they themselves are, from *extrinsic* properties, which they have in virtue of their relations or lack of relations to other things. How to draw this distinction? Some approaches fail, some fall into circularity. (See my 'Extrinsic Properties'.) But if we start by distinguishing natural from unnatural properties, then the distinction between intrinsic and extrinsic properties is not far away. It cannot be said that all intrinsic properties are perfectly natural – a property can be unnatural by reason of disjunctiveness, as the property of being tripartite-or-liquid-or-cubical is, and still it is intrinsic if its disjuncts are. But it can plausibly be said that all perfectly natural properties are intrinsic. Then we can say that two things are *duplicates* iff (1) they have exactly the same perfectly natural properties, and (2) their parts can be put into correspondence in such a way that corresponding parts have exactly the same perfectly natural properties, and stand in the same perfectly natural relations. (Maybe the

---

so that a property might be natural at one world but not at another. I do not mean to suggest any such thing. A property is natural or unnatural *simpliciter*, not relative to one or another world.

second clause is redundant. That depends on whether we acknowledge some *structural* properties – properties having to do with the way a thing is composed of parts with their own properties and relations – as perfectly natural.) Then we can go on to say that an *intrinsic* property is one that can never differ between two duplicates.

There is a corresponding distinction among relations. An *internal* relation is one that supervenes on the intrinsic natures of its *relata*: if X_1 and Y_1 stand in the relation but X_2 and Y_2 do not, then there must be a difference in intrinsic nature either between the Xs or else between the Ys. If X_1 and X_2 are duplicates (or identical), and so are Y_1 and Y_2, then the pairs $\langle X_1, Y_1 \rangle$ and $\langle X_2, Y_2 \rangle$ stand in exactly the same internal relations. Relations of similarity or difference in intrinsic respects are internal; for instance, the relations of closeness of worlds that figured in my accounts of counterfactuals and of verisimilitude. (See section 1.3.)

Some other relations, notably relations of spatiotemporal distance, are not internal; they do not supervene on the natures of the *relata*. If X_1 and X_2 are duplicates (or identical), and so are Y_1 and Y_2, it may yet happen that the pairs $\langle X_1, Y_1 \rangle$ and $\langle X_2, Y_2 \rangle$ stand in different relations of distance. Consider a (classical) hydrogen atom, which consists of an electron orbiting a proton at a certain distance. If we take a duplicate of the electron and a duplicate of the proton, then they needn't exhibit the same distance – they may not comprise an atom, they may be in different galaxies or different worlds.

However there is a different way in which relations of distance do supervene on intrinsic character. If, instead of taking a duplicate of the electron and a duplicate of the proton, we take a duplicate of the whole atom, then it will exhibit the same electron–proton distance as the original atom. Although distance fails to supervene on the intrinsic natures of the *relata* taken separately, it does supervene on the intrinsic nature of the composite of the *relata* taken together – in this case, the composite hydrogen atom.

There are other relations for which not even that much is true, for instance the relation of having the same owner. It involves more than the *relata* taken either separately or together, since it also drags in the owner and however much of the rest of the world it takes for there to be the institution of ownership. Thus we don't just have the internal relations versus all the rest; we have a three-way classification. I shall say that a relation is *external* iff it does not supervene on the natures of the *relata* taken separately, but it does supervene on the nature of the composite of the *relata* taken together. A relation of intrinsic similarity is internal; a relation of distance is external; but the relation of having the same owner is neither internal nor external.

I distinguish *duplication* from *indiscernibility*. Two things are duplicates iff they have the same intrinsic qualitative character; and that is a matter of the perfectly natural (hence *ex officio* intrinsic) properties of those things and their parts, and of the perfectly natural external relations of their parts. Two things are *indiscernible* iff they have the same intrinsic and extrinsic qualitative character. Extrinsic qualitative character, wherein duplicates may differ, consists of extrinsic properties that are, though not perfectly natural, still somewhat natural in virtue of their definability from perfectly natural properties and relations. Indiscernibles share all their somewhat natural properties. They do not, of course, share all their properties without exception – not if we admit, for any set, a property of belonging to that set, as we automatically do if we identify properties with sets.

To illustrate, contrast two kinds of eternal recurrence. Some worlds exhibit *one-way* eternal recurrence: there is a beginning of time and then there is a first epoch, a second epoch just like the first, a third, and so *ad infinitum*. Then corresponding inhabitants of the different epochs are duplicates – they differ in no intrinsic respect – but they are not indiscernible. They differ in their extrinsic qualitative character in that one inhabits the first epoch, another inhabits the seventeenth, and so on. Other worlds exhibit *two-way* eternal recurrence: there is no last epoch and no first, the epochs are ordered like the integers rather than the natural numbers. Then the corresponding inhabitants of different epochs are not only duplicates but indiscernibles. But still they don't share all their properties, because for any two of them there are sets which contain one without the other.

Many philosophers are sceptical about the distinction between natural and gruesome properties. They think it illegitimate, unless it can somehow be drawn in terms that do not presuppose it. It is impossible to do that, I think, because we presuppose it constantly. Shall we say that natural properties are the ones that figure in laws of nature? – Not if we are going to use naturalness of properties when we draw the line between laws of nature and accidental regularities. Shall we say that they are the ones that figure in the content of thought? – Not if we are going to say that avoidance of gratuitous gruesomeness is part of what constitutes the correctness of an ascription of content. Shall we say that they are the ones whose instances are united by resemblance? – Not if we are going to say that resemblance is the sharing of natural properties. Unless we are prepared to forgo some of the uses of the distinction between natural and unnatural properties, we shall have no easy way to define it without circularity. That is no reason to reject the distinction. Rather, that is a reason to accept it – as primitive, if need be.

I would willingly accept the distinction as primitive, if that were the only way to gain the use of it elsewhere in our analyses. The contribution to unity and economy of theory would be well worth the cost. But I think there are two attractive alternatives: theories which, for some price both in ontology and in primitives, give us resources to analyse the distinction without forgoing any of its applications. I have two such theories in mind. One is a sparse theory of immanent universals, more or less as presented in D. M. Armstrong's *Universals and Scientific Realism*. The other is a theory of tropes, more or less as in D. C. Williams's 'On the Elements of Being', but made sparse in a way that imitates Armstrong's theory.[45] In the contest between these three alternatives – primitive naturalness, universals, or tropes – I think the honours are roughly even, and I remain undecided.

The two theories go as follows. To each perfectly natural property there corresponds a universal, or else a set of tropes. Wherever the property is instantiated, there the corresponding universal, or one of the corresponding tropes, is present. Let us assume that unit positive charge is a perfectly natural property, which is instantiated by momentary stages of various particles. For short: charge is instantiated by particles. Wherever there is a charged particle, there the universal of charge, or else one of the tropes of charge, is present. It is located there, just as the particle itself is. Indeed, it is part of the particle. It is not a spatiotemporal part: the universal or trope occupies the whole of the spatiotemporal region, point-sized or larger, that the particle itself occupies. Besides the universal or trope of charge, other universals or tropes also will be present as further non-spatiotemporal parts of the same particle. For instance, there will be a universal or trope of mass.

The difference between universals and tropes comes when we consider two instances of the same perfectly natural property – for instance, two particles each having unit positive charge. Each one contains a non-spatiotemporal part corresponding to charge. But if this non-spatiotemporal part is a universal, then it is the same universal for both particles. One and the same universal recurs; it is multiply located; it is wholly present in both particles, a shared common part whereby the two particles overlap. Being alike by sharing a universal is 'having something in common' in an absolutely literal sense. If the non-spatiotemporal part whereby a charged particle is charged is a trope, on the other hand, then there are different tropes for different charged particles. There is no recurrence, no sharing of a multiply located non-spatiotemporal part. Instead, we say that the charge-trope of one particle and the charge-trope of another are *duplicate* tropes, in a way that a charge-trope and a mass-trope, say, are not.

---

[45]A somewhat similar theory of universals is the principal system of Goodman, *The Structure of Appearance*, provided we take it to apply not only to appearance but to things generally. Other advocates of trope theory – under a variety of names, and with various differences of doctrine – include Stout, Campbell, and Johnston.

If there are universals, we can say that the particle is composed partly of its several universals. But not entirely; because another particle exactly like it would have the very same universals, and yet the two particles would not be the same. We can say that the particle consists of its universals together with something else, something non-recurrent, that gives it its particularity. Then we need a primitive notion to say how that something gets united with the universals. I shall call this union 'instantiation'. (I trust there will be no confusion with the 'instantiation' of a property-taken-as-a-set by its members.) We can either say that the universal is instantiated by the whole of a particular; or that it is instantiated by the part that gives the particularity, the residue which is left if we take an ordinary particular and subtract its universals.

(It cannot be said, unfortunately, that a universal is instantiated by just anything that has it as a part. For one thing, the relation of part to whole is transitive; so if a universal of charge is part of a particle which is part of an atom, then the universal in turn is part of the atom; but it is the particle, not the atom, which instantiates the universal. And so on up; the universal is part of everything, however big, that the particle is part of. Further, suppose there are disunified wholes composed of miscellaneous parts, as indeed I believe (see section 4.3). These might include universals which they do not instantiate.)

If there are tropes, we might say that the particle is composed entirely of its tropes; there is no problem with a second particle exactly like it, since that second particle is composed not of the same tropes but of duplicate tropes. Then we need a primitive notion – 'instantion' in yet another sense – to say how the tropes that comprise the particle are united. It is an advantage of tropes over universals that we need no special thing to confer particularly – that is, non-recurrence – since the tropes are particular already. The companion drawback is that we need the primitive notion of duplicate tropes, whereas with universals we just say that it is one and the same universal throughout the charged particles.[46]

A theory of universals might attempt to analyse all similarity in terms of shared universals. (Whether it can succeed depends on what can be said about similarity between universals themselves; see Armstrong, *Universals and Scientific Realism*, chapters 22 and 23.) A theory of tropes must be less ambitious. It cannot analyse all similarity, because duplication of tropes is itself a primitive relation of similarity. But duplication of tropes is much better behaved than other relations of similarity that we

---

[46]A universal recurs; a trope has duplicates. We could also imagine an intermediate thing that sometimes recurs and sometimes has duplicates. A trope theorist who also believes in strict identity over time might say that charge recurs along the world-line of one persisting particle, but is duplicated between one persisting particle and another. Campbell and Johnston favour this sort of theory.

might contemplate taking as primitive. The similarity of particles is a messy business: particles can be alike in one respect and not in another, for instance when they are alike in mass but opposite in charge. A theory that starts with similarity-in-some-respect and attempts to recover the respects of comparisons by analysis will run into serious trouble. (See Armstrong, chapter 5; and Goodman, *The Structure of Appearance*, chapter V.) It's simpler with tropes: two charge tropes are alike or not, and that's that. If you will not countenance primitive similarity in any form, then trope theory is not for you. But if you will, then duplication of tropes is an especially satisfactory form for primitive similarity to take.

A universal unifies the set of all and only those particulars that instantiate it. A maximal set of duplicate tropes – that is, a set of tropes that are duplicates of one another but not of any other trope not included in the set – likewise unifies the set of all and only those particulars which instantiate some trope in the set. If we accept a theory of universals or of tropes, we can define a perfectly natural property (of particulars) as any set that is thus unified.

This may seem roundabout. If indeed we accept a theory of universals, why not give up the plan of identifying properties with sets of their instances, and say that the universal itself is the property? Or if we accept a theory of tropes, why not say that the set of duplicate tropes is the property? Surely these things, if they exist, are fine candidates for the role of properties – and no *possibilia* are needed.

Yes and no. In the first place, we would still need *possibilia* if we wanted to acknowledge uninstantiated properties alien to this world. Universals and tropes are present in their instances, and so must have instances if they are to be present at all. If uninstantiated properties are universals, they are other-worldly universals. If they are sets of tropes, they are sets of other-worldly tropes.

In the second place, universals or sets of duplicate tropes would be fine for the role of *sparse* properties, but the sparse properties are not enough. There may be no urgent need to quantify over all of the very abundant and very gruesome properties that modal realism has on offer as sets of *possibilia*. But certainly we want to go well beyond the perfectly natural properties. When we speak of the various properties that a believer ascribes to himself and the things around him, or when we say that Fred hasn't many virtues, or when we say that sound taxonomy will take account of the biochemical as well as the anatomical properties of organisms, then we quantify over properties that are neither flagrantly gruesome nor perfectly natural. We would not wish to repudiate all properties that are in any way disjunctive or negative or extrinsic. However, universals or tropes are credible only if they are sparse. It is quite easy to believe that a point particle divides into a few non-spatiotemporal parts in such a way that one of them gives the particle its charge, another gives it its mass, and so on. But it is just absurd to think that a thing has (recurring or non-recurring) non-spatiotemporal parts for *all* its countless abundant properties! And it is little better to think that a thing has a different non-spatiotemporal part for each one of its properties that we might ever mention or quantify over. The most noteworthy property of this bed is that George Washington slept in it – surely this is true on some legitimate conception of properties – but it is quite unbelievable that *this* property corresponds to some special non-spatiotemporal part of the bed! This is not one of the perfectly natural properties that might correspond to a universal or a trope; rather, it is a property that gains a degree of derivative naturalness, because it is definable in a not-too-complicated way from the perfectly natural properties. The universals or sets of duplicate tropes would not be good candidates to serve as the abundant properties, or even the not-too-abundant-and-not-too-sparse properties. They make a useful adjunct to a broader theory of properties, not a replacement for it.

(A note on terminology. Sometimes 'universal' becomes just another rough synonym for 'property'. The two words are used loosely and interchangeably, equally infected with indecision between rival versions of the definitive theoretical role. On that usage, any candidates whatever for the role of properties, abundant or sparse, could equally deserve the name of universals. But I do not use the two words loosely and interchangeably. (I regret to say that I once did, in 'An Argument for the Identity Theory'.) Instead, I reserve the word 'universal' strictly for the things, if such there be, that are wholly present as non-spatiotemporal parts in each of the things that instantiate some perfectly natural property.)

Just as monadic universals or tropes might serve to single out the perfectly natural properties, so polyadic universals or tropes might serve to single out the perfectly natural relations. Indeed, if we buy into universals or tropes just in order to avoid taking naturalness as primitive, it seems that we had better be able to cover the relations as well as the properties.[47] Suppose we have a dyadic universal or trope corresponding

---

[47]There just might be another way to define naturalness of relations: by a very short list, fixed once and for all. It seems a little strange to discuss naturalness of relations in a general way when we have only one really clear example: the spatiotemporal relations. Maybe a few more: maybe part–whole and identity. Maybe set membership. Maybe, if we're unlucky, an irreducible relation of causal or lawful connection. But it's still a short list. If we tried to define the natural properties once and for all by a short list – there are the mass properties, the charge properties, the quark colours and flavours, . . . – we ought to suspect that we had left off not only the this-worldly natural properties we have yet to discover, but also the nameless alien natural properties that are found only at other worlds. It seems a bit less clear that we need to leave room for alien natural relations. What if the few natural relations of this-worldly things are the only ones to be found at any world? I regard this hypothesis as far-fetched, but not altogether absurd.

to the relation of being a certain minute distance apart; and suppose a proton and an electron are that distance apart, and together comprise an atom. Then the dyadic universal or trope is present as a non-spatiotemporal part of the atom. It has the same divided location that the atom itself has. But in a different way; unlike the atom, the universal or trope is not itself divided. It doesn't have one part in the proton and another in the electron. If we accept this theory, we just have to accept that an undivided thing can have a divided location. It is part of the atom; but no part of it is part of the proton or part of the electron. If we accept this theory, we must say that the proton and the electron do not exhaust the atom.[48] All this is disturbingly peculiar, much more so that the monadic case, but if the price is right we could learn to tolerate it.

The atom has the structural property of consisting of a proton and an electron a certain distance apart. Is there a structural universal or a structural trope to correspond to this property? If so, that too is present as a non-spatiotemporal part of the atom. We might think that if sparseness is wanted, then this extra thing is superfluous. We already have the monadic universals or tropes of the two particles, and the dyadic universal or trope of distance between them. The presence of these already settles the atom's structure – so what would a structural universal or trope add? But just as the atom itself is not some extra thing over and above its proton and its electron and their distance, so we might say that the atom's structural universal or trope is no extra thing. It is somehow composed of the simpler universals or tropes, and so is nothing over and above them; so we needn't complain of its redundancy. It is not entirely clear how the composition of structural universals would work and so I think it doubtful whether a theory of universals ought to admit them.[49] Structural tropes, on the other hand, seem unproblematic.

The question of primitive naturalness versus universals or tropes is

---

[48]I said that an external relation, although it does not supervene on the intrinsic natures of its *relata* taken separately, does supervene on the intrinsic nature of the composite of its *relata* – for instance, the electron–proton distance supervenes on the intrinsic nature of the whole atom. To make this work under a theory of universals or tropes, 'composite' has to be understood in a special way. The *relata* are just the electron and the proton, but their composite has to be augmented to include also their distance-universal or distance-trope, and any other dyadic universals or tropes that may connect the electron and the proton. (See Williams, 'Necessary Facts', pages 603–5.) Might we throw in too much, and falsely certify the relation of having the same owner as external because we had thrown in a corresponding universal or trope? No fear! – The alleged universal or trope would be superfluous, so a sparse theory will deny its existence. Just as we can safely say that all perfectly natural properties are *ex officio* intrinsic, so we can say that all perfectly natural relations are external, and those will be the only relations to which there correspond dyadic universals or tropes.

[49]See my 'Against Structural Universals'; and Armstrong, *Universals and Scientific Realism*, volume II, pages 69–70.

peripheral to the defence of modal realism which is the main business of this book; I have nevertheless taken it up here for several reasons. First, because of a question I have already considered: whether the benefits of modal realism are diminished if we believe in universals or tropes and therefore have less need of properties taken as sets of *possibilia*. Second, because of the question how satisfactory it might be to replace my genuine possible worlds and individuals by ersatz ones constructed out of this-worldly universals or tropes; I take up this question in section 3.2. And third, because universals or tropes turn out to complicate many of our discussions of the tenets of modal realism and the difference between varieties of it. To take one example: I noted above that a universal is part of anything that a particular that instantiates it is part of. That makes it a common part of all worlds wherein it is instantiated; which means that so long as I remain neutral about the existence of universals, I need to qualify my denial of trans-world identity. (See section 4.2.)

1.6 Isolation

I hope that by saying what theoretical purposes it is meant to serve, I have helped to make clear what my thesis of plurality of worlds is. Now I shall address some further questions of formulation and state some further tenets of my position.

A possible world has parts, namely possible individuals. If two things are parts of the same world, I call them *worldmates*.[50] A world is the mereological sum[51] of all the possible individuals that are parts of it, and so are worldmates of one another. It is a maximal sum: anything that is a worldmate of any part of it is itself a part. (This is just a consequence of my denial that worlds overlap.) But not just any sum of parts of worlds is itself a world. It might, of course, be only part of a world. Or it might consist of parts of two or more different worlds; thus it might be spread

---

[50]Worldmates are compossible in the strongest sense of the word. Two things are compossible in another sense if they are vicariously worldmates, in virtue of their counterparts; that is, iff some one world contains counterparts of both of them. Two things are compossible in yet another sense iff some one world contains intrinsic duplicates of both. In this third sense, any two possible individuals are compossible (except, perhaps, when one is too big to leave room for the other); see section 1.8.

[51]The *mereological sum*, or *fusion*, of several things is the least inclusive thing that includes all of them as parts. It is composed of them and of nothing more; any part of it overlaps one or more of them; it is a proper part of anything else that has all of them as parts. Equivalently: the mereological sum of several things is that thing such that, for any X, X overlaps it iff X overlaps one of them. For background on the mereology that I shall be using extensively in this book, see Leonard and Goodman; or Goodman, *Structure of Appearance*, section II.4.

over logical space, not wholly within any one world, and its parts might not all be worldmates of one another.

What, then, is the difference between a sum of possible individuals that is a possible world, and one that is not? What makes two things worldmates? How are the worlds demarcated one from another? Why don't all the *possibilia* comprise one big world? Or, at the other extreme, why isn't each possible neutrino a little world of its own? In Perry's terminology: what is the unity relation for possible worlds?[52]

I gave part of the answer in my opening section, when I said that nothing is so far away from us in space, or so far in the past or the future, as not to be part of the same world as ourselves. The point seems uncontroversial, and it seems open to generalisation: whenever two possible individuals are spatiotemporally related, they are worldmates. If there is any distance between them – be it great or small, spatial or temporal – they are parts of one single world.

(Better: for any two possible individuals, if every particular part of one is spatiotemporally related to every particular part of the other that is wholly distinct from it, then the two are worldmates. This formulation avoids difficults that might be raised concerning partial spatiotemporal relatedness of trans-world mereological sums; difficulties about multiply located universals; and difficulties about whether we ought to say that overlapping things are spatiotemporally related.)

This is perhaps more controversial than it seems. Didn't I speak, in connection with predetermination, of worlds that diverge? That is, of worlds that are exactly alike up to some time, and differ thereafter? Doesn't that presuppose trans-world comparison of times, simultaneity or succession between events of different worlds? Trans-world spatiotemporal relations between the participants in those events, or the spacetime regions in which they happen?

I think not. Trans-world comparisons, yes; trans-world spatiotemporal relations, no.

Suppose two worlds are exactly alike up to a certain time, and diverge thereafter. I explain it thus. There is an initial segment of one world, and there is an initial segment of the other, which are perfect duplicates. They are maximal such segments: they are not respectively included in two larger initial segments which are also duplicates. There is a correspondence between the parts of these two segments under which the corresponding parts also are duplicates; and under which corresponding parts are related alike spatiotemporally, and as whole to part. Therefore the corresponding parts are excellent counterparts. They are so whether you take a counterpart relation that stresses similarity of intrinsic

---

[52]The question is raised by Richards. I am grateful to him, and to David Johnson, for helpful discussion of it.

character, or one that stresses extrinsic match of origins, or even one that stresses historical role. (Except insofar as something that is part of the duplicated region has a historical role lying partly outside that region.) Temporal cross-sections of the worlds, for instance, are excellent counterparts: there are counterpart centuries, or weeks, or seconds. Likewise there are counterpart places: galaxies, planets, towns. So things that are parts of the two worlds may be simultaneous or not, they may be in the same or different towns, they may be near or far from one another, in very natural counterpart-theoretic senses. But these are not genuine spatiotemporal relations across worlds. The only trans-world relations involved are internal relations of similarity; not indeed between the very individuals that are quasi-simultaneous (or whatever) but between larger duplicate parts of the two worlds wherein those individuals are situated.

Suppose you discovered – say, from a well-accredited oracle – that large parts of human history were re-enacted, with interesting variations, in remote galaxies at times in the distant past and future. In speaking of these re-enactments, you would surely introduce counterpart-theoretic comparisons of place and time. You might say that a remarkable event in one of them took place last year in Headington; when you would also say, without any conflict, that it will take place about 6.4×10^{12} years hence, 3.8×10^9 light years away in the general direction of the constellation Centaurus. You should have no greater difficulty in squaring talk about other-worldly goings-on last week in Didcot with my denial that there are any spatiotemporal relations between parts of different worlds.

So we have a sufficient condition: if two things are spatiotemporally related, then they are worldmates. The converse is much more problematic. Yet that is more or less the doctrine that I propose. Putting the two halves together: things are worldmates iff they are spatiotemporally related. A world is unified, then, by the spatiotemporal interrelation of its parts. There are no spatiotemporal relations across the boundary between one world and another; but no matter how we draw a boundary within a world, there will be spatiotemporal relations across it.

A first, and simplest, objection is that a world might possibly consist of two or more completely disconnected spacetimes. (Maybe *our* world does, if indeed such disconnection is possible.) But whatever way a world might be is a way that some world is; and one world with two disconnected spacetimes is a counterexample against my proposal. Against this objection, I must simply deny the premise. I would rather not; I admit some inclination to agree with it. But it seems to me that it is no central part of our modal thinking, and not a consequence of any interesting general principle about what is possible. So it is negotiable. Given a choice between rejecting the alleged possibility of disconnected spacetimes within a single world and (what I take to be the alternative) resorting to a primitive worldmate relation, I take the former to be more credible.

I cannot give you disconnected spacetimes within a single world; but I can give you some passable substitutes. One big world, spatiotemporally interrelated, might have many different world-like parts. *Ex hypothesi* these are not complete worlds, but they could seem to be. They might be four-dimensional; they might have no boundaries; there might be little or no causal interaction between them. Indeed, each of these world-like parts of one big world might be a duplicate of some genuinely complete world. There are at least four ways for one big world to contain many world-like parts. Each is a way that a world could be; and so, say I, each is a way that some world is.

(1) The spacetime of the big world might have an extra dimension. The world-like parts might then be spread out along this extra dimension, like a stack of flatlands in three-space.

(2) The world-like parts might share a common spacetime. There might be several populations, interpenetrating without interaction in the single spacetime where all of them live. If so, of course the inhabitants had better not interact with the shape of their spacetime as we do with the shape of ours; else this interaction enables the different populations to interact indirectly with one another.

(3) Time might have the metric structure not of the real line, but rather of many copies of the real line laid end to end. We would have many different epochs, one after another. Yet each epoch would have infinite duration, no beginning, and no end. Inhabitants of different epochs would be spatiotemporally related, but their separation would be infinite. Or instead there might be infinitely many infinite regions laid out side by side in space; then there would have to be infinite spatial distances between points in different world-like regions.

(4) Or time might have the metric structure of the real line, as we normally suppose. And yet there might be infinitely many world-like epochs one after the other. Each might be of finite duration; but their finitude might be hidden from their inhabitants because, as the end of an epoch approaches, everything speeds up. Suppose that one generation lives and dies in twelve months, the next in six, the next in three, . . . so that infinitely many generations fit into the last two years of their epoch. Similarly, world-like regions of finite diameter might be packed spatially, with shrinkage as things approach the edge.

If you thought, as I did too, that a single world might consist of many more or less isolated world-like parts, how sure can you be that you really had in mind the supposed possibility that I reject? Are you sure that it was an essential part of your thought that the world-like parts were in no way spatiotemporally related? Or might you not have had in mind, rather, one of these substitutes I offer? Or might your thought have been sufficiently lacking in specificity that the substitutes would do it justice?

A second objection concerns spirits, and episodes in the mental lives of spirits, which are traditionally supposed to be outside of space. However sure we are that no such deficient things are worldmates of ours, is it not at least possible that the traditional story might be true? If so, then some world is populated by such spirits. But that is no objection. I do not say that all worlds are unified by spatiotemporal interrelatedness in just the same way. So the interrelation of a world of spirits might be looser than that of a decent world like ours. If the spirits and their doings are located in time alone, that is good enough. (To make sense of that, maybe time and space would have to be more separable at the world of the spirits than they are at our world; but that is surely possible.) I can even allow marvellous Spirits who are spatiotemporally related to other things by being omnipresent – for that is one way among others to stand in spatiotemporal relations. I am not sure why I need to defend the possibility of spirit tales – after all, people have been known to accept impossible theories, as witness naive set theory – but in fact I think I give them at least as much room in logical space as they deserve.

A third objection concerns the possibility that there might be nothing, and not rather something. If a world is a maximal mereological sum of spatiotemporally interrelated things, that makes no provision for an absolutely empty world. A world is not like a bottle that might hold no beer. The world *is* the totality of things it contains, so even if there's no beer, there's still the bottle. And if there isn't even the bottle, there's nothing there at all. And nothing isn't a very minimal something. Minimal worlds there can indeed be. There can be nothing much: just some homogeneous unoccupied spacetime, or maybe only one single point of it. But nothing much is still something, and there isn't any world where there's nothing at all. That makes it necessary that there is something. For it's true at all worlds that there is something: it's true whenever we restrict our quantifiers to the domain of parts of a single world, even if the only part of some world is one indivisible nondescript point. Of course, if we don't restrict quantifiers from the standpoint of one world or another, then all the more is it true that there is something rather than nothing: there is logical space, the totality of the worlds in all their glory.

How bad is this? I think the worst of it is the fear that I might offer to *explain* why there is something rather than nothing, just by saying that this is a necessary truth. But don't fear; I do not think that would be an explanation. For an explanation, I think, is an account of etiology: it tells us something about how an event was caused. Or it tells us something general about how some, or many, or all events of a certain kind are caused. Or it explains an existential fact by telling us something about how several events jointly make that fact true, and then perhaps something about how those truthmaker events were caused. So I think there is nothing I might say that could count as explaining why there is something rather than nothing; and that includes saying, truly, that there is no world where there is nothing.[53]

So far I am stonewalling. I accept the unwelcome consequences of my thesis, and claim they are not as bad as you might think. But there is one more objection to consider, and this one really does seem to me to call for a retreat. The last resort would be a primitive worldmate relation, but I think it won't be necessary to fall back that far.

Imagine a theory of spacetime that is built for Newtonian mechanics, or for common sense. (Old-fashioned Newtonian mechanics, as opposed to recent reformulations that are still in a sense Newtonian, but do away with absolute rest.) This theory will say that any two spacetime points are related by a spatial distance and a temporal distance: two different distances. One but not both of these distances may be zero, thus absolute simultaneity and absolute rest both are well defined. I suppose this is a way the world might have been, therefore it is a way that some world is. But we have good reason to think that our world is different. In our relativistic world, any two spacetime points have only one distance between them; it may be a spatial distance, it may be a temporal distance, or it may be a zero distance which is neither spatial nor temporal ('space-like' interval coded by a positive real, 'time-like' interval coded by a positive imaginary, or 'light-like' interval). Of course there are other differences between Newtonian and relativistic spacetime, but this difference of two distances versus one is the difference that matters to ontology.

We name the properties and relations that figure in our world; so what we call 'spatiotemporal relations' are relations that behave in the relativistic way, with spatial or temporal distance but not both. Now when we talk about the Newtonian world, are we talking about the possibility of different behaviour on the part of those same relations? Is it that those very relations might double up to give us two distances, one of each kind, between the same two points? Or are we talking instead about some different relations that might take the place of the spatiotemporal relations of our world?[54]

---

[53] I find it pleasing that another view, the one I like second best after my own, also seems to make it come out necessary that there is something rather than nothing. This is the 'combinatorial' view: in place of other worlds, we have constructions in which the elements of this world – elementary particulars and universals, perhaps – are put together in different combinations. (See section 3.2, in which I present this as a form of 'linguistic ersatzism'.) But as D. M. Armstrong has noted in discussion, there is no way to combine elements and make nothing at all. So there is no combinatorial possibility that there might be nothing.

[54] What does this question mean? Maybe one thing, maybe another, depending on our underlying theory of natural properties and relations; and on that question I am staying

If it is the former, no worries. The Newtonian world is just as much spatiotemporally interrelated as ours is, even if the spatiotemporal relations behave differently there. But if it is the latter, then strictly speaking I cannot say that the Newtonian world is *spatiotemporally* interrelated. It has its system of external relations, whereby its parts are arranged, which are analogous to the spatiotemporal relations whereby the parts of our world are arranged. But these Newtonian impostors are not to be called the 'spatiotemporal relations', because that is the name we gave to the different relations that hold between the parts of our world. (It is beside the point that when we named the relations of our world, we may have thought they behaved in the Newtonian rather than the relativistic way. However much we intended to name relations that conformed to some theory, doubtless we intended much more to name relations that are pervasive in our world.) Similarly, *mutatis mutandis*, if the inhabitants of a Newtonian world talk about the possibility of a world like ours. Suppose they did pretty much what we did in naming what they call 'spatiotemporal relations'; and suppose it is not so that the very same relations behave in the Newtonian way at one world and in the relativistic way at the other. Then they should not say, strictly speaking, that our world is 'spatiotemporally interrelated'.

I do not know how to answer the question whether we have the same relations in the different worlds. It might even have different answers in different cases: some pairs of a Newtonian and a relativistic world use the same relations (doubled up for the Newtonian world), other pairs don't. Also, I suppose some worlds are interrelated by systems of external relations that differ more, at least in their behaviour, than Newtonian doubled-up distances differ from relativistic distances. It would be nice to suppose that all worlds are interrelated by the very same relations, namely the ones that we call 'spatiotemporal', despite whatever behavioural differences there may be. I do not reject this supposition. But I am unwilling to rely on it.

What I need to say is that each world is interrelated (and is maximal with respect to such interrelation) by a system of relations which, if they are not the spatiotemporal relations rightly so called, are at any rate analogous to them. Then my task is to spell out the analogy. At least some of the points of analogy should go as follows. (1) The relations are

---

neutral between three alternatives. (See section 1.5.) (1) Maybe naturalness is a primitive, applied to properties or relations understood as sets. Then we have families of relations that can serve as the common spatiotemporal relations of all the worlds, and we have other families of less inclusive relations that can serve as the different special spatiotemporal relations for different kinds of worlds, and the question is which relations are more natural. (2) Maybe a relation is natural when its instances share a relational universal; then the question is what universals there are. (3) Maybe a relation is natural when its instances contain duplicate tropes; then the question is what tropes there are.

natural; they are not gruesome gerrymanders, not even mildly disjunctive. (2) They are *pervasive*: mostly, or perhaps without exception, when there is a chain of relations in the system running from one thing to another, then also there is a direct relation. (3) They are *discriminating*: it is at least possible, whether or not it happens at every world where the relations are present, that there be a great many interrelated things, no two of which are exactly alike with respect to their place in the structure of relations. (4) They are *external*: they do not supervene on the intrinsic natures of the *relata* taken separately, but only on the intrinsic character of the composite of the *relata*. (See section 1.5. The definition of what it is for a relation to be external involved *possibilia* but not yet possible worlds, and so is available at this point without circularity.) When a system of relations is analogous to the spatiotemporal relations, strictly so called, let me call them *analogically* spatiotemporal.[55]

I have some hope that it might be possible to bypass the messy idea of analogically spatiotemporal relations. A much simpler alternative would be that worlds are unified by *external* interrelatedness, of whatever sort. On this suggestion, *any* natural external relations will do to unify a world. Every part of a world bears some such relation to every other part; but no part of one world ever bears any such relation to any part of another.

---

[55]There are three different conceptions of what the spatiotemporal relations might be. There is the dualist conception: there are the parts of spacetime itself, and there are the pieces of matter or fields or whatnot that occupy some of the parts of spacetime. Then the spatiotemporal relations (strict or analogical) consist of distance relations that hold between parts of spacetime; relations of occupancy that hold between occupants and the parts of spacetime they occupy; and, derivatively from these, further distance relations between the occupants, or between occupants and parts of spacetime.

There are two simpler monistic conceptions. One of them does away with the occupants as separate things: we have the parts of spacetime, and their distance relations are the only spatiotemporal relations. The properties that we usually ascribe to occupants of spacetime – for instance, properties of mass, charge, field strength – belong in fact to parts of spacetime themselves. When a part of spacetime has a suitable distribution of local properties, then it is a particle, or a piece of a field, or a donkey, or what have you.

The other monistic conception does the opposite: it does away with the parts of spacetime in favour of the occupants (now not properly so called), so that the only spatiotemporal relations are the distance relations between some of these. I tend to oppose the third conception, at least as applied to our world, for much the reasons given in Nerlich, *The Shape of Space*. I tend, more weakly, to oppose the dualist conception as uneconomical. I suppose it may be, however, that there are worlds of all three sorts; if so, that would give more reason than ever to doubt that the same system of spatiotemporal relations serves to unify all the worlds. Throughout this book, I shall presuppose that there are such things as spatiotemporal regions, whether or not there also are distinct things that occupy those regions. But I believe this presupposition plays no important role, and I could have been more neutral at the cost of clumsier writing. I certainly don't mean to suggest that the existence of spacetime and its parts is an essential tenet of modal realism.

Never mind whether the relations in question are spatiotemporal, either strictly or analogically.

If the simplification is to have a hope, the restriction to natural relations must bear a good deal of weight. It will have to exclude more than just the gruesome gerrymanders. For what about the relation of *non-identity*? (Here I am indebted to discussion with James Grieve.) It qualifies on my definition as an external relation, and it obtains invariably between the particular parts of different worlds. However, we may fairly deny it a place in our select inventory of the natural relations. It would be superfluous to include it if we have the resources to introduce it by definition; and we do, since X and Y are non-identical iff there is a class that one of X and Y belongs to and the other does not. (If you think there is need to cover non-identity of 'proper classes' you should add a clause: '. . . or there is something that belongs to one of X and Y but not the other'.)

I find it hard to say whether this simplification could succeed. My problem is a lack of test cases. What natural external relations could there be besides the (strictly or analogically) spatiotemporal relations? I would reject some candidates for further external relations that might be offered: for instance, primitive genidentity relations, non-qualitative counterpart relations (see section 4.4), or a primitive worldmate relation.

Perhaps the following will do as a test case. If so, it looks unfavourable for the simplification. We tend to think that positive and negative charge are natural intrinsic properties of particles; but suppose not. Suppose instead there are natural external relations of like-chargedness and opposite-chargedness. (Then we can introduce extrinsic versions of the charge properties. To be neutral is to be like-charged to some particles and opposite-charged to none; to be negative is to be like-charged to most of the lightweight particles that orbit much heavier clumps of particles hereabouts; and to be positive is to be opposite-charged to a negative particle.) On this view, as opposed to the standard view, the relations of like- and opposite-chargedness do *not* supervene on the intrinsic natures of two particles taken separately; an electron and a positron may be perfect intrinsic duplicates. That is the point of calling the relations external. They are natural *ex hypothesi*. They are pervasive (at least, given the appropriate laws) in what whenever two particles are connected by a chain of such relations, they are connected directly. But they are very far from discriminating (again, given the appropriate laws): if there are as few as three particles, there must be two of them that are alike so far as these relations are concerned. If this story, or something like it, could be true, then here we have external relations that are not strictly or analogically spatiotemporal.

Could two particles in different worlds stand in these external relations of like- or opposite-chargedness? So it seems, offhand; and if so, then the simplification fails. I would welcome a reason why particles at different worlds cannot stand in these relations – other than a verificationist reason that I would find unpersuasive – but failing such a reason, I am inclined to reject the simplification. Then I must stick instead with my underdeveloped suggestion that the unifying external relations have to be, if not strictly spatiotemporal, at least analogically spatiotemporal.

There is a second way in which the worlds are isolated: there is no causation from one to another. If need be, I would put this causal isolation alongside spatiotemporal isolation as a principle of demarcation for worlds. But there is no need. Under a counterfactual analysis of causation, the causal isolation of worlds follows automatically. Therefore it contributes nothing to the demarcation of one world from another. No matter how we solve the demarcation problem, trans-world causation comes out as nonsense.

When we have causation within a world, what happens is roughly as follows. (For simplicity I ignore complications having to do with causal pre-emption and overdetermination, and with the idealisation of supposing that we always have closest antecedent-worlds. Taking these matters into account would do nothing in favour of trans-world causation.) We have a world W where event C causes event E. Both these events occur at W, and they are distinct events, and it is the case at W that if C had not occurred, E would not have occurred either. The counterfactual means that at the closest worlds to W at which C does not occur, E does not occur either.

Try to adapt this to a case of trans-world causation, in which the events of one world supposedly influence those of another. Event C occurs at world W_C, event E occurs at world E_E, they are distinct events, and if C had not occurred, E would not have occurred either. This counterfactual is supposed to hold – where? It means that at the closest worlds to – where? – at which C does not occur, E does not occur – where? – either.

Normally the counterfactual is supposed to hold at the world where the one event causes the other; so maybe if the causation goes between two worlds, the counterfactual ought to hold at both. So we have:

(1) at the closest worlds to W_C at which C does not occur, E does not occur either, and

(2) at the closest worlds to W_E at which C does not occur, E does not occur either.

But (1) looks wrong: since we are looking at a supposed case of trans-world causation, it is irrelevant to ask whether we get E at worlds close to W_C; we ought to be looking at worlds close to W_E, the world where the supposed effect did take place. And (2) looks even worse: we ought to be hypothesising the removal of C from a world like W_C: removing it from a world like W_E is irrelevant. In fact, the closest world to W_E at which C does not occur might very well be W_E itself!

So should we make sure that we make our revisions to the right worlds by specifying explicitly which worlds the events are to be removed from? Like this:

(1′) at the closest worlds to W_C at which C does not occur at W_C, E does not occur at W_E, and

(2′) at the closest worlds to W_E at which C does not occur at W_C, E does not occur at W_E.

But this is worse than ever. What can these double modifications mean: at *this* world, an event does not occur at *that* world? C just *does* occur at W_C, E just *does* occur at W_E; there is no world at which these facts are otherwise. You might as well say that in Auckland it rains in Melbourne, but in Wellington it doesn't rain in Melbourne. There is no way to make literal sense of this, unless by taking the outer modifier as vacuous. (That is why you instantly thought of two ways to make *non-literal* sense of it: in Auckland they say it rains in Melbourne, but they don't say so in Wellington; it rains a lot in Melbourne compared to Auckland, but not compared to Wellington.)

Try this. As the one world is to ordinary causation, so the pair of worlds is to trans-world causation. So put pairs for single worlds throughout:

(3) at the closest world-pairs to the pair ⟨W_C, W_E⟩ such that C does not occur at the first world of the pair, E does not occur at the second world of the pair.

This makes sense, but not I think in a way that could make it true. For I suppose that the closeness of one world-pair to another consists of the closeness of the first worlds of the pairs together with the closeness of the second worlds of the pairs. We have to depart from W_C for the first world of a closest pair, since we have to get rid of C. But we are not likewise forced to depart from W_E for the second world of a closest pair, and what is so close to a world as that world itself? So the second world of any closest pair will just be W_E, at which E does occur, so (3) is false.

(If there were significant external relations between worlds, that might provide another respect of comparison for world-pairs. But to this I say, first, that even if trans-world external relations are not absolutely forbidden by our solution to the problem of demarcation, the permitted ones would be such things as our imagined relations of like- and opposite-chargedness, which don't seem to do anything to help (3) to come true;

and second, that if our special world-pair counterfactuals are supposed to make for causal dependence, they had better be governed by the same sort of closeness that governs ordinary causal counterfactuals, but ordinary closeness of worlds does not involve any trans-world external relations that might make world-pairs close.)

When it seems to us as if we can understand trans-world causation, I think that what must be happening is as follows. We think of the totality of all the possible worlds as if it were one grand world, and that starts us thinking that there are other ways the grand world might have been. So perhaps what we really have in mind is:

(4) at the closest alternative grand worlds to ours where C does not occur in the part corresponding to W_C, E does not occur in the part corresponding to W_E.

But this is thoroughly misguided. If I am right, the many worlds already provide for contingency, and there is no sense in providing for it all over again. Or else I am wrong, and the many worlds do not provide for genuine contingency. (As some think; see section 2.1.) But then it makes no sense to repeat the very method you think has failed, only on a grander scale. The worlds are all of the maximal things that are suitably unified. If they fall into grand clusters, and yet grander clusters of clusters, and so on, that is neither here nor there. By 'worlds' I still mean *all* the worlds. (And how could they fall into clusters – what sort of relation could unify a cluster without also merging the worlds within it?) There is but one totality of worlds; it is not a world; it could not have been different. Therefore (4) is nonsense, intelligible only if taken as vacuous.

So there isn't any trans-world causation. And not because I so stipulate as a principle of demarcation, but as a consequence of my analyses of causation and of counterfactuals. This is the real reason why there couldn't be a very powerful telescope for viewing other worlds. The obstacle isn't that other worlds are too far away, as Kripke jokingly says; and it isn't that they're somehow 'abstract', as of course he really thinks. (See *Naming and Necessity*, pages 44 and 19.) Telescopic viewing, like other methods of gathering information, is a *causal* process: a 'telescope' which produced images that were causally independent of the condition of the thing 'viewed' would be a bogus telescope. No trans-world causation, no trans-world telescopes.

Likewise, if there is no trans-world causation, there is no trans-world travel. You can't get into a 'logical-space ship' and visit another possible world. You could get into what you confusedly think is a logical-space ship, turn the knob, and disappear. And a perfect duplicate of you at your disappearance, surrounded by a perfect duplicate of your ship, could appear *ex nihilo* at some other world. Indeed, there are plenty of worlds where aspiring logical-space travellers disappear, and plenty of worlds where they appear, and plenty of qualitative duplications between ones that disappear and ones that appear. But none of this is travel unless there is one surviving traveller who both departs and arrives. And causal continuity is required for survival; it is a principal part of what unifies a persisting person. It is so within a single world: if there is a demon who destroys people at random, and another who creates people at random, and by a very improbable coincidence the creating demon replaces a victim of the destroying demon, the qualitative continuity could be perfect, but the lack of causal dependence would still make it not be a genuine case of survival. Likewise across worlds. No trans-world causation, no trans-world causal continuity; no causal continuity, no survival; no survival, no travel. All those people in various worlds who meet their ends in 'logical-space ships', as well as the more fortunate ones who appear *ex nihilo* in such ships, are sadly deluded.

But if you'd like to see a world where Napoleon conquered all, don't give up hope. Maybe ours is one of those big worlds with many world-like parts, spatiotemporally related in some peculiar way. Then you might get your wish, near enough, by means of a special telescope or a special spaceship that operates entirely within our single world. You won't see the world-like part where Napoleon himself is, of course; you're there already, and he didn't conquer all. But I presume you'd be content with a world-like part where the conqueror was an excellent counterpart of Napoleon. I would be the last to denounce decent science fiction as philosophically unsound. No; tales of viewing or visiting 'other worlds' are perfectly consistent. They come true at countless possible worlds. It's just that the 'other worlds' that are viewed or visited never can be what *I* call 'other worlds'.

1.7 Concreteness

Because I said that other worlds are of a kind with this world of ours, doubtless you will expect me to say that possible worlds and individuals are concrete, not abstract. But I am reluctant to say that outright. Not because I hold the opposite view; but because it is not at all clear to me what philosophers mean when they speak of 'concrete' and 'abstract' in this connection. Perhaps I would agree with it, whatever it means, but still I do not find it a useful way of explaining myself.

I can say this much, even without knowing what 'concrete' is supposed to mean. I take it, at least, that donkeys and protons and puddles and stars are supposed to be paradigmatically concrete. I take it also that the division between abstract and concrete is meant to divide entities into fundamentally different kinds. If so, then it is out of the question that an abstract entity and a concrete entity should be exactly alike, perfect duplicates. According to my modal realism, the donkeys and protons and puddles and stars that are parts of this world have perfect duplicates that are parts of other worlds. This suffices to settle, whatever exactly it may mean, that at least some possible individuals are 'concrete'. And if so, then at least some possible worlds are at least partly 'concrete'.

A spectator might well assume that the distinction between 'concrete' and 'abstract' entities is common ground among contemporary philosophers, too well understood and uncontroversial to need any explaining. But if someone does try to explain it, most likely he will resort to one (or more) of four ways.[56]

First, the Way of Example: concrete entities are things like donkeys and puddles and protons and stars, whereas abstract entities are things like numbers. That gives us very little guidance. First, because we have no uncontroversial account of what numbers are. Are the paradigms of abstractness meant to be the von Neumann ordinals – certain pure sets? Are they meant to be structural universals, instantiated here and there within our world, like the tripartiteness that is instantiated wherever there is a proton composed of quarks (if quarks themselves are mereological atoms)? Are they 'irreducible *sui generis* abstract entities'? And even given a useful account of the nature of numbers, there are just too many ways that numbers differ from donkeys *et al.* and we still are none the wiser about where to put a border between donkey-like and number-like.

At least the Way of Example has something to say about some parts of other worlds. As noted above, some parts of other worlds are *exactly* like donkeys, because they are donkeys, so those at any rate are paradigmatically concrete. Likewise for other-worldly puddles and protons and stars. So far, so good. But other parts of other worlds are, for instance, chunks of other-worldly spacetime – are those paradigmatically concrete? And if ordinary particulars contain universals or tropes as (non-spatiotemporal) parts, then worlds composed of ordinary particulars will in turn have universals or tropes as parts; in which case not all the parts of worlds are paradigmatically concrete. Indeed we might contemplate a theory of numbers – one which says, for instance, that the number three is the structural universal of tripartiteness – according to which some parts of worlds would turn out to be paradigmatically abstract.

And what of a whole world? Is it sufficiently donkey-like, despite its

---

[56]I shall pass over a fifth way, offered by Dummett in chapter 14 of *Frege: Philosophy of Language*, in which the distinction between abstract and concrete entities is drawn in terms of how we could understand their names. Even if this fifth way succeeds in drawing a border, as for all I know it may, it tells us nothing directly about how the entities on opposite sides of that border differ in their nature. It is like saying that snakes are the animals we instinctively most fear – maybe so, but it tells us nothing about the nature of snakes.

size? And perhaps despite the fact that it consists mostly of empty spacetime? I am inclined to say that, according to the Way of Example, a world is concrete rather than abstract – more donkey-like than number-like. I am also inclined to say that a world is more like a raven than a writing-desk; and that it is ping rather than pong. But I know not why.

Second, the Way of Conflation: the distinction between concrete and abstract entities is just the distinction between individuals and sets, or between particulars and universals, or perhaps between particular individuals and everything else. That accords well enough with our examples. It is safe to say that donkeys and the like are particular individuals, not universals or sets. It is a defensible, if not trouble-free, view that numbers are sets; alternatively, it is arguable that they are universals. So far, so good. I say that worlds are individuals, not sets. I say that worlds are particulars, not universals. So according to the Way of Conflation in either version, I say that worlds are concrete.

Third, the Negative Way: abstract entities have no spatiotemporal location; they do not enter into causal interaction; they are never indiscernible one from another.

The Negative Way and the Way of Conflation seem to disagree rather badly. As for the first part, the denial that abstract entities are located, I object that by this test some sets and universals come out concrete. Sets are supposed to be abstract. But a set of located things *does* seem to have a location, though perhaps a divided location: it *is* where its members *are*. Thus my unit set is right here, exactly where I am; the set of you and me is partly here where I am, partly yonder where you are; and so on. And universals are supposed to be abstract. But if a universal is wholly present in each of many located particulars, as by definition it is, that means that it is where its instances are. It is multiply located, not unlocated. You could just declare that an abstract entity is located only in the special way that a set or a universal is located – but then you might as well just say that to be abstract is to be a set or universal. Your talk of unlocatedness adds nothing. Maybe a *pure* set, or an *uninstantiated* universal, has no location. However these are the most dispensable and suspect of sets and universals. If it is said that sets or universals generally are unlocated, perhaps we have a hasty generalisation. Or perhaps we have an inference: they're unlocated because they're abstract. If so, we had better not also say that they're abstract because they're unlocated.

As for the second part, the denial that abstract entities enter into causal interaction, this too seems to disagree with the Way of Conflation. Is it true that sets or universals cannot enter into causal interaction? Why shouldn't we say that something causes a set of effects? Or that a set of causes, acting jointly, causes something? Or that positive charge causes effects of a characteristic kind whenever it is instantiated? Many authors have proposed to identify an event – the very thing that most surely can cause and be caused – with one or another sort of set. (For instance, in 'Events' I propose to identify an event with the set of spacetime regions where it occurs.) Must any such identification be rejected, regardless of the economies it may afford, just because sets are supposed to be 'abstract'?

As for the third part, the denial that abstract entities can be indiscernible, indeed I do not see what could be said in favour of indiscernible universals. But as for sets, I should think that if two individuals are indiscernible, then so are their unit sets; and likewise whenever sets differ only by a substitution of indiscernible individuals. So, *pace* the Way of Conflation, it seems that the Negative Way does not classify universals, or sets in general, as abstract.

What does it say about worlds? Other worlds and their parts certainly stand in no spatiotemporal or causal relations to *us*. Worlds are spatiotemporally and causally isolated from one another; else they would be not whole worlds, but parts of a greater world. But by the same token, we stand in no spatiotemporal or causal relation to *them*. That doesn't make us abstract. It's no good saying that, for us, we are concrete and an other-worldly being is abstract; whereas, for that other-worldly being, he is concrete and we are abstract. For one thing is certain: whatever the abstract–concrete distinction is, at least it's supposed to be a very fundamental difference between two kinds of entities. It has no business being a symmetrical and relative affair.

So the right question is: do other worlds and their parts stand in spatiotemporal and causal relations to anything? Parts of worlds do: they stand in (strictly or analogically) spatiotemporal relations, and in causal relations, to other parts of their own worlds. (With exceptions. Maybe a tiny world might have only one part. A chaotic and lawless world might have no causation. But I presume we don't want to say that parts of worlds are abstract in these special cases, concrete otherwise.) Whole worlds, however, cannot stand in spatiotemporal and causal relations to anything outside themselves, and it seems that nothing can stand in such relations to its own parts. Should we conclude that worlds – including the one we are part of – are abstract wholes made of concrete parts? Perhaps, indeed, divisible exhaustively into concrete parts? That seems unduly literalistic – presumably the Negative Way should be construed charitably, so that wholes can inherit concreteness from their parts. As for indiscernibility, I have no idea whether there are indiscernible worlds; but certainly there are indiscernible parts of worlds, for instance indiscernible epochs of a world of two-way eternal recurrence. So according to the Negative Way, charitably read, I say that worlds and their parts – including the universals, if such there be! – are concrete.

Fourth, the Way of Abstraction: abstract entities are abstractions from concrete entities. They result from somehow subtracting specificity, so that an incomplete description of the original concrete entity would be a complete description of the abstraction. This, I take it, is the historically and etymologically correct thing to mean if we talk of 'abstract entities'. But it is by no means the dominant meaning in contemporary philosophy.

A theory of non-spatiotemporal parts of things, whether these be recurring universals or non-recurring tropes, makes good sense of some abstractions. We can say that unit negative charge is a universal common to many particles, and is an abstraction from these particles just by being part of each of them. Or we can say that the particular negative charge of this particular particle is part of it, but a proper part and in that sense an abstraction from the whole of it. But we cannot just identify abstractions with universals or tropes. For why can we not abstract some highly extrinsic aspect of something – say, the surname it bears? Or its spatiotemporal location? Or its role in some causal network? Or its role in some body of theory? All these are unsuitable candidates for genuine universals or tropes, being no part of the intrinsic nature of the thing whence they are abstracted.

We can also make good sense of abstractions, or an adequate imitation thereof, by the stratagem of taking equivalence classes. For instance, we abstract the direction of a line from the line itself by taking the direction to be the class of that line and all other lines parallel to it. There is no genuine subtraction of specific detail, rather there is multiplication of it; but by swamping if not by removal, the specifics of the original line get lost. For instance, the direction comprises many located lines; it is located where its members are, namely everywhere; so it is not located more one place than another, and that is the next best thing to not being anywhere. But sets in general cannot be regarded thus as abstractions: most sets are equivalence classes only under thoroughly artificial equivalences. (And the empty set is not an equivalence class at all.) Further, if we abstract by taking equivalence classes, we need not start with paradigmatically concrete things. Thus directions may be abstracted from lines, but the lines themselves may be taken as certain sets of quadruples of real numbers.

So even if universals and equivalence classes are abstractions, it remains that the Way of Abstraction accords badly with the Ways of Example and of Conflation. It accords no better with the Negative Way: if we can abstract the spatiotemporal location of something, that abstraction will not be unlocated; rather, there will be nothing to it except location. Likewise if we can abstract the causal role of something, then the one thing the abstraction will do is enter into causal interactions.

Unless understood as universals or tropes or equivalence classes, abstractions are obviously suspect. The inevitable hypothesis is that they are verbal fictions: we say 'in the material mode' that we are speaking about the abstraction when what's true is that we are speaking abstractly about the original thing. We are ignoring some of its features, not introducing some new thing from which those features are absent. We purport to speak of the abstraction 'economic man'; but really we are speaking of ordinary men in an abstract way, confining ourselves to their economic activities.

According to the Way of Abstraction, I say that worlds are concrete. They lack no specificity, and there is nothing for them to be abstractions from. As for the parts of worlds, certainly some of them are concrete, such as the other-worldly donkeys and protons and puddles and stars. But if universals or tropes are non-spatiotemporal parts of ordinary particulars that in turn are parts of worlds, then here we have abstractions that are parts of worlds.

So, by and large, and with some doubts in connection with the Way of Example and the Negative Way, it seems that indeed I should say that worlds as I take them to be are concrete; and so are many of their parts, but perhaps not all. But it also seems that to say that is to say something very ambiguous indeed. It's just by luck that all its disambiguations make it true.

1.8 Plenitude

At the outset, I mentioned several ways that a world might be; and then I made it part of my modal realism that

(1) absolutely every way that a world could possibly be is a way that some world is, and

(2) absolutely every way that a part of a world could possibly be is a way that some part of some world is.

But what does that mean? It *seems* to mean that the worlds are abundant, and logical space is somehow complete. There are no gaps in logical space; no vacancies where a world might have been, but isn't. It seems to be a principle of plenitude. But is it really?

Given modal realism, it becomes advantageous to identify 'ways a world could possibly be' with worlds themselves. Why distinguish two closely corresponding entities: a world, and also the maximally specific way that world is? Economy dictates identifying the 'ways' with the worlds.

But as Peter van Inwagen pointed out to me, that makes (1) contentless. It says only that every world is identical to some world. That would be true even if there were only seventeen worlds, or one, or none. It says nothing at all about abundance or completeness. Likewise for (2).

Suppose we thought a maximally specific 'way' should be the same kind of things as a less specific 'way': namely a property, taken as a set. Then a maximally specific 'way' would be a unit set. Now indeed the 'ways' are distinct from the worlds. Further, they are abstract in whatever sense sets are. But this does nothing to restore content to (1). A 'possible way' is a *non-empty* set, and (1) now says trivially that each of the unit sets has a member.[57]

Or perhaps a 'way' should be not a unit set, but an equivalence class under indiscernibility. I am agnostic about whether there are indiscernible worlds. If there are, I myself would wish to say that there are indiscernible ways a world could be, just as I would say that a world of two-way eternal recurrence affords countless indiscernible ways – one per epoch – for a person to be. But others might not like the idea of indiscernible 'ways'. They might therefore welcome a guarantee that, whether or not worlds ever are indiscernible, 'ways' never will be. Now (1) says trivially that each of the equivalence classes has a member.

Or suppose we thought a 'way' should be the intrinsic nature of a world, a highly complex structural universal (as in Forrest, 'Ways Worlds Could Be'.) Given that thesis, a 'possible way' is an *instantiated* universal. Now (1) says trivially that each of these has a world to instantiate it.

We might read (1) as saying that every way we *think* a world could possibly be is a way that some world is; that is, every seemingly possible description or conception of a world does fit some world. Now we have made (1) into a genuine principle of plenitude. But an unacceptable one. So understood, (1) indiscriminately endorses offhand opinion about what is possible.

I conclude that (1), and likewise (2), cannot be salvaged as principles of plenitude. Let them go trivial. Then we need a new way to say what (1) and (2) seemed to say: that there are possibilities enough, and no gaps in logical space.

To which end, I suggest that we look to the Humean denial of necessary connections between distinct existences. To express the plenitude of possible worlds, I require a *principle of recombination* according to which patching together parts of different possible worlds yields another possible

---

[57]Some critics have thought it very important that the 'ways' should be 'abstract' entities and distinct from the worlds. For instance, see Stalnaker, 'Possible Worlds'; and van Inwagen, who writes 'the cosmos, being concrete, is not a way things could have been. . . . And surely the cosmos cannot itself be identical with any way the cosmos could have been: to say this would be like saying that Socrates is identical with the way Socrates is, which is plain bad grammar.' ('Indexicality and Actuality', page 406.) But to me, the choice whether to take a 'way' as a unit set or as its sole member seems to be of the utmost unimportance, on a par with the arbitrary choice between speaking of a set or of its characteristic function.

world. Roughly speaking, the principle is that anything can coexist with anything else, at least provided they occupy distinct spatiotemporal positions. Likewise, anything can fail to coexist with anything else. Thus if there could be a dragon, and there could be a unicorn, but there couldn't be a dragon and a unicorn side by side, that would be an unacceptable gap in logical space, a failure of plenitude. And if there could be a talking head contiguous to the rest of a living human body, but there couldn't be a talking head separate from the rest of a human body, that too would be a failure of plenitude.

(I mean that plenitude requires that there could be a separate thing *exactly like* a talking head contiguous to a human body. Perhaps you would not wish to call that thing a 'head', or you would not wish to call what it does 'talking'. I am somewhat inclined to disagree, and somewhat inclined to doubt that usage establishes a settled answer to such a far-fetched question; but never mind. What the thing may be called is entirely beside the point. Likewise when I speak of possible dragons or unicorns, I mean animals that fit the stereotypes we associate with those names. I am not here concerned with Kripke's problem of whether such animals are rightly called by those names.)

I cannot altogether accept the formulation: anything can coexist with anything. For I think the worlds do not overlap, hence each thing is part of only one of them. A dragon from one world and a unicorn from a second world do not themselves coexist either in the dragon's world, or in the unicorn's world, or in a third world. An attached head does not reappear as a separated head in some other world, because it does not reappear at all in any other world.

Ordinarily I would replace trans-world identity by counterpart relations, but not here. I cannot accept the principle: a counterpart of anything can coexist with a counterpart of anything else. Counterparts are united by similarity, but often the relevant similarity is mostly extrinsic. In particular, match of origins often has decisive weight. Had my early years gone differently, I might be different now in ever so many important ways – here I envisage an other-worldly person who is my counterpart mainly by match of origins, and very little by intrinsic similarity in later life. It might happen (at least under some resolutions of the vagueness of counterpart relations) that nothing could be a counterpart of the dragon unless a large part of its surrounding world fairly well matched the dragon's world; and likewise that nothing could be a counterpart of the unicorn unless a large part of its surrounding world fairly well matched the unicorn's world; and that no one world matches both the dragon's world and the unicorn's world well enough; and therefore that there is no world where a counterpart of the dragon coexists with a counterpart of the unicorn. Considered by themselves, the dragon and the unicorn are compossible. But if we use the method of counterparts, we do not consider them by themselves; to the extent that the counterpart relation heeds extrinsic similarities, we take them together with their surroundings.

It is right to formulate our principle of recombination in terms of similarity. It should say, for instance, that there is a world where something like the dragon coexists with something like the unicorn. But extrinsic similarity is irrelevant here, so I should not speak of coexisting *counterparts*. Instead, I should say that a *duplicate* of the dragon and a *duplicate* of the unicorn coexist at some world, and that the attached talking head has at some world a separated duplicate.

Duplication is a matter of shared properties, but differently situated duplicates do not share all their properties. In section 1.5, I defined duplication in terms of the sharing of perfectly natural properties, then defined intrinsic properties as those that never differ between duplicates. That left it open that duplicates might differ extrinsically in their relation to their surroundings. Duplicate molecules in this world may differ in that one is and another isn't part of a cat. Duplicate dragons in different worlds may differ in that one coexists with a unicorn and the other doesn't. Duplicate heads may differ in that one is attached to the rest of a human body and the other isn't.

Not only two possible individuals, but any number should admit of combination by means of coexisting duplicates. Indeed, the number might be infinite. Further, any possible individual should admit of combination with itself: if there could be a dragon, then equally there could be two duplicate copies of that dragon side by side, or seventeen or infinitely many.

But now there is trouble. Only a limited number of distinct things can coexist in a spacetime continuum. It cannot exceed the infinite cardinal number of the points in a continuum. So if we have more than continuum many possible individuals to be copied, or if we want more than continuum many copies of any single individual, then a continuum will be too small to hold all the coexisting things that our principle seems to require.

Should we keep the principle of recombination simple and unqualified, follow where it leads, and conclude that the possible size of spacetime is greater than we might have expected? That is tempting, I agree. And I see no compelling reason why a possible spacetime can never exceed the size of a continuum. But it seems very fishy if we begin with a principle that is meant to express plenitude about how spacetime might be occupied, and we find our principle transforming itself unexpectedly so as to yield consequences about the possible size of spacetime itself.

Our principle therefore requires a proviso: 'size and shape permitting'. The only limit on the extent to which a world can be filled with duplicates of possible individuals is that the parts of a world must be able to fit together within some possible size and shape of spacetime. Apart from that, anything can coexist with anything, and anything can fail to coexist with anything.

This leaves a residual problem of plenitude: what are the possible sizes and shapes of spacetime? Spacetimes have mathematical representations, and an appropriate way to state plenitude would be to say that for every representation in some salient class, there is a world whose spacetime is thus represented. It is up to mathematics to offer us candidates for the 'salient class'. (See section 2.2 for further discussion.)

We sometimes persuade ourselves that things are possible by experiments in imagination. We imagine a horse, imagine a horn on it, and thereby we are persuaded that a unicorn is possible. But imaginability is a poor criterion of possibility. We can imagine the impossible, provided we do not imagine it in perfect detail and all at once. We cannot imagine the possible in perfect detail and all at once, not if it is at all complicated. It is impossible to construct a regular polygon of nineteen sides with ruler and compass; it is possible but very complicated to construct one of seventeen sides. In whatever sense I can imagine the possible construction, I can imagine the impossible construction just as well. In both cases, I imagine a texture of arcs and lines with the polygon in the middle. I do not imagine it arc by arc and line by line, just as I don't imagine the speckled hen speckle by speckle – which is how I fail to notice the impossibility.

We get enough of a link between imagination and possibility, but not too much, if we regard imaginative experiments as a way of reasoning informally from the principle of recombination. To imagine a unicorn and infer its possibility is to reason that a unicorn is possible because a horse and a horn, which are possible because actual, might be juxtaposed in the imagined way.

In 'Propositional Objects' Quine suggested that we might take a possible world as a mathematical representation: perhaps a set of quadruples of real numbers, regarded as giving the coordinates of the spacetime points that are occupied by matter. His method could be extended to allow for various sizes and shapes of spacetime, for occupancy by different kinds of matter and by point-sized bits of fields, and perhaps even for occupancy of times by non-spatial things. In section 3.2, I shall argue that we should not *identify* the worlds with any such mathematical representations. However we should accept a *correspondence*: for every Quinean ersatz world, there is a genuine world with the represented pattern of occupancy and vacancy. This is just an appeal to recombination. But we are no longer applying it to smallish numbers of middle-sized things, horses or horns of heads. Instead, we are applying it to point-sized things, spacetime points themselves or perhaps point-sized bits of matter or of fields. Starting with point-sized things that are uncontroversially possible, perhaps because actual, we patch together duplicates of them in great number (continuum many, or more) to make an entire world. The mathematical representations are a book-keeping device, to make sure that the 'size and shape permitting' proviso is satisfied.

Another use of my principle is to settle – or as opponents might say, to beg – the question whether laws of nature are strictly necessary. They are not; or at least laws that constrain what can coexist in different positions are not. Episodes of bread-eating are possible because actual; as are episodes of starvation. Juxtapose duplicates of the two, on the grounds that anything can follow anything; here is a possible world to violate the law that bread nourishes. So likewise against the necessity of more serious candidates for fundamental laws of nature – perhaps with the exception of laws constraining what can coexist at a single position, for instance the law (if such it be) that nothing is both positive and negative in charge. It is no surprise that my principle prohibits strictly necessary connections between distinct existences. What I have done is to take a Humean view about laws and causation, and use it instead as a thesis about possibility. Same thesis, different emphasis.

Among all the possible individuals there are, some are parts of this world; some are not, but are duplicates of parts of this world; some, taken whole, are not duplicates of any part of this world, but are divisible into parts each of which is a duplicate of some part of this world. Still other possible individuals are not thus divisible: they have parts, no part of which is a duplicate of any part of this world. These I call *alien* individuals. (That is, they are alien *to* this world; similarly, individuals could be alien to another world. For instance, many individuals in this world are alien to more impoverished worlds.) A world that contains alien individuals – equivalently, that is itself an alien individual – I call an alien world.

In 'New Work for a Theory of Universals', I defined an alien natural property as one that is not instantiated by any part of this world, and that is not definable as a conjunctive or structural property build up from constituents that are all instantiated by parts of this world.[58] Anything that instantiates an alien property is an alien individual; any world within which an alien property is instantiated is an alien world.

But not conversely: we could have an alien individual that did not instantiate any alien properties, but instead combined non-alien properties

[58]Perhaps, as Armstrong has suggested in discussion, I should have added a third clause: '. . . and that is not obtainable by interpolation or extrapolation from a spectrum of properties that are instantiated by parts of this world'.

in an alien way. Suppose that positive and negative charge are not, strictly speaking, incompatible; but suppose it happens by accident or by contingent law that no this-worldly particle has both these properties. Then an other-worldly particle that does have both is an alien individual but needn't have any alien properties.

A world to which no individuals, worlds, or properties are alien would be an especially rich world. There is no reason to think we are privileged to inhabit such a world. Therefore any acceptable account of possibility must make provision for alien possibilities.

So it won't do to say that all worlds are generated by recombination from parts of this world, individuals which are possible because they are actual. We can't get the alien possibilities just by rearranging non-alien ones. Thus our principle of recombination falls short of capturing all the plenitude of possibilities.

A principle which allowed not only recombination of spatiotemporal parts of the world but also recombination of non-spatiotemporal parts – universals or tropes – would do a bit more. It would generate those alien individuals that do not instantiate alien properties. But I say (1) that such a principle, unlike mine, would sacrifice neutrality about whether there exist universals or tropes, and (2) that it still wouldn't go far enough, since we also need the possibility of alien properties.

Although recombination will not generate alien worlds out of the parts of this world, it nevertheless applies to alien worlds. It rules out that there should be only a few alien worlds. If there are some, there are many more. Anything alien can coexist, or fail to coexist, with anything else alien, or with anything else not alien, in any arrangement permitted by shape and size.

1.9 Actuality

I say that ours is one of many worlds. Ours is the actual world; the rest are not actual. Why so? – I take it to be a trivial matter of meaning. I use the word 'actual' to mean the same as 'this-worldly'. When I use it, it applies to my world and my worldmates; to this world we are part of, and to all parts of this world. And if someone else uses it, whether he be a worldmate of ours or whether he be unactualised, then (provided he means by it what we do) it applies likewise to his world and his worldmates. Elsewhere I have called this the 'indexical analysis' of actuality and stated it as follows.

> I suggest that 'actual' and its cognates should be analyzed as *indexical* terms: terms whose reference varies, depending on relevant features of the context of utterance. The relevant feature of context, for the term 'actual', is the

world at which a given utterance occurs. According to the indexical analysis I propose, 'actual' (in its primary sense) refers at any world w to the world w. 'Actual' is analogous to 'present', an indexical term whose reference varies depending on a different feature of context: 'present' refers at any time t to the time t. 'Actual' is analogous also to 'here', 'I', 'you', and 'aforementioned' – indexical terms depending for their reference respectively on the place, the speaker, the intended audience, the speaker's acts of pointing, and the foregoing discourse. ('Anselm and Actuality', pages 184–5.)

This makes actuality a relative matter: every world is *actual at* itself, and thereby all worlds are on a par. This is *not* to say that all worlds are actual – there's no world at which that is true, any more than there's ever a time when all times are present. The 'actual at' relation between worlds is simply identity.

Given my acceptance of the plurality of worlds, the relativity is unavoidable. I have no tenable alternative. For suppose instead that one world alone is *absolutely* actual. There is some special distinction which that one world alone possesses, not relative to its inhabitants or to anything else but *simpliciter*. I have no idea how this supposed absolute distinction might be understood, but let us go on as if we did understand it. I raise two objections.

The first objection concerns our knowledge that we are actual. Note that the supposed absolute distinction, even if it exists, doesn't make the relative distinction go away. It is still true that one world alone is ours, is this one, is the one we are part of. What a remarkable bit of luck for us if the very world we are part of is the one that is absolutely actual! Out of all the people there are in all the worlds, the great majority are doomed to live in worlds that lack absolute actuality, but we are the select few. What reason could we ever have to think it was so? How could we ever know? Unactualised dollars buy no less unactualised bread, and so forth. And yet we *do* know for certain that the world we are part of is the actual world – just as certainly as we know that the world we are part of is the very world we are part of. How could this be knowledge that we are the select few?

D. C. Williams asks the same question. Not about 'actuality' but about 'existence'; but it comes to the same thing, since he is discussing various doctrines on which so-called 'existence' turns out to be a special status that distinguishes some of the things there are from others. He complains that Leibniz 'never intimates, for example, how he can tell that *he* is a member of the existent world and not a mere possible monad on the shelf of essence' ('Dispensing with Existence', page 752).

Robert M. Adams, in 'Theories of Actuality', dismisses this objection. He says that a simple-property theory of absolute actuality can account for the certainty of our knowledge of our own actuality by maintaining

that we are as immediately acquainted with our own absolute actuality
as we are with our thoughts, feelings, and sensations. But I reply that
if Adams and I and all the other actual people really have this immediate
acquaintance with absolute actuality, wouldn't my elder sister have had
it too, if only I'd had an elder sister? So there she is, unactualised, off
in some other world getting fooled by the very same evidence that is
supposed to be giving me my knowledge.

This second objection concerns contingency. (It is due to Adams, and
this time he and I agree.) Surely it is a contingent matter which world
is actual. A contingent matter is one that varies from world to world.
At one world, the contingent matter goes one way; at another, another.
So at one world, one world is actual; and at another, another. How can
this be *absolute* actuality? – The relativity is manifest!

The indexical analysis raises a question. If 'actual' is an indexical, is
it or is it not a rigidified indexical? In a context where other worlds are
under consideration, does it still refer to the world of utterance, or does
it shift its reference? Compare 'now', which is normally rigidified, with
'present', which may or may not be. So you say 'Yesterday it was colder
than it is now', and even in the scope of the time-shifting adverb, 'now'
still refers to the time of utterance. Likewise you say 'Yesterday it was
colder than it is at present', and the reference of 'present' is unshifted.
But if you say 'Every past event was once present', then the time-shifting
tensed verb shifts the reference of 'present'. I suggest that 'actual' and
its cognates are like 'present': sometimes rigidified, sometimes not. What
if I'd had an elder sister? Then there would have been someone who
doesn't actually exist. (Rigidified.) Then she would have been actual,
though in fact she is not. (Unrigidified.) Then someone would have been
actual who actually isn't actual. (Both together.) In the passage just quoted
I called the unrigidified sense 'primary'; but not for any good reason.[59]

I said that when I use it, 'actual' applies to my world and my
worldmates; that is, to the world I am part of and to other parts of that
world. Likewise, *mutatis mutandis*, when some other-worldly being uses
the word with the same meaning. But that left out the sets. I would not
wish to say that any sets are *parts of* this or other worlds,[60] but
nevertheless I would like to say that sets of actual things are actual.
Sometimes we hear it said that sets are one and all unlocated; but I don't
know any reason to believe this, and a more plausible view is that a set

[59]For various examples that require or forbid rigidification if they are to make sense,
see my *Philosophical Papers*, volume I, page 22; for further discussion, see Hazen, 'One
of the Truths about Actuality' and van Inwagen, 'Indexicality and Actuality'.
[60]But not because I take it that the part–whole relation applies only to individuals and
not sets, as I said in *Philosophical Papers*, volume I, page 40; rather, because I now take
it that a set is never part of an individual.

is where its members are. It is scattered to the extent that its members are scattered; it is unlocated if, but only if, its members are unlocated. That applies as much to location among the worlds as it does to location within a single world. Just as a set of stay-at-home Australians is in Australia, so likewise a set of this-wordly things is this-worldly, in other words actual. In the same way, a set of sets that are all in Australia is itself in Australia, and likewise a set of actual sets is itself actual; and so on up the iterative hierarchy.

I might sometimes prefer to use the word 'actual' a bit more broadly still. There is no need to decide, once and for all and inflexibly, what is to be called actual. After all, that is not the grand question: what is there? It is only the question which of all the things there are stand in some special relation to us, but there are special relations and there are special relations. Suppose there are things that are not our world, and not parts of our world, and not sets built up entirely from things that are parts of our world – but that I might nevertheless wish to quantify over even when my quantification is otherwise restricted to this-worldly things. If so, no harm done if I sometimes call them 'actual' by courtesy. No harm done, in fact, if I decline to adopt any official position on the question whether they are actual or whether they are not! It is no genuine issue.

The numbers, for instance, might well be candidates to be called 'actual' by courtesy. But it depends on what the numbers are. If they are universals, and some or all of them are non-spatiotemporal parts of their this-worldly instances which in turn are parts of this world, then those numbers, at least, are actual not by courtesy but because they are parts of this world. Likewise for other mathematical entities.

Properties, taken as sets of all their this- and other-worldly instances, are another candidate. By what I said above about actuality of sets, only those properties are actual whose instances are confined to the actual world. But most of the properties we take an interest in have instances both in and out of this world. Those ones might be called 'partly actual'; or they might as well just be called 'actual', since very often we will want to include them in our otherwise this-worldly quantifications.

Events fall in with the properties; for I see no reason to distinguish between an event and the property of being a spatiotemporal region, of this or another world, wherein that event occurs. (See my 'Events'.) An event that actually occurs, then, is a set that includes exactly one this-worldly region. That makes it partly actual, and we may as well just call it 'actual'.

Propositions, being sets of worlds, also fall in with the properties taken as sets. A proposition is partly actual at just those worlds where it is true, for it has just those worlds as its members. So we might call at least the true propositions 'actual'; or we might just call all propositions 'actual', distinguishing however between those that are and are not actually true.

Not only sets but individuals may be partly actual – big individuals, composed of parts from more worlds than one, and so partly in each of·several worlds. If there are any such trans-world individuals that are partly in this world, hence partly actual, should we call them 'actual' *simpliciter*? – That depends. We needn't, if we think of them just as oddities that we can mostly ignore. I think they are exactly that. (See section 4.3.) But if we were reluctant to ignore them in our quantifying, perhaps because we thought that we ourselves were among them, then we might appropriately call them 'actual'.[61]

[61]In *Philosophical Papers*, volume I, pages 39–40, I distinguished three ways of 'being in a world': (1) being *wholly* in it, that is, being part of it; (2) being *partly* in it, that is, having a part that is wholly in it; and (3) existing *from the standpoint of* it, that is, 'belonging to the least restricted domain that is normally – modal metaphysics being deemed abnormal – appropriate in evaluating the truth at that world of quantifications'. If the world in question is actual, that is almost my present distinction between being actual, being partly actual, and being actual by courtesy; the only difference in the terminologies being that I would not now throw all sets into the lower grade. I distinguish all of the above from (4) existing *according to* a world: I claim that something exists according to a world – for instance, Humphrey both exists and wins the presidency according to certain worlds other than ours – by having a counterpart that is part of that world. On being part of versus existing according to, see section 4.1.

2

Paradox in Paradise?

2.1 Everything is Actual?

In this chapter of objections and replies, I begin with four objections meant to show that my modal realism, with the aid of uncontroversial auxiliary premises, leads to outright paradox. I reply by controverting the auxiliary premises. They may have something going for them intuitively, but I think they are not so compelling that I need count their rejection as any great cost.

One line of argument holds that I misrepresent my own position. I ought to say not that there are many possible worlds, and that ours is actual and the rest are unactualised. Instead I ought to say that actuality is much bigger and much more fragmented than we ordinarily think. For it is a trivial matter of meaning that whatever there is, is actual. The word 'actual' is a blanket term, like 'entity' or 'exists': it applies to everything. Not just everything hereabouts, or everything suitably related to us, as I would have it; but *everything* without restriction. To say as I do that some things are unactualised is nonsense on a par with saying that some things do not exist, or with Meinong's shocker: 'there are objects of which it is true to say that there are no such objects' ('Über Gegstandstheorie', section 3). Actualism, the thesis that everything is actual, is not some metaphysical thesis that one is free to affirm or deny; it is a trivial analytic truth. Its denial is unintelligible. Maybe there are 'other worlds' just as I say there are, spatiotemporally and causally isolated from us and all our surroundings. But if there are, then they are just some more of actuality.

The objection has a second part. Since everything is actual, the other worlds, if such there be, actually exist. Then it is not merely possible that they exist. They are not unactualised possibilities. In fact they have nothing to do with possibility. For possibility concerns not the far reaches of actuality – not even the reaches of actuality that are spatiotemporally isolated from us, if such there be – but rather it concerns *alternatives* to actuality. Actuality – all of it, no matter how much of it there is – might have been different, and that is what modality is all about. More of actuality is no substitute for unactualised possibility.

This second part of the objection is less commonly made than the first. But it may be what Peter van Inwagen is driving at when, after asking why I believe in (more than one of) the things I call worlds, he goes on to say that I 'face the problem of explaining what these things would have to do with modality if there were any of them' ('Plantinga on Trans-World Identity', page 119). You might think that I have often explained what these things have to do with modality, for instance by saying that the modal operators are quantifiers over them. Perhaps van Inwagen's implicit point is that the modal operators, as ordinarily understood, cannot be quantifiers over subdivisions of actuality. If so, I agree – but that is not how I do explain them since, *contra* the first part of the objection, you may take me at my word when I deny that other worlds are actual. The second part of the objection relies on the first part, so if I answer the first part I thereby deal with both.

Many philosophers have stated the first part of the objection in some form or other (two of the first were Richards and Haack), but none more vigorously than Lycan. He first distinguishes what he calls 'our original, actuality-indicating quantifier' from my so-called 'Meinongian' quantifier which does not indicate actuality. (He is not suggesting that I claim to quantify over incomplete or inconsistent Meinongian objects – of course I do not – but only that I claim to quantify beyond actuality.) Then he goes on to make very heavy weather over the latter.

> I have to take my place among those who find *Relentlessly* (i.e., *genuinely* or *primitively*) Meinongian quantification simply unintelligible. . . . I mean that I really cannot understand Relentlessly Meinongian quantification at all; to me it is *literally* gibberish or mere noise. ('The Trouble with Possible Worlds', page 290).

I think that what gives Lycan such bother is not the way I quantify. I quantify just the way he or anyone else does: over all the entities I think there are, or over less than all of them whenever it's convenient to impose some restriction. Our quantifiers are common property. We don't need to learn them anew whenever we change our opinions about what there is to quantify over. Lycan's real trouble is with what I mean by 'actual'. He insists that it must be a blanket term. It must extend just as far as the quantifiers themselves, when least restricted, however far that may be. If so, then 'Meinongian' quantification beyond the actual is nonsense indeed. I myself do not use 'actual' as a blanket term. I have already explained that I use it to mean 'this-worldly': it is an indexical, relative term, and as used by us it distinguishes our world and our worldmates from all the other worlds and their inhabitants. But I do use 'entity' as a blanket term, and if ever you hear me claim to be quantifying over nonentities – quantifying genuinely and primitively, and without first restricting my use of 'entity' somehow – then you may fairly echo Lycan's protests.

Just as Lycan makes heavy weather over 'actual', someone could make equally heavy weather over 'this-worldly', saying that there can be only one world, because – as a trivial matter of meaning – 'world' is a blanket term for the totality of everything. Thus Richards: 'In short, the world is what exists, and we cannot muck about with that' ('The Worlds of David Lewis', page 108). Likewise Skyrms claims that whenever we have a class of truths, there must be one single world that they all describe – even if what they *purport* to do is to describe *many* worlds! ('Possible Worlds, Physics and Metaphysics', pages 324–5.) If by definition 'the world' comprises all there is, then to speak as I do of things that are out of this world is tantamount to speaking of things that are outside of all there is – which is nonsense. But of course I do *not* use 'world' as a blanket term; as Richards very well understands, since he challenges me to say what demarcates the worlds one from another. A very proper question, which I have taken up in section 1.6; I hope that discussion went some way toward showing what 'world' could sensibly mean if it is not a blanket term.

Nobody could have thought that I *meant* to use either 'actual' or 'world' as blanket terms. So if critics complain of paradox when I say that some things are unactualised and out of this world, it must be because they think those words are blanket terms willy-nilly. I cannot use them any other way and still retain any contact with their common meaning. But is that really so? Suppose we interviewed some spokesman for common sense. I think we would find that he adheres firmly to three theses:

(1) Everything is actual.

(2) Actuality consists of everything that is spatiotemporally related to us, and nothing more (give or take some 'abstract entities'). It is not vastly bigger, or less unified, than we are accustomed to think.

(3) Possibilities are not parts of actuality, they are alternatives to it.

The first two theses cannot both be mere matters of meaning, trivial analytic truths. Taken together, they say too much for that. My critics claim that the first is analytic, its denial is paradoxical or 'mere noise'; whereas the second is up for grabs. But I think the two theses, indeed all three, are on an equal footing. Together they fix the meaning of 'actual', but they go far beyond just fixing meanings. I don't see any evidence that the analyticity is concentrated more in some of them than in others. Common sense could have made up its communal mind where the analyticity resided – if we are right not to Quine the very idea of analyticity – but it had no need to settle that question, so very sensibly it didn't bother to. Or so it seems to me; and after all, I speak as party to the conventions of the community in question.

If so, then I am within my rights in standing with common opinion about the unification and the extent of actuality, at the expense of common opinion that everything is actual. I no more abandon the ordinary meaning than I would if I did the opposite, as the critics advise. In denying that everything is actual, I do of course disagree with common opinion. I acknowledge that as a fair objection (see section 2.8) but it is far less serious than the charge of paradox that was before us. I am not trying to quantify over things such that there are no such things; so what I am saying is not 'literal gibberish' – or even figurative.

Let us call the first and second theses together *metaphysical actualism*; that is a substantive thesis about what there is. Let us call the first thesis by itself *terminological actualism*; that is more a proposal for how to speak than a thesis of any kind. And let us call the thesis that terminological actualism is analytic, and so may not intelligibly be rejected, *analytic actualism*. I reject all three. Metaphysical and analytic actualism I reject as false. Terminological actualism I reject as inadvisable, if we reject metaphysical actualism; and as not compulsory if we reject analytic actualism.

It is a mere matter of terminology whether to use 'actual' and 'world' as I do; but it does matter, because of the third of our three theses of common sense. Analytic or not, it seems compelling. I too would find it very peculiar to say that modality, as ordinarily understood, is quantification over parts of actuality. If I were convinced that I ought to call all the worlds actual – in which case also I might be reluctant to call them worlds – then it would become very implausible to say that what might happen is what does happen at some or another world. If there were a place left for unactualised possibilities at all, they would be possibilities of a grander sort – not differences between the worlds, but other ways that the grand world, the totality that includes all my little worlds, might have been. It would be useless to try again just as before, and believe in a plurality of grand worlds; for if a plurality of worlds falls victim to analytic actualism, then a plurality of grand worlds does too.[1] All this would be a great defeat, given the theoretical benefits that

---

[1]Skyrms conjures up the spectre of a regress from a plurality of worlds to a plurality of grand worlds to a plurality of yet grander worlds . . . ('Possible Worlds, Physics and

modal realism brings. So it is fortunate indeed that there is no convincing reason to think it analytic that everything is actual.

We have not seen the last of terminological and analytic actualism. As we proceed through other objections, often the critics will urge that I ought to think of all the worlds together in some way that we are accustomed to thinking of the actual world; and then they will say, rightly, that it would be very peculiar to think in such a way. Well, why do I have to think things that would be so peculiar? I suppose their underlying idea is that I should because I *must*: because it is a trivial analytic truth that everything is actual.

2.2   All Worlds in One?

Another line of argument seeks to entrap modal realism in paradoxes akin to those that refute naive set theory. Plausible premises about what is possible turn out to afford ways of mapping arbitrary classes of worlds one to one onto single worlds, which leads at once to contradiction. In reply, I must deny the plausible premises. Fortunately, I think I can argue that they are suspect for independent reasons.

Forrest and Armstrong, in 'An Argument against David Lewis' Theory of Possible Worlds', rely on an unqualified principle of recombination to produce one such paradox. Say that a world *copies* a class of possible individuals, perhaps from various different worlds, iff it contains non-overlapping duplicates of all the individuals in that class. The principle of recombination that I endorsed in section 1.8 says that, given a class of possible individuals, there is some world which copies that class. However I insisted on qualifying the principle by the proviso: 'size and shape permitting'. The reason I gave for the proviso – and it seems to me a sufficient reason all on its own – was that without it, the principle would deliver proofs that there are very large spacetimes, since if we had a class of more than continuum many possible individuals, they could not be copied into any merely continuum-sized spacetime; however 'it seems very fishy if we begin with a principle that is meant to express plenitude about how spacetime might be occupied, and we find our principle transforming itself unexpectedly so as to yield consequences about the possible size of spacetime itself.'

Metaphysics', pages 331–2.) The regress works by cycling around three assumptions: (1) that 'reality' is the totality of everything, (2) that reality might have been different, and (3) that possible difference is to be understood in terms of a plurality of alternatives. I reply that (1) and (2) aren't both right. Which one is wrong depends on whether we choose to take 'reality' as a blanket term for everything, or as yet another word for the this-worldly part of everything. That choice may be left unmade.

Forrest and Armstrong show that the unqualified principle is worse than fishy. It leads to disaster. Even if we were content to follow where it leads, we could not just concede that some worlds have enormously big spacetimes – far beyond the cardinality of the continuum – and leave it at that. There is no equilibrium: the more we concede, the more the insatiable principle demands. The more possible individuals there are, the bigger can a class of them be. The bigger those classes can be, the bigger some worlds must be, if there is a world to copy every class. But the bigger some worlds are, the more possible individuals there are – and around we go again. There is no stable resting place.

In more detail, their argument is as follows. Start with all the possible worlds. Each one of them is a possible individual. Apply the unqualified principle of recombination to this class of possible individuals. Then we have one big world which contains duplicates of all our original worlds as non-overlapping parts. But we started with all the worlds; so our big world must have been one of them. Then our big world is bigger than itself; but no matter how big it is, it cannot be that.

The conclusion that the big world is bigger than itself requires clarification, and a subsidiary argument. It is not good enough just to complain that it has an exact duplicate of the whole of itself as a proper part of itself. That is not objectionable; it happens at some perfectly decent possible worlds. For instance, take a world of one-way eternal recurrence: its proper part consisting of all but the first epoch (or the first seventeen, or any number) is an exact duplicate of the whole of it.

Therefore Forrest and Armstrong suggest that we measure the size of a world by the cardinality of the set of its electrons. Suppose the big world has K electrons in it; we may safely assume that K is some large infinite cardinal. Then there are $2^K - 1$ non-empty subsets of the electrons of the big world; and for every such subset, there is a world rather like the big world in which just those electrons remain and the rest have been deleted. (I take this to be a subsidiary appeal to recombination.) Call these worlds *variants* of the big world. (The big world itself is one of them.) There are $2^K - 1$ variants; there are non-overlapping duplicates of all these variants within the big world; each variant contains at least one electron, therefore so does each duplicate of a variant; so we have at least $2^K - 1$ electrons in the big world; but *ex hypothesi* we had only K electrons in the big world; and $2^K - 1$ must exceed K; so the big world has more electrons in it than it has. For a world to be bigger than itself in that sense is indeed impossible; which completes the *reductio*.

I see Forrest and Armstrong as giving me a second reason, even more conclusive than my previous reason (which was already good enough), why the principle of recombination needs its qualifying proviso. Their *reductio* shows that the proviso may not be dropped. But they insist that it must be dropped; it is the simpler, unqualified form of the principle that is intuitively compelling. My proviso, if spelled out, would have to put some restriction on the possible size of spacetime. Among the mathematical structures that might be offered as isomorphs of possible spacetimes, some would be admitted, and others would be rejected as oversized. Forrest and Armstrong say that such a restriction 'seems to be *ad hoc*'. Maybe so; the least arbitrary restriction we could possibly imagine is none at all, and compared to that any restriction whatever will seem at least somewhat *ad hoc*. But some will seem worse than others. A restriction to four-dimensional, or to seventeen-dimensional, manifolds looks badly arbitrary; a restriction to finite-dimensional manifolds looks much more tolerable. Maybe that is too much of a restriction, and disqualifies some shapes and sizes of spacetime that we would firmly believe to be possible. If so, then I hope there is some equally natural break a bit higher up: high enough to make room for all the possibilities we really need to believe in, but enough of a natural break to make it not intolerably *ad hoc* as a boundary.

My hope, notice, is just that some such break *exists*. I do not claim to make the worlds, and I do not claim to have some way of finding out all about them, therefore I will not be at all troubled if I cannot say just what break is right. My thesis is existential: there is *some* break, and the correct break is sufficiently salient within the mathematical universe not to be *ad hoc*. If study of the mathematical generalisations of ordinary spacetime manifolds revealed one salient break, and one only, I would dare to say that it was the right break – that there were worlds with all the shapes and sizes of spacetime below it, and no worlds with any other shapes and sizes. If study revealed no suitable breaks, I would regard that as serious trouble. If study revealed more than one suitable break, I would be content to profess ignorance – incurable ignorance, most likely.

There is an alliance between what remains of the present objection – namely, a complaint that there must be something arbitrary about the needed restriction on shapes and sizes – and the objection considered in the previous section. For when something seems arbitrary, we are apt to think that it might well have been different. If the restriction is an arbitrary feature of the totality of all possible worlds, then we are apt to think that this totality could have been different. But if so, then there is a possible way for it to be which differs from the way it actually is – and we are back to thinking of the worlds not as genuine alternative possibilities, but as parts of one big disunified actuality. All the more reason, I think, why the restriction had better be some extremely natural break, so that (if we could know what it was) it would not strike us as arbitrary.

Forrest and Armstrong leave a loophole. Their premise that any number of worlds can be copied into a single world – their appeal to recombination –

is meant to apply only if the worlds to be copied comprise a set or aggregate. So if there are the worlds, but there is no set or aggregate of all of them, then the contradiction is dodged. Does this loophole give me a way to do without the unwelcome proviso? I think not. (1) If we say that a set or aggregate of possible individuals always can be copied into a single world, but we do not say the same for other classes, that is already to qualify recombination in a way that detracts from its plausibility. (2) Some uses of *possibilia*, for instance in constructing semantic values for sentential modifiers (as in section 1.4), will require the forbidden sets. (3) How could the worlds possibly fail to comprise a set? We do say that according to the iterative conception of sets, some classes are 'too big to be sets', but this is loose talk. Sheer size is not what matters; rather, the obstacle to sethood is that the members of the class are not yet all present at any rank of the iterative hierarchy. But all the individuals, no matter how many there may be, get in already on the ground floor. So, after all, we have no notion what could stop any class of individuals – in particular, the class of all worlds – from comprising a set. (4) Likewise we have no notion what could stop any class of individuals from comprising an aggregate.

So I continue to accept a set of all worlds, indeed a set of all individuals. The Forrest–Armstrong *reductio* stands; but a *reductio* against the unqualified principle of recombination is not a *reductio* against my theory of possible worlds, as they say it is. I do not accept the unqualified principle, and there is no strong reason why I should. It is a gift that I do best to refuse.

2.3   *More Worlds Than There Are?*

Another paradox likewise works by embedding sets of worlds within single worlds, but the embedding works differently. The set is embedded not by duplicating all its members into a single world, but rather by making it the set of worlds that characterises the content of somebody's thought. I believe the paradox is due to David Kaplan; I learned it from him *circa* 1975. Recently it has been presented in Martin Davies's *Meaning, Quantification, Necessity*, page 262, with credit to Kaplan and to Christopher Peacocke. Davies states it roughly as follows:

(1) Suppose that the cardinality of the set of possible worlds is K.

(2) Each subset of this set is a proposition, namely the proposition which would be expressed by a sentence which was true with respect to precisely the worlds in that subset.

(3) There are 2^K such propositions, and 2^K is strictly greater than K.

(4) Consider some man and time. For each proposition, it is possible that he should have been thinking a thought at that time whose content would be specifiable by a sentence expressing that proposition; and that this should have been his only thought at that time.[2]

(5) So there is a distinct possible situation corresponding to each such proposition.

(6) So there are at least 2^K possible worlds, contradicting the assumption with which we began.

Kaplan remarked that we could replace the thinker by a speaker, to give a semantic version of the paradox; in which case, (4) would say that for each proposition, it is possible that the man at the time should have been uttering a sentence that expressed that proposition, and that this should have been his only utterance at that time.

(In section 1.4 I suggested that a content of thought should be given by a set of possible individuals, not worlds, since the thought might be egocentric; or that it should be given not by a set of possibilities but by a probability distribution, to allow for partial belief; or that it should be given not by one set or one distribution but by a class of them, since the man might be a compartmentalised doublethinker, or the content of his thought might be not fully determinate; or that all these amendments should be made together. The amendments only make matters worse. If they make a difference, it is by increasing the number of possible contents of the thinker's thought and the number of different possible situations. I ignore them henceforth.)

I reply by denying (4). Not just any set of worlds is a set that might possibly give the content of someone's thought. Most sets of worlds, in fact all but an infinitesimal minority of them, are not eligible contents of thought. It is absolutely impossible that anybody should think a thought with content given by one of these ineligible sets of worlds.

In my usage, any set of worlds is by definition a proposition. (See section 1.5.) That is why I deny (4) and accept (2). But there is a conflicting usage,

---

[2]My only substantive change from Davies is the addition of this final clause in (4), which seems to be required if (5) is to follow. Or else we could understand that the man's thought is to be his *total* thought at the time; perhaps that is what Davies intended, in which case his original formulation will serve.

In a recent lecture (at the Seventh International Conference of Logic, Methodology and Philosophy of Science, Salzburg, 1983) Kaplan has presented a more cautious version of the paradox. Instead of affirming (4), he only insists that logicians *qua* logicians ought not implicitly deny (4). Their systems should be metaphysically neutral. 'As logicians, we strive to *serve* philosophical ideologies not to constrain them.' Agreed – but I am not a logician, and metaphysical neutrality is not among my aims. Doubtless Kaplan, *qua* neutral logician, does not intend his paradox to impose any constraint adverse to the 'ideology' of modal realism. Its proper moral is that the way of the neutralist is hard.

equally well established, on which the propositions are by definition the possible contents of thought, whatever those may be. On that usage, (4) is unexceptionable, and I deny (2) instead. The terminological issue is avoided so long as I just say: not all sets of worlds, in fact only very few of them, are possible contents of thought.

I would take the paradox as reason enough to deny that just any set of worlds gives the content of some possible thought. But I think that I have independent reason as well.

My reason does not rest on our human limitations: that we are only just so smart, we have only just so many neurons, we live only just so many years, ... For the 'man' in the paradox needn't be subject to human limitations. He can be as smart as any man could possibly be; and smarter than any man could possibly be under the actual laws of nature, since he might live under other laws. He needn't be a man at all; he might be a god. Not an impossible god, because there are none of those thinking anything at any worlds at all; but he can be as smart as a god can possibly be. He can have as much ability to think many different thoughts as it is possible for any thinker to have.

Instead, I ask: what makes it so that a thinker has a thought with a certain content? And to this question, I take it that a broadly functionalist answer is right. A man or a beast or a god, or anything that is a thinker at all, has a thought with a certain content in virtue of being in a state which occupies a certain functional role. This definitive functional role has to do with the causal relations of that state to the thinker's sensory input, his behavioural output, and his other states. At least with these causal relations as they are for that thinker at that moment; and perhaps also as they are for that thinker at other times, and for his counterparts who lived divergent lives, and even for other beings of the same kind as he. For my present purpose, most of the debated differences between varieties of functionalism do not matter; except that of course I require some sort of analytic functionalism, not just a contingent connection between contents and roles. If it were a contingent connection, the worlds posited in the paradox might be worlds where that connection does not hold.

If the functional role of the thinker's state determines the content of his thought, then there can be only as many different possible contents of thought as there are different definitive functional roles. The different functional roles are the relevantly different ways of thinking; other differences between thinkers do not distinguish their contents of thought. (Here, of course, I mean the 'narrowly psychological' contents; but if the abundance the paradox requires cannot be found already among the narrow contents, I do not see how broad contents will serve my opponent better.) Maybe it is just possible that the definitive functional roles might be infinite in number. But there is infinity and there is infinity. I cannot see the slightest *prima facie* reason to think that there are even uncountably many of the definitive roles, let alone that there are as many as there are propositions (beth-three, on the lowest reasonable estimate). The paradox settles that there are not, but that conclusion should come as no surprise.

It's all very well to say that there must be unthinkable contents because there aren't enough functional roles to go around; but it would be nice to say what an unthinkable content would be like. Of course I cannot get you to think one, nor can I express one in language that gets its meaning ultimately in virtue of the content of our thoughts. (Thus the semantic version of the paradox fails along with the psychological version.) Still, I think I can say something about what the omitted contents are, drawing on the sketch of a functionalist theory of content that I offered in section 1.4.

Such a theory, I said, should have two parts. One part says what it is for an assignment of content to states to fit the functional roles of the states; the constraints are principles of rationality, for instance a principle to the effect that a state which is assigned content consisting of some system of beliefs and desires ought to be a state that tends to produce conduct that would serve those desires according to those beliefs. But principles of fit can be expected to underdetermine the assignment of content very badly. Given a fitting assignment, we can scramble it into an equally fitting but perverse alternative assignment. Therefore a theory of content needs a second part: as well as principles of fit, we need 'principles of humanity', which create a presumption in favour of some sorts of content and against others.

For instance, one fitting assignment might be that I want a pot of beer, and I think it can be had at the nearest pub. But an equally fitting assignment might be that I suddenly want a saucer of mud, and I expect the pub to serve me that. Extend the perverse assignment to make it cohere; part of it must be that I follow a queer sort of inductive 'reason', on which all my previous experience of pubs supports my peculiar expectation. If both those assignments fit equally, then the first is right and the second is wrong. I don't mean that the first is the more likely hypothesis. Rather I mean that the principles that favour the first are among the principles constitutive of content.

If I had behaved differently, would that have made the second assignment right in virtue of its better fit? No; because *ex hypothesi* the two assignments fit the same behaviour. If I behaved differently, that would not favour the second assignment over the first, but rather would detract from the fit of both. There is nothing that could favour the second and make it correct. If the second fits well enough to be in the running, then so does the first. Then the first wins. There aren't enough functional roles to go around; the first and second assignments are rival claimants to the same role; and the first is the more deserving claimant by reason of the perversity of the second; so that role belongs to the first, and the second must go without. So the second assignment, taken as a whole, affords an example of unthinkable content.

That's a tame example; there are countless fitting assignments that would be more perverse still. The contents they assign could not be expressed finitely; they would require infinitely gruesome gerrymanders of the more or less natural properties that we have words for. They are ineligible contents of thought because they are utterly unpatterned and miscellaneous. I suggest that an unthinkable content is one that can never be correctly assigned because, whenever it fits the functional roles of the thinker's states, some more favoured content also fits. If so, you just cannot think a thought with that content. Being smart wouldn't help. Maybe you are already smart enough to make the unfavoured content fitting; it still isn't right if some more favoured rival also fits.

2.4   How Can We Know?

Another line of argument is epistemic. I began with our abundant modal knowledge, particular and general. We know that there might be a talking donkey; and we know a general principle which tells us, for instance, that if there might be a talking donkey and there might be a philosophising cat, then there might be both together side by side. I want to incorporate this knowedge into a systematic theory. Accordingly, I uphold modal realism. But thereby – so says the objection – I betray the modal knowledge I began with. For if modal realism gives the right account of the content of what we know, then it could not possibly be known at all!

Thus Richards: 'while possible-worlds semantics does yield truth-conditions for possibility statements . . . the truth-conditions are such that, for any given statement, it is impossible in general to determine whether they are met and hence whether the statement is true. . . . How shall I determine whether *A* is true in some world or other? Unless it is true in my world, direct inspection is ruled out' ('The Worlds of David Lewis', pages 109–10). Lycan concurs, asking how in particular we can tell without inspection whether there is a world where Saul Kripke is the son of Rudolf Carnap.

The objection echoes Benacerraf's famous dilemma for philosophy of mathematics. It would seem that we have abundant mathematical knowledge, including knowledge of the existence of countless mathematical objects not open to direct inspection. We might very well want to take the content of this knowledge at face value; or in Benacerraf's less loaded words, we might want our account of mathematical truth to be motivated by 'the concern for having a homogeneous semantical theory in which semantics for the propositions of mathematics parallels the semantics for the rest of the language'. But 'accounts of truth that treat mathematical and nonmathematical discourse in relevantly similar ways do so at the cost of leaving it unintelligible how we can have any mathematical knowledge whatsoever; whereas those which attribute to mathematical propositions the kinds of truth conditions we can clearly know to obtain, do so at the expense of failing to connect these conditions with any analysis of the sentences which shows how the assigned conditions are conditions of their *truth*.' The trouble is that knowledge requires some sort of causal connection between the knower and the subject matter of his knowledge. But a standard, straightforward account of mathematical truth 'will depict truth conditions in terms of conditions on objects whose nature, as normally conceived, places them beyond the reach of the better understood means of human cognition (e.g. sense perception and the like)' ('Mathematical Truth', pages 661–2 and 667–8).

I think it is very plain which horn of Benacerraf's dilemma to prefer. To serve epistemology by giving mathematics some devious semantics would be to *reform* mathematics. Even if verbal agreement with mathematics as we know it could be secured – and that is doubtful – the plan would be to understand those words in a new and different way. It's too bad for epistemologists if mathematics in its present form baffles them, but it would be hubris to take that as any reason to reform mathematics. Neither should we take that as any reason to dismiss mathematics as mere fiction; not even if we go on to praise it as very useful fiction, as in Hartry Field's instrumentalism. Our knowledge of mathematics is ever so much more secure than our knowledge of the epistemology that seeks to cast doubt on mathematics.

So mathematics will do as a precedent: if we are prepared to expand our existential beliefs for the sake of theoretical unity, and if thereby we come to believe the truth, then we attain knowledge. In this way, we can even attain knowledge like that of the mathematicians: we can know that there exist countless objects causally isolated from us and unavailable to our inspection. Causal accounts of knowledge are all very well in their place, but if they are put forward as *general* theories, then mathematics refutes them.

(In taking mathematics as my precedent for knowledge beyond the reach of our causal acquaintance, I run some risk. What if it turns out that somehow, after all, we can interpret mathematics as ontologically innocent, not committed to any special, unobservable mathematical objects? And what if we can do this in an entirely acceptable fashion – that is, without at all reforming the content of mathematics, without dismissing any part of it as mere useful fiction, and without imposing any devious semantics that seems remote from our ordinary understanding of the idioms of quantification? I have no idea how this could be done, but perhaps that is just a failure of imagination on my part. If it could be done, that would be a great triumph for philosophy of mathematics, and I would join in the celebration. But wouldn't it wreck my precedent for knowledge of the other worlds? – Not altogether. It could not be said that really we understood mathematics all along in the wonderfully innocent way. (Else what made it so hard to give any account of our understanding?) So I still have a conditional judgement to cite as my precedent. Even if there does turn out to be some ontologically innocent way to understand mathematics, still we have judged – and judged rightly, say I – that we did not require any such thing before we could have mathematical knowledge; we *would* have had mathematical knowledge even if it *had* been knoweldge of a causally inaccessible realm of special objects.)

You might grant that we have knowledge of a vast realm of mathematical objects beyond the reach of our causal acquaintance; no causal account covers this part of our knowledge. But you might want to distinguish the mathematical and modal cases: the mathematical objects are *abstract*, whereas the other worlds are supposed to be *concrete*. And you might think this distinction has something to do with how things can and cannot be known. Thus Skyrms:

> *If* possible worlds are supposed to be the *same* sorts of things as our actual world; *if* they are supposed to exist in as concrete and robust a sense as our own; *if* they are supposed to be as real as Afghanistan, or the center of the sun or Cygnus A, *then they require the same sort of evidence for their existence as other constituents of physical reality.* ('Possible Worlds, Physics and Metaphysics', page 326.)

Presumably he thinks that different rules of evidence would apply if worlds were supposed to exist in some delicate sense, or if they were abstract and not at all like Afghanistan.

If modal knowledge is what I say it is, and if we have the modal knowledge that we think we do, then we have abundant knowledge of the existence of concrete individuals not causally related to us in any way. For instance, we know *a priori* that besides the donkeys among our worldmates there are countless other donkeys, spread over countless worlds. They are other-worldly donkeys, unactualised donkeys, 'merely possible' donkeys, but donkeys nonetheless. But aren't donkeys just the sort of thing whose existence can only be known *a posteriori*, by means of causal acquaintance?

(Maybe causal acquaintance with donkeys themselves is not required – we need no backward causation to know that there will be donkeys in the next century – but in that case we are causally acquainted with the past causes of future donkeys. In the case of other-worldly donkeys, though, we can no more be acquainted with the donkeymakers than with the donkeys themselves.)

I don't really know what is meant by someone who says that mathematical objects are abstract whereas donkeys, even other-worldly ones, are concrete. But in section 1.7 I listed four Ways, by no means equivalent, in which such a statement might be meant. Way of Example: donkeys are donkey-like, mathematical objects are number-like. Way of Conflation: donkeys are particular individuals, whereas mathematical objects are sets or perhaps universals. Negative Way: donkeys stand in spatiotemporal and causal relations, mathematical objects don't. Way of Abstraction: mathematical objects are abstractions from something or other, donkeys are not. Whichever is meant, I can more or less agree, except that the last applies to some mathematical objects more clearly than to others. (I see how a rational number is an abstraction: it is an equivalence class of ratios. But what about an arbitrary set of miscellaneous integers?) But I do not see how any of these different statements supports the alleged connection between different ways of knowing and different kinds of entities to be known. The Negative Way does at least make a relevant distinction: the entities it calls abstract cannot be known by causal acquaintance. That gives us no help in understanding how else they can be known. To say that abstract entities alone are known without benefit of causal acquaintance seems unprincipled: they'd *better* be, or they can't be known at all! Could 'abstract' just mean 'don't worry'?

I think it is true that causal acquaintance is required for some sorts of knowledge but not for others. However, the department of knowledge that requires causal acquaintance is not demarcated by its concrete subject matter. It is demarcated instead by its contingency. Here, the relevance is plain. If I know by seeing, for instance, my visual experience depends on the scene before my eyes; if the scene had been different, within limits, my experience and my subsequent belief would have been correspondingly different. Likewise other channels of causal acquaintance set up patterns of counterfactual dependence whereby we can know what is going on around us. But nothing can depend counterfactually on non-contingent matters. For instance nothing can depend counterfactually on what mathematical objects there are, or on what possibilities there are. Nothing sensible can be said about how our opinions would be different if there were no number seventeen, or if there were no possibility for dragons and unicorns to coexist in a single world. All counterfactuals with impossible antecedents may indeed be vacuously true. But even so, it is seldom sensible to affirm them.

Our knowledge can be divided into two quite different parts. As best we can, I think by seeking a theory that will be systematic and devoid of arbitrariness, we arrive at a conception of what there is altogether: the possible worlds, the possible individuals that are their parts, and the mathematical objects, even if those should turn out to be pure sets not made out of the parts of the worlds. This conception, to the extent that it is true, comprises our modal and mathematical knowledge. But a conception of the entire space of possibilities leaves it entirely open where in that space we ourselves are situated. To know that, it is necessary to observe ourselves and our surroundings. And observation of any sort, whether sensory or by means of instruments and traces and signals and records that can put us into dependence on our more distant surroundings, is a matter of causal dependence of one contingent matter of fact upon another. We do not find out by observation what possibilities there are. (Except that if we notice that logical space as we conceive it contains no very plausible candidates to be ourselves, that might be a good reason to reconsider our conception.) What we do find out by observation is what possibilities *we* are: which worlds may be ours, which of their inhabitants may be ourselves.

So we have the desired boundary between knowledge that does and that doesn't require causal contact with the subject matter. It is a principled boundary, though motivated within the very modal realism that is in dispute. (I am mounting a defensive operation, and will be content with a standoff.) Modal and mathematical knowledge together fall on the right side of the line. Our *contingent* knowledge that there are donkeys at *our* world requires causal acquaintance with the donkeys, or at least with what produces them. Our *necessary* knowledge that there are donkeys at *some* worlds – even talking donkeys, donkeys with dragons as worldmates, and what have you – does not require causal acquaintance either with the donkeys or with what produces them. It requires no observation of our surroundings, because it is no part of our knowledge of which possible world is ours and which possible individuals are we.

If you think that all knowledge requires causal acquaintance with the subject matter, I think that is just hasty generalisation. But if you concede that knowledge of mathematical objects does not, and yet you insist that knowledge of other-worldly donkeys does, then I doubt that you really do regard the latter as non-contingent modal knowledge. I suspect that you suspect that the other worlds must really be parts of actuality, not alternative possibilities. We considered this as an objection in its own right in section 2.1. It is right or it is wrong. If it is right, it is decisive as it stands. If it is wrong, it should be rejected altogether. Either way, it is better to take it straight than to entangle it with issues about knowledge. If the other worlds would be just parts of actuality, modal realism is kaput. If not, then the knowledge we have concerning donkeys at other possible worlds is not on a par with the knowledge we lack concerning donkeys in remote or hidden parts of this world. We should not be misled by a false analogy between the two. The former is part of our modal knowledge of what worlds there are. The latter would be part of our knowledge about which world is ours; we gain such knowledge by interacting causally with the world around us, and the problem is that we interact mainly with its nearby and unhidden parts.

If we don't know by causal interaction that other worlds and their donkeys exist, how *do* we know? – I can take that question three ways. (1) I can take it as a request for an analysis of knowledge; and for a fully general analysis, one that applies to the whole range of our knowledge, modal and mathematical knowledge included. That is a fair request, and I regret that I cannot deliver the goods. But I don't see that this is especially my problem. It is a problem for everyone (certain sceptics and conventionalists excepted) and it is not worsened by a modal realist construal of the content of our modal knowledge.

   (I do have one suggestion to offer. The analysis of knowledge is plagued with puzzles about truths believed for bad reasons: because you were told by a guru, because you made two mistakes that cancelled out, because by luck you never encountered the persuasions or evidence that would have misled you, ... In each case, the puzzle is introduced by one or two examples; but we then suppose that an analysis needs to deal with the problem across the board. Maybe not. Maybe some of the familiar puzzles don't arise in connection with knowledge of simple non-contingent matters. Can you *really* not know that $2+2=4$, or that there are no true contradictions, when you fully understand and accept the statement? I doubt it. Would your acceptance of *these* statements fail to be knowledge if you only accepted them because the guru told you to? Or because two of your mistakes cancelled out? Or because you chanced to miss the lecture by the persuasive sophist who would have changed your mind? Not so, I think, or not clearly so.)

   (2) Or I can take the question how we know as a request for 'naturalistic epistemology'. Never mind what makes our modal opinions count as knowledge; how do we come by the modal opinions that we do in fact hold? ('You say the dollar will be devalued tomorrow – *how do you know*?' Imagine that the question is asked *not* by a doubter or an epistemologist, but by an official seeking your help in plugging leaks. He wants to know how you came to think so.) In the mathematical case, the answer is that we come by our opinions largely by reasoning from general principles that we already accept; sometimes in a precise and rigorous way, sometimes in a more informal fashion, as when we reject arbitrary-seeming limits on the plentitude of the mathematical universe. I suppose the answer in the modal case is similar. I think our everyday modal opinions are, in large measure, consequences of a principle of recombination – something along the lines discussed in section 1.8, though doubtless there is room to improve my formulation of it. One could imagine reasoning rigorously from a precise formulation of it, but in fact our reasoning is more likely to take the form of imaginative experiments.

We try to think how duplicates of things already accepted as possible – for instance, because they are actual – might be arranged to fit the description of an alleged possibility. Having imagined various arrangements – not in complete detail, of course – we consider how they might aptly be described. If things of these kinds were arranged like this, would *that* be a world where Saul Kripke is the son of Rudolf Carnap?

For more far-fetched possibilities, recombination is less useful. But there are other principles that we can apply. A rejection of arbitrary-seeming limits on the plenitude of worlds, for instance, might lead us to conclude that if any worlds have seventeen dimensions then others have eighteen; or that it is highly unlikely that every natural property instantiated at any world is instantiated here at our world. On still other questions, there seems to be no way at all of fixing our modal opinions, and we just have to confess our irremediable ignorance. I think one question of this kind concerns incompatibility of natural properties. Is it absolutely impossible for one particle to be both positively and negatively charged? Or are the two properties exclusive only under the contingent laws of nature that actually obtain? I do not see how we can make up our minds; or what guarantee we have that there must be some way to settle the question. Certainly we are not entitled just to make the truth be one way or the other by declaration. Whatever the truth may be, it isn't up to us.

Certainly the way to come by modal opinions is not to inspect the worlds one at a time, not only because we cannot inspect the worlds at all, but because we would have to work very fast to run through all of them within a conveniently short time.[3] You might as well think that our knowledge of the real numbers comes from inspecting *them* one at a time! No; our methods must be general, in both the mathematical and the modal cases. Certainly when we reason from recombination by means by imaginative experiments, the method is general; we imagine only some salient features, and thereby cover an infinite class of worlds all in one act of imagining.

(3) Finally, I can take the question how we know as a sceptical challenge: put this alleged knowledge on a firm foundation, show that it is derived by an infallible method. My first response would be to say that here, as elsewhere, it is unreasonable to hope for firm foundations or infallible methods. But on second thought, it seems that infallible methods *can* be had, and with the greatest of ease. Probably the right thing to say is that the demand for an infallible method does not make very good sense for knowledge of non-contingent matters, because it is too easily trivialised. For if it is a necessary truth that so-and-so, then believing that so-and-so *is* an infallible method of being right. If what I believe

---

[3]Richards makes this point; as does McGinn, after making me a handsome gift of a faculty of 'mental vision' which works like the notorious powerful telescope.

is a necessary truth, then there is no possibility of being wrong. That is so whatever the subject matter of the necessary truth, and no matter how it came to be believed. So perhaps an infallible *general* method is what is demanded. But that too is suspiciously easy. How about the method of reasoning from certain specified premises which are themselves non-contingent? In the modal case, the reasoning might be highly informal, consisting mainly of imaginative experiments implicitly premised on a principle of recombination; in the mathematical case, the reasoning might proceed more or less rigorously from axioms of iterative set theory, or from the axioms of some limited branch of mathematics. Suppose, for example, that you accept every theorem you can deduce from the Peano axioms within a certain deductive system. If in fact the axioms are necessarily true (as they are), and the deductive system necessarily preserves truth, then you cannot possibly go wrong. You are following a method of arriving at arithmetical opinions that is both infallible and general. Never mind that you follow this method only because your guru told you to; it is still infallible and general.

So what is *really* wanted? Is it that we must put our firm foundations on still firmer foundations, and subsume our general infallible methods under still more general infallible methods, *ad infinitum*? Surely there must be an end sooner or later, and why not sooner? Is it that we must be reasonable? I think the procedure of revising our opinions piecemeal, guided in part by theoretical conservatism and in part by the pursuit of theoretical unity, is what we call 'being reasonable'; and it is by this procedure that we can accept the Peano axioms, the axioms of iterative set theory, the principle of recombination, and so forth. Is it that we must prove that it is reasonable to be reasonable? That proof should be a one-liner. Is it that we must find something to say that would, of necessity, make anyone who heard it become reasonable forthwith? That would be a spell, not an argument. Must we prove, from no questionable premises, that those who are reasonable will never fall into error? That is not to be expected.

2.5 A Road to Scepticism?

I now turn to three milder objections. They say not that modal realism leads to outright paradox, but that it somehow demands momentous changes in the way we think and live. I may in consistency be a modal realist – but only if I am prepared to change my life in extreme and eccentric ways to suit my philosophy. I am not prepared to do any such thing, and don't see why I should.

The first of these objections has been raised by Peter Forrest, in 'Occam's Razor and Possible Worlds'; by George Schlesinger; and (in discussion) by Robert M. Adams and J. J. C. Smart. They say that a modal realist ought to be a sceptic; because there are ever so many deceptive worlds, full of people very like us – counterparts or duplicates of us – who learn from experience in exactly the same way that we do, but who learn falsehoods.

Some of our deceived counterparts expect the future to resemble the past in the appropriate ways; but they live in worlds where the future does not at all resemble the past. Such worlds exist by recombination: graft any future onto any past. For some of the deceived, things will go wrong in a subtle and insidious way: new observations will tend to confirm the ether drift after all. Those are the lucky ones. For others, things will degenerate into utter chaos all around them. Others will never learn of their errors, for one reason or another. They will never be disappointed, but they will have been no less deceived.

Some are deceived not about the future but about the past: they live in brand-new worlds full of false traces and records of a past that never was. There might have been a Falsifier to make the false traces. But there needn't have been – for any possible state, there are worlds that begin in just that state.

Some are deceived even about their present. Some wield Occam's razor just as we do; they favour the most parsimonious theory that fits their observations, but unfortunately their worlds are full of epiphenomenal rubbish that does not interact in any way with them or with anything they can observe. Some are the playthings of powerful field linguists, who irradiate their surfaces so as to prompt assent to falsehoods. Some are brains in vats. However reasonably they theorise, their theories are almost entirely wrong.[4]

Shouldn't the sad fate of all these counterparts and duplicates of ours be a warning to us? What business have we to trust what we call 'reasonable' methods of forming beliefs and expectations, if we know how those methods betray so many others so like ourselves? Why should we expect better luck than theirs? A modal realist has no right to trust induction – he should turn sceptic forthwith.

(I shall use the word 'induction' broadly, to cover all the methods we deem reasonable for forming beliefs about the unobserved parts of our world on the basis of experience with the observed parts. Induction narrowly speaking – the extrapolation of frequencies from samples to the populations sampled – is, of course, an important part of induction. But

---

[4]I reject recent arguments that brains in vats would not be deceived. The arguments only show how we must take some care in saying what the brains are and are not wrong about. See my 'Putnam's Paradox'.

what I mean in general is a complicated matter of inheriting, devising, testing, revising, and applying hypotheses; of judging the *a priori* credibility of alternative possibilities, and of continually reapportioning our credence among them under the impact of new evidence; done sometimes thoughtfully, more often by habit, sometimes betwixt and between.)

I have no intention of becoming a sceptic. What we call 'inductive reason' is rightly so called; and I, as a modal realist, have no more reason to foresake inductive reason than anyone else has. I *do* have the reason that everyone has; and I agree with common opinion that this reason is insufficient.

The reason that everyone has is that induction is fallible. It is possible, and it is possible in very many ways, that by being reasonable we shall be led into error. By trusting induction we run a risk, and we proceed in the confident hope that the genuine possibilities of error will seldom be realised. All that, I say, is quite independent of any theory of the nature of possibilities. I recognise the possibilities of error that everyone else recognises; they are no more and no less possibilities of error for being understood as other worlds of a kind with our own. They give me no more and no less reason to foresake inductive reason than they give to someone who holds a rival metaphysical view of their nature, or to someone who holds no particular view. Even if someone says there are no such entities as possibilities at all, but still he says it is possible in very many ways that we might be deceived (I have no idea what he thinks there are many of!), I think that he and I have equal reason, and equally insufficient reason, to distrust induction.

Why should the reason everyone has to distrust induction seem more formidable when the risk of error is understood my way: as the existence of other worlds wherein our counterparts are deceived? It should not. But why does it? I have two conjectures. The first is that we are in an unstable condition. We have not become altogether reconciled to our predicament, though we have got in the habit of not fussing about it. Outside the philosophy room, it is inevitable that we give our trust to a fallible method. But underneath, we really do not like to do such a thing. And calling the fallible method 'inductive reason' – as we are right to do, because that is indeed the name we have given it – does not make us like it any better. But there are not a lot of things to be said one way or the other about our disagreeable predicament, we have said those things quite often enough, and so we put our attention elsewhere. But if that is our condition, our discontent is always ready to come alive again if the same old thing – namely, that there are abundant possibilities of error – can be said in a new and different way. And one way to give it a new and different look is to tie it to a controversial account of the metaphysical nature of the possibilities in question. That can make it come back to haunt us as vigorously as if it were brand new. Modal realism creates no new reason for scepticism, but it revivifies the old reason.

A different conjecture is that once again we are being influenced by the thought that everything is actual. That means that if I am right that there are other worlds, they are not the alternative possibilities I say they are; so what they present is not the mere possibility of error. Instead, the other worlds are more of actuality, and whatever inductive deception occurs therein occurs actually. But if we knew that many people were actually being deceived, that would not be just the old reason for scepticism: distrust induction because it is fallible. No; that would be a good *inductive* reason to distrust induction. It's not that we should trust induction while it teaches us that it is not to be trusted; rather, our attempt to trust it would destroy itself. If a prophet says: 'Buy cheap, sell dear, and never heed the word of the likes of me!' then however much you might wish to follow his counsel, there is no way you can. It's not just that you would find it difficult to take him seriously; the trouble is that if you follow either part of his counsel you thereby disregard the other part.

I claim once more that I am within my rights to call the other worlds possible, not actual. If so, they give us no cases of actual inductive error, so they give us no inductive reason to distrust induction. Insofar as the present objection relies on setting induction against induction, it is either wrong (if I am right) or superfluous (if I am wrong); since if the other worlds are not alternative possibilities then the present objection is the least of my troubles.

We might ask how the inductively deceptive worlds compare in abundance to the undeceptive worlds. If this is meant as a comparison of cardinalities, it seems clear that the numbers will be equal. For deceptive and undeceptive worlds alike, it is easy to set a lower bound of beth-two, the number of distributions of a two-valued magnitude over a continuum of spacetime points; and hard to make a firm case for any higher cardinality. However, there might be a sense in which one or the other class of worlds predominates even without a difference in cardinality. There is a good sense, for instance, in which the primes are an infinitesimal minority among the natural numbers, even without any difference in cardinality: their limiting relative frequency is zero. We cannot take a limiting relative frequency among the worlds, for lack of any salient linear order; but perhaps there is some third way, not cardinality and not relative frequency, to make sense of the question how abundant are the deceptive worlds.

In 'Occam's Razor and Possible Worlds', Peter Forrest argues ingeniously that there is a certain sense in which deceptive worlds predominate, though without a difference in cardinality. If he were right, a predominance of possibilities of error could support scepticism in a way that a mere abundance of such possibilities could not.

He concentrates on only one sort of possibility of error: the world full of epiphenomenal rubbish, in which we go wrong by relying on Occam's razor. Consider only worlds with observers like ourselves; by 'epiphenomenal', let us mean things that do not interact with those observers or with anything they observe. A *clean* world is one with nothing epiphenomenal; clean worlds are not deceptive in the way under consideration, though of course some of them are deceptive in other ways. All other worlds are *rubbishy*. If epiphenomenal rubbish is present it can be here but not there, or there but not here, or . . . . But if it is absent it is nowhere, and that's that. So there are countless ways for it to be present, and only one way for it to be absent. This suggests that we can associate each clean world with infinitely many rubbishy worlds. We can: let us call worlds *equivalent* iff they are exactly alike except for whatever epiphenomenal rubbish they may contain. Each clean world is equivalent to infinitely many rubbishy worlds, but not to any clean worlds except itself. (Or a world indiscernible from itself. But let me grant to Forrest, for the sake of the argument, that there are no indiscernible worlds. I do not know whether this is true, but I do agree with Forrest that an attempt to avoid his conclusion by appeal to indiscernible worlds would be outrageously *ad hoc*.) The equivalence classes partition the relevant worlds, and in each equivalence class the rubbishy worlds outnumber the clean worlds by infinity to one. In each class, rubbishy worlds predominate and clean worlds are an infinitesimal minority.

Class by class, rubbishy worlds predominate; so, in some reasonable sense, they predominate *simpliciter*. Call this Forrest's *direct argument*. He regards it as intuitively plausible, but lacking in rigour. I regard it as lacking in force altogether, because it can be paralleled to its discredit. Here is an infinite table in which each number appears once. The left-hand column is an enumeration of the non-primes; the rest is an enumeration of the primes, folded up to fill a two-dimensional array.

$$
\begin{array}{lllll}
4 & 1 & 2 & 11 & 13 \ldots \\
6 & 3 & 7 & 17 & 41 \ldots \\
8 & 5 & 19 & 37 & 59 \ldots \\
 & \cdot\cdot\cdot
\end{array}
$$

The rows partition the numbers; and in each row, the primes outnumber the non-primes by infinity to one. Class by class, the primes predominate. Shall we conclude that the primes predominate *simpliciter*? – We would not have thought so, accustomed as we are to thinking that (in the sense of limiting frequency) the primes are the infinitesimal minority!

If we really have found a sense in which the primes predominate, we must acknowledge that in the same sense the non-primes also predominate, or the squares, or the odds, or the evens, or whatever infinite subclass of the numbers you please. For in each case we can build a table on the same principle: the alleged minority squeezes into one column, the alleged majority is folded to fill the rest of the table.

Forrest seems prepared to grant that even if the rubbishy worlds predominate in some sense, they do not have any greater cardinality. But if this be granted, then we can fight fire with fire. To be sure, there is Forrest's partition of worlds. But if the cardinalities are the same, then there must also exist a *counter-partition*: a different way of dividing the relevant worlds into classes, such that in each class there are infinitely many clean worlds, and only one rubbishy one! So it is the clean worlds that predominate class by class, and in that sense predominate *simpliciter*; and thereby we argue in support of Occam's razor. It might be harder to describe an equivalence relation that generates a counter-partition than it was to describe the one that generates Forrest's partition, but what is the relevance of that?

Forrest backs up his direct argument with a 'more rigorous' indirect argument, in two steps. Again we refer to the equivalence classes, within which worlds are alike except perhaps for their epiphenomenal rubbish.

First step. Suppose, *per impossibile*, that you knew which equivalence class contains the actual world. In that class, whichever it is, rubbishy worlds predominate by infinity to one. So you should then conclude, with almost perfect certainty, that the actual world is rubbishy.

Second step. But all the classes are on a par. Whatever the correct class should turn out to be, if you knew it you should conclude that the actual world is rubbishy. Why wait for information when its content could make no difference? You should *already* conclude that the actual world is rubbishy.

But this 'more rigorous' argument has no more force than the merely 'plausible' version. Like the direct argument before it, the indirect argument can be paralleled to its discredit. We can put a counter-partition in place of Forrest's original partition, thereby supporting Occam's razor. Or we can parallel it, as before, in a numerical case. Suppose your task is to guess whether the mystery number, selected you know not how, is prime. Primes predominate, by infinity to one, in every row of our previous table; and all the rows are on a par. If, *per impossibile*, you knew which row contained the mystery number, you should then conclude that it is almost certainly prime. Why wait? You should *already* conclude that the mystery number is prime – or non-prime, or square or odd or even or what you will.

Unlike the direct argument, Forrest's indirect argument is an interesting paradox. In view of the discrediting parallels, it is plain that one step or the other must be wrong, but it is not at all clear which one is at fault. To fault the first step is, in effect, to endorse extreme inequalities in our distribution of initial credence. We might have hoped for at least some vestige of a principle of indifference: equal distribution over the worlds might be uncalled for, it might not even have any clear meaning in the infinite case, but at least we shouldn't have one single world outweighing an infinite class! To fault the second step is to give up an infinitary version of an additivity principle for credence. That also is quite unwelcome. But that, it seems, is the choice.

But however Forrest's paradox can best be solved, it is everybody's problem. It has nothing to do with modal realism. You cannot refute a thesis just by hooking it up to a paradox with a life of its own.

Forrest thinks the paradox does not have a life of its own: modal realism enters as one of its premises. He thinks that if the rubbishy worlds somehow predominate among all the relevant worlds (as in the direct argument), or if they outnumber the clean worlds by infinity to one in a class which *ex hypothesi* is known to contain the actual world (as in the first step of the indirect argument), that is not by itself a decisive reason to conclude that the actual world is rubbishy. It is only a defeasible reason. If it is reasonable to believe *a priori* that the actual world is clean, then the defeasible reason is defeated. That is a reasonable thing to believe, says Forrest; but only if you are not a modal realist. You have to think that the actual world is special, not only in its relation to you, but absolutely. Here I disagree; I think it is just as reasonable for a modal realist as for anyone else to believe *a priori* that the actual world is clean. It is true that there are many reasonable modal realists who believe this and are mistaken because they inhabit rubbishy worlds. But nobody ever said that inductive reason was guaranteed to succeed.

But we needn't dispute the point; because the discreditable parallels show that something else is wrong, apart from what Forrest says about the alleged relevance of modal realism. Suppose he is right that given modal realism, there is nothing to defeat the first step of his indirect argument. Then equally there is nothing to defeat the first step of the parallel argument that uses a counter-partition to defend the razor. We end with two opposite conclusions about what a modal realist ought to believe; and that is enough to discredit both arguments. Similarly in the case of the mystery number, we may suppose if we like that there are countably many guessers, and each has a personal mystery number selected especially for him, and every number is the mystery number for someone. Your mystery number is in no way special, except in its relation to you. Then there is nothing to defeat the first step of a Forrest-style argument that you should be certain that your mystery number is prime, or that it is non-prime, or square or odd or even or what you will.

Jonathan Bennett and John Bigelow have suggested, in quite different connections,[5] that abundance of possibilities might be measured by variety. There are distances between points in Australia that are far greater than any distances between points in Sydney (even counting the western suburbs) and that has something to do with the fact that Sydney is a comparatively small part of Australia. Likewise, suppose we have a region in the space of all possibilities, and there are far greater dissimilarity distances between points in the whole space than there ever are between points in the region; that would suggest that in some sense the given region is a comparatively small part of the entire space. (Of course this is the merest sketch: so far as what I've just said goes, for instance, we could be fooled by smallish regions with long thin tentacles. Improvements are feasible, as Bennett and Bigelow show.) Here, as the spatial analogy shows, our comparisons of size have nothing to do with comparisons of cardinality. Does this approach give us a new way to say that rubbishy worlds predominate? Clean worlds can be dissimilar. But rubbishy worlds can be dissimilar in new and different ways. Are there far greater dissimilarities between rubbishy worlds than there ever are between clean worlds? If so, would that make it reasonable to believe that ours is a rubbishy world rather than an equivalent clean world?

I think not. Within limits, I defend the notion of comparative similarity. Within limits, and given suitably ordinary contextual background, we surely are prepared to weigh respects of similarity and difference against one another and say, for instance, that some world where the scratched match lights is more like this world (where the unscratched match doesn't light) than is any world where the scratched match fails to light because the scratching is done underwater. But I insist on the limits, and I protest against an appeal to comparative similarity that goes beyond them. We have no settled way to weigh ordinary similarities and differences against unconsidered similarities and differences having to do with the epiphenomenal rubbish. Why should we? For any ordinary counterfactual, we may as well say that the closest antecedent worlds are those where the rubbish is just as it is here – namely absent, or so we may reasonably believe. There's no such trade-off as we had between similarity in respect of lighting and similarity in respect of being dry, wherefore we have had no occasion to establish terms of trade. There is no fact of the matter about whether dissimilarities involving the rubbish are greater than dissimilarities between clean worlds – to say such a thing is to pretend that terms of trade have been settled. Among the nearby worlds, where comparative similarity is comparatively determinate, it seems quite a good

---

[5]Bennett, 'Killing and Letting Die'; Bigelow, 'Possible Worlds Foundations for Probability'.

idea to measure abundance by variety. But to claim that rubbishy worlds predominate by reason of their variety would be to go too far.

2.6 A Road to Indifference?

Likewise it is argued that modal realism should change the way in which we care about what happens. Robert M. Adams puts the point as follows. He is comparing a thesis of 'absolute actuality', on which the world we are part of is a fundamentally different kind of thing from alternative possibilities, with my indexical theory of actuality, on which the worlds are all of a kind and to call one world actual is only to say that it is the one we are part of.

> We may be moved by the joys and sorrows of a character known to be fictitious; but we do not really believe it is bad that evils occur in a nonactual possible world, or good that joys occur in a nonactual possible world, though of course it would be bad and good, respectively, for them to be actual. I think that our very strong disapproval of the deliberate actualizing of evils similarly reflects a belief in the absolutely, and not just relatively, special status of the actual as such. Indeed, if we ask, 'What is wrong with actualizing evils, since they will occur in some other possible world anyway if they don't occur in this one?', I doubt that the indexical theory can provide an answer which will be completely satisfying ethically. ('Theories of Actuality', pages 215–16; Loux, page 195.)

Thus a modal realist should be indifferent to this-worldly evils. There would be the same sum total of good and of evil throughout the worlds, no matter which world is ours. And he needn't bother what he does; there would be the same sum total no matter how he acted.[6]

There would indeed be the same sum total. (And not just because the amounts of good and evil throughout the worlds will in any case be undefined infinite sums.) If I had acted otherwise, for instance by taking to a life of crime, each and every good or evil that is present somewhere in the totality of worlds would still have been present, and none would have been added. It is wrong to think: then this world would have been a little worse, and the rest would have been no different, so the totality of worlds would have been a little worse. No; if I had turned to crime, a different world would have been actual. The closest world where my

---

[6]Similarly, D. C. Williams (in a lecture at the University of Notre Dame in 1974) complains that my view is 'complete fatalism, because the sum total of being is absolutely necessary'. What's more, this sum total of being involves a variety of miseries horrible to think of. And it is futile to lead a good life and attempt to eradicate evil – the evil you have gone to the trouble of preventing just happens off in another world.

counterpart turns to crime is one where a different world is actual. If this is world W and it is world V, then this is a world where W is actual, whereas the closest world where my counterpart turns to crime is a world where V is actual. But it is true at both worlds that both worlds, with all their goods and evils, are part of the totality of worlds.[7]

Perhaps the confusion is caused by a *de re* counterfactual: this world is such that if I had turned to crime, it would have been worse. I interpret that as follows: the closest world where my counterpart turns to crime is one where this world's counterpart is worse than this world is. The counterpart of W at V presumably is V itself, which presumably *is* worse than W, making the *de re* counterfactual true. Or perhaps the confusion is caused by our old enemy, the thought that really the other worlds are just parts of actuality, so counterfactuals ought to be about different ways the totality of worlds might have been. I say again: that's right or wrong, if right needn't be brought against me in a roundabout fashion, if wrong shouldn't be brought against me at all.

The point comes in a prudential as well as a moral version. Consider only the goods that I myself want, apart from whatever moral concerns I may have. I have various more or less personal aspirations. At the moment, I want very much to get this book done. And I hope that afterward it will meet with some approval; not necessarily that it will win converts to modal realism, but at least that other people will come to share my understanding of what they stand to gain and lose by declining the conversion. This hope moves me to labour day and night in front of an ugly green screen. Why bother? For if I am right on this matter, I know that there are ever so many worlds where the book gets written, ever so many more where it doesn't, still more where it does but is full of vile errors, ... The book I want to have written will be written in any case – of necessity, it will be written countless times over, word for word the same. (And countless more times over, with more or less significant variations.) Among my counterparts and myself are many who succeed in writing it, and many who fail. What does it matter where I myself fall?

A story by Larry Niven even suggests that knowledge of a plurality of worlds might reasonably undermine the will to live. Every decision you ever make is made in all the myriad ways it might be made. It is made one way by you, other ways by your other-worldly counterparts who are exactly like you up to the moment of the decision. Not only difficult and momentous decisions will be made all different ways; but also easy decisions, even decisions too easy to take any thought, like the decision whether to kill yourself on the spur of the moment for no reason

---

[7]Here is a case, exceptional but not problematic, where something foreign to a world itself can sensibly be said to be true at that world. As I said in section 1.2, a restricting modifier 'in Australia' or 'at world W' imposes its restriction only defeasibly.

at all. Given that the decision will in any case be made all different ways, what does it matter whether you are one of the ones who makes it one way or one of the ones who makes it another way?

(Three qualifications. (1) Niven's story is not strictly a story of many possible worlds, but of many world-like parts of one big world; for he posits travel between them. (See section 1.6.) (2) Niven may be talking about branching worlds, in which one present decider has many futures that are all equally his. If so, I grant his point. That really would make nonsense of decision. (See section 4.2.) But let me assume instead that he is talking about the case of many different deciders, each with his own single future, who are exactly alike up to the moment of decision. (3) Part of Niven's argument may be the sceptical point of the previous section; not only will things come about in all the myriad ways no matter what you choose to do, but also you are not entitled to have any expectations about consequences to you.)

I reply that the argument for indifference relies on a false premise. It is so in all three cases, moral and prudential alike, but most obviously so in the third case. Wanting to live is not wanting that a kind of thing happen, somewhere in the worlds and never mind where; it is an egocentric want, a want that *I myself* should have a certain property. The appropriate way to give the content of my desire is not by a condition that I want the entire system of worlds to satisfy, but by a condition that I want myself to satisfy. It is futile to want the entire system of worlds to satisfy a condition, because it is not contingent what conditions the entire system of worlds does or doesn't satisfy. You might as well want the number seventeen to be prime, or to be even – satisfied or unsatisfiable, your wish is equally idle either way. It is not idle to want continued life for yourself; you may have it or not, and you will not get what you want if you make the wrong decision about whether to kill yourself on the spur of the moment. It will not matter to reality as a whole how you decide – there will in any case be many just like you who decide one way and many who decide the other – but it still matters to you. An egocentric want is *prima facie* a different thing from a want as to how the world should be. Elsewhere I have argued that the *prima facie* difference is genuine. The first sort of want is not in general reducible to the second. (In the terminology of my 'Attitudes *De Dicto* and *De Se*', some wants are irreducibly *de se*.) All the more is an egocentric want a different thing from a want about how the entire plurality of worlds should be.

We do have irreducibly egocentric wants. There is no difficulty in understanding how that is possible; or if there is, it only arises when we stubbornly insist that seemingly egocentric wants cannot be what they seem. Nor can I think of any good reason why we ought not to have them. Your egocentric desire to survive cannot be satisfied vicariously by the survival of your counterparts, and that is why you should not be indifferent to whether you live or die.

Likewise, I do not just idly want someone in some world to have written this book I have in mind; I want to have written it myself, and that is what motivates me to keep going. And I do not just idly want someone at some world to be wiser through learning its lessons; I want to change the thinking of my worldmates. That is doubly egocentric: I want my worldmates to be among the people who learn, and I want to be the one to teach them. That is why it matters to me whether I am one of those among my counterparts who labour on, or one of those who quit.[8]

In the moral case, I *do* say that an other-worldly evil is just as much an evil as a this-worldly one, and an other-worldly good is just as much a good. If it is a matter simply of judgement, parity of reasoning must prevail. The Hitler-counterpart of a world that differs from ours mainly with respect to affairs on the fourth planet of Vega is morally on a par with the Hitler we know and hate. If to believe it is bad that evils occur in a non-actual possible world is to believe that those evils are bad, or, in other worlds, that those bad things are evils, of course I believe it; and in the same way, of course I believe it is good that joys occur in a non-actual possible world.

But, judgements aside, do I really *care* about other-worldly goods and evils? Is it a matter of wants: should I want there to be less evil and more good in total, throughout the worlds? It would be an idle wish, since the character of the totality of all the worlds is not a contingent matter. I see no reason why I ought to have so utterly idle and pointless a wish. But what is more, I have no idea whether or not I *do* have it. It is so disconnected from any guidance of conduct that I cannot tell how it would be manifest in my thought or action whether I had it or not. Perhaps

---

[8]Mark Johnston has questioned whether I am in a position to insist that my desires for the future are egocentric, given the theory I hold of persistence through time. I think that persisting things such as myself are divisible into temporal parts, or stages; and the stage who now wants the book finished is not the stage who will finish it for me. Then don't I really just want it to get finished somehow, never mind by whom? Wouldn't it be just as well if a benign impostor took over, if he'd do the job the way I want it done? And if we agree thus far, why does it matter if the benign impostor, and those he teaches, are part of some other world?

In reply, I agree that my view makes it fair to think of the desires as belonging in the first instance to my present stage, and derivatively to the persisting sum of many stages. And I agree that what my present stage wants is not to finish the book itself – it's a sensible stage, so it knows that can't be expected. But that's not to say that it only cares what happens, never mind how. There is a middle ground. My present stage wants the book to be finished in the fulfilment of *its* present intentions – there's the egocentric part – and that will happen only if the proper sort of causal continuity binds together my present stage with the one that finishes the book. The continuity thus desired is part of the continuity that unifies mereological sums of person-stages into persisting people.

it would be no different from my cool judgement that the evils and goods of other worlds are no less evils and goods – and if it is that, then I do have it. Perhaps it would manifest itself in efforts to do the impossible and improve the affairs of other worlds. If so, I do not have it. Or I suppose not – but I have no real idea what efforts to do such impossible feats would look like, so for all I know, I might be attempting them daily. Perhaps it would manifest itself in idle thought: should I lie awake at night bemoaning the evils of other worlds, and should I celebrate their joys? I see no reason why I should bemoan the evils and celebrate the joys even of remote parts of this world, which I believe in along with everyone else. I suppose the cancer patients in the tenth century suffered as much as cancer patients do today – ought I to spend time bemoaning their suffering?

'Concern' and 'caring' are muddled conglomerates of judgement, preference, conduct, and attention. To the question whether a modal realist ought to be concerned about the joys and sufferings and evils and goods that go on in other worlds, I answer in four parts. As to judgement, yes; not to judge them as what they are would be mistaken. As to preference, no; a preference that non-contingent things be otherwise is idle. As to conduct, the question is empty; when no possible conduct would be relevant, there is no sense asking whether the relevant things ought to be done. As to attention, no; there are better ways to spend your life than in brooding about the fortunes of perfect strangers, even perfect strangers who are counterparts of yourself or those you love.

'What is wrong with actualising evils, since they will occur in some other possible world anyway if they don't occur in this one?' – If you actualise evils, you will be an evil-doer, a causal source of evil. That is something which, if you are virtuous, you do not want to be. Other-worldly evils are neither here nor there. They aren't your evils. Your virtuous desire to do good and not evil has nothing to do with the sum total of good and evil throughout reality. It has to do with what befalls you and your worldmates, and in particular it has to do with the way in which what befalls yourself and others depends causally on what you do.

For those of us who think of morality in terms of virtue and honour, desert and respect and esteem, loyalties and affections and solidarity, the other-worldly evils should not seem even momentarily relevant to morality. Of course our moral aims are egocentric. And likewise all the more for those who think of morality in terms of rules, rights, and duties; or as obedience to the will of God.

If modal realism makes a problem for anyone, it is for utilitarians. But not even for commonplace utilitarians, who might go in for a certain amount of generalised benevolence under the heading of solidarity with humanity, or out of kindness to those whom they are in a position to help. The problem belongs only to utilitarians of an especially pure sort. Only if morality consists of maximising the total of good, absolutely regardless of where and to whom the good may accrue, can it lose its point because the sum total of good throughout the plurality of worlds is non-contingently fixed and depends not at all on what we do. I agree with J. J. C. Smart's statement of the point:

> In fact on a realistic theory of possible worlds they are all going to exist anyway, and so a truly universalistic ethics collapses . . . . The only sort of ethics that a realistic theory of possible worlds would allow would be an ethics of the speaker's own world, and this would be a particularist ethics, much as an ethics that considered only the good of one's own tribe or nation would be. (*Ethics, Persusasion and Truth*, pages 88–9.)

But if modal realism subverts only a 'truly universalistic ethics', I cannot see that as a damaging objection. What collapses is a philosophers' invention, no less remote from common sense than modal realism itself. An ethics of our own world is quite universalistic enough. Indeed, I dare say that it is already far too universalistic; it is a betrayal of our particular affections. If my modal realism has any bearing at all on matters of value and morality, it pushes me toward common sense, not away.

2.7   Arbitrariness Lost?

Peter Unger has argued that modal realism permits us to see the world as far less arbitrary than we are accustomed to suppose.[9] It is not clear that this would be an objection – Unger regards it rather as a point in modal realism's favour – but at any rate it is convenient to group it with other arguments that, for better or worse, modal realism should change our thinking about this-worldly matters. I myself, being conservatively inclined, do take it as an objection. The fewer remarkable implications, the better for plausibility. There may indeed be a sense in which modal realism makes us more comfortable with the arbitrary, brute facts of the world – no harm in that – but I insist that they remain arbitrary and they remain unexplained.

Suppose some chance process goes on – a genuine chance process, not a deterministic process in which the predetermining conditions are beyond our ability to observe – and it gives one outcome rather than another. Or suppose that according to the prevailing laws of nature, particles of a certain kind cannot in any way be created or destroyed; there are finitely many of them; and we have one number rather than another of these

[9]"Minimizing Arbitrariness'; see also Schlesinger, 'Possible Worlds and the Mystery of Existence'.

particles. Or suppose that a certain (dimensionless) physical constant figures in the laws of nature; and it has one value rather than another. For that matter, suppose the fundamental laws of nature can be codified in a system of equations, and these equations take one form rather than another.

All these seem arbitrary, 'quirky' facts about the world. In each case, we have a range of alternatives and the world selects one alternative out of the range. It is contingent that one alternative is selected rather than another. There is no sufficient reason why it happened that way. In the best possible organisation of the whole truth about the world into a deductive system, such a fact would have to come in as an axiom, not a theorem. It seems to cry out for explanation when there is no explanation to be had. It will distress a rationalist to hear such cries go unanswered; whereas to someone like me, inured to brute contingency, it seems only to be expected. In fact it would arouse my suspicion to be told that, after all, explanation does *not* inevitably terminate in brute matters of fact.

Under modal realism, these arbitrary features simply distinguish our world from others. Different worlds have all different outcomes of the chance process; all different numbers of the conserved particles; all different values of the physical constant; all different forms of equations for the fundamental laws. The entire system of worlds, in which all the different alternatives in each range are chosen, different ones at different worlds, does not display the arbitrariness of the worlds considered individually. As Unger puts it, 'by localizing our specificity, we minimize the arbitrariness that is associated with it' ('Minimizing Arbitrariness', page 31). The same would have been true if all different alternatives had appeared in different parts of one big world. That opportunity to minimise arbitrariness by localising specificity within our world is not to be had, so far as we know. But by localising specificity within the entire system of worlds, we gain the same effect: the arbitrariness seems to vanish.

You might protest: 'it does not vanish, it is only relocated. Different worlds select different alternatives in each range, so the entire system of worlds displays no arbitrariness. But then one only of all these worlds is actualised, and it is arbitrary which one that is. And this one arbitrary selection out of a range vaster than ever subsumes all the arbitrariness that we saw before.' But if modal realism is true, there is no special thing that happens to an arbitrary one out of all the worlds; rather, each world alike is actual from the standpoint of its own inhabitants.

But then isn't it an arbitrary matter which world is ours? – It seems not. We just are the inhabitants of one world rather than another. We have counterparts whereby we vicariously inhabit other worlds, and in that sense we could have inhabited other worlds; but there is no other world of which we ourselves, literally, are part. Here are we; there are other people elsewhere in space, elsewhere in time, elsewhere among the worlds. To call it arbitrary that we are of this world rather than another is like calling it arbitrary that we are who we are, rather than any of those other people who live elsewhere.

It is as if I were to call it arbitrary, for instance, that I am David Lewis rather than being Peter Unger. Is that arbitrary? It is a selection of just one alternative out of a range, sure enough. And I would say that it is in a sense contingent: just as other worlds are alternative possibilities for a world, so other individuals are alternative possibilities for an individual; and in particular, Unger is an alternative possibility for me. This is so despite the fact that he is my worldmate, not a part of some other world. (See sections 1.2 and 4.4, and my 'Individuation by Acquaintance and by Stipulation'.) But it is not a fact about the world that I am David Lewis rather than being Peter Unger. *A fortiori* it is not a fact that cries out for explanation. If it is a fact at all, it is an *egocentric* fact about *me*, not at all a fact about the world. We have no notion of what it could possibly mean to explain an egocentric fact like this one. So, very sensibly, we do not crave any such explanation.

(If you suggest that this fact might indeed be explained in terms of the causes that associated my soul with one body rather than another, you misunderstand the problem. If indeed we were embodied souls, the question would not be one about how a certain soul came to inhabit a certain body and lead a certain life. Rather, the egocentric fact would be that I am one soul rather than another – and again, for the supposed souls just as for ordinary people, we have no notion of what it could possibly mean to explain a fact like that.)

Likewise for the fact of which world is ours. It is an egocentric fact, on a par with the fact of which person is me – in fact, the latter subsumes the former. Since this egocentric fact cannot have an explanation, neither can it cry out for one.

So we have, first, the non-contingent fact that there are a plurality of worlds, wherein the alternatives are selected all different ways. There is nothing arbitrary there, and nothing that cries out for explanation. (At least, not if there exists some sufficiently natural break to serve as a limit on the possible sizes and shapes of spacetime; see section 2.2.) And we have, second, the egocentric fact that we are these people who live in this world, rather than other people who live in other worlds. Maybe that is in some sense arbitrary, but it also does not cry out for explanation. But take the two together, and they yield the arbitrary facts about this world that caught our attention: the outcome of the chance process, the number of the conserved particles, the value of the physical constant, the form of equations for the fundamental laws. So where has the arbitrariness gone?

Nowhere. It remains where it always was. In whatever sense those facts were arbitrary before we embedded them in a modal realist ontology, they are arbitrary still. It remains true that they involve selection of one alternative out of a large range. It remains true that they are contingent, which we now take to mean that they vary from world to world. It remains true that they are the sort of facts that it would make sense to explain, and that we would like to explain if we could. And it remains true that we cannot explain them. Their derivability from a non-contingent fact together with an egocentric fact, neither of which cries out for explanation, does not stop them from crying out for explanation.

Why should it even seem to? Perhaps because explanation is seen too much in terms of sufficient reasons, not in terms of information about how things are caused. According to modal realism, the non-contingent fact and the egocentric fact give us what is in some sense a sufficient reason for every contingent fact about our world. But that sufficient reason, if we may call it so, is no substitute for the information about causes that we call 'explanation'. (See my 'Causal Explanation'.) Sometimes we seek information about causes, and we find what we seek. If we learn how hurricanes are caused, we gain some knowledge of the causal ways of our world. No such knowledge could have been gained just by thinking that some worlds have hurricanes and some do not, and that we are who we are, and we are inhabitants of a world with hurricanes. Sometimes we seek information about causes, and we are disappointed to learn that the only information to be had is negative. We learn that nothing at all distinguishes the actual causal history of the actual outcome of a chance process from the hypothetical causal history of a hypothetical alternative outcome, in other words nothing causes the one thing to happen rather than the other. Then what we wanted is not to be had at all; and it is not to be had by thinking that some worlds have one outcome and some have the other, and that we are who we are, and we are inhabitants of a world with this outcome rather than that. Or we learn that the number of the conserved particles has no cause except, of course, for the number of the particles at earlier times. Again, nothing that modal realism has to offer can take the place of the kind of interesting causal information that we sought but did not find.

Sometimes the pursuit of explanation is more the pursuit of unified and general fundamental laws than of information about the causal histories of events. We may hope to explain the value of the arbitrary-seeming physical constant, or to explain the form of the equations, by deriving the most fundamental laws we know from still more fundamental laws that we may hope to discover. We may hope; but we have no guarantee of success. It might be that the most fundamental laws we know are the most fundamental laws there are. What is sought is information about the nomological ways of our world. Once more, nothing that modal realism has to offer can take the place of that.

If arbitary-seeming facts cry out for explanation and no explanation is forthcoming, modal realism may somehow provide solace and remove our stubborn conviction that there *must* be some further explanation, if only we could find it. If so that is all to the good, since that conviction was unreasonable in the first place. But what modal realism cannot do is to provide an explanation of its own, suited to take the place of the missing this-worldly explanation.

The same can be said when the facts about our world seem not so much arbitrary as remarkably lucky. A case can be made that the evolution of life is possible only if the values of the fundamental physical constants and the boundary conditions on the cosmos are exactly right – and lo, they *are* exactly right![10] Merely arbitrary facts may cry out for explanation, but this remarkable luck cries much more loudly. There are explanations in terms of divine creation or natural teleology to be proposed, of course – and to be resisted as *obscurum per obscurius*. But if these are to be resisted, what can take their place?

A modal realist can appeal to the 'anthropic principle': we ought to find it not at all remarkable that the physical constants and boundary conditions turn out to permit the evolution of intelligent life, no matter how exceptional the required values may be. For there are many worlds, with all different values of the constants and boundary conditions. Intelligent life is found only at those of the worlds where the constants and conditions permit it, or where other-worldly laws make it less sensitive to the constants and the conditions. Of course, any inhabitant of a world will find that his world is a habitable one. That is only to be expected. It does not cry out for further explanation.

(You don't have to be a modal realist to appeal to the anthropic principle. You don't need genuine other worlds, suitably isolated, as opposed to world-like parts of this world. You don't need worlds, or world-like parts, that are all the ways they could possibly be; you only need enough variety to make it unremarkable that habitats for intelligent life are included. Sciama speaks of an 'extreme form' of the anthropic principle which answers the question why we are here by 'invoking the existence of all conceivable logically self-consistent universes' ('Issues in Cosmology', page 395). It is this extreme form that modal realism offers. However I cannot advance this as much of a selling point for modal realism, since more moderate forms might do to meet whatever need there is for an anthropic principle in cosmology.)

It's all very well to invoke the anthropic principle when the remarkable habitability of our world seems to cry out for explanation. But I do not think that this invoking of the anthropic principle is *itself* an explanation. Rather it is a reason why we may be content, if need be, to do without

[10]See *inter alia* Gale, Leslie, and Sciama.

one. It is not an explanation because it gives no information about the causal or nomological ways of our world. It tells us nothing about how any event was caused; it does nothing to subsume laws under still more unified and general laws.

It may be said that an anthropic 'explanation' deserves that name because it makes its explanandum less surprising. That it does, to be sure. But that is not what explanations do, or at any rate not always. Explanations give causal or nomological information. That information often does make the explanandum less surprising, but it may make it more surprising, or may leave it about as surprising as before. Suppose you check into a hotel room, and there you find a new-looking pack of cards. They turn out to be ordered neatly: they go from ace to king of clubs, then ace to king of diamonds, then ace to king of hearts, then ace to king of spades. Not surprising – maybe it's a brand new deck, or maybe whoever left them had won at solitaire. Not so. What's true is that they got into that order by being well and fairly shuffled. The explanation, if known, would make the explanandum much more surprising than it was before.

2.8   The Incredulous Stare

I once complained that my modal realism met with many incredulous stares, but few argued objections. (*Counterfactuals*, page 86.) The arguments were soon forthcoming. We have considered several of them. I think they have been adequately countered. They lead at worst to standoffs. The incredulous stares remain. They remain unanswerable. But they remain inconclusive.

Modal realism *does* disagree, to an extreme extent, with firm common sense opinion about what there is. (Or, in the case of some among the incredulous, it disagrees rather with firmly held agnosticism about what there is.) When modal realism tells you – as it does – that there are uncountable infinities of donkeys and protons and puddles and stars, and of planets very like Earth, and of cities very like Melbourne, and of people very like yourself, . . . small wonder if you are reluctant to believe it. And if entry into philosophers' paradise requires that you do believe it, small wonder if you find the price too high.

I might ask, of course, just what common sense opinion it is with which my modal realism disagrees. Is it the opinion that there do not *actually* exist an uncountable infinity of donkeys? I don't disagree at all with *that* – to actually exist is to be part of this world, and I dare say that there are only finitely many donkeys among our worldmates. Or is it, simply, the opinion that there do not exist an uncountable infinity of donkeys – with the quantifier wide open, entirely unrestricted, and no 'actually' either explicit or tacit in the sentence? *That* opinion I do indeed deny. But if you ask a spokesman for common sense, out of the blue, which opinion it is that he holds, doubtless he will say that he cannot tell the difference between the two. He thinks actuality is all there is; I disagree. (We have considered this question in section 2.1.) I make a distinction where he makes none. Then who is to say whether his undifferentiated opinion is the one I accept or the one I reject? If it is the former, no worries.

Unfortunately, I think it is both. If he doesn't distinguish the two opinions, he holds both or neither; he certainly doesn't hold neither; so he holds both. So I do have a severe disagreement with him. It is true that I also agree with him, and that he himself cannot distinguish the point of agreement from the point of disagreement. But I can. To the extent that I respect common sense, that's trouble. And I do respect common sense, within limits.

In trying to improve the unity and economy of our total theory by providing resources that will afford analyses, for instance of modality as quantification over worlds, I am trying to accomplish two things that somewhat conflict. I am trying to *improve* that theory, that is to change it. But I am trying to improve *that* theory, that is to leave it recognisably the same theory we had before. For it is pointless to build a theory, however nicely systematised it might be, that it would be unreasonable to believe. And a theory cannot earn credence just by its unity and economy. What credence it cannot earn, it must inherit. It is far beyond our power to weave a brand new fabric of adequate theory *ex nihilo*, so we must perforce conserve the one we've got. A worthwhile theory must be credible, and a credible theory must be conservative. It cannot gain, and it cannot deserve, credence if it disagrees with too much of what we thought before. And much of what we thought before was just common sense. Common sense is a settled body of theory – unsystematic folk theory – which at any rate we *do* believe; and I presume that we are reasonable to believe it. (*Most* of it.)

Common sense has no absolute authority in philosophy. It's not that the folk know in their blood what the highfalutin' philosophers may forget. And it's not that common sense speaks with the voice of some infallible faculty of 'intuition'. It's just that theoretical conservatism is the only sensible policy for theorists of limited powers, who are duly modest about what they could accomplish after a fresh start. Part of this conservatism is reluctance to accept theories that fly in the face of common sense. But it's a matter of balance and judgement. Some common sense opinions are firmer than others, so the cost of denying common sense opinion differs from one case to the next. And the costs must be set against the gains. Sometimes common sense may properly be corrected, when the earned credence that is gained by making theory more systematic more than makes up for the inherited credence that is lost. It is not to be demanded that a philosophical theory should agree with anything that the man on the street would insist on offhand, uninformed and therefore uninfluenced by any theoretical gains to be had by changing his mind. (Especially not if, like many men on the streets nowadays, he would rise to the occasion and wax wildly philosophical at the slightest provocation.) The proper test, I suggest, is a simple maxim of honesty: never put forward a philosophical theory that you yourself cannot believe in your least philosophical and most commonsensical moments.

The incredulous stare is a gesture meant to say that modal realism fails the test. That is a matter of judgement and, with respect, I disagree. I acknowledge that my denial of common sense opinion is severe, and I think it is entirely right and proper to count that as a serious cost. How serious is serious enough to be decisive? – That is our central question, yet I don't see how anything can be said about it. *I* still think the price is right, high as it is. Modal realism ought to be accepted as true. The theoretical benefits are worth it.

Provided, of course, that they cannot be had for less.

3

Paradise on the Cheap?

3.1 The Ersatzist Programme

And so the quest for paradise on the cheap. There is a popular and formidable alternative to my own view, *ersatz modal realism*,[1] that promises us just that. The ersatzers say that instead of an incredible plurality of concrete worlds, we can have one world only, and countless abstract entities representing ways that this world might have been. Likewise we can have abstract entities representing ways that donkeys or whatnot might have been. We need not disagree extravagantly with common sense about how many worlds, donkeys, atoms, or gods there are. The abstract representations are not worlds, donkeys, atoms, or gods. So there is no affront to common sense ideas about what there is.

According to ersatzism, we have a well-understood division of all there is into the concrete and the abstract. On the concrete side, common sense opinion about what there is must be respected. There is one concrete world, and one only. It includes all the concrete beings there are. There are no other worlds, and no other-worldly possible individuals – not, at any rate, if those are understood as concrete (or partly concrete) entities. Further, the one concrete world is not any more extensive, and not any less of a spatiotemporal unity, than common sense opinion supposes it to be. (Or if it is, that is another story – an unlikely story! – and irrelevant to modality. The ersatzer certainly will not *accept* heterodox views about the extent of concrete reality, but he may prefer agnosticism to rejection.)

I too might be heard to say that there is only one world, that there are only finitely many donkeys, or that there is no God. But when I say such things, I am restricting my quantifiers, just as when I look in the

---

[1] Or 'moderate' modal realism, as Stalnaker calls it – but in what dimension does its moderation lie?

fridge and say that there is no beer. I do not deny that there is beer outside the fridge, but I ignore it in my speech. Likewise I may ignore the other worlds, and the other-worldly donkeys and gods, without at all denying that – speaking unrestrictedly – they do exist. Not so for the ersatz modal realist. When *he* says that there are no other worlds, and no other-worldly possible individuals, he says it with his quantifiers wide open. He means to quantify over *everything*, without *any* restriction whatever, ignoring *nothing*. (And these quantifiers too are meant to be entirely unrestricted. I doubt that any perfect disambiguation is possible: all our idioms of quantification alike are flexible, subject to tacit restriction. But I think that, wilful misunderstanding aside, my meaning should be clear.)

If we stand firmly with common sense opinion, it seems that the concrete realm affords no room for a paradise of *possibilia*. But perhaps the abstract realm will prove more accommodating. There, it seems, we have license to believe in what we please. Scarcely anyone protests when the mathematicians believe in a vast hierarchy of pure sets, beside which our cosmos is scarcely better than finite. So why should not metaphysicians make us free, provided we say as the mathematicians do: no worries, it's all abstract! (And if asked what that means, say: you know, abstract the way mathematical entities are abstract.) Maybe we can get by with the mathematical entities themselves; or maybe we need other abstract entities. But either way, we can rely on common sense opinion not to stand in the way of the needs of systematic theory. For common sense is opinionated mostly about what there is in the concrete realm.

What does the abstract realm have to offer? According to ersatz modal realism, there are abstract surrogates fit to play the same theoretical roles as the concrete *possibilia* that are to be rejected. These are abstract entities capable, somehow, of representing concrete entities. They represent in a double sense. (1) They are representations, so that it somehow makes sense to speak of what is the case *according to* them; and thereby (2) they are representatives, taking the place of what they purport to represent.

Some of them are the *ersatz worlds*. These represent the entire concrete world in complete detail, as it is or as it might have been. One ersatz world is *actualised*: it represents the concrete world correctly. The rest are *unactualised*. Any one of them could have been the one to represent the concrete world correctly; it would have been, if the concrete world had been suitably different. But as is, there is nothing they represent correctly. They misrepresent the concrete world as it is. They could have represented other concrete worlds correctly, but *ex hypothesi* there are none of those to represent.

Not only the entire concrete world, but lesser concrete individuals as well, have abstract representations: these are the *actualised ersatz individuals*. In addition there are *unactualised ersatz individuals*: these might have represented concrete individuals had things been different, but as is they represent nothing.

Unactualised ersatz worlds and individuals differ from actualised ones only by their failure to represent anything correctly. They exist just as much, and they belong just as much to the one and only world. So the ersatzer can happily call all of them actual, and call himself an actualist; and this is not the merely terminological actualism that I challenged in section 2.1. (He may or may not think it a trivial analytic truth that everything is actual – that is a separate question.) But if he does call all of them actual, he must take care to distinguish that from actual*isation* – for out of all the ersatz worlds and individuals there actually are, all but one of the worlds and the great majority of the individuals are unactualised.

How different this is from my own usage: I say that the other worlds and other-worldly individuals are neither actual nor actualised, and I analyse both 'actual' and 'actualised' as indexical terms meaning 'this-worldly'. And for me, unactualised other-worldly things may indeed be said not to exist – but only when we speak with our quantifiers restricted. I do not distinguish actuality from actualisation; and I insist that it is a relative matter, and that absolute actuality is open to decisive objections. (See section 1.9).

As I have my relative actuality, so the ersatzer has relative actualisation: every ersatz world is actualised according to itself and no ersatz world is actualised according to any other ersatz world. For just as unactualised ersatz worlds misrepresent the truth on other matters, so they – implicitly if not explicitly – misrepresent the truth about which one of them it is that represents correctly. Each ersatz world E represents the concrete world to be a certain way such that, if it were that way, then E would be the ersatz world that represents correctly; and thereby E implicitly represents itself as actualised. So far as relative actualisation is concerned, all the ersatz worlds are on an equal footing: just as, for me, all the worlds are on an equal footing in that each is actual relative to itself and none is actual relative to any other.

But the ersatzer has not only relative actualisation but absolute actualisation besides, so his ersatz worlds are not on an equal footing after all. The one that represents the concrete world correctly isn't just actualised according to itself – it is actualised *simpliciter*. Every ersatz world claims to be uniquely accurate – this one really is. *I* might say that the accuracy of ersatz worlds is still relative, since one of them accurately represents one concrete world, and another another. Not so for the ersatzer, because he says there is only the one concrete world to be represented.

If absolute actuality is open to serious objection, as I said, how does the ersatzer get away with it? By not really accepting a plurality of worlds in the first place. I asked how we could know it if the world we are part of is the one that is absolutely actual – after all, if there's a special status to be had, plenty of other-worldly people have as much reason as we do to think their worlds are the special ones. The ersatzer replies thus.

> Everything is *actual*. No problem there. Only one ersatz world is absolutely actua*lised*. We aren't part of *that*, since we are concrete and it's an abstract representation. Rather, we are part of the concrete world that it accurately represents. As for your deceived other-worldly people, they don't exist. People are concrete, ersatz worlds are abstract. What exist are not other-worldly people but abstract misrepresentations.

Then I asked how it could be contingent which world was actual, unless actuality were relative rather than absolute. The ersatzer replies thus.

> Exactly as you explain the contingency in terms of relative actuality of worlds, so I explain it in terms of relative actualisation of ersatz worlds. A contingent matter is disputed: it comes out different according to different ersatz worlds. Each ersatz world is actualised according to itself and not according to the others, thereby they disagree about which one is actualised, therefore that is a contingent matter. You think you objected to absolute actualisation; but really you objected to doing without relative actualisation. But I don't do without it; I needn't choose between relative and absolute, I have them both.

I cannot fault these replies. Not given their theoretical setting: the single concrete world, the one correct abstract representation, the many misrepresentations.[2] I can only insist that they would make no sense at all in the different setting to which I objected; the many worlds, no duality of concrete world versus abstract representations, and an alleged absolute distinction that singles out one of the many worlds.[3]

It is plain how ersatz *possibilia* may replace the real thing in our various analyses. It is possible that donkeys talk iff there is some abstract ersatz world according to which donkeys talk – no other-worldly talking donkeys are required, only a false abstract representation. Humphrey might have won the election iff some abstract ersatz world falsely represents him as winning – but however he may be misrepresented, our Humphrey the loser

---

[2]In 'Attitudes *De Dicto* and *De Se*' I objected that the ersatzer seemed to make it a non-contingent matter which ersatz world is actualised. I had not fully appreciated the difference between his theoretical setting and my own. I thank John G. Bennett for setting me right.

[3]I worded the ersatzer's replies in my own way; but I think almost every recent ersatzist author has said something similar. See, among others, Adams in 'Theories of Actuality' and Stalnaker in 'Possible Worlds'.

is still the only Humphrey there is. And so on, across the board. *Mutatis mutandis*, the analyses survive. Therefore genuine modal realism may safely be rejected, since we have a way to match its theoretical benefits and leave its 'crazy' ontology behind. Why pay? You can enter philosophers' paradise on the cheap.

So say the ersatzers. But not exactly so; few would state the position quite as I have done. Most of them would say not that possible worlds are to be replaced by abstract representations, but rather that possible worlds *are* abstract representations. This is a mere issue of terminology. Even so, I think it matters. It's wrong to say that the ersatz modal realists and I agree at least that possible worlds exist, and disagree only about whether those worlds are abstract or concrete. That understates the extent to which they disagree with me (and with one another). We agree that there are entities fit to occupy certain theoretical roles, but that is all. The ersatzers just do not believe in what I call worlds; and sometimes – depending on which version of ersatzism we consider – I just do not believe in what they call worlds. Compare the foolish suggestion that all of us at least agree that God exists, although we disagree about His nature: some say He's a supernatural person, some say He's the cosmos in all its glory, some say He's the triumphal march of history, ... Given *that* much disagreement about 'His' nature, there's nothing we all believe in!

Further, it would be wrong for the ersatzers to say in general that abstract representations are to be called 'worlds', unless they say it even when there is a concrete claimant to the name. Then what of the actualised ersatz world versus the concrete world it represents? Will they say that some abstract representation is a 'world', and the concrete totality we are part of is not? Not a good position for the would-be friends of common sense! So I think the ersatzers would do better to say that they reject possible worlds and know how to do without them.[4]

Ersatzism is indeed attractive. I must agree that the ersatzers have the advantage in agreement with common sense about what there is, and this is an advantage well worth having. And their abstract ersatz *possibilia* can indeed do much of the work of the real thing. But I insist that they pay a high price. I cannot say, once and for all, what that price is; because ersatzism comes in different versions, which have different advantages and different drawbacks. I do not offer any serious objection that applies across the board. But I do claim that each version, in its own way, is in serious trouble. In different ways for different versions, the ersatzers

---

[4]Van Inwagen, in *An Essay on Free Will*, pages 232–3, cites C. S. Lewis to the effect that a 'world' may be a 'state of affairs'. But Lewis meant a state of affairs distinctive of some historical epoch, as when the new world is revealed after the saints come marching in. That usage is irrelevant to the contest between concrete and abstract worlds.

must resort to primitive facts where genuine modal realists can offer analyses; or their ways of making ersatz worlds distort the facts of modality; or their ontology is after all not so safe and sane. On balance, I think ersatzism is somewhat worse off than the genuine modal realism that I favour. Paradise on the cheap, like the famous free lunch, is not to be had. Make of this what you will. Join the genuine modal realists; or foresake genuine and ersatz worlds alike.

(Or rather, foresake all-purpose ersatz worlds, capable of replacing the genuine ones throughout our analyses. It will remain possible to use ersatz worlds for limited purposes, for instance when it is harmless to conflate certain possibilities which a construction of ersatz worlds has difficulty in distinguishing.)

One question seems to me crucial in dividing the versions: how is it that the ersatz worlds represent? In other words, how is it that such-and-such is the case according to a certain ersatz world? Different answers to that question lead to different views about the metaphysical nature of the ersatz worlds and individuals, about their power to replace genuine *possibilia*, and about the primitives that ersatzism will require. Different answers thereby yield ersatzisms with different advantages and drawbacks.

I distinguish three principal versions: *linguistic*, on which ersatz worlds are like stories or theories, constructions out of words of some language, and represent in virtue of meanings given by stipulation; *pictorial*, on which they are like pictures, or scale models, and represent by isomorphism; and *magical*, on which they just represent, it is simply their nature to do so, and there's nothing to be said about how they do it.

Three versions of ersatzism; but I distinguish only two main kinds of ersatzist authors. There are some who explicitly support various forms of linguistic ersatzism: for instance Jeffrey, Carnap, Skyrms, and (at one point) Quine. I know of none who explicitly support the pictorial or magical versions. Instead, there are authors who favour nondescript ersatzism. These authors – Plantinga, Stalnaker, and many others – keep silent, or explicitly decline to commit themselves, on the questions that seem to me crucial in dividing the versions. In particular, they do not say how the representing works. Hence I tend to think of them as favouring the magical version. But that's not quite fair: they never say that their ersatz worlds have the sort of internal structure that would permit linguistic or pictorial representation, but they don't deny it either. Since the different versions meet with different objections, that makes it hard to pin any objection at all on an author who keeps neutral. His position may seem to have the advantages of all the versions and the drawbacks of none! Thus I will do better to examine the versions than the authors; and when I attack a position that nobody has ever explicitly supported, you must see me as putting a trilemma against the neutralists. I promise not to waste your time on any version that I myself think is unworthy of respectful attention; and not to knowingly overlook any version that escapes all my objections.

3.2   Linguistic Ersatzism

Linguistic ersatzism typically constructs its ersatz worlds as maximal consistent sets of sentences. The language in which the worlds are made might just be ordinary language, more or less; as in Richard Jeffrey's proposal to take ersatz worlds as 'complete, consistent novels'. Such a novel

> describes a possible world . . . in as much detail as is possible without exceeding the resources of the agent's language. But if talk of possible worlds seems dangerously metaphysical, we can focus attention on the novels themselves, and speak of a complete, consistent novel as actually *being* a possible world. (*The Logic of Decision*, section 12.8.)

The ersatz worlds represent by saying. If the worldmaking language is plain English, for instance, then it is the case according to a novel that a donkey talks iff that novel contains the sentence 'A donkey talks'. If the language is not plain English, the ersatzer will have to specify an interpretation for it. That done, he can say that it is the case according to a novel that a donkey talks iff that novel contains a sentence which, as interpreted, means that a donkey talks. Call this *explicit* representation that a donkey talks. But there might not be any one sentence which means exactly that; there may not even be any set of sentences which jointly mean exactly that a donkey talks and nothing more. If so, we must say that it is the case according to a novel that a donkey talks iff the novel contains several sentences (in the worst case, an infinite set) which, as interpreted, jointly imply that a donkey talks. Call this *implicit* representation that a donkey talks.

The worldmaking language had better not be plain English. Jeffrey mentions the need to idealise the language somewhat 'in the sense that the (declarative) sentences of that language have fixed . . . truth values, independent of the contexts of their utterance'. (Unlike me, an ersatzer would not take that to prohibit contingency. He does not believe in other-worldly contexts of utterance.) Some further idealisation is needed to make sure there are determinate truth values at all: the worldmaking language had better be disambiguated and precise.

We might take a sentence as a sequence of its words. Or, for the sake of disambiguation, we might do better to take the sentences as parsed: let a sentence be the sequence of phrases which are its immediate constituents, let each phrase be the sequence of phrases which are *its* immediate constituents, and so on down to phrases which are single words. Thus ersatz worlds turn out to be set-theoretic constructions out of words. A word in turn might be taken as the set of its particular inscriptions; or as the set of spatiotemporal regions wherein it is pronounced. Thus the ersatz worlds are set-theoretic constructions out of parts of the concrete world.

That is how linguistic ersatzism fulfils its promise of safe and sane ontology: it relies on ontology that most philosophers are committed to in any case. There it does indeed have the advantage over my modal realism. The point is not that its ersatz worlds should be easy to believe in, because they are in some ill-defined sense abstract; the point is that we believe in them already. If such constructions are properly called 'abstract', well and good. If not, no harm done.

(What shall a would-be ersatzer do if he regards set theory with scepticism, and prefers to avoid any ontological commitment to sets? Must he reject linguistic ersatzism just because of its set-theoretic constructions? I think not. For surely set-theoretic talk does make *some* kind of sense, and its seeming existential quantifications do mean *something* true. The question is how they are to be understood. If they can be understood only at face value, then I conclude that the project of disbelieving in sets is hopeless; in which case the sceptical ersatzer may as well give in and use set theory. But if they can be understood in some more innocent way, as the sceptic must hope, then again he may use set theory, for then his use of it is innocent.)

I once raised a problem of cardinality against linguistic ersatzism. 'If we take "language" at all literally, so that sentences are finite strings over a finite alphabet, there are not enough sets of sentences to go around' (*Counterfactuals*, page 90). There are at most continuum many sets of strings, *a fortiori* at most continuum many ersatz worlds. The same is true if we take sentences as parsed, provided the language has a finite vocabulary and each phrase has finitely many immediate constituents. But it is easy to argue that there are more than continuum many possibilities we ought to distinguish. It is at least possible to have continuum many spacetime points; each point may be occupied by matter or may be vacant; since anything may coexist with anything, any distribution of occupancy and vacancy is possible; and there are more than continuum many such distributions. So either there are different distributions that get described alike, or there are distributions that do not get described at all. Either different possibilities are misrepresented as the same, or some possibilities are misrepresented as impossible. That just gets the facts of modality wrong.[5]

---

[5] This complaint is not addressed to Jeffrey. His novels will not do as general-purpose ersatz worlds, but they may be well suited for the limited purpose for which he introduced

My argument was right, for what it is worth. But it is not a problem. There is no reason why linguistic ersatzism needs to 'take "language" at all literally' and burden itself with the two assumptions of finitude that make the problem. It is necessary that the ersatzer should be able to present his worldmaking language, using his original natural language to specify its syntax and interpretation, when he presents his theory. But it is not necessary that the worldmaking language should itself be anything like a natural language, or that there should be any way to speak or write its sentences, or that its vocabulary should be finite, or that its sentences should be finite in length. All we need is language in a generalised sense: a system of structures that can be parsed and interpreted. The words can be anything that safe and sane ontology has to offer. They can be individuals that are part of the concrete world, or set-theoretic constructions out of those, or pure sets, or anything else we believe in. It does not matter what they are, if they get their role in representing by arbitrary stipulation. So we could have an infinite number of words: let all the real numbers serve as words, or all the points or regions of spacetime, and stipulate in some wholesale way what they are to mean. Alternatively, we can use infinitary connectives to build infinitely long sentences from the resources of a finite vocabulary. Either method would give us a way to build sentences that say explicitly, about each of a continuum of points, whether it is vacant or occupied.[6] This is well-explored ground: model theory normally treats finitary language with finite vocabulary as a special case. Cardinality problems do not threaten linguistic ersatzism, though they do teach us how to go about it.

Carnap made extensive use of linguistic ersatz worlds in his writings on logic, semantics, and probability. At first he took the ersatz worlds as sets which contain, for every atomic sentence of a certain interpreted formal system, either that sentence or its negation but not both; and which contain no other sentences. These are maximal consistent sets of sentences of a worldmaking language which is a fragment of the given system. This language may have an infinite vocabulary of predicates and names, so

---

them: to serve as points in a structure that represents an agent's system of belief and desire. More generally, many of the objections I shall be putting forward later in this section, either against linguistic ersatzism generally or against particular forms of it, would not apply to certain special-purpose uses of linguistic ersatz worlds. When I complain, as I shall, that there are various ways for different possibilities to get conflated in their linguistic descriptions, that may be harmless when we want to use ersatz *possibilia* to characterise the content of thought for a subject who has no way to distinguish the conflated possibilities in his perception and conduct. (Stalnaker makes this point, though not in defence especially of linguistic ersatzism.) And when I complain about problems with possibilities that involve alien natural properties, those problems will not hinder the treatment of not very far-fetched counterfactual suppositions, for instance in a counterfactual analysis of causation.

[6]See Roper, 'Toward an Eliminative Reduction of Possible Worlds', page 51; and Bricker, *Worlds and Propositions*, pages 174–89.

we needn't worry about cardinality; but except for (single) negation, it is devoid of resources for compounding its sentences. (We shall consider later why such impoverishment of the worldmaking language might be wanted.) Such a set 'is called a *state-description* . . . , because it obviously gives a complete description of a possible state of the universe of individuals with respect to all properties and relations expressed by predicates of the system. Thus the state-descriptions represent Leibniz' possible worlds or Wittgenstein's possible states of affairs' (*Meaning and Necessity*, page 9).

Note two difficulties with this method. Everything must have a name, else our state-descriptions will be silent about the nameless things; and nothing may have two names, else our state-descriptions may both affirm and deny, of the same thing under different names, that it satisfies a predicate.

One solution, the *Lagadonian* method, exploits our freedom to take the words as anything we please. Do we need one and only one name for everything in some large domain? Just declare that each of these things names itself. A Lagadonian language is inconvenient for some uses, as Gulliver observed; but it's handy for making state-descriptions. A state-description in a Lagadonian language will be a set-theoretic construction out of the predicates and the negation symbol, whatever those are, together with the members of the given domain, each one serving as its own name. In effect, this is the solution Carnap adopted in his later writings. In 'A Basic System of Inductive Logic', for instance, he takes ersatz worlds as models, in the standard model-theoretic sense. A model consists of a domain, together with an assignment to each n-ary predicate of a set of n-tuples of members of the domain; these being the n-tuples that satisfy that predicate according to that model. If we hold the domain fixed (as Carnap stipulates) models correspond one to one with state-descriptions in the Lagadonian language. We could think of the model as a transformed 'surface structure' of the sentence obtained from the state-description by infinite conjunction. Or we could just think directly of the model as an infinitary sentence: a structure that can be parsed and interpreted, a linguistic representation or misrepresentation of the world.

(If models are to serve thus as ersatz worlds, they had better not be regarded at the same time as interpreting the language. An assignment of extensions to predicates depends partly on what the predicates mean, partly on contingent matters of fact. If it is to represent the latter, the former must be settled beforehand. Carnap is clear that the worldmaking language is presented complete with interpretation. This double role of models has been well discussed by Etchemendy.)

If we also believe in universals as constituents of the concrete world, as perhaps we should, we can carry the Lagadonian scheme one step further.[7]

---

[7]Similar constructions would be possible starting with tropes; they are discussed in Johnston, *Particulars and Persistence*.

Suppose that the concrete world is somehow divisible into 'elementary' particulars and universals, in such a way that the whole truth about it supervenes on the truth about which of these particulars instantiate which of these universals. Let these universals and particulars serve as the vocabulary of a language. Just as we can use each particular as its own name, so we can use each universal as its own predicate. It is satisfied by just those particulars that instantiate it. Then a pair of a particular and a universal can serve as an atomic sentence according to which that particular instantiates that universal. More generally, if some of the universals are polyadic, a 'tuple consisting of an n-ary universal followed by n particulars can serve as an atomic sentence according to which those particulars jointly instantiate that universal. And a state description or model in that language can serve as an ersatz world. (We don't even need a negation sign: take all sets of atomic sentences as state-descriptions, and stipulate that all *and only* the atomic sentences included in a given state-description are true according to it, and the rest are false acording to it.) An ersatz world so constructed purports to represent the various elementary particulars instantiating the various elementary universals, and we run through all consistent alternatives as to which instantiate which.

Such a scheme, minus my gloss on it as in a sense linguistic, is considered in Brian Skyrms's 'Tractarian Nominalism'. As in the *Tractatus*, the actual world is the totality of facts; and likewise for other worlds, except that the 'facts' of which they are totalities sometimes are false, so not really facts. Atomic facts suffice to build the worlds; others supervene. Strictly speaking, facts are 'primitive entities' for Skyrms. But we may 'in the vulgar way, think of an atomic fact as associated with a representation consisting of . . . an n-ary relation followed by n objects' (page 200). Thus, setting aside the 'primitive entities' themselves, we get vulgar representations which amount to maximal consistent sets of sentences of a Lagadonian language.

A language that is interpreted in the Lagadonian way is, nevertheless, interpreted. The ersatzer who presents his worldmaking language must still stipulate how it is interpreted, even if what he stipulates is that it has a Lagadonian interpretation. That is not, of course, the only interpretation the language could bear. It is just an especially easy one to specify. A real number could serve as a name for itself, but it could equally well serve as a name for itself plus seventeen. I could be my own name, but alternatively I could be yours; or I could be put to some other use in a language, say as a punctuation mark.

There is another way we might take advantage of our freedom to use anything we like as words. Provided we believe in the mathematical universe, understood perhaps as the realm of pure sets, we can draw our vocabulary from there. Thus linguistic ersatzism merges with what might seem to be a rival plan: the use of mathematical representations as our ersatz worlds. Take a simple example. Suppose we have a coordinate system for a flat spacetime. Then we can associate with each point a quadruple of real numbers. Suppose we think there are only two ways a point can be: occupied or vacant. And suppose we think that it is enough to specify the distribution of matter over the points: all else supervenes on that. Then a mathematical ersatz world could be a set of quadruples, specifying the set of points that are occupied. Equivalently, we could take the characteristic function of the set: the ersatz world is a set of pairs, and it pairs a quadruple with 1 to represent a point as occupied, or with 0 to represent it as vacant. This mathematical representation is equally a linguistic representation: the worldmaking language uses 1 and 0 as predicates meaning 'occupied' and 'vacant', the quadruples name the points, name–predicate pairs are atomic sentences, two sentences that predicate occupancy and vacancy of the same point are inconsistent, and thus the ersatz world turns out to be a maximal consistent set of sentences.

Quine is not known as a friend of possible worlds, ersatz or otherwise. But in his 'Propositional Objects' he briefly proposed that classes of ersatz worlds might characterise the attitudes of an animal without language. (It was not his final proposal; he went on to transform his ersatz worlds first into ersatz possible individuals – centred worlds – and then into stimulation patterns.) His illustrative construction, based on fictitious 'Democritean' physics, was roughly as above.

There was one further step. What do we think when one set of quadruples, or the characteristic function thereof, differs from another only by some transformation of coordinates? Do we have two possibilities represented, or one possibility represented two ways? Quine, as we would expect of him, takes the latter view for a wide range of transformations. He therefore factors out the artificial differences by taking equivalence classes. It is possible, albeit tiresome, to describe what he does in linguistic terms, as follows. Begin with the characteristic functions rather than the sets. Interpret 1 and 0 as predicates, as before. Interpret a quadruple now as an open term, with a tacit free variable which ranges over coordinate systems. Relative to any given coordinate system, the quadruple denotes the point with the proper coordinates in that system. The pair of a quadruple with 1 or 0 now becomes an open formula, with the same tacit variable, satisfied by some coordinate systems and not others. An entire characteristic function, which is a set of these formulae, is interpreted as the existential quantification of the infinitary conjunction of its members. Two of the characteristic functions that differ only by appropriate transformations of coordinates imply one another; whereas two that differ otherwise are inconsistent. Thus an equivalence class of characteristic functions turns out to be a maximal consistent set of sentences.

Democritean physics is very simplified indeed; but my point applies to other systems of mathematical representation, more realistic and more versatile. (I don't think we could specify one versatile enough to cover *all* possibilities, however, for reasons given at the end of this section.) If mathematical ersatz worlds take the form of trajectories through purely mathematical phase spaces, or vectors in purely mathematical Hilbert spaces, or what have you, I take it that it will still be possible to interpret them linguistically: as sets of sentences, or as single infinitary sentences, in some suitable worldmaking language. My point is not that we will understand mathematical ersatzism better by seeing it as linguistic in a fairly general, and hence fairly empty, sense. It's just that when I come to criticise linguistic ersatzism, I would like my objections to apply as widely as possible.

It is worth mentioning one trick that is possible in the Democritean special case, though so far as I know it doesn't generalise. We are assuming that only the abstract realm could provide the makings of a paradise of ersatz *possibilia*; and in this section, we are supposing that the ersatz worlds will be set-theoretic constructions, impure or pure. But if you are not only a Democritean but also a haecceitist (see section 4.4) about spacetime points, you can have *concrete* ersatz worlds. Presumably a spacetime point is concrete; a spatiotemporal region is just the mereological sum of its points; so presumably a region also is concrete. That goes for any region, however bizarrely shaped. Take any region as an ersatz world according to which exactly the points of that region are occupied and all other points are vacant. The ersatz worlds overlap greatly, since they are all built from the same constituents in the way that is characteristic of linguistic representation. Thus they all fit into the single spacetime of the concrete world. The region consisting of all and only the occupied points is the actualised ersatz world. Something very like this appears in Cresswell's 'The World is Everything that is the Case'. (He offers it as an example only, insisting that various different constructions would equally well serve his purposes.) However Cresswell takes his regions as sets rather than mereological sums of points; thereby declining, as is only right, to take advantage of the peculiarities of the special case.

Besides the ersatz possible worlds, we also need ersatz possible individuals: representations of how an individual that is less than an entire world might be. My modal realism provides possible individuals simply as the proper parts of possible worlds; for instance small parts, such as people. They figure prominently in the applications of *possibilia*. Especially so if, as I advocate, haecceitism is rejected and the diversity of possibilities for an individual is understood as the diversity of possible individuals in worlds, not as diversity of worlds. (See section 4.4.) Linguistic ersatzism cannot follow the same plan. Its ersatz worlds are sets of sentences, and their parts are just their subsets. These are incomplete descriptions (or misdescriptions) of the whole world, not complete descriptions of parts of the world.

Just as we make linguistic ersatz worlds as complete descriptions of an entire world, so we should make our linguistic ersatz possible individuals as complete descriptions of parts of the world. We can take them as maximal consistent sets of open sentences of the worldmaking language, with a free pronoun or variable; or, equivalently, as maximal consistent sets of complex predicates. Just as a set of sentences is consistent if they might all be true, so a set of open sentences is consistent if they might all be true *of* something, taken as value of the common pronoun or variable; and a set of predicates is consistent if something might fall under all of them. Our previous discussion of ersatz worlds carries over, *mutatis mutandis*, to ersatz individuals.

On my own view, a possible individual exists at a possible world by being part of it. But a linguistic ersatz individual is in no sense part of an ersatz world; what we have instead is that an ersatz individual may be actualised according to an ersatz world. That is so if the ersatz individual and the ersatz world *mirror* one another. Suppose the ersatz world consists of sentences P, Q, R, . . .; then the mirroring ersatz individual might consist in part of open sentences:

x is part of a world where P,

x is part of a world where Q,

x is part of a world where R,

   . . . .

Thus the ersatz individual is by no means a purely intrinsic description; the description is extrinsic in a big way. By the time we are done describing an individual completely, we have *en passant* described the world wherein it is situated. In the other direction, suppose the ersatz individual consists of open sentences Fx, Gx, Hx, . . .; then the mirroring ersatz world might consist in part of sentences:

For some x, Fx,

For some x, Fx and Gx,

For some x, Fx and Gx and Hx,

   . . . .

(If we have infinitary conjunction, one infinite sentence can serve instead of this sequence of finite approximations.) By the time we are done describing a world completely, we have *en passant* described all the individuals within it.

Just as we distinguish explicit and implicit representation generally, so we can distinguish explicit and implicit mirroring. The mirroring is explicit if the mirroring sentences – sentences of the worldmaking language with the appropriate meanings, as shown above – appear as members of the ersatz world and the ersatz individual; it is implicit if those sentences do not themselves appear, but if they are implied by sentences that do appear.

(What if the worldmaking language lacks the logical resources to formulate the mirroring sentences, as happens, for instance, if its only sentences are atomic and negated atomic? Then the implication in implicit mirroring must go from sets of sentences in the original worldmaking language to sentences of a richer language in which the missing resources have been supplied.)

As ersatz worlds and ersatz individuals mirror one another, so likewise do two different ersatz individuals that are actualised according to the same ersatz world. Suppose one of them consists of the open sentences Fx, Gx, Hx, . . . and the other one consists of Lx, Mx, Nx, ... Then the first will contain open sentences that mean or that imply:

x coexists with something y such that Ly,

x coexists with something y such that Ly and My,

x coexists with something y such that Ly and My and Ny,

   . . . .

And the second will contain open sentences that mean or that imply:

x coexists with something y such that Fy,

x coexists with something y such that Fy and Gy,

x coexists with something y such that Fy and Gy and Hy,

   . . . .

Likewise, in a more complicated way, for the mutual mirroring of infinitely many ersatz individuals all actualised according to a single ersatz world.

This completes my exposition of linguistic ersatzism. It is a popular approach, and deservedly so. It relies on a familiar and well-understood method of representing; and it delivers ersatz worlds and individuals by means of ontology that is almost uncontroversial. However it is open to two serious objections.

My first objection is that modality must be taken as primitive. This happens in one or both of two different ways. First, via consistency. Not any set of sentences of the worldmaking language is an ersatz world. It has to be a consistent set. Else it could not describe the concrete world correctly, no matter how the concrete world was. An inconsistent set might be an ersatz impossible world, but it is not an ersatz possible world. Further, an ersatz world must be maximal consistent. That is, it must be a consistent set whose consistency would be destroyed by the addition of any other sentence of the worldmaking language. Else it may describe the world incompletely, conflating two different possibilities that would be distinguished if we extended it to a larger consistent set; or if not that, it may leave implicit something that the language has the resources for representing explicitly. So in order to say which things of the right nature – which sets of sentences of the worldmaking language – are the ersatz worlds, we need to distinguish the consistent ones. That is *prima facie* a modal distinction: a set of sentences is consistent iff those sentences, as interpreted, *could* all be true together.

The second need for primitive modality comes via implicit representation. It may be that so-and-so, according to a certain ersatz world, not because there is a sentence included in that world which just means that so-and-so, no more and no less; but because there are sentences which jointly imply that so-and-so. There might be a single sentence which implies that so-and-so but doesn't just mean that so-and-so because it implies more besides; or there might be a finite or infinite set of sentences which jointly imply that so-and-so. This implication is *prima facie* modal: a set of sentences implies that so-and-so iff those sentences, as interpreted, *could* not all be true together unless it were also true that so-and-so; in other words, if it is *necessary* that if those sentences are all true together, then so-and-so.

In section 3.1, I called attention to one case of implicit representation: each ersatz world E represents that the concrete world is as E says it is, and not as any other ersatz world says it is; and thereby E implicitly represents that it alone succeeds in correctly representing the concrete world, therefore that it alone is actualised. This is a special case, because here it seems that the representation almost *has* to be implicit. How could an ersatz world *explicitly* represent its own success and the others' failures? It would have to explicitly represent the concrete world, and itself correctly representing the concrete world, and countless other ersatz worlds incorrectly representing the concrete world. But each ersatz world thus represented must itself represent, *inter alia*, all of the ersatz worlds. It is as if we had a library, and every book in the library describes fully – say, by unabridged direct quotation – every book in the library. Books being the finite things they are, of course that is impossible. It is not clear to me how it would be for ersatz worlds. At any rate, there's no sense going to extremes to avoid implicit representation in this case. Even if we did, we would still need primitive modality elsewhere, to define consistency or to define implicit representation or both.

It is clear that we have some choice about where the carpet is to bulge. The worldmaking language can be rich or poor in its expressive resources. If it is rich, like an idealisation of plain English, the problem of consistency gets hard and the problem of implicit representation gets easy. The more the language has the power to tell us explicitly what is so according to the ersatz world, the less need we have for implicit representation. But the more the language can say explicitly, the more opportunities it has to say one thing and imply the contrary – that is, to fall into inconsistency. In fact, an inconsistent set of sentences can simply be regarded as one that represents explicitly that so-and-so while it also represents implicitly that not so-and-so; and the more can be represented explicitly, the more ways such a conflict can arise.

That is why we might prefer an impoverished worldmaking language that lacks the resources to explicitly represent anything very complicated. Such are Carnap's languages of state-descriptions or models. These worldmaking languages are excised from richer systems by removing the logical vocabulary, except perhaps for (single) negation. It seems easy to define maximal consistency in a language with nothing but atomic and negated atomic sentences. Just make sure you have a state-description. That is, make sure that for each atomic sentence you have either it or its negation but not both. Likewise if we have a Lagadonian language in which the names are self-naming elementary particulars and the predicates are self-predicating elementary universals, or if we code distributions of matter by pairing coordinate quadruples with 0 or 1, it seems that a straightforward combinatorial definition could suffice to tell us which sets of sentences are maximal consistent. But in return the problem of implicit representation becomes difficult, since there's precious little that these languages can represent explicitly.

It matters little whether we take a rich language and face a problem of saying which sets of its sentences are consistent, or whether instead we take a poor language and face the problem of saying what its sets of sentences imply. Either way, the same remedy comes to mind: we could replace primitive modality by a syntactic surrogate. We define consistency or implication in terms of formal deduction, and we define our ersatz worlds or their implicit representation from that. Our syntactic surrogate might be limited to the worldmaking language, if that language is rich and our goal is to characterise its maximal consistent sets. Or our surrogate might have to apply to an enrichment of the worldmaking language – the union of the worldmaking language and English, perhaps – if the worldmaking language is poor and our goal is to characterise implicit representation.

Of course, our syntactic surrogate had better not yield narrowly logical consistency or narrowly logical implication – that is, consistency under some reinterpretation or other of all but the logical vocabulary, or implication that is invariant under all such reinterpretations. That would falsify the facts of modality by yielding allegedly consistent ersatz worlds according to which there are married bachelors, numbers with more than one successor, and suchlike impossibilities; or by giving us no ersatz worlds which, when they explicitly represent a distribution of matter over spacetime or what have you, thereby implicitly represent such supervenient global facts as that there is a talking donkey. However, it is permissible to specify that certain sentences of the worldmaking language (or an enrichment of it) are axiomatic; then narrowly logical consistency or implication can take us the rest of the way. A putative ersatz world in a rich language should (1) be logically consistent, and (2) contain all the specified axioms. An ersatz world in a poor language implicitly represents that a donkey talks iff its sentences, together with the specified axioms in an enriched language, logically imply a sentence of the enriched language which means that a donkey talks. (If the enrichment combines the worldmaking language with a substantial part of English, we can simply require that the ersatz world plus the axioms imply the very sentence 'A donkey talks'.)

The question is whether we can specify the proper axiom set without covertly relying on primitive modality. I think we cannot. But before I offer good reasons why not, I must disown two bad reasons.

The first bad reason is one that I advanced in *Counterfactuals* (page 85). We don't want logically consistent but mathematically inconsistent ersatz worlds; and we don't want to lose mathematically implicit representation. So the axiom set had better include the mathematical truths, so far as these are expressible in the vocabulary of the language in question. Either the worldmaking language itself, or else its enrichment for implicit representation, had better be rich enough to express quite a lot of mathematics. But then how are we to specify the set of mathematical truths? It is impossible, of course, to specify them as exactly the sentences that meet some effective syntactic test; or even as exactly the theorems of some formal system. To specify them modally is to give up on the plan of providing syntactic surrogates for primitive modality. How else? I used to think this decisive. But Roper, in 'Toward an Eliminative Reduction of Possible Worlds', asks why we may not specify the mathematical axioms model-theoretically. Why aren't we free to say, for instance, that the arithmetical truths are those sentences of the arithmetical part of the language that are true in standard models of arithmetic? Why indeed? I think Roper is right to insist that we may. There is indeed a serious philosophical problem about how we can refer unequivocally to the standard models, but we do seem to manage it somehow. If we can refer to standard models, never mind how, then we may do so when we specify our axioms, and thereby define our surrogates for primitive modality, and thereby define our ersatz worlds and our implicit representation. The task is to bypass primitive modality in our analyses. Effectiveness is not in the bargain.

The second bad reason arises out of a misunderstanding about what circularity is. When he specifies his axioms, as a step toward defining ersatz worlds and implicit representation and eventually modality itself, the ersatzer presumably is guided by his pre-existing modal opinions. He adds this truth to his axioms because he takes it to be necessary, declines to add that one because he takes it to be contingent. Then even if he ends with a correct definition of necessity and contingency, isn't his procedure circular? – No. Circularity is a matter of what you analyse in terms of what; it is not a matter of why you think your analysis is right. It is not circularity if you build your analysis to give the answers it ought to, excercising your understanding of the *analysandum* as you go. You might as well say that an analysis of 'cousin' in terms of 'parent' was circular, because you wouldn't have given that analysis if you hadn't already had a working command of the word 'cousin'! The object of analysis is to reduce our burden of primitive notions, and to make tacit understanding explicit – not to bootstrap ourselves into understanding what we didn't understand at all beforehand.

Now for the good reasons. I think there are at least two places where primitive modality will not go away. The axioms to do the job may exist, but the ersatzer will not be in a position to specify them. He can only declare: the axioms shall include whichever sentences of such-and-such form are necessarily true. Once he says that, all his analyses from there on are modal.

The first place has to do with the fundamental properties and relations of simple things: as it might be, the positive and negative charge of point particles. Even a stripped-down worldmaking languge had better be able to speak explicitly of such matters, so our present problem concerns the consistency of ersatz worlds, rather than implicit representation. Suppose we have predicates meaning 'positive' and 'negative'. Then it is consistent, in the narrowly logical sense, to say that something is both positive and negative. If our ersatz worlds were state-descriptions in the given language, for which the only test of consistency is that no atomic sentence should be included along with its own negation, we would have ersatz worlds according to which some particles are both positive and negative. This seems wrong: here we seem to have an inconsistency which is not narrowly logical, but arises because positive and negative charge are two determinates of one determinable. (Thus stripping down the worldmaking language doesn't altogether smooth out this bulge in the carpet.) The remedy is plain: we need an axiom. Not in the stripped-down worldmaking language itself, but in a suitable enrichment of it, we can form a sentence to say that nothing is both positive and negative: call this the *axiom of unique charge*. We can declare that only those state-descriptions shall count as ersatz worlds that are logically consistent with this axiom.

(Or we could declare outright that no ersatz world shall include two atomic sentences that predicate 'positive' and 'negative' of the same thing; but, for convenience, let's suppose the problematic part of the project to be concentrated in the choice of axioms.)

But wait! Maybe it is just a matter of contingent fact that positive and negative charge never coexist. Lawful fact, but that is still contingent. If so, then inclusion of the proposed axiom of unique charge would misrepresent the facts of modality. But if not, if positive and negative charge really are incompatible determinables, then omission of the axiom would misrepresent the facts. It is risky to write the axiom in, it is risky to leave it out. If the ersatzer knew the facts of modality, he would know what to do. But he doesn't and he can't. What is he supposed to do – make them up out of whole cloth? *That* gets the facts wrong even if he guesses right! The only safe course is to resort to primitive modality. The declaration must be conditional: *if* it is impossible for any one particle to be both positively and negatively charged, *then* let there be an axiom of unique charge.

Mind you, it would be no small advance if we could explain modality in general by taking one very special case of it – the incompatibility between determinates of one determinable, and even that only for the special case of a few 'fundamental' properties and relations – as primitive. If that were to be had, the offer of safe and sane ontology with just a smidgin of primitive modality would indeed be hard to refuse. But it is not to be had. There is another place where primitive modality will not go away, and there the need is more extensive. The ontological gain would have to be worth not a little primitive modality but a lot.

The second place has to do with the relation of global to local descriptions. We describe the spatiotemporal arrangement and fundamental properties of point particles in infinite detail – and lo, we have implied that there is a talking donkey, or we have fallen into inconsistency if we also say explicitly that there is not. The implication or inconsistency is not narrowly logical, thanks to a difference in vocabulary. We need to cover it somehow. We have a problem about consistency if the worldmaking language speaks both of local and global matters, both of particles and of donkeys. Or we have a problem about implicit representation if the worldmaking language speaks only of local matters, and yet the ersatz worlds implicitly represent global matters. We need *connecting axioms*: conditionals to the effect that *if* – here follows a very long, perhaps infinitary, description of the arrangement and properties of the point particles – *then* there is a talking donkey. If we are not to get the facts of modality wrong, such axioms had better be written into the definitions of consistency and implication.

That would be impossible in practice, of course. Maybe the axioms would be infinite both in length and in number; I would suppose not, but at any rate it is safe to say that nobody could produce them. So no linguistic ersatzer can complete his theory. Unless, of course, he does the obvious thing: declares wholesale that among all conditionals with local antecedents and global consequents, exactly those shall be axioms that are necessarily true.

Suppose, *per impossibile*, that the ersatzer did produce the requisite axioms; and, what is still more marvellous, that he persuaded us that he had them right. I am still inclined, though hesitantly, to raise an objection of principle. The job was to analyse *modality* (and also several other things for which genuine or ersatz *possibilia* come in handy). It was not also part of the job to analyse 'talking donkey'. But he did; for he needed axioms that would tell him, for every possible arrangement of particles, whether or not that arrangement would make there be a talking donkey. In fact, before he could finish with modality, he had to complete a wholesale analysis of the global in terms of the local! Why should the analysis of modality have to wait on *that*? Surely it ought to be possible to take 'talking donkey' and whatnot as primitive when we are analysing modality, whatever other project we might care to undertake on another day. That's how *I* do it: I say it's possible for there to be a talking donkey iff some world has a talking donkey as part – no utopian analysis of 'talking donkey' in terms of arrangements of particles is required.

I conclude that linguistic ersatzism must indeed take modality as primitive. If its entire point were to afford an analysis of modality, that would be a fatal objection. But there are many theoretical services left for a version of ersatzism to render, even if it cannot analyse modality away. So it is open to an ersatzer to pay the price, accept modality as primitive, and consider the proposal well worth it on balance. Many ersatzers, of various sorts, see the contest between genuine and ersatz modal realism in just that way: there is a choice between unwelcome ontology and unwelcome primitive modality, and they prefer the latter. That seems to me a fair response on their part, but of course not conclusive.

(Frank Jackson has suggested that resort to primitive modality, and the circularity that would ensue if we went on to analyse modality in terms of ersatz worlds, is no price at all. 'Circularity is a crucial defect in explicatory philosophical analyses. . . . But the situation is quite different with paraphrases directed to ontological questions.' If we take 'virtuous' as primitive in paraphrasing away a seeming reference to virtue, that 'is unacceptable as a final explication of virtue because it is circular, but it does . . . show that we need not believe in the existence of an entity called "virtue"' ('A Causal Theory of Counterfactuals', page 18). Right; *if* our work is directed to ontological questions only, we may help ourselves to any primitives we please, so long as we somehow understand them. But if our work is directed to ontological questions and analytic questions both, as I think it usually is, then we are trying at once to cut down on questionable ontology and to cut down on primitives, and it is fair to object if one goal is served at too much cost to the other.)

My second objection concerns the descriptive power of the worldmaking language. If it is a language that can be specified, complete with interpretation, by a this-worldly theorist, then it must have limited descriptive resources; and then it cannot distinguish all the possibilities it should. Here I am no longer speaking of the shortfall of cardinality; as we have seen, that can be set right by introducing infinite vocabulary or infinitary connectives. But two problems of descriptive power remain. Each one divides into (what I take to be) a harmless part and a serious part.

First is a problem about indiscernibles. If ersatz possible worlds and individuals are linguistic descriptions, then we will never have two of them exactly alike. If an ersatz possibility *is* its description, there can be only one for any given description. Our ersatz worlds and individuals will obey a principle of identity of indiscernibles. So if ever we ought to acknowledge a plurality of indiscernible *possibilia*, our linguistic ersatz *possibilia* will be unsatisfactory. We will have to regard them as equivocal, as ambiguously representing many different possibilities. But then the possibilities of which there are many cannot be the linguistic descriptions of which there is only one.

The problem of indiscernible possible worlds is the harmless part. My modal realism does not say whether or not there are indiscernible worlds; and I can think of no very weighty reason in favour of one answer or the other. No application of modal realism seems to require indiscernible worlds, and none would be hindered by them. It is an eminently negotiable question. If linguistic ersatzism has no place for indiscernible worlds, and is otherwise attractive, so be it.

The problem of indiscernible possible individuals, on the other hand, is serious. Certainly it is at least possible that there should be many indiscernible individuals – alike in their intrinsic natures, and in their extrinsic properties as well. That would be so if there were two-way eternal recurrence. Or it would be so if the universe consisted of a perfect crystalline lattice, infinite in all directions. According to an ersatz world that represents such repetition in time or space, there are many indiscernible individuals. But we do not have correspondingly many indiscernible ersatz possible individuals, all actualised according to this ersatz world. One must do for all. What the ersatz world says, or implies, is that the one ersatz individual is actualised many times over. So where we ought to have many indiscernible possibilities for an individual, we have only one. Imagine a full description of a world of eternal recurrence, with a certain role – say, that of a conqueror rather like Napoleon – filled once in every indiscernible epoch. There are infinitely many indescernible possibilities for filling the Napoleonic role in such a world. Or so it surely seems. But no: there is only the one ersatz individual, only the one linguistic description of a filler of the role.

Is it so or not that there are many possibilities? Neither choice is satisfactory. Say yes, and the possibilities cannot be the ersatz individuals. Then what else is there for them to be? Say no, and we lose what seems to be a valid implication: if there is a possibility according to which there are many different individuals, then there are many different possible individuals associated with that possibility.

You might say: 'if multiplicity is wanted, no sooner said than done – let's make many ordered pairs, pairing the one linguistic ersatz individual with each of the infinitely many integers.' But multiplicity was not all I wanted. This is an irrelevant multiplicity. We have the infinitely many new representations, differing now by the integers built into them; and we have the infinitely many indiscernible possibilities that ought to be acknowledged. But the many representations do not represent the many possibilities unambiguously, one to one. Rather, each of the many new representations is ambiguous over all the many possibilities, just as the one original representation was. Nothing has been gained.

The second problem of descriptive power is that if a worldmaking language is specifiable by a this-worldly theorist, then it cannot be expected to have a rich enough vocabulary to describe and to distinguish all the different possibilities there are.[8]

Part of this problem is well known. If we build ersatz worlds out of actual things, linguistically or otherwise, how can we represent possibilities that involve extra individuals? For linguistic ersatzism, this is a problem about naming. If the extra individuals do not exist for us to name (or for us to declare them to be names of themselves) how can we possibly have any names for them? And without names for the extra individuals, how do we distinguish ersatz worlds that do not differ at all in what roles are played – in what sort of individuals there are, with what properties, how related – but differ only in which extra individuals occupy those roles?

I consider this to be the harmless part of the problem. It is a haecceitist's problem, and I reject haecceitism. I think any intuitions in its favour can be met by other means. (See section 4.4.) I think we characterise a

---

[8]Here I am indebted to Lycan, 'The Trouble with Possible Worlds'; Skyrms, 'Tractarian Nominalism'; and especially Bricker, *Worlds and Propositions*, pages 189–94.

possibility quite well enough by describing what kinds of individuals there are and how they are related. We omit no information if we fail to say, by name, who is who. The information we could give only by naming unactualised extra individuals is no genuine information at all. If *per impossibile* we had all the names, and could say by name who it is that plays this role and who plays that, we would merely make distinctions without differences. What matters is that we give a description according to which such-and-such roles are filled.

It is otherwise for properties. Here, what correspond to haecceitistic differences are genuine differences in how things might be; for they are differences in what properties things might have. I complain that if we only have words for the natural properties that are instantiated within our actual world, then we are not in a position to describe completely any possibility in which there are extra natural properties, alien to actuality. It is reasonable to think there are some such possibilities; and I do not see how we could have words for the alien properties they involve. Therefore these possibilities cannot be identified with their linguistic descriptions in any language that could be available to us. Our best linguistic ersatz worlds sometimes are incomplete, and conflate possibilities that differ only in respect of their alien natural properties.

Think of an ersatzist philosopher who lives in a simpler world than ours. The protons and neutrons (if we may call them that) of his world are indivisible particles. There are no quarks; and so the distinctive properties of quarks, their so-called flavours and colours, are not instantiated by anything at all in his simpler world. Nor, let us suppose, are these properties analysable in terms of properties and relations that are instantiated in the simpler world. They are alien to that world. Likewise, perhaps some properties instantiated within richer worlds than ours are alien to our world. Maybe there are some especially opulent worlds that do have instances of all the natural properties there could possibly be. (By the principle of recombination advanced in section 1.8, there are such worlds if, but only if, it is possible to have a spacetime big enough to make room for instances of all the different natural properties from all the worlds.) But those worlds are special, and we have no reason to think we live in one of them. More likely we are in the same position as the philosopher who lives in a simpler world than ours. Then if we failed to acknowledge the possibility of alien natural properties, we would be just as wrong as he would be. But that is exactly what will happen under linguistic ersatzism. There is no way the theorist can specify his worldmaking language so that it will have words – names or predicates – for properties alien to his world. So any language he can specify will be inadequate to distinguish some of the possibilities there are.

The point is simplest if we believe in universals to which the perfectly natural properties correspond, and we adopt the Lagadonian scheme and let each universal serve as a predicate for itself. If only the universals that appear in this world are available to serve as predicates, then plainly there are no predicates for alien universals. But it doesn't help if we adopt some other scheme of interpretation. It still seems clear that if we had been in the position of the philosopher in the simpler world, we would have had no way at all to name the quark flavours and colours. And we may very well be in a predicament parallel to his. It is at any rate a possible predicament – he is in it. It seems arbitrary and absurd to admit that it is possible to be in such a predicament if you are a simple creature whose protons do not consist of quarks, and then to deny that it is possible to be in a parallel predicament if you are one of the more complex creatures that we take ourselves to be.

Or so I think. Of course, I have explained the problem in modal realist terms: here are we, there are the alien natural properties (or universals) only instantiated off in other worlds, and we have no way to introduce words for them. An ersatzer will not agree that there are any properties instantiated off in other worlds, since he does not believe that there are any other worlds. Nevertheless he somehow understands modality; and I should hope he would find it compelling to say, simply, that there might have been other natural properties (or universals) than there are. If not, I say that he gets the facts of modality wrong. And I hope he would agree, also, that there is no way for us to introduce words for those properties that there might have been, but actually are not.

Here I expect a protest. I have spoken indifferently of properties that there actually are, or of properties that are actually instantiated; and of properties that there only might have been, or of properties that only might have been instantiated. It is open to reply that the properties there actually are go beyond the properties that are actually instantiated; and that the properties that only might have been instantiated are nevertheless among the properties that there are. The reply invokes uninstantiated properties: it claims that each and every property that might have been actualised does exist, as part of (the abstract side of) actuality. Then by the Lagadonian scheme, if not otherwise, we have a name for all the extra properties that might have been instantiated but aren't. Ersatz worlds are to be constructed out of the resources of actuality, including the uninstantiated properties that actually exist.

(Such a position, minus my gloss on it as linguistic in a generalised sense, would be one natural way to develop the rather noncommital 'world-story' ersatzism of Robert M. Adams. His world-stories are sets of entities with quasi-syntactic structure. These entities sometimes have individuals, or else their 'thisnesses', as constituents; so it seems that properties, in some sense, might well be wanted as further constituents.)

In reply, I must raise a question that I have been passing by: what does the ersatzer mean by 'property'? As I said in section 1.5, there are many different conceptions of properties; and not all of these are available to an ersatzer. He cannot mean what I mean: the set of all the instances, at this world or any other. For a property uninstantiated at this world has no this-worldly instances; he doesn't believe in other-worldly instances; so the set is empty. But he does not wish to conflate all the uninstantiated properties. Is a property, for him, some sort of abstraction from a predicate? From a this-worldly predicate, it will have to be; for he believes in no others. Then he will first have to find some other way to introduce words for the alien properties, before he can name them by the Lagadonian method. Are his properties universals? Or sets of duplicates tropes? All very well for an elite minority of instantiated properties, perhaps. But no good for uninstantiated properties – universals or tropes are supposed to be present in their instances, and there is nothing for uninstantiated ones to be present in. Not, at any rate, here in what the ersatzer takes to be the one and only world. (I have no parallel problem. Alien universals or tropes could be present in their other-worldly instances.) Is it that, although the uninstantiated ones among his properties do not technically qualify as universals or tropes, at any rate they are *of a kind with* the instantiated universals or tropes that really are present in things? But what does 'of a kind' mean here? I don't suppose it is to be explained in terms of the sharing of second-order universals, or the exact duplication of second-order tropes! I might perhaps take 'of a kind' as primitive, as an alternative to believing in universals or tropes. But if you take it as primitive on top of your universals or tropes, you're buying a dog and doing the barking yourself. Are his properties the sort of magical entities that I shall discuss in section 3.4? In that case it will be enough, for now, to say that he ought not to believe in such things because there is no acceptable account of how they do their stuff; but that if nevertheless he does believe in them, he could make them serve the ersatzist cause more simply than as words in a Lagadonian language. So (with the magical properties left as unfinished business) I think my conclusion stands: neither the philosopher in the simpler world, nor we in ours, have any words for the missing properties.

What we can do, however, is to speak of them by quantification. The ersatzer in the simple world can introduce a language in which he can say, what is false in his world:

Protons are tripartite. And there are natural properties X, Y, Z, of which each least part of a proton has exactly one, which enter as follows into the laws of nature that govern the binding together of protons and their least parts: – X – Y – Z –. And the properties X, Y, and Z are different from charge, different from spin, ...

where the dashed part is an open sentence in which the variables occur free, and the dotted part is completed with difference clauses for all the natural properties he is in a position to name. That is, he can introduce a language in which to formulate existential quantifications over properties. Such a quantification is false at his world, but it could be made true by suitably behaved properties alien to his world; and, thanks to the last clause, it could be made true only by there being alien properties. Such sentences can be members of, and true according to, his linguistic ersatz worlds. Ramsey taught us to use existential quantifications over properties to express the content of hypotheses about this world; and the same method is available for use in describing unactualised possibilities. The ersatzer in the simpler world can construct Ramsified ersatz worlds which contain (or imply) existential quantifications that could be made true by there being alien natural properties, and only so.

And we can do the same. Some of our linguistic ersatz worlds should be Ramsified; so that they say by quantification, if not by name, that there are extra nameless properties, alien to our world, which are have instances distributed in so-and-so way and which play such-and-such nomological role. Then we have ersatz worlds according to which there are extra, alien properties. Thereby we acknowledge the possibility. What more could I ask?

Well, I could ask not only that possibilities not be omitted, but also that different possibilities not be conflated. When that unfortunate philosopher in his simpler world constructs Ramsified ersatz worlds using the limited resources at his disposal, every world is at least partially described by one of them. But I say that the worlds with the alien properties – I mean worlds with natural properties that are alien to *him*, for instance our world – are described incompletely. He has said what roles for properties are occupied, but he has not said – and he could not possibly say – which properties occupy which roles. Here we are, with names for properties that he cannot name. We can distinguish our world from one in which, say, one of the quark colours has traded places with one of the flavours. The two possibilities are isomorphic, yet different. There are more ways than one to make one of his Ramsey sentences, or one of his Ramsified ersatz worlds, come true. Therefore such an ersatz world does not describe any of the relevant possibilities completely.

(Here I expect a rejoinder. Is it really possible that a quark colour and a flavour should trade places? Or do such properties as these have their nomological roles or their causal powers essentially? If so, as has been suggested by Shoemaker and by Swoyer, then a property with the nomological role of a certain quark colour would have to be that quark colour, and could not be one of the flavours instead. Then it may be, after all, that the philosopher in the simpler world has the resources to describe our world – or any world – completely; it is enough if he can specify the relevant nomological roles. And if he has adequate resources to describe any world, so *a fortiori* do we. So my objection rests on denying the thesis of essential nomological roles. I support this denial by means of the principle of recombination (see section 1.8). Start with a world where the quark colours and flavours do figure in the laws that are supposed to be essential to them. By patching together duplicates of things from that world, we can presumably describe a world where those laws are broken; yet perfectly natural properties are intrinsic *ex officio*, and so they never can differ between duplicates. The principle of recombination seems to me very compelling indeed; and it ought to be no less compelling when reformulated in ersatzist fashion. If an ersatzer answers me by sacrificing recombination so that nomological roles can be essential, I say that he leaves the frying pan for the fire.)

In arguing that a Ramsified ersatz world made from the resources of the simple world can come true in more ways than one, I have again spoken as the modal realist that I am. But I have not been begging the question against the linguistic ersatzer. He should agree with me that such an ersatz world, though it is the very best that could be made by the philosopher in the simpler world, is incomplete. For it conflates possibilities that even an ersatzer can distinguish, if he has the luck to live at this world. It conflates different ones of the richer ersatz worlds that we can make, therefore it is incomplete.

But how is it with one of the very best Ramsified ersatz worlds that *we* can make? Is this ersatz world complete? Is it so or not that there are many possible ways for it to come true? Neither choice is satisfactory. Say yes, and those many possibilities cannot be the one ersatz world that stops with Ramsey sentences. Then what else is there for them to be? Say no, and I ask what guarantees our luck? As before, there is a possible predicament – the philosopher in the simpler world is in it – in which some of one's very best Ramsified ersatz worlds will be incomplete. It seems arbitrary and absurd to admit that it is possible to be in such a predicament if you are a simple creature whose protons do not consist of quarks, and then to deny that it is possible to be in a parallel predicament if you are one of the more complex creatures that we take ourselves to be.

You might say: 'if multiplicity is wanted, no sooner said than done – let's make many ordered pairs, pairing the one Ramsified linguistic ersatz world with each of the infinitely many integers.' But again, as in the case of indiscernible possible individuals, multiplicity was not all I wanted. This seems like an irrelevant multiplicity. We have the infinitely many new representations, differing now by the integers built into them; and we have the infinitely many possibilities, differing by permutations of the alien properties, that ought to be acknowledged. But the many representations do not represent the many possibilities unambiguously, one to one. Rather, each of the many new representations is ambiguous over all the many possibilities, exactly as the one original representation was. Nothing has been gained.

The ersatzer's problem is that he denied, quite implausibly, that there are many ways that one of his Ramsified ersatz worlds could come true. He might try to soften that denial as follows.

> For each of my Ramsified ersatz worlds, there *is* only the one possibility; because – say I, standing firm – the ersatz world *is* the possibility. So I deny that there are many ways that such an ersatz world could come true. But I am willing to say, since I help myself to primitive modality – I'd better! – that *if* my ersatz world did come true, *then* there would be many ways for it to come true. For then there would be more properties to name, so there would be a richer worldmaking language, so the missing distinctions could be provided. There is only the one possibility, but there might have been the many.

I am not content. This sounds better than it is. It sounds as if he is meeting me half-way: when I demand many possibilities he does not offer me that, but at least he offers me many *possible* possibilities. Then I could very well say: call them what you will, at least we have many of something. Not so. There is no such thing in his ontology as an unactualised possible possibility. He has gone no part of the way toward granting what I took to be plainly true. I say there are many ways that something might have happened. He denies that there are many of anything relevant, though he grants that there might have been.

At least, I hope that is what he does. But he could turn very devious, agreeing with me verbally while disagreeing in substance. He could *say* 'there are many' and *mean* 'there might have been many'. Does the pot call the kettle black? No; when *I* say interchangeably 'there are many talking donkeys – other-worldly ones' and 'there might have been many talking donkeys', that is because on my view the thing can be said either way equivalently, without at all departing from the ordinary quantificational meaning of 'there are many'. (Remember that part of the ordinary meaning of any idiom of quantification consists of susceptibility to restrictions; and that restrictions come and go with the pragmatic wind.) But if the ersatzer turns devious, his 'there are many' has come loose altogether from its ordinary quantificational meaning. 'There are many ways the Ramsified ersatz world could come true' could mean what you please, for instance that God is great. But so long as it is meant quantificationally, the ersatzer hasn't any right to affirm it as I do. He would do better to bite the bullet: to say outright that, strange as it may seem, each of our Ramsified ersatz worlds could come true in only one way.

Skyrms is one philosopher who is prepared to bite the bullet. As I noted above, his 'Tractarian Nominalism' is linguistic ersatzism of the Lagadonian sort. He stops short of declaring his allegiance to it, but he does consider it a 'live metaphysical option, and an attractive one'. He sees that the position has the consequence that 'we think about possible facts and possible worlds in two quite different ways. For possible worlds whose objects and relations are subsets of this world our possibilities are essentially *combinatorial*. We rearrange some or all of our relationships between some or all of the objects to get our possibilities. . . .' But 'there might be more, or other objects than there are. There might be other forces in nature, other physical properties and relations. To cash these intuitions we must think of possibilities *analogically*. In the analogical phase . . . the game is quite different. . . . at this stage, haecceitism fails' (for objects and relations alike) 'and a kind of Ramsey sentence . . . approach to the "new" objects prevails' ('Tractarian Nominalism', pages 201–2). Evidently Skyrms finds it acceptable that a Ramsey sentence approach should prevail, not only for the more or other objects – as to that, I agree with him – but also for the other forces in nature, other physical properties and relations.

Linguistic representation gave us three problems, none of which arise for my genuine modal realism. (1) Some descriptions are inconsistent, so we need resources to distinguish the consistent ones; whereas there is no such thing as an inconsistent world. (2) We cannot have two indiscernible descriptions; whereas maybe there are indiscernible worlds, and in any case there certainly are indiscernible parts of worlds. (3) What can be described is limited by what we can have words for; whereas worlds can outrun our means of describing them. These three drawbacks of linguistic ersatzism, taken together, seem to me to be rather more damaging than the incredulous stares that greet my own plurality of worlds. But if, fully aware of its advantages and drawbacks, you judged linguistic ersatzism to be the better theory, that would not be contrary to reason. I take this to be a question for weighing and balancing – not for knockdown refutation.

It is otherwise with pictorial and magical ersatzism, to be considered in the rest of this chapter. Those may seem to have advantages both over genuine modal realism and over linguistic ersatzism, but I think their merits are illusory and they are to be rejected. The best ersatzism by far is linguistic.

3.3 Pictorial Ersatzism

If the problems of linguistic representation do not arise for genuine modal realism, then perhaps the ersatzer would be better served by ersatz worlds which are made more in the image of genuine worlds. Perhaps, apart from its abstractness, an ersatz world should be like a picture. Let it be like a picture in a generalised sense: a sense in which a statue counts as a three-dimensional picture, and a working model counts as a four-dimensional picture. And let it be an idealised picture, infinite in extent and many-dimensional if need be, which represents the concrete world in its entirety and in all its detail. We want no projection into too few dimensions, no omission of hidden or minute parts, no spurious structure that is in the picture but plays no part in the representing.

A picture represents by isomorphism. We have a cat on a mat, and we have a picture of it. There is a part of the picture that corresponds to the cat; it is composed of parts that correspond in turn to parts of the cat: to the paws, the tail, the whiskers, ... This part of the picture is mostly black, except for one white bit that corresponds to a bit of the cat's throat; therefore the picture represents the cat as being black except for a white patch on the throat. The part of the picture that corresponds to the cat touches another part of the picture that corresponds to the mat; therefore the picture represents the cat as being on the mat.

With our ordinary pictures, the isomorphism is limited. For instance the part of the picture that corresponds to the cat is not furry; instead it is streaky in a certain way, and that is how it represents the cat as furry. Distances correspond not by identity but by a scaling factor: the parts of the picture are all closer together than the corresponding parts of the cat and mat. The opposite side of the cat, and its innards, are not pictured at all; no part of the picture is isomorphic to them; and yet the cat is represented as a proper complete cat, or at any rate is not represented as incomplete. Even with working models there are limits to isomorphism. A model locomotive does not represent its prototype as being made of plastic (with overscale atoms), or as having an electric motor in the boiler. These practical limitations of isomorphism are patched over by means of extensive and complicated conventional understandings; at this point pictorial representation is language-like. We don't want that. We were looking for an *alternative* to linguistic ersatz worlds, so let us have something as different as we can. Since we think of our new ersatz worlds as *idealised* pictures, we may safely suppose that they represent entirely by isomorphism. The only remaining limits are those, if any, that are inescapable given our project of using abstract entities to picture concrete ones.

Isomorphic representation, pure and simple, works by composition of parts and by identity of properties and relations. So our pictorial ersatz world must consist of parts, with diverse properties, arranged in a certain way. Thereby it represents the concrete world as isomorphic to it: as consisting of corresponding parts, with the same properties, arranged in the same way. One ersatz world pictures the concrete world correctly.

(One only, unless there is duplication among the ersatz worlds.) In the case of that ersatz world, the abstract picture and the concrete world really are isomorphic. Any other ersatz world pictures the concrete world incorrectly. It misrepresents the world as isomorphic to it, but in fact the concrete world is not isomorphic to it, and nothing else – or nothing an ersatzer would believe in – is either. The ersatz world that pictures the concrete world correctly is the actualised ersatz world. Any other could have been actualised instead: had the concrete world been different in the arrangement and properties of its parts, it would thereby have been isomorphic to a different ersatz world.

Just as one part of the picture of the cat on the mat is isomorphic (within limits) to the cat, and smaller parts are isomorphic to parts of the cat, so the parts of the actualised ersatz world are isomorphic to parts of the concrete world. Some parts of some other ersatz worlds also are isomorphic to parts of the concrete world – the misrepresentation in those ersatz worlds lies elsewhere. Other parts of ersatz worlds are not isomorphic to anything there is, but they would have been had things been different. Just as the parts of genuine possible worlds are the possible individuals, so the parts of pictorial ersatz worlds are the ersatz possible individuals. And when an entire ersatz world is isomorphic to the concrete world, and thereby is actualised as a whole, then also the various ersatz individuals that are part of that ersatz world are actualised by their respective concrete isomorphs.

The big advantage of pictorial over linguistic ersatzism is that there is no problem about possibilities that involve alien natural properties. Just as I say that alien properties are instantiated by parts of other worlds, so the pictorial ersatzer can say that they are instantiated by parts of his abstract pictures. He can have his alien ersatz worlds, full of ersatz individuals instantiating diverse alien natural properties beyond the reach of our thought and language. Unlike the linguistic ersatzer, he neither omits nor conflates these possibilities.

However, I have three objections. The first and second resemble objections to linguistic ersatzism, but in both cases the problems arise in a changed form. The third is new, and I think is the most serious.

The first is that we still need primitive modality. Not, as before, in order to require consistency when we select the ersatz worlds out of a wider class of candidates; we have indeed bypassed that problem. Pictorial ersatzism, like genuine modal realism and unlike linguistic ersatzism, needn't filter out inconsistent candidates, because there aren't any in the first place. For instance, we noticed that it is all too easy to *say* that the same particle is both positive and negative in charge. But if in fact these are incompatible determinates, whether or not we have any way to know it, then nothing whatever – be it a concrete particle or be it part of an abstract picture – has them both. And if the way to represent that a particle is both positive and negative is for part of a picture also to be both positive and negative, we can rest assured that coexistence of charges will be pictured only if it is indeed possible.

I know there are so-called 'inconsistent pictures', mostly by Escher. But what makes their inconsistency possible is that the representation is not perfectly pictorial. It isn't all done by isomorphism; for instance, there are conventions of perspective to be abused. But the more is done by isomorphism, the less opportunity there is for any inconsistency – can a statue be inconsistent? And our pictorial ersatz worlds are uncompromisingly pictorial. It is *all* done by isomorphism.

Implicit representation, on the other hand, is still with us and still creates a need for primitive modality. An analysis of modality in pictorial ersatzist terms would be circular. To see why, let us try to analyse the modal statement that there might be a talking donkey. That is so iff there is some ersatz world according to which there is a talking donkey. Such an ersatz world is one that has a part – an ersatz possible individual – which is an ersatz talking donkey. But what does it mean to call something an ersatz talking donkey? After all, it is *not* isomorphic to any talking donkey, because there is no talking donkey for it to be isomorphic to. At any rate, there is none within the one and only concrete world the ersatzer believes in. The picture represents falsely; the ersatz talking donkey, and likewise the ersatz world it is part of, are unactualised. What makes the thing an ersatz talking donkey is just that it *could* have been isomorphic to a talking donkey that was part of the concrete world, and it *would* have been if the concrete world had been different, and it *couldn't* have been isomorphic to any part of the concrete world that was not a talking donkey.

In short, there might be a talking donkey iff there might be a talking donkey isomorphic to some part of some ersatz world. That is no advance toward an analysis of the modal statement we began with.

If an ersatz talking donkey were literally a talking donkey, we would have no problem. (That is why there is no parallel problem for me: I say that an other-worldly talking donkey *is* literally a talking donkey.) But that, I take it, is not to be said. The sharing of properties across the divide between concrete and abstract must have its limits. Concreteness and abstractness themselves obviously cannot be properties shared across the divide. And neither can donkeyhood. Whatever 'concrete' may mean, at least one thing is certain: a donkey is the very sort of thing that is paradigmatically concrete. Therefore an abstract ersatz donkey, talking or not, is no donkey. In the properties and arrangement of its parts, all but those properties that cannot be shared across the divide, it is just like a donkey. It is like a donkey except for being abstract rather than concrete. But that is a treacherous way to put it. To say that something is 'like a donkey' is not to say that there is any donkey it is like. In this case there is not, or so the ersatzer supposes. Our ersatz donkey is unlike any donkey there is, even apart from its lack of concreteness. For no donkey talks. Only in the modal sense is it donkey-like: it is like donkeys that might be, not donkeys that are.

(We might do a bit better with simpler things. Suppose we had asked what an abstract ersatz proton is. The answer 'something just like a proton except that it isn't concrete' need not be taken in the unhelpful modal sense. Unlike donkeys, protons have little scope for differing one from another. So we might well accept not only that any ersatz proton is proton-like, but also that there is some proton that it is like. That is not beyond dispute – is it too essentialist about proton-kind? – but if it is not yet right for protons, it might be right for still simpler things, spacetime points perhaps. Then we can go further: for we have structural definitions of kinds of atoms in terms of subatomic particles, kinds of molecules in terms of atoms, and so on. (Sometimes these definitions are disjunctive, as when there are isotopes of an element or isomers of a compound.) So I will grant that we can say what it is to be an ersatz paradichloro-benzene molecule. It won't matter if there are no concrete paradichloro-benzene molecules for an ersatz one to be isomorphic to: we characterise the ersatz molecules not by their isomorphism to the concrete, but by their structural definition in terms of ersatz things – ersatz protons, and the like – that we can characterise by isomorphism to the concrete. But at some point the method gives out: what is the structural definition of a talking donkey? If we have to know that before we can analyse the statement that there might have been a talking donkey, and likewise for the statement that there might have been a philosophising cat, or a laughing cow, the analysis of modality will long remain unfinished.)

Extending our earlier contrast of explicit and implicit representation, we can say that a pictorial ersatz world represents *explicitly* that the concrete world consists of parts arranged in a certain way and with certain properties. The properties here are limited to those that can be shared across the divide, therefore we can have no explicit representation that there are donkeys or protons or puddles or stars – not if such things are paradigmatically concrete. (Thus the representation just envisaged of a proton or a paradichlorobenzene molecule, though perhaps unproblematic, does not count as explicit.) And an ersatz world represents *implicitly* all that is implied by what it represents explicitly. The implication is modal: we have implicit representation that there is a talking donkey because, necessarily, if the properties and arrangement of the parts of the concrete world are as they are explicitly represented to be, then there must be a talking donkey. Indeed, whenever it is represented that there are concrete things of such and such kind, or instances of properties not shared across the divide, the representation must be implicit.

(Another sort of implicit representation, noted in the linguistic case, is still with us: representation by an ersatz world that it is the actualised one. To make this representation explicit we would have to let each ersatz world picture not only the concrete world but also the entire system of ersatz worlds, including itself. This would make the ersatz worlds enormously complex. And worse, if the ersatz worlds picture one another picturing one another . . . , that would mean that each ersatz world has many different parts which could be isormorphic to the concrete world. Then what distinguishes the part that is supposed to be the picture of the concrete world from all the parts that are parts of the pictures of various ersatz worlds?)

This is very like the problem that arose for linguistic ersatzism if we chose an impoverished worldmaking language, capable of describing local but not global matters. We need primitive modality to get from what is explicitly represented to what is implied about, as it might be, whether there is a talking donkey. So we might look in the same direction for a remedy: introduce a language for which implication can be defined in deductive, purely syntactic terms. (Not the worldmaking language, since we no longer have one.) As part of that definition, it will be necessary to specify a list of axioms. Again, I do not think that can be done without covertly relying on primitive modality. We will need conditional axioms to the effect that *if* – here follows a very long, perhaps infinite, description in terms of properties that can be shared across the divide – *then* there is a talking donkey. Again, it would be impossible in practice to give the axioms, so no pictorial ersatzer can complete his theory. (And even if, *per impossibile*, the job could be done, I would still find it very peculiar if it turned out that before we can finish analysing modality, we have to analyse talking-donkeyhood as well!) Unless, of course, he does the obvious thing: declares that among conditionals of the proper form, exactly those shall be axioms that are necessarily true.

My second objection is that we still have a problem of conflation of indiscernible possibilities, though it takes a new form. For pictorial, as opposed to linguistic, ersatzism, possibilities certainly do not obey any principle of identity of indiscernibles. There might be indiscernible ersatz worlds; and there certainly will be indiscernible ersatz individuals. An ersatz world according to which there is two-way eternal recurrence will consist of many indiscernible ersatz epochs, and within these will be found indiscernible ersatz Napoleonic conquerors. The problem is with the actualisation of indiscernible possibilities. If one ersatz world is isomorphic to the concrete world, then so is any other that is indiscernible from it; whereas it ought to be that one and only one ersatz world is actualised. Likewise, more seriously, for indiscernible ersatz individuals. Suppose the concrete world undergoes eternal recurrence, with a Napoleonic conqueror in every epoch. Consider one of these conquerors: Napoleon himself. He is isomorphic to *all* those indiscernible ersatz individuals. So we have plenty of indiscernible possibilities for him, as we should; but instead of actualising one of them, he actualises them all! That is not right. Should we therefore take possibilities to be not the ersatz worlds and individuals themselves, but equivalence classes of them under indiscernibility? No, that gives back unique actualisation at the cost of conflating the indiscernible possibilities. I have no corresponding problem: isomorphism doesn't distinguish indiscernibles but identity does. If this is a world of eternal recurrence, Napoleon actualises only one of the indiscernible possible individuals: himself.

My third, and most serious, objection is that pictorial ersatzism does not really get rid of unwelcome ontology. Its 'abstract' ersatz worlds and individuals are not abstract in any customary sense of the word, or in any sense that makes them easier to believe in than my 'concrete' *possibilia*.

In section 1.7, I complained that the supposed distinction between abstract and concrete is in disarray. I listed four ways of trying to explain it, and I complained that these ways disagreed with one another. Let us review them to see if we can find any useful sense in which a pictorial ersatz world might be 'abstract'.

First we had the Way of Example: concrete entities are things like donkeys and puddles and protons and stars, whereas abstract entities are things like numbers. This Way is unhelpful if we are told that pictorial ersatz donkeys are quite donkey-like in the arrangement and properties of their parts, but nevertheless are abstract.

Second was the Way of Conflation: the distinction between concrete and abstract entities is just the distinction between individuals and sets, or between particulars and universals, or perhaps between particular individuals and anything else. This Way is useless: pictorial ersatz worlds have to be particular individuals, but abstract even so. For if they are to be fit for their work, they must be composed of parts capable of extensive sharing of properties and of relations with the particular individuals that are parts of the concrete world. But – aside from hoked-up disjunctive and extrinsic classifications – there seem to be few shared properties of universals and particulars, or of sets and individuals. So ersatz worlds had better be composed of particulars rather than universals, and individuals rather than sets. (I do not rule out that *some* parts of the ersatz world, and of the concrete world as well, might be universals. But if so, both the ersatz and the concrete worlds would nevertheless divide exhaustively into particulars, since the universals would be parts of the particulars that instantiate them.) And if so, then the ersatz worlds must themselves be particular individuals. For a universal cannot be composed of particular parts: universals recur, particulars don't, but if the whole recurs then so do its parts, for the parts must be present wherever the whole is. And a set cannot be composed mereologically out of individual parts. For two things can never be composed of exactly the same parts – that is the difference between mereological composition and the generating of sets – and there is already an individual composed of those parts. Mereology does apply to sets, I think; but we have to take the parts of a set to be its subsets, rather than any individuals.

Third was the Negative Way: abstract entities have no spatiotemporal location; they do not enter into causal interaction; they are never indiscernible one from another. Since our abstract ersatz worlds are supposed to represent pictorially, by means of the properties and arrangement of their parts, it seems that their parts must enter into spatiotemporal relations. Perhaps they stand in no spatiotemporal relations to us; but if so, then equally we stand in no spatiotemporal relations to them, and that doesn't make *us* abstract. (The difference between abstract and concrete is supposed to be a difference in kind, so not a relative matter.) Likewise for causal interaction: the parts of ersatz worlds do not enter into causal interaction with us, but they seem to enter into causal interaction with one another. Or at least into something just like causal interaction: it would be covered by a counterfactual analysis of causation, with the counterfactuals in turn explained in terms of closeness of ersatz worlds. Perhaps we might insist on denying that parts of ersatz worlds are located, or enter into causal interaction, for the very reason that they are not concrete; but only if we had some independent reason why they are not. As for indiscernibility: an ersatz world that pictures two-way eternal recurrence will have indiscernible parts. So on all three counts, pictorial ersatz worlds consist of parts which the Negative Way cannot classify as abstract. Therefore the Negative Way does not support any contention that the ersatz worlds themselves are abstract.

Fourth was the Way of Abstraction: abstract entities are abstractions from concrete entities. They result from somehow subtracting specificity, so that an incomplete description of the original concrete entity becomes a complete description of the abstraction. But our pictorial ersatz worlds and individuals do not seem to be at all lacking in specific detail. Maybe you could say that the actualised ersatz world is somehow an abstraction from the concrete world; though it doesn't seem to be *specificity* that has been subtracted. But how about the unactualised ersatz worlds? Are they somehow abstractions from other concrete worlds? – No, because according to the ersatzer there aren't any other concrete worlds for them to be abstractions from.

Still, I think the Way of Abstraction affords our only hope of finding a sense in which the pictorial ersatz worlds and their parts are 'abstract'. The best sense I can make of that claim is as follows. First, *some* of them are literally abstractions. There is a special ingredient of the concrete world –

vim, I shall call it – which is entirely absent from all the ersatz worlds and their parts. The actualised ersatz world is just like the concrete world with its vim left out, so in that sense it is an abstraction. Likewise any ersatz individual that is isomorphic to part of the concrete world is a vimless abstraction. Second, the rest of the ersatz worlds and individuals are not literally abstractions. There is nothing they are abstractions from. We nevertheless call them abstract because, like the ones that literally are abstractions, they are devoid of vim. Being vimless makes them abstraction-like.

(Genuine abstractions, we recall, might well be treated as innocent verbal fictions: to speak of the abstraction, economic man, is really just to speak in an abstract way of ordinary men. No hope for such a strategem in the present case. Not for the abstraction-like entities which are not genuine abstractions: we cannot really be talking about the things whence they were abstracted if there are no such things. And not even for the genuine abstractions that the others are supposed to be like: to make those things abstraction-like, we need *genuine* abstractions for them to be like. Non-abstractions spoken of in an abstract way – ordinary men, for instance – would not make things of a kind with them be abstraction-like.)

You may be tempted to give vim a different name. Should you call it 'concreteness'? No; for when unactualised ersatz worlds lack vim, they are not genuine abstractions, merely abstraction-like. (And perhaps some things with vim are genuine abstractions. Why not abstract from the concrete world by leaving out not its vim but something else?) Should you call it 'actualisation'? No; *ex hypothesi* it is missing even from the actualised ersatz world. Should you call it 'existence'? No; the abstract ersatz realm, however lacking in vim, nevertheless exists.

The concrete world and the pictorial ersatz worlds alike are highly complex particular individuals. One of these individuals is the one we ourselves are part of. And one of them is distinguished because it has vim, and for that reason – for that reason *only*, so it seems – is called 'concrete'. Why should we think we are part of the one with vim? How could we tell and why should we care? *Ex hypothesi*, we could have otherwise the same properties, and the parts of ourselves and our surroundings could be arranged alike, whether we had vim or not.

Almost, we have made our way back to genuine modal realism. To the extent that pictorial ersatzism is different, its differences are not to its credit. Its ontology is no more commonsensical than my own: it is just the same except for the vim, that mystery ingredient added to one world. Maybe the addition of vim does give us a sense in which we can say that there is only one concrete world – we can only hope we are part of it! – but any connection with our reasons for wanting to say so are long gone. The ersatz worlds are not sets or universals, 'abstract' entities that we might believe in already. The parts of what we are asked to believe in are donkeys, puddles, protons, stars, or what have you, in all but name. And the reason for withholding the names is flimsy in the extreme.

Pictures represent by having a lot in common with what they represent. Our problem is that they have altogether too much in common. Pictorial ersatzism is to be rejected.

3.4   Magical Ersatzism

For linguistic and pictorial ersatzism alike, there is supposed to be an account of how representation works. This account relies on the structure, set-theoretic or mereological, of the ersatz world. What is true *according to* it depends on what is true *of* it; and what is true of it is, mainly, that it is built up in a certain way from constituents of certain kinds. The same could be said of the representation in my genuine modal realism: it is true according to another world that there is a talking donkey because it is true of that world that it has a talking donkey as one of its parts.

When we insisted on giving some structural account of representation, it seemed that we faced a choice of evils: insufficient power to represent, or else sufficient power by means of unwelcome ontology. Perhaps that should teach us not to pursue structural accounts of representation. Perhaps we need some wholly different account of representation, or no account at all.

Let us suppose, then, that ersatz worlds have no relevant inner structure. We may as well suppose they have no structure at all. They are not sets, so they have no members. They are mereologically atomic, so they have no proper parts. They are simples.

And they are abstract simples. In what way 'abstract'? – Presumably the Negative Way. For *ex hypothesi* they are not sets, in particular not equivalence classes. Nor are they to be understood as non-spatiotemporal parts – universals or tropes – of the particles or donkeys or whatnot that are parts of the concrete world; because surely there are not enough of those to supply as many ersatz worlds as we need. But the ersatz worlds are not *sui generis* among abstract entities; they are distinguished members of a broader class of abstract simples. You might prefer to give these simples some tendentious name, but I shall call them simply *elements*.

There is an important distinction among the elements. Again I want a neutral word for it; so I shall just say that some of them are *selected*, others are not. Which ones are selected depends on what goes on within the concrete world. For instance, there are some elements that cannot be selected unless there is a talking donkey included as a part within the concrete world. And there is one element such that, necessarily, it is selected if and only if there is a talking donkey. Since the selection of elements depends on the concrete world, we may take it as a binary relation that the concrete world bears to whichever elements it selects.

It may happen that, necessarily, if the concrete world selects element E, then also it selects element F; if so, let us say that E *implies* F. We assume that this relation of implication between the elements satisfies various formal principles: suffice it to say that the elements, taken under implication, comprise a complete, atomic Boolean algebra. In this Boolean algebra, there are many elements, called *maximal*, that are not implied by other elements (except that there is one special 'null' element that implies every element, even the maximal ones). We could call two elements *incompatible* iff they cannot both be selected; then a maximal element is incompatible with exactly those elements that it does not imply (and is not null), and this is an alternative way to characterise the maximal elements. Necessarily, no matter what goes on within the concrete world, one and only one of the maximal elements will be selected. Then the selected elements will be exactly those which the selected maximal element implies. Since every (non-null) element is implied by at least one maximal element, it is possible for any (non-null) element to be selected.

(A more complicated version of the theory, considered by Bricker, might permit there to be clusters of two or more elements, within which all the elements imply one another; we get a Boolean algebra only when we throw out all but any one element from each cluster. For simplicity, I will suppose we have no such clusters, so we have a Boolean algebra already.)

An element E *represents* that so-and-so, or it is the case that so-and-so *according to* E, iff, necessarily, if E is selected, then so-and-so. This is how maximal elements, in particular, represent. The maximal elements are the *ersatz worlds*. End of theory.

Suppose that an ersatzer presented his theory to me just like that. Some forseeable and indecisive skirmishing would ensue. Let us hasten through it.

Say I: this is no theory. This is a theory-schema, which any number of different theories could fit. Even my own: maybe the elements are the sets of worlds, the concrete world – or *any* concrete world – selects just those elements that have it as a member, and it is the case according to an element that a donkey talks iff each world in that element has a talking donkey as a part. Equally, any sort of linguistic or pictorial ersatzism could fit your schema.

Says he: not so. You have paid attention to the positive side of my theory and overlooked my denials. I deny that the elements are concrete. I deny that they have structure. I deny that they have parts or members. That rules out the interpretations you mentioned. (Fair enough. But had his denials been left out, my point would have been well taken.)

Say I: you make a great mystery, because you tell me nothing at all about the nature of the elements.

Says he: I told you that they are abstract and they are simple. That was not what you wanted to hear. You wanted to be told that they had some sort of complex structure, as if they were linguistic descriptions or pictures. I deny that they have any such structure. Why is my denial any less informative than some positive story about their structure would have been?

Say I: you make a second mystery, because you don't tell me what it is for the concrete world to 'select' an element.

Says he: that's primitive. All theories have their primitives, and 'selects' and 'elements' are mine.

Say I: you cannot explain modality, because you took that as primitive also.

Says he: I did. I don't pretend to explain modality, but there are plenty of other purposes for the theory to serve. (Fair enough.) The choice is between primitive modality and crazy ontology like yours, and I choose the former.

Say I: what's so sane about your ontology? You multiply entities at least as much as I do.

Says he: your ontology flies in the face of common sense, mine doesn't. You require a lot of extra donkeys, and so forth; everybody knows what that means, and nobody believes it. I require a lot of abstract simples; common sense has no opinion about them one way or the other.

Say I: you're taking refuge in your denials. If you'd come clean and say something positive about the nature of your abstract simples, then we'd see what common sense might have to say about them.

Says he: there's nothing positive I could say that would be true.

So far, a deadlock. But I think I can advance my case by asking him to tell me something more about the primitive apparatus of his theory. In particular, I want to know more about the relation whereby the concrete world 'selects' some elements, maximal and otherwise. I ask: is selection an internal relation or an external relation? That is: is it determined by the two intrinsic natures of its two *relata*? Or is it determined not by the intrinsic natures of the *relata* taken separately, but only by the intrinsic nature of the composite of both of them: element plus concrete world?

It would be unfair asking the ersatzer to define his primitive. But I am not demanding definition, only classification. Compare my own case. I might well take predicates of distance as primitive; but primitive or no, I would say that distances are external relations *par excellence*. I might well take some sort of similarity relation as primitive;[9] but primitive or

---

[9]As in the 'adequate nominalism' considered as one option in my 'New Work for a Theory of Universals', pages 347–8.

no, any sort of similarity is an internal relation. I can fairly ask the ersatzer to classify his primitive in the same way.

Suppose first that the relation of selection is internal: when the concrete world selects an element, that is so in virtue of what goes on within the concrete world together with the intrinsic nature of the selected element. If part of what goes on within the concrete world is that there is a talking donkey, that will mean that elements with some intrinsic natures will be selected and elements with others will not be. There is one element which, in virtue of its distinctive intrinsic nature, necessarily will be selected if and only if there is a talking donkey within the concrete world. Selection may remain unanalysed, but we have at least a schema that gives the form of an analysis. Element E is selected iff

$$F_1(E) \text{ and } P_1 \text{ or } F_2(E) \text{ and } P_2 \text{ or } \ldots$$

where the Fs have to do with the intrinsic natures of the elements and the Ps have to do with goings-on within the concrete world. If we are not in a position to spell out the analysis, that is because our language lacks some of the requisite Fs and Ps, or because there are infinitely many disjuncts, or both.

Now we know more about the elements. They are not all alike; they differ one from another. In fact, there is a great deal of difference among them. The intrinsic natures available to them must be rich enough to permit enormous variation. For there must be enough elements, all with different distinctive natures, to provide a sufficient plenitude of possibilities. Now it is fair to renew my request to be told something about what the elements are like, and how they differ one from another. What are the properties in virtue of which one or another of them is selected?

Suppose the ersatzer replies to me: their intrinsic properties are *representational* properties. For instance, some elements have the property: *representing that a donkey talks*, or in other words, *being an element according to which a donkey talks*. It is in virtue of these representational properties that some elements are selected and some are not. For instance, there is one element that has the aforementioned property of representing that a donkey talks, and no other representational properties. Necessarily, that one is selected iff a donkey talks. Thus one of the disjuncts in the analysis-schema shown above is:

$$F_j(E) \text{ and } P_j$$

where F_j is 'represents that a donkey talks' and P_j is 'a donkey talks'. And so it goes in general, for a great many corresponding Fs and Ps. However, it isn't always this easy. Sometimes the distinctive representational property of an element will have no finite expression in ordinary English; and sometimes – in cases involving nameless alien natural properties, for example – it cannot be expressed, not even infinitarily, for lack of vocabulary. So we haven't any general analysis of how it is that the concrete world selects certain elements. But at least we have illustrations; so we should now understand what sort of properties are involved, and how it is that the concrete world selects elements in virtue of their representational properties.

No. All this helps us not at all. We have danced around a tiny circle. There is an element such that, necessarily, it is selected iff a donkey talks; that element has some distinctive intrinsic property; that property is named 'representing that a donkey talks'; the property with that name singles out the element that, necessarily, is selected iff a donkey talks. Not a thing has been said about what sort of property that might be; still less, about which property of the appropriate sort it might be. The property that plays the role is: the property that plays the role. It is no use telling me by name what property it is, if it bears that name exactly because it plays that role. The names may give the impression that we know what we are talking about, but the impression is bogus. We have not the slightest idea what the 'representational properties' are; except that they are properties whereby a vast flock of abstract simples differ one from another. Equally, we have not the slightest idea what the primitive internal relation of selection is. Never mind a general understanding; we haven't even one simple illustration of how the concrete world might select some element in virtue of its intrinsic nature. Because the most we can ever say about the nature of the element is: it is of a nature to be selected iff . . . .

Bring on the 'representational properties' by name, and we might suppose that they are on a par with other properties that we have named by acquaintance with their instances. It is not so. We cannot have named them by acquaintance with the instances that now concern us: the abstract simple elements. The elements are abstract in the sense of the Negative Way, so we have no causal acquaintance with them whatsoever. Can it be that the 'representational properties' are instantiated also by parts of the concrete world, so that we could have named them by acquaintance with their concrete instances? There are not very many candidates, since they must be properties capable of being instantiated by simples. Properties of charge, mass, quark colour and flavour, and the like might perhaps do. (If somehow they could be shared by abstract simples. But I don't see why they couldn't be.) But there are not nearly enough of those properties to make all the differences we need. So at least the great majority of the 'representational properties' must lie entirely outside our acquaintance. Then it is a mystery how anyone could have understood the predicate 'selects', which is supposed to express an internal relation that involves these properties. If the ersatzer has understood his own primitive, he must have done it by magic.

Our isolation from the 'representational properties', on this view, resembles our isolation from the other-worldly alien natural properties on my own view. So I willingly grant that some properties lie beyond the reach of our thought and language. And I willingly grant that there are various internal relations which hold in virtue of such properties, and which therefore also lie beyond the reach of our thought and language. What will not do is the pretence that we have somehow reached the unreachable, and got hold of a word for a specific one of the internal relations that lie beyond our reach.

So perhaps it would be better to suppose that the relation of selection is not internal but external. When the concrete world selects some of the abstract elements, that is not in virtue of the distinctive intrinsic natures of the selected elements. Selection is like a distance relation between spacetime points: when one point is a mile or a year away from another, that is not at all because of the distinctive natures of the two related points. Indeed the points may well all be exactly alike. If they are distinct from the point-sized bits of matter or fields that occupy them, then they haven't much intrinsic nature at all. Likewise if selection is an external relation, we can do away with all mystery about the distinctive natures of the elements. We may as well suppose that the elements are all exactly alike; they are as uniform and impoverished in intrinsic nature as the points are. Then it becomes fair once again for the ersatzer to offer us nothing but denials when we ask him what the elements are like. The name of 'elements' becomes more appropriate than before: all there is to them is their place in a relational system.[10]

My problem this time is not with the elements, but with the supposed external relation of selection. For one thing, I wonder as before how an ersatzer could possibly understand his own primitive. So far as we are told, selection is not any external relation that is ever instantiated entirely within the concrete world; whenever it is instantiated, one term of the relationship is abstract in the sense of the Negative Way, causally isolated from us, and therefore beyond our acquaintance. I wonder how such a relation ever can come within the reach of our thought and language. But I will not press this objection. There is another that seems even more serious.

My main objection is that selection is not any ordinary external relation; it is a *modal* relation. I have been tolerant – maybe too much so – toward primitive modality; but here, the primitive modality is especially repugnant.

---

[10]I take it we would then have a case of 'constitutive relations', as denounced by John Anderson. It does seem very peculiar that there should be a relational system of things with no intrinsic natures to speak of. But I see no decisive objection. Besides, I fear we may have the spacetime points as a precedent.

The concrete world selects various elements. We are now supposing that this selection has nothing to do with the distinctive natures of the selected elements – they haven't any – but it still has to do with what goes on in the concrete world. Necessarily, if a donkey talks, then the concrete world selects these elements; if a cat philosophises, it selects those; and so on. I ask: how can these connections be necessary? It seems to be one fact that somewhere within the concrete world, a donkey talks; and an entirely independent fact that the concrete world enters into a certain external relation with this element and not with that. What stops it from going the other way? Why can't anything coexist with anything here: any pattern of goings-on within the concrete world, and any pattern of external relations of the concrete world to the abstract simples?

What makes a relation external, I would have thought, exactly is that it holds independently of the natures of the two *relata*. We wanted the relation to be independent of the intrinsic nature of the elements, because – once we see past the empty words – those alleged natures turn out to be an utter mystery. But now we want the relation not to be independent of what goes on within the concrete world. How can we have it both ways?

Suppose someone told us that in outer space there are many very special particles. They surround the earth in a certain spatial arrangement: they are at various distances from the earth and from one another. Their arrangement corresponds, of necessity, to what goes on here on earth. For instance there are some of them such that, if a donkey talks somewhere on earth, they spell out the word 'yes'; if not, they spell out the word 'no'. It's not that this correspondence between heavenly and earthly affairs is ordained by the laws of nature, which are, after all, contingent. No: it is *absolutely* necessary. In no sense at all is it possible that the arrangement of the particles might fail to be thus correlated with the vicissitudes of earthly affairs. The connections between heavenly and earthly affairs thus obtain by more than merely natural necessity. They are supernatural.

I would not believe such a tale for a moment, and I hope you wouldn't either. If we know anything at all about what's possible, we know that the spatiotemporal relations of the extraterrestrial particles to the earth and to one another can vary quite independently of whether there are talking donkeys here below. Supernatural necessary connections between the one thing and the other are flatly impossible. But the tale of an external relation of selection is no better. The extraterrestrial particles have been replaced by abstract simples altogether outside of space and time; the earth has been replaced by the concrete world in its entirety; and the familiar external relations of distance have been replaced by the supposed external relation of selection. None of these changes help. All they do is kick up dust: no worries, it's all abstract!

I would like to complain, in Humean fashion, about necessary connections between distinct existences. But it's not quite that simple. After all, the concrete world that may or may not have a talking donkey as part is the same thing as the concrete world that may or may not select a certain element. Nevertheless, I take it that we are dealing with something akin to our Humean principle of recombination (see section 1.8) which requires that anything can coexist with anything, and which thereby prohibits a necessary connection between the intrinsic character of a thing and the intrinsic character of distinct things with which it coexists. We equally need a companion principle which prohibits a necessary connection between the intrinsic character of a thing and its external relations to other things. It cannot be, for instance, that there is an absolutely necessary connection (as opposed to a contingent law of nature) whereby every charged particle must be exactly a certain distance from another particle. It's one thing for the particle to be charged, another thing for two particles to be at a certain distance – the common involvement of the same particle is not enough to make the alleged connection intelligible.

So long as we know of no external relations except the (strictly or analogically) spatiotemporal ones, it would be good enough to stick to the special case. We can just require that spatiotemporal arrangement may vary independently of the intrinsic nature of the things arranged. Given any possible way for things to be arranged – that is, any way that some or other things at some or other world *are* arranged – things of any intrinsic nature whatever (shape and size permitting) may be arranged in just that way. We said that if there are a unicorn at one world and a dragon at another, then (size and shape permitting) there is a third world where duplicates of the dragon and the unicorn coexist. In just the same way we may say that if seventeen unicorns stand in a certain arrangement at one world and there are seventeen dragons at another world, then (size and shape permitting) there is a third world where duplicates of the dragons are arranged just as the unicorns in the first world are. This is really just part of our original principle of recombination.

Once we suppose that there are further external relations, for instance the one by which the concrete world allegedly selects abstract simple elements, then our principle of independence needs to be generalised. No matter what novel external relations there may be, it remains unintelligible that the intrinsic nature of a thing should constrain the external relations in which it stands.

Given modal realism, I can understand these principles of independent variation in terms of duplicate individuals in different possible worlds. The ersatzer cannot be expected to understand them in that way. But he had better have some way to understand them – if not, so much the worse for his position – and *mutatis mutandis*, he too should find them compelling.

In short: if the concrete world selects elements by an internal relation, we have no conception whatever of the differences among elements in virtue of which some are selected rather than others; and it is only by magic that 'selects' could be our word for any such relation. If, on the other hand, the concrete world selects elements by an external relation, it is the relation itself that is magical: what spell constrains it to correspond rigidly to goings-on in the concrete world? Either way, ersatzism that relies on such a relation is justly called 'magical'; and is to be rejected.

Some further hypotheses may be considered, but I do not think they do any better.

(1) Selection is an external relation, magically constrained to correspond to goings-on in the world; however, there are irrelevant differences between the elements, so they are not all exactly alike.

(2) Selection is a mixed relation: it is the conjunction of an internal relation that relies on differences of elements, whereof we have no conception, with an external relation that is magically constrained to correspond to goings-on in the world.

(3) Selection is not even an external relation. It is not even determined by the intrinsic nature of the composite, element plus concrete world, taken as a whole; still less by the intrinsic natures of the two *relata* taken separately. It is like the relation of belonging to a common owner, as my watch and my wallet do, which involves not only the two *relata* but also the owner and a certain amount of the social environment. This would presumably make it equivalent to an external relation of elements to something even more inclusive than the entire concrete world, but the magical constraining is still there.

(4) Selection is not any kind of natural relation. There is nothing to it but a list – a list entirely out of reach of our thought and language. Element E is selected iff:

E is N_1, and P_1; or E is N_2, and P_2; or . . .

where the Ns are mere proper names of elements. No such names could possibly be available to us; so again it's magic if the ersatzer understands his own primitive.

I expect protest from the magicians. Not indeed from this-worldly magicians – there aren't any, or if there are, you can't prove it from their published writings.* However, many leading philosophers of modality favour nondescript ersatzism. They offer, more or less fully, what amounts to the positive side of the magician's story: the elements, selection of elements by the concrete world, implication among elements, the Boolean

*(Added in proof): True when written; but Peter van Inwagen's 'Two Concepts of Possible Worlds', soon to appear in *Mid-West Studies in Philosophy* 11, will be an explicit and formidable defence of magical ersatzism.

algebra with its maximal elements that serve as ersatz worlds. They tell us little about the nature of the elements, except that somehow they are abstract. They tell us, in effect (in one terminology or another), that the elements represent; but they don't say how. But they do not offer the denials of structure that distinguish a magical ersatzer from a linguistic or pictorial one. So what they give us is a schema to fit a variety of theories. (Including my own, as noted above, if sets of worlds count as 'abstract'.) However these nondescript ersatzers have close counterparts at other worlds who *do* offer the denials, and therefore are genuine magicians. It is these other-worldly magicians who will protest. (Not against me, of course, since they have no telescopes to read my writings; rather, against any of their own worldmates who write as I do; but let us ignore that.) They say –

> You have taken such pains to state our views in an austere and unfamiliar way! That is just a cheap trick to alienate the reader from something perfectly commonplace. He would know very well what the 'elements' and the 'selecting' of them are, if only you would give them their customary names.

Different other-worldly magicians would offer different suggestions about what the customary names are. Thereby they would remind us of different this-worldly nondescript ersatzist authors: for instance Plantinga, Stalnaker, van Inwagen, Slote,[11] Prior and Fine,[12] and Forrest. But I doubt that they would attach great importance to their disagreements with one another. They say –

> Elements are *states of affairs*, or *ways things might be*, or *possibilities*, or *propositions*, or *complex structural properties* (for short: *structures*) that might belong to the entire concrete world. Selected elements are states of affairs that *obtain*, or *ways things are*, or *realised* possibilities, or *true* propositions, or structures that the concrete world *has*. One state of affairs is *there being a talking donkey*, or one way things might be is *that there might be a talking donkey*, or one possibility is *that there be a talking donkey*, or one proposition is *that there is a talking donkey*, or one structure is *including a talking donkey*. Necessarily, iff there were a talking donkey, then that state of affairs would

[11] *Metaphysics and Essence*, pages 146–56.

[12] Their work raises further complications which I ignore when placing them in the company of the others listed. (1) Prior elsewhere suggests that his 'quantification' over propositions somehow carries no ontological commitment (*Objects of Thought*, pages 31–9). (2) Even if propositions exist, Prior and Fine suggest that some of them exist only contingently, because they involve individuals that exist contingently; and just as there might have been other individuals than there are, so there might have been other propositions. Then iterated modality cannot be quantification over ersatz worlds taken as maximally specific propositions that actually exist.

obtain, or that way things might be would be a way things are, or that possibility would be realised, or that proposition would be true, or that structure would be had by the concrete world. And what could be easier than that?

This seems to help, but I think it just covers up the problem. Yes, we have all those customary names: 'states of affairs', 'ways things might be', and the rest. We have no difficulty at all in using them correctly; or at least, we have thoroughly mastered a limited repertory of uses. Our use of the names associates them in the first instance with roles in our thought. I suppose it is a firm commitment of common sense that there are some entities or other that fill the roles, and therefore deserve the names. But that is not to say that we have much notion what sort of entities those are. We can toss the names around and never think what manner of entities we are talking about. Only when we want to improve on common sense, and get something more systematic and unified and definite, does the question arise. The entities that deserve the names are the entities best suited to fill the roles. To figure out what those are, we must survey the candidates according to our best systematic theory of what there is. It's no good saying: which are they? – why, they are the states of affairs! (Or the ways things might be, or . . . .) You might as well interrupt a serious discussion of how to cast a play and say: who shall be Polonius? – Let it be Polonius!

The magicians' protest is just like the bogus assistance we got in understanding the supposed internal relation of selection. We were told that the relevant intrinsic properties of the elements were such 'representational properties' as, for instance, the property of representing that a donkey talks. But we were none the wiser. For we saw that the property of representing that a donkey talks was none other than the property – we knew not what – that distinguishes the element such that, necessarily, it is selected iff a donkey talks. If at that point, we had been told that this element was called *there being a donkey that talks*, that also might have seemed helpful. But it would have been just as empty. The name is reserved for that which occupies a role. But it does not occupy the role just by bearing the name, any more than you can rule the world just by being named 'Donald'. The naming does nothing at all toward telling us what entity occupies the role, or how it manages to do what it must do to deserve the name. If I cannot see how something can do what it *must* do to deserve a name, it's no answer to be told that it just does; and it's no answer to be given a tendentious name for it that presupposes that it somehow does. If I cannot see how an abstract simple, for instance, could deserve the name 'state of affairs' or 'there being a talking donkey', because I don't see what we could have for a relation of selection, it's no answer just to stipulate that it is so named.

Understand that I am *not* opposed to states of affairs, ways things might be, possibilities, propositions, or structures. I believe in all those things. That is to say, I believe in entities that deserve the names because they are well suited to play the roles. The entities I put forward as candidates are the same in every case: sets of worlds. Worlds as *I* understand them: us and all our surroundings, and other things like that. The set of all and only those worlds that include a talking donkey as a part, for instance, is the state of affairs *there being a talking donkey*. This same set is also a way things might be, namely *that there might be a talking donkey*. It is also the possibility *that there be a talking donkey*. It is the proposition *that there is a talking donkey*. And it is the structure *including a talking donkey*. The concrete world – or rather, any concrete world – selects just those sets of worlds that have it as a member. That is what it is for a state of affairs to obtain, or for a way things might be to be a way things are, or for a possibility to be realised, or for a proposition to be true, or for a structure to be had – all relative to a given concrete world, ours or another.

I do not mean to wax monopolistic, claiming that sets of worlds are the *only* candidates suited to play the roles and deserve the names. Among the entities I am most committed to, possible individuals and set-theoretic constructions out of them, there are plenty of other candidates. It might even be, sometimes, that other candidates are preferable to the sets of worlds. For the roles associated with the names are by no means fully and uncontroversially settled. Sets of worlds are well suited to some versions of the roles, other constructions are better suited to other versions.

Recall, for instance, the versions of the proposition-role that we distinguished in section 1.5. If it is central to the conception you associate with 'proposition' that there should be some sort of quasi-syntactic structure, so that it makes sense to speak of subject–predicate propositions or negative or conjunctive or quantified propositions, then sets of worlds would not do; but there are more complicated set-theoretic constructions out of possible individuals that could serve instead. Or if it is crucial that 'propositions' should serve as contents of belief and desire, I would recommend not sets of possible worlds but sets of possible individuals.

Likewise there is room for different versions of 'ways things might be' or 'possibilities' or 'structures'. If you mean to include ways that something less than an entire world might be, then again you need sets of possible individuals. If part of the role you associate with these terms is a principle of identity of indiscernibles, you had better take not just any sets but only those that include both or neither of any pair of indiscernible individuals. If, on the other hand, you want to confine your attention to *maximal* 'ways', and you do not require guaranteed identity of indiscernibles, then you might as well replace unit sets by their sole members. If you associate with 'state of affairs' a role involving predication, I would recommend individual–property pairs, where the property in turn is taken as a set of possible individuals. And so on.

All this is a matter of fitting suitable entities to the various rather ill-defined roles that we rather indecisively associate with various familiar names. Don't think of it as a matter of discovering which entities *really are* the states of affairs, or the ways things might be, or the possibilities, or the propositions, or the structures!

Of course, these many candidates for the playing of roles and the deserving of names are not available to an ersatzer. *I* could construct excellent ersatz worlds in ever so many ways, drawing on the genuine worlds for raw material; but he who believes in one concrete world only has no use for any of these constructions.

When the ersatzer needs his own candidates to play the roles and deserve the names, let him introduce them to us properly. If he offers set-theoretic constructions out of the parts of the concrete world, on the linguistic plan, that is fair play. I have argued that the candidates so produced will be defective owing to false conflations, but maybe their defects are tolerable. And if he tells us about some other entities he believes in that he deems suited to the roles, that too is fair play – if he really does tell us about them. What is not fair is just to declare: the entities that play the roles are none other than the entities that play the roles! Or, equivalently: none other than the states of affairs, the ways things might be, the possibilities, the propositions, the structures.

If the magical ersatzer wants his 'customary names' for the elements, he can have them. I can still put my dilemma against him. He says these two simples are states of affairs; he says this one is *there being a talking donkey*, while that one is *there being a philosophising cat*. I ask: why is it that way around? What makes it so that the first, rather than the second, is rightly called by the name he gives it? What makes it so that the first, rather than the second, is the one such that, necessarily, it obtains iff there is a talking donkey? Does he say it is because of the distinctive intrinsic nature of the first? But the second has a distinctive nature too. And I cannot see how the distinctive nature of the first could have anything especially to do with talking donkeys. It's not as if the first consists in part of a talking donkey, or of the words 'talking donkey', or of something which could have been isomorphic to a talking donkey if only there had been one for it to be isomorphic to. To be a magician is exactly to renounce all such answers as these. Or does he say it is because of the distinctive necessary connections of the first? But why is it the first rather than the second that has those necessary connections? And how can anything have them?

And if it were an ersatz world, a maximal state of affairs that could not be named by any finite phrase, the dilemma would be no different. What makes this one, but not that one, be an ersatz world according to which a donkey talks? Is it a matter of distinctive intrinsic natures? What can the distinctive nature of a simple have to do with whether a donkey talks? Or is it a matter of how this one, as opposed to that, is hooked up in the network of necessary connections?

I must put my question by example: how is it represented that a donkey talks? Or schematically: how is it represented that so-and-so? I cannot put my question as a proper generalisation, else it might get a trifling answer. I cannot ask: what is it, in general, for proposition P to be true at ersatz world E? For then the magician might say (unless he is the sort who calls the elements themselves 'propositions') that just as I take propositions as sets of worlds, so he takes propositions as sets of ersatz worlds; and P is true at E iff E is a member of P. This gets us nowhere. A certain set of ersatz worlds is the proposition that a donkey talks rather than being, say, the proposition that a cat philosophises. What makes it so? – Having as members exactly those ersatz worlds which represent that a donkey talks. And which are those? – We are back to our previous problem. We have only taken it from singular to plural. It used to be: how does an ersatz world represent that a donkey talks? What makes this ersatz world be one according to which a donkey talks? Now it is: how do all and only these ersatz worlds represent that a donkey talks? What makes this set be the one that is the proposition that a donkey talks?

As yet, we have considered only magical ersatz worlds: abstract simples that can somehow be selected by the entire concrete world. As with other versions of ersatzism, we also need ersatz possible individuals. The individuals cannot be parts of the worlds, as happens in genuine modal realism or pictorial ersatzism, because our magical ersatz worlds are simples. Instead they must be further abstract entities, of a kind with the ersatz worlds, as happens in linguistic ersatzism.

The theories of ersatz worlds and ersatz individuals will be parallel. We have more elements, more abstract simples different from the ones considered before. Again, some of them are selected; but this time, elements are selected not by the entire concrete world but by various individuals that are parts of it. The selection of elements depends on what sort of individual does the selecting. Thus there are some elements that cannot be selected by any individual unless it is a talking donkey; and there is one such that, necessarily, it is selected by an individual iff that individual is a talking donkey. We take selection as a binary relation which each individual bears to the elements it selects. Element E implies element F iff, necessarily, any individual that selects E also selects F. Again, the elements taken under implication comprise a complete, atomic Boolean algebra. And in the algebra are maximal elements, not implied by other (non-null) elements. Necessarily, an individual selects one and only one maximal element; it also selects all elements implied by that maximal element. Every (non-null) element is implied by at least one maximal element, and can therefore be selected. So far, all is as before.

And now for something a little different: representing turns relational. An element E *represents* that individual X does so-and-so, or X does so-and-so *according to* E, iff, necessarily, if X selects E, then X does so-and-so. (I use 'does so-and-so' as schematic for an arbitrary predicate; it needn't have anything to do with activity.) This is how maximal elements, in particular, represent. The new maximal elements are the *ersatz individuals*.

As genuine possible individuals may be worldmates, so ersatz individuals may be ersatz worldmates. We can have this as a special case of something more general: call elements E and F *compatible* iff it is possible that there are individuals that select both E and F. (Not necessarily the same, not necessarily different, but both part of the one and only concrete world.)

There's no need to keep our new batch of elements distinct from the old batch; because there are some of our new elements that can be selected only by the entire concrete world – which is, after all, one big individual – and those ones may be identified with our old elements. We can say that an ersatz individual *inhabits* an ersatz world iff the two are compatible. End of theory.

The preliminary skirmishing goes just as before. And so does my principal dilemma. Is selecting an internal relation? – Then I think we have no conception of the 'representational properties' of the elements in virtue of which it obtains. And it's no help saying, for instance, that one element has *the property of representing as a talking donkey*, if all we can mean by that is that it has whatever intrinsic nature distinguishes the element such that, necessarily, it is selected by an individual iff that individual is a talking donkey. Is selecting an external relation? – Then how can it fail to be possible for the character of the selecting individual to vary independently of which elements it selects? One way there is magic in the ersatzer's supposed understanding of his primitive, the other way there is magic in the working of the primitive itself, and either way the theory is to be rejected.

Again I expect a magicians' protest. But this time, I think the other-worldly magical ersatzers will find themselves allied (if there can be such a thing as a trans-world alliance) with some this-worldly friends of the forms. For this time, after they say that there would have been no mystery if I had given the elements their customary names, they will say –

Elements are *properties*, or *ways a thing might be*, or *possibilities for an individual*. Elements selected by an individual are properties which that individual *has*, or *ways it is*, or possibilities it *realises*. One property is *being a talking donkey*, or one way a thing might be is *that it might be a talking donkey*, or one possibility for an individual is *that it be a talking donkey.* Necessarily, iff some individual is a talking donkey, then it would have that property, or that way a thing might be would be a way it is, or it would realise that possibility. And what could be easier than that?

The previous magicians' protest is subsumed if we say, as we well might, that to a state of affairs or a proposition there corresponds the property of being a concrete world wherein that state of affairs obtains or which makes that proposition true; that a way 'things' might be is better called a way the entire concrete world might be; that because the concrete world is a big individual, a possibility for it is a special case of a possibility for an individual; and that a complex structural property which might belong to the entire concrete world is just one kind of property among others.

My reply is as before. 'Property', and the rest, are names associated in the first instance with roles in our thought. It is a firm commitment of common sense that there are some entities or other that play the roles and deserve the names, but our practical mastery of uses of the names does not prove that we have much notion what manner of entities those are. That is a question for theorists. I believe in properties. That is, I have my candidates for entities to play the role and deserve the name. My principal candidates are sets of possible individuals. (But I can offer you alternatives – other set-theoretic constructions out of possible individuals – to suit different versions of the role. I can offer you entities with quasi-syntactic structure, if you like; or candidates for properties that are had to a degree, or relative to a time, or relative to a place – though I think it better to call such things 'relations'.) My candidates to play the role and deserve the name of properties are, of course, unavailable to the ersatzer. When he needs his own, let him introduce them properly. Set-theoretic constructions out of parts of the actual world are fair, suffer from false conflations, but might be good enough. If he tells us about some other entities he believes in that he deems suitable to play the role of properties, let him *really* tell us. It's unfair just to declare: the entities that play those roles are none other than the properties!

But all is not quite as before, because this time we have a red herring: what about universals? Or sets of duplicate tropes? I have granted that I find theories of universals or tropes intelligible, though I suspend judgement about their truth. What's more, universals would be in a sense abstract, though not according to the Negative Way, and at least some of them well might be simples; likewise for tropes. And universals or tropes would not be constructions out of the possible individuals that the ersatzer rejects. So here he has just what he needs to play the role and deserve the name of properties, and I am in no position to complain. – Not so. I insist once again: the theoretical roles we associate with various familiar names are by no means fully settled. In section 1.5, I distinguished various legitimate conceptions of properties; and in particular, I distinguished the roles of *abundant* versus *sparse* properties. What the ersatzer needs are candidates for the role of abundant properties. He needs enough of the maximal ones to serve as all the ersatz individuals, and then there are all the non-maximal ones besides. Universals, or sets of duplicate tropes, would never do as abundant properties – it is just absurd to think that an individual has all its countless abundant properties as non-spatiotemporal parts! They could be candidates only for the role of sparse properties.

So magical ersatzism is no better off for ersatz possible individuals in general than it is for ersatz possible worlds. If abstract simples are to serve as abundant properties, and in particular as the maximal ones that are the ersatz individuals, then we need a selection relation that individuals bear to these abstract simples, and we are not given the needed relation just by being told to call it 'having a property'.[13]

Now I can return to a piece of unfinished business from section 3.2. We were imagining a linguistic ersatzer who built his worldmaking language on the Lagadonian plan. I said his language was inadequate, because it had no words for natural properties alien to this world. He replied that the needful uninstantiated properties were part of this world, and he declared them one and all to be names of themselves. I wondered what he could mean by 'properties' and eliminated various candidates: my sets of possible individuals, abstractions from (non-Lagadonian) predicates, universals, sets of duplicate tropes. But I left it open that he might mean the sort of magical elements we have just been discussing. Now I have

---

[13]In asking how the selection relation could possibly work if abstract simples – abstract in the sense of the Negative Way – are supposed to play the role of properties, I have in part restated familiar arguments against properties understood as transcendent forms. Thus when I ask why, if the relation is external, it is impossible for the character of things to vary independently of the elements they select, I take this to be much the same point that Armstrong makes when he writes: 'Is it not clear that *a*'s whiteness is not determined by *a*'s relationship with a transcendent entity? Perform the usual thought-experiment and consider *a* without the Form of Whiteness. It seems obvious that *a* might still be white' (*Universals and Scientific Realism*, volume I, page 68). Armstrong imagines away the form itself: I leave the form and imagine away the thing's relationship to it, but otherwise the point is the same. As Armstrong says, and I agree, the force of the thought-experiment depends on the transcendence of the form. If unit charge is supposed to be a non-spatiotemporal part of the particle itself – an immanent universal rather than a transcendent form, therefore located and *not* abstract in the sense of the Negative Way – it would seem not in the least obvious that we could imagine away the unit charge and yet leave the particle as charged as ever. Nor, *pace* Armstrong (volume I, page 37), does the point apply to properties understood as sets; at least, not if they are sets of possible individuals, as I would have them. You cannot consider the thing in question to fall outside the set of all actual and possible white things, and leave it still white.

raised objections against that alternative as well. Properties understood as abundant abstract simples, instantiated by means of a relation that either cannot be understood unless by magic or else works by magical necessary connections, are no better as building blocks for a set-theoretic construction of ersatz worlds than they are for the more direct uses we have been considering. The position is a hybrid of linguistic and magical ersatzism. It avoids some of the disadvantages of the former by giving itself the worse disadvantages of the latter.

It is somewhat of an artificial exercise to evaluate magical ersatzism, since it is not at all clear that we have any theory here to evaluate. Still, if there *were* such a theory, how well might it meet the objections I have raised against linguistic and pictorial ersatzism?

Does it take modality as primitive? – Yes, overtly and abundantly. And if we take the version in which selection is an external relation, its primitive modality is of an especially repugnant sort: necessary connections where there ought to be independent variation.

Does it conflate indiscernible possibilities? – Perhaps. I see no reason why it should if selection is an external relation. If selection is an internal relation, however, there may well be a problem. If we had two elements with exactly the same 'representational properties', there is no way that one could be selected and the other not; so they would not be *alternative* possibilities. (Further, the mutual implication of the indiscernibles violates the assumption that we have a Boolean algebra. But no doubt that part of the theory is negotiable.)

Does it ignore or conflate possibilities involving alien natural properties? – I see no reason why it should.

Is its ontology more credible than my own? – It is certainly quite different. And we are told so little that incredulity cannot gain a foothold.

I suppose that is one way to gain credibility. It is not a good way.

4

Counterparts or Double Lives?

4.1 Good Questions and Bad

Peter van Inwagen has written that anyone who is rightly taught – that is, anyone who has read Plantinga –

> will see that there is no problem of trans-world identity. He will find that all attempts he knows of to formulate the supposed problem are either incoherent or else have such obvious 'solutions' that they do not deserve to be called problems. He will realize that it was all done with mirrors – that is, with empty words and confused pictures. There is, therefore, no longer any excuse for talking as if there were a 'problem of trans-world identity'. ('Plantinga on Trans-World Identity', page 101.)

Nevertheless, I shall devote the whole of this final chapter to the problem of trans-world identity.

Still, to a great extent I agree with van Inwagen's harsh judgement. Very often we do meet formulations that probably manifest confusion, and that are apt to cause it. I shall begin by separating questions. I think there are some good ones to be found, as well as the incoherent ones and the ones with uncontroversial 'solutions'.

The first thing to say is that our topic, like the Holy Roman Empire, is badly named; we may continue to use the customary name, but only if we are careful not to take it seriously. In the first place we should bear in mind that Trans-World Airlines is an intercontinental, but not as yet an interplanetary, carrier. More important, we should not suppose that we have here any problem about *identity*.

We never have. Identity is utterly simple and unproblematic. Everything is identical to itself; nothing is ever identical to anything else except itself. There is never any problem about what makes something identical to itself;

nothing can ever fail to be. And there is never any problem about what makes two things identical; two things never can be identical. There might be a problem about how to define identity to someone sufficiently lacking in conceptual resources – we note that it won't suffice to teach him certain rules of inference – but since such unfortunates are rare, even among philosophers, we needn't worry much if their condition is incurable.

We *do* state plenty of genuine problems in terms of identity. But we *needn't* state them so. Therefore they are not problems about identity. Is it ever so that an F is identical to a G? That is, is it ever so that the same thing is an F, and also a G? More simply, is it ever so that an F is a G? The identity drops out. Thus it is a good question whether a river is something you can bathe in twice; or whether a restaurant is something that can continue to exist through a simultaneous change in ownership and location and name; or whether numbers are von Neumann ordinals; or whether there is something that all charged particles have in common; or whether there could be a time traveller who meets his younger self; or whether there was ever a genuine nation that included both Austria and Hungary. All of these questions could be stated in terms of identity – harmlessly, unless that way of stating the questions confused us about where to seek for answers.

Likewise for the question whether worlds ever overlap; that is, whether two worlds ever have a common part; that is, whether any part of one world is ever part of another as well; that is, whether there is ever identity between parts of different worlds. This is a good question, but not a question about identity. Or rather, it is a good question for genuine modal realists; it makes little sense as a question for ersatzers. I consider this question in section 4.2, where I shall defend a qualified negative answer.

It is also a good question, but it is a different good question, whether there is anything that overlaps two different worlds, and so is in both in the way that a highway may be in two different states. Again, I could state it in terms of identity: is there ever identity between things that are (partly) in different worlds? Really it is not a question about identity, but about mereology: is there any reason to restrict mereological summation so that several things have a mereological sum only if all of them are parts of a single world? The follow-up question concerns semantics: if summation is unrestricted, so that indeed there are trans-world individuals, are these mere oddities? Are they nameless, do they fall outside the extensions of ordinary predicates and the domains of ordinary quantification? Or do they include things of importance to us, such as ourselves? I consider these questions in section 4.3, where I shall acknowledge the existence of trans-world individuals but dismiss them as oddities.

It is yet another good question, and this time it is a good question for genuine modal realists and ersatzers alike, whether it ever happens that anything exists according to two different (genuine or ersatz) worlds. If you like, I can state this question too in terms of identity: does it ever happen that something which exists according to one world and something which exists according to another are identical? The answer to that ought to be uncontroversial: yes, that very often happens. Take our worldmate Hubert Humphrey, for instance. The Humphrey who exists according to our world and the Humphrey who exists according to some other worlds are identical. (It is too bad that grammar demands the plural.) That is, Humphrey exists according to many different (genuine or ersatz) worlds. According to ours, he exists and he lost the presidential election; according to others, he exists and he won. This is a question that, as van Inwagen says, does not deserve to be called a problem.

But what *does* deserve to be called a problem is the follow-up question: what is it for Humphrey to exist according to a world? What is representation *de re*? How does a world, genuine or ersatz, represent, concerning Humphrey, that he exists? This one is *not* a question for genuine modal realists and ersatzers alike. Or rather, it is not *one* question for both. The available answers for genuine and for ersatz worlds will look quite different.

A genuine world might do it by having Humphrey himself as a part. That is how our own world represents, concerning Humphrey, that he exists. But for other worlds to represent in the same way that Humphrey exists, Humphrey would have to be a common part of many overlapping worlds, and somehow he would have to have different properties in different ones. I reject such overlap, for reasons to be considered shortly. There is a better way for a genuine world to represent, concerning Humphrey, that he exists. Humphrey may be represented *in absentia* at other worlds, just as he may be in museums in this world. The museum can have a waxwork figure to represent Humphrey, or better yet an animated simulacrum. Another world can do better still: it can have as part a Humphrey of its own, a flesh-and-blood counterpart of our Humphrey, a man very like Humphrey in his origins, in his intrinsic character, or in his historical role. By having such a part, a world represents *de re*, concerning Humphrey – that is, the Humphrey of our world, whom we as his worldmates may call simply Humphrey – that he exists and does thus-and-so. By waving its arm, the simulacrum in the museum represents Humphrey as waving his arm; by waving his arm, or by winning the presidential election, the other-worldly Humphrey represents the this-worldly Humphrey as waving or as winning. That is how it is that Humphrey – our Humphrey – waves or wins according to the other world. This is counterpart theory, the answer I myself favour to the question how a world represents *de re*.[1]

---

[1] See my 'Counterpart Theory and Quantified Modal Logic'; 'Counterparts of Persons

(The same goes in reverse. Our Humphrey is a counterpart of many Humphreys of many other worlds. I deny that the counterpart relation is always symmetrical, but surely it often is. So here are many other-worldly Humphreys who win the presidency, but who lose according to this world. They are represented as losing by the presence here of Humphrey the loser.)

There are various ways that an ersatz world might represent, concerning Humphrey, that he exists, or that he waves, or that he wins. It depends on what sort of ersatz world we are dealing with. A linguistic ersatz world might include English sentences that mention Humphrey by name: 'Humphrey exists', 'Humphrey waves', 'Humphrey wins'. Or it might include sentences of some other worldmaking language, which mention Humphrey by some other name. Or it might instead include sentences of the worldmaking language which say explicitly that there is someone of a certain description who exists, and waves, and wins; and this could qualify as representation *de re* concerning Humphrey if the description sufficiently resembles the description of Humphrey as he actually is. Or, instead of saying explicitly that there is someone of the appropriate description, a linguistic ersatz world might say it implicitly, by means of many sentences having to do with the vacancy or occupation of spacetime points, or with the instantiating of various elementary universals by various elementary particulars. A pictorial ersatz world might have a part which is a picture, made out of stuff that is in some mysterious sense abstract, of Humphrey waving and winning. A magical ersatz world might represent that Humphrey exists and waves and wins by having some ineffable distinctive intrinsic nature. Or it might do it by means of brute necessary connections: necessarily, if some simple element stands in some unanalysable relation to the concrete world then Humphrey exists and waves and wins.

It is sometimes thought that ersatzism is better off than counterpart theory in respecting certain intuitions: intuitions that *de re* modality has to do with the *res* itself, not some imitation or substitute or counterpart. Thus Kripke makes his famous complaint that on my view

> . . . if we say 'Humphrey might have won the election (if only he had done such-and-such),' we are not talking about something that might have happened to *Humphrey*, but to someone else, a 'counterpart'. Probably, however, Humphrey could not care less whether someone *else*, no matter how much resembling him, would have been victorious in another possible world. (*Naming and Necessity*, page 45.)

---

and Their Bodies'; and *Counterfactuals*, pages 39–43; also David Kaplan, 'Transworld Heir Lines'.

Coming from an advocate of genuine modal realism with overlap, this complaint might have some force. But here it comes only a page away from Kripke's equally famous remark that

> A possible world isn't a distant country that we are coming across, or viewing through a telescope. (Page 44.)

Joking aside (he does say that 'another possible world is too far away'), Kripke's point seems to be that we are supposed to respect Humphrey's intuition that it is *he himself* who would have been victorious in another world, and we are supposed to do this by declining to think of that other world as the sort of thing that he himself could even be part of! What is going on?

I think counterpart theorists and ersatzers are in perfect agreement that there are other worlds (genuine or ersatz) *according to* which Humphrey – he himself! (stamp the foot, bang the table) – wins the election. And we are in equal agreement that Humphrey – he himself – is not *part* of these other worlds. Somehow, perhaps by containing suitable constituents or perhaps by magic, but anyhow not by containing Humphrey himself, the other world represents him as winning. If there were any genuine modal realists who believed in overlap of worlds, they would indeed be in a position to insist that at another world we have Humphrey himself winning the presidency. That might indeed be a point in their favour. But it is not a point in favour of any other view but theirs, and in particular it is not a point in favour of any kind of ersatzism.

Counterpart theory does say (and ersatzism does not) that someone else – the victorious counterpart – enters into the story of how it is that another world represents Humphrey as winning, and thereby enters into the story of how it is that Humphrey might have won. Insofar as the intuitive complaint is that someone else gets into the act, the point is rightly taken. But I do not see why that is any objection, any more than it would be an objection against ersatzism that some abstract whatnot gets into the act. What matters is that the someone else, or the abstract whatnot, should not crowd out Humphrey himself. And there all is well. Thanks to the victorious counterpart, Humphrey himself has the requisite modal property: we can truly say that *he* might have won. There is no need to deny that the victorious counterpart also makes true a second statement describing the very same possibility: we can truly say that a Humphrey-like counterpart might have won. The two statements are not in competition. Therefore we need not suppress the second (say, by forbidding any mixture of ordinary modal language with talk of counterparts) in order to safeguard the first.[2]

---

[2] Here I am indebted to Mondadori; see his 'Counterpartese, Counterpartese*, Counterpartese_D.' But I disagree with him at one point. He grants that I may truly say

I said that counterpart theory and ersatzism are alike in denying that Humphrey himself is part of the other world which represents him as winning. But that was a little too quick. Counterpart theory and ersatzism are also alike in having trick ways to dodge the conclusion. In both cases there is a loophole to exploit, but exploiting the loophole does nothing to satisfy the alleged intuition that it must be Humphrey himself who wins. For the counterpart theorist, the trick is to say that 'Humphrey' names not the Humphrey of our world, and not the Humphrey of another, but rather the trans-world individual who is the mereological sum of all these local Humphreys. If that is what Humphrey is (but I shall argue in section 4.3 that it isn't), then indeed he himself is partly in this world and partly in that and not wholly in any. Part of him loses and part of him wins. But presumably the losing part cares what might have happened to *it*; it could not care less what happens to some *other* slice off the same great salami – unless, of course, the world containing that other-worldly slice of Humphrey can be taken as a world that represents the this-worldly slice as winning.

For the ersatzer (of the linguistic persuasion) the trick is to remember that anything you please can serve as a word of the worldmaking language. Humphrey might as well be used as his own name, in Lagadonian fashion. Then he will be, if not a part, at least a set-theoretic constituent of the ersatz world which is a set of sentences saying *inter alia* that he wins. So what? Presumably he could not care less what words of what languages are assembled with him into what set-theoretic structures – unless, of course, we get a linguistic structure that represents him as winning. Let him by all means care how he can be consistently represented, but not about the words of the representation. It is perfectly arbitrary whether he serves as a word. And if he does, it is perfectly arbitrary what he means. If Humphrey is to be made a word, there is no need to make him be his own name. He would do just as well as a name for Checkers, or as a preposition or adverb. Or he could be the negation sign in a sentence that denies his existence.

There are at least two more good questions that can be extracted from the topic of trans world identity, though again they have nothing special to do with identity. I merely state these questions here; I shall take them

---

that Humphrey himself might have won; but then he insists that if we ask 'who would have had the property of *winning*,' my answer must be 'not Humphrey, but one of his counterparts' (page 81). Not so. The modal predicate 'would have had the property of winning' is on a par with the modal predicate 'might have won'. I can apply either predicate in one sense to Humphrey, in another sense to the victorious counterpart. If there is an objection to be raised, it must be that I *can* say *un*wanted things, not that I *cannot* say *wanted* things. I reply that the unwanted things are not seriously objectionable in the way that lack of the wanted things would be.

up in sections 4.4 and 4.5. Again they are questions for genuine modal realists and ersatzers alike. For the sake of neutrality, I shall formulate them in terms of representation *de re*; that is, in terms of truth according to a world, genuine or ersatz, concerning some actual individual such as Humphrey.

One is the question of haecceitism. We can distinguish representation of the way things are qualitatively (in a broad sense of that world) from representation *de re*. It may be the case according to a world that there are things of certain kinds, arranged in certain ways, and with certain causal relationships; these are matters of qualitative character. But also it may be the case, according to a world, concerning the individual Humphrey, that he exists and waves and wins. Can these two kinds of representation vary independently? Or does what a world represents concerning matters of qualitative character determine what that world represents *de re*?

The other is the question of constancy. Do we have a settled answer, fixed once and for all, about what is true concerning a certain individual according to a certain (genuine or ersatz) world? Or can different answers be right in different contexts? Can two opposed answers even be right together, in a single context? Can it happen sometimes that no answer is determinately right?

4.2 Against Overlap

The simplest way that part of another world could represent Humphrey – our Humphrey – is by identity. He might lead a double life, in two worlds at once. He himself, who is part of the actual world, might be part of the other world as well. He could be a common part of both, in the same way that a shared hand might be a common part of two Siamese twins. The other world represents him as existing because he is part of it. He exists at the other world because, restricting our quantification to the parts of that world, he exists. This leading of double lives is what best deserves to be called 'trans-world identity'.

I cannot name one single philosopher who favours trans-world identity, thus understood. The philosophers' chorus on behalf of 'trans-world identity' is merely insisting that, for instance, it is Humphrey himself who might have existed under other conditions, who might have been different, who might have won the presidency, who exists according to many worlds and wins according to some of them. All that is uncontroversial. The controversial question is *how* he manages to have these modal properties. The answer now mooted is that he has them by being a shared part common to many worlds, and by having different properties relative to different worlds that he is part of. Despite its lack of supporters, this answer deserves our attention. First, because it is agreeably simple. Second, because it is the only view that fully respects the 'he himself' intuition: rival views say that Humphrey himself *might* have won, and that he himself is somehow *represented* as winning, but only this view says that he himself *does* win. And third, because it is congenial to haecceitism; but I shall postpone that issue to section 4.4.

The advantages are genuine. Nevertheless trans-world identity, in the sense of overlap of worlds, is to be rejected. Or rather, it is to be rejected as a general theory of representation *de re*. There are one or two special cases of overlap that might be tolerated, but they fall far short of meeting all our needs for representation *de re.*

My main problem is not with the overlap itself. Things do have shared parts in common, as in the case of the Siamese twins' hand. Given the unrestricted mereology I favour, sharing of parts is altogether commonplace. Indeed, any part of any world is part of countless mereological sums that extend beyond that world. But what I do find problematic – inconsistent, not to mince words – is the way the common part of two worlds is supposed to have different properties in one world and in the other.

Hubert Humphrey has a certain size and shape, and is composed of parts arranged in a certain way. His size and shape and composition are intrinsic to him. They are simply a matter of the way he is. They are not a matter of his relations to other things that surround him in this world. Thereby they differ from his extrinsic properties such as being popular, being Vice-President of the United States, wearing a fur hat, inhabiting a planet with a moon, or inhabiting a world where nothing goes faster than light. Also, his size and shape and composition are accidental, not essential, to him. He could have been taller, he could have been slimmer, he could have had more or fewer fingers on his hands.[3]

Consider the last. He could have had six fingers on his left hand. There is some other world that so represents him. We are supposing now that representation *de re* works by trans-world identity. So Humphrey, who is part of this world and here has five fingers on the left hand, is also part of some other world and there has six fingers on his left hand. *Qua* part of this world he has five fingers, *qua* part of that world he has six. He himself – one and the same and altogether self-identical – has five fingers on the left hand, and he has not five but six. How can this be? You might as well say that the shared hand of the Siamese twins has five fingers as Ted's left hand, but it has six fingers as Ned's right hand! That is

---

[3]The next several paragraphs are mostly adapted from my 'Individuation by Acquaintance and by Stipulation', pages 21–2, with the kind permission of the editors of *The Philosophical Review*.

double-talk and contradiction. Here is the hand. Never mind what else it is part of. How many fingers does it have? What shape is it?

(You might say that five fingers and the palm are common to Ted and Ned, however the sixth finger belongs to Ned alone; and likewise with Humphrey. But no: a proper five-fingered hand differs in shape and composition from a proper six-fingered hand less one of its fingers, and likewise a proper six-fingered hand differs from a proper five-fingered hand with an extra finger stuck on.)

I expect protest: though it would be contradiction to say, simply, that Humphrey had five fingers on the left hand and also that he had not five but six, that is *not* what was said. He has five *at this world*; he has six *at that world*. – But how do the modifiers help? There are several ways for modifiers to remove a contradiction. But none of them apply here.

(1) If a tower is square on the third floor and round on the fourth floor, no worries; it's just that one segment differs in cross-sectional shape from another. The modifiers direct us to consider the shapes of the segments, not of the whole tower. But the thesis we are considering is that the *whole* of Humphrey is part of different worlds, with different properties at different ones. It is exactly the trans-world identity that spoils this way out.

(2) If a man is honest according to the *News* and crooked according to the *Times*, no worries; different papers tell different stories about him, they represent him differently, and at least one of them gets it wrong. But the thesis we are considering is a form of genuine, not ersatz, modal realism: the way that Humphrey has a property according to a world is that Humphrey himself, having that very property, is a part of that world.

(3) If a man is father of Ed and son of Fred, no worries; he bears different relations to different individuals, and the extrinsic properties he thereby has – being a father, being a son – are compatible. Likewise if the wisest man in the village is by no means the wisest man in the nation. But our problem does not concern Humphrey's relationships to the things that accompany him in one or another world. Rather, we are dealing with his intrinsic nature; and the only relations relevant to that are those that obtain between his own parts. (And if he is part of two worlds, so in turn are his parts.) If you say that Humphrey has five fingers at this world and six fingers at that, and you take the modifiers to cure the contradiction, most likely you mean to suggest that having five or six fingers is not an intrinsic property after all, but a relation. (And an external relation – not one that supervenes on the intrinsic properties of the *relata*.) Then the right thing to say would be that Humphrey bears the five-finger relation to this world and the six-finger relation to that world. Or you might say it by coining transitive verbs: he five-fingers this world, but he six-fingers that world. But what are these relations? I know what to say if I want

to make believe formally that shapes are relations rather than intrinsic properties, but I know better. If you say that a shape – sphericality, or five-fingeredness – is just what we always thought it was, except that it is a relation which something may bear to some but not all of the wholes of which it is part, that will not do. What would it be to five-finger one thing while six-fingering another? How can these supposed relations be the shape of something?

They cannot be; and so there is no solution. If indeed Humphrey – he himself, the whole of him – is to lead a double life as part of two different worlds, there is no intelligible way for his intrinsic properties to differ from one world to the other. And it will not do just to declare, when we know better, that such things as his size and shape and composition are after all not among his intrinsic properties.

Call this *the problem of accidental intrinsics*. It would not arise for Humphrey's essential properties, however intrinsic. For the problem is how he can have different properties as part of different worlds, and in the case of essential properties there is no variation to worry about. It is very hard to see how Humphrey could be a man as part of one world and an angel as part of another, but if he is essentially human that difficulty does not arise.

Neither would it arise for Humphrey's extrinsic properties, however accidental. There are two ways to think of his extrinsic properties: as relations in disguise, or as genuine properties. (See my discussion in section 1.5 of 'properties' that are had relative to this or that.) First, take them as relations. He is related to his surroundings, and we are not supposing that his surroundings also are common from world to world. Perhaps he owns four dogs who are part of this world, and he owns only three dogs who are part of that other world. That is how the accidental extrinsic 'property' of owning four dogs can be a property that he has at this world, but lacks at that other world of which he is also a part. Owning four dogs is covertly a relation: Humphrey bears it to the worlds that have himself and four dogs he owns as parts, and not to any other worlds. It is as easy for him to have this 'property' at one world and not another as it is for a man to be father of Ed and not of Fred.

Second, take his extrinsic properties instead as genuine properties. Then he has them *simpliciter*, and they cannot vary from world to world. But what can vary from world to world is the way we name them, and predicate them of him – which may give an illusion that the properties themselves vary. Thus he has, *simpliciter*, the extrinsic property of owning four dogs who are part of this world; and he has, *simpliciter*, the property of not owning four dogs who are part of that world. These properties are compatible, if indeed there is overlap; having both of them is part of what it is to lead a double life in two worlds. But the restricting modifier 'at this world' or 'at that world' enables us to refer to these two extrinsic properties by shortened names. In the scope of 'at this world', we can drop the final clause from the name 'the property of owning four dogs who are part of this world'; and in the scope of 'at that world' we can likewise drop the final clause from the name 'the property of not owning four dogs who are part of that world'; and that is how it can be true at this world that he has the property of owning four dogs, and true at that world that he has the property of not owning four dogs, although his extrinsic properties – properties rightly speaking, as opposed to disguised relations – do not vary from world to world.

There is no problem of accidental intrinsics for rival theories. Not for my own theory, genuine modal realism with counterparts instead of overlap: counterparts need not be exact intrinsic duplicates, so, of course, Humphrey and his counterparts can differ in their intrinsic properties. Not for the theory that Humphrey is a vast trans-world individual, composed of distinct parts from different worlds: one part of the vast Humphrey can differ in its intrinsic properties from other parts. Not for any sort of ersatzism: in whatever way it is that ersatz worlds represent or misrepresent Humphrey, they can misrepresent him as having intrinsic properties that in fact he does not have, just as lying newspapers can do.

Our question of overlap of worlds parallels the this-worldly problem of identity through time; and our problem of accidental intrinsics parallels a problem of temporary intrinsics, which is the traditional problem of change.[4] Let us say that something *persists* iff, somehow or other, it exists at various times; this is the neutral word. Something *perdures* iff it persists by having different temporal parts, or stages, at different times, though no one part of it is wholly present at more than one time; whereas it *endures* iff it persists by being wholly present at more than one time. Perdurance corresponds to the way a road persists through space; part of it is here and part of it is there, and no part is wholly present at two different places. Endurance corresponds to the way a universal, if there are such things, would be wholly present wherever and whenever it is instantiated. Endurance involves overlap: the content of two different times has the enduring thing as a common part. Perdurance does not.

(There might be mixed cases: entities that persist by having an enduring part and a perduring part. An example might be a person who consisted of an enduring entelechy ruling a perduring body; or an electron that had a universal of unit negative charge as a permanent part, but did not consist entirely of universals. But here I ignore the mixed cases. And when I speak of ordinary things as perduring, I shall ignore their enduring universals, if such there be.)

[4]My discussion of this parallel problem is much indebted to Armstrong, 'Identity Through Time', and to Johnston. I follow Johnston in terminology.

Discussions of endurance versus perdurance tend to be endarkened by people who say such things as this: 'Of course you are wholly present at every moment of your life, except in case of amputation. For at every moment all your parts are there: your legs, your lips, your liver . . . .' These endarkeners may think themselves partisans of endurance, but they are not. They are perforce neutral, because they lack the conceptual resources to understand what is at issue. Their speech betrays – and they may acknowledge it willingly – that they have no concept of a temporal part. (Or at any rate none that applies to a person, say, as opposed to a process or a stretch of time.) Therefore they are on neither side of a dispute about whether or not persisting things are divisible into temporal parts. They understand neither the affirmation nor the denial. They are like the people – fictional, I hope – who say that the whole of the long road is in their little village, for not one single lane of it is missing. Meaning less than others do by 'part', since they omit parts cut crosswise, they also mean less than others do by 'whole'. They say the 'whole' road is in the village; by which they mean that every 'part' is; but by that, they only mean that every part cut lengthwise is. Divide the road into its least lengthwise parts; they cannot even raise the question whether those are in the village wholly or only partly. For that is a question about crosswise parts, and the concept of a crosswise part is what they lack. Perhaps 'crosswise part' really does sound to them like a blatant contradiction. Or perhaps it seems to them that they understand it, but the village philosophers have persuaded them that really they couldn't, so their impression to the contrary must be an illusion. At any rate, *I* have the concept of a temporal part; and for some while I shall be addressing only those of you who share it.[5]

Endurance through time is analogous to the alleged trans-world identity of common parts of overlapping worlds; perdurance through time is analogous to the 'trans-world identity', if we may call it that, of a trans-world individual composed of distinct parts in non-overlapping worlds. Perdurance, which I favour for the temporal case, is closer to the counterpart theory which I favour for the modal case; the difference is that counterpart theory concentrates on the parts and ignores the trans-world individual composed of them.

The principal and decisive objection against endurance, as an account of the persistence of ordinary things such as people or puddles, is the problem of temporary intrinsics. Persisting things change their intrinsic properties. For instance shape: when I sit, I have a bent shape; when I stand, I have a straightened shape. Both shapes are temporary intrinsic

---

[5] I attempt to explain it to others in *Philosophical Papers*, volume I, pages 76–7. But I have no great hopes, since any competent philosopher who does not understand something will take care not to understand anything else whereby it might be explained.

properties; I have them only some of the time. How is such change possible? I know of only three solutions.

(It is *not* a solution just to say how very commonplace and indubitable it is that we have different shapes at different times. To say that is only to insist – rightly – that it must be possible somehow. Still less is it a solution to say it in jargon – as it might be, that bent-on-Monday and straight-on-Tuesday are compatible because they are 'time-indexed properties' – if that just means that, somehow, you can be bent on Monday and straight on Tuesday.)

First solution: contrary to what we might think, shapes are not genuine intrinsic properties. They are disguised relations, which an enduring thing may bear to times. One and the same enduring thing may bear the bent-shape relation to some times, and the straight-shape relation to others. In itself, considered apart from its relations to other things, it has no shape at all. And likewise for all other seeming temporary intrinsics; all of them must be reinterpreted as relations that something with an absolutely unchanging intrinsic nature bears to different times. The solution to the problem of temporary intrinsics is that there aren't any temporary intrinsics. This is simply incredible, if we are speaking of the persistence of ordinary things. (It might do for the endurance of entelechies or universals.) If we know what shape is, we know that it is a property, not a relation.

Second solution: the only intrinsic properties of a thing are those it has at the present moment. Other times are like false stories; they are abstract representations, composed out of the materials of the present, which represent or misrepresent the way things are. When something has different intrinsic properties according to one of these ersatz other times, that does not mean that it, or any part of it, or anything else, just *has* them – no more so than when a man is crooked according to the *Times*, or honest according to the *News*. This is a solution that rejects endurance; because it rejects persistence altogether. And it is even less credible than the first solution. In saying that there are no other times, as opposed to false representations thereof, it goes against what we all believe. No man, unless it be at the moment of his execution, believes that he has no future; still less does anyone believe that he has no past.

Third solution: the different shapes, and the different temporary intrinsics generally, belong to different things. Endurance is to be rejected in favour of perdurance. We perdure; we are made up of temporal parts, and our temporary intrinsics are properties of these parts, wherein they differ one from another. There is no problem at all about how different things can differ in their intrinsic properties.

Some special cases of overlap of worlds face no problem of accidental intrinsics. One arises on the hypothesis that there are universals, wholly present recurrently as non-spatiotemporal parts of all their particular instances. If so, these universals must recur as freely between the worlds as they do within a world. For there is qualitative duplication between the worlds, by the principle of recombination; and universals are supposed to recur whenever there is duplication. Doubtless there are electrons in other worlds than ours. If a universal of unit negative charge is part of each and every this-worldly electron, then equally it is part of the other-worldly electrons; in which case, since parthood is transitive, it is a common part of all the worlds where there are electrons; and that is overlap. We expect trouble with the accidental intrinsic properties of the common part. But what are those properties in this case? I cannot think of any. There isn't much to the intrinsic nature of a universal. Maybe it's intrinsically simple, or maybe it's intrinsically composed, somehow, of other universals; but if so, that seems to be an essential matter, so we still have no intrinsic accidents to trouble us. (Likewise these seem to be no temporary intrinsics to trouble us, so there is no problem about universals enduring through time.) If indeed there are no accidental intrinsics to raise a problem, then overlap confined to the sharing of universals seems entirely innocent. And also it seems inevitable, if there are universals at all. So my rejection of overlap must be qualified: whatever the universals may do, at any rate no two worlds have any particular as a common part.

If there are universals, identical between worlds as they are between instances within a world, then for them we may as well help ourselves to the simplest method of representation *de re*: what is true of a universal according to a world is what is true of *it*, when we restrict quantifiers to that world. What is true of it at a world will then be, first, that it has its constant essential intrinsic nature; and, second, that it has various relationships – notably, patterns of instantiation – to other things of that world. For instance it will be true of unit negative charge, at one world, that it is instantiated by exactly seventeen things, which are close together; and at another world, that it is instantiated by infinitely many widely scattered things. Thus its extrinsic 'properties', taken as disguised relations, vary. Its extrinsic properties, properly speaking, do not. But the way we name them does, so that for instance we can say that at one world but not the other, the universal has the property of being instantiated by seventeen close-together things.[6]

[6]A universal can safely be part of many worlds because it hasn't any accidental intrinsics. But mightn't the same be said of some simple particulars – tropes, if such there be, or fundamental particles, or momentary slices thereof? Maybe these things have no accidental intrinsic properties – it certainly seems hard to think of plausible candidates. If they haven't, then they too could safely be shared between overlapping worlds. We would not face a problem of accidental intrinsics. But I suggest that we would face a parallel problem of accidental external relations. Suppose we have a pair of two of these simple

Another special case of overlap would be, if not altogether innocent, at least safe from the problem of accidental intrinsics. This is simply the case in which something does have accidental intrinsic properties, but they are constant within a limited range of worlds, and the proposed overlap is confined to the worlds in that limited range. Such limited overlap could not give us all we need by way of representation *de re*. For the thing does have some accidental intrinsic properties; so there must be some world which represents it as lacking some of these properties; that must be a world outside the limited range of overlap; so when that world represents the thing as lacking the properties, that representation *de re* must work not by trans-world identity but in some other way. Limited overlap would have to be combined with some other treatment of representation *de re*, presumably some form of counterpart theory.

Even so, limited overlap might be wanted. The most likely case would be limited overlap when branching worlds share a common inital segment. I distinguish *branching* of worlds from *divergence*. In branching, worlds are like Siamese twins. There is one initial spatiotemporal segment; it is continued by two different futures – different both numerically and qualitatively – and so there are two overlapping worlds. One world consists of the initial segment plus one of its futures; the other world consists of the identical initial segment plus the other future.

In divergence, on the other hand, there is no overlap. Two worlds have two duplicate initial segments, not one that they share in common. I, and the world I am part of, have only one future. There are other worlds that diverge from ours. These worlds have initial segments exactly like that of our world up to the present, but the later parts of these worlds differ from the later parts of ours. (Or we could make it relativistic: what is duplicated is the past cone from some spacetime point, as it might be from here and now.) Not I, but only some very good counterparts of me, inhabit these other worlds.

I reject genuine branching in favour of divergence. However there might

---

particulars A and B, both of which are common parts of various worlds. A and B are a certain distance apart. Their distance, it seems, is a relation of A and B and nothing else – it is not really a three-place relation of A, B, and this or that world. That means that A and B are precisely the same distance apart in all the worlds they are both part of. That means (assuming that we explain representation *de re* in terms of trans-world identity when we can) that it is impossible that A and B should both have existed and been a different distance apart. That seems wrong: it is hard to suppose that the distance is essential to the pair, equally hard to suppose that distance is not the plain two-place relation that it seems to be. So trans-world identity, even for simple particulars without accidental intrinsic properties, is *prima facie* trouble. An advocate of it will have some explaining to do, both as to how he gets around the problem of accidental external relations, and also as to what motivates it when it cannot provide a fully general account of representation *de re*. Such explaining may be found in Johnston, *Particulars and Persistence*, chapter 4.

be some reason to go the other way. Consider the philosophers who say that the future is unreal. It is hard to believe they mean it. If ever anyone is right that there is no future, then that very moment is his last, and what's more is the end of everything. Yet when these philosophers teach that there is no more time to come, they show no trace of terror or despair! When we see them planning and anticipating, we might suspect that they believe in the future as much as anyone else does. Maybe they only insist on restricting their quantifiers, and all they mean is that nothing future is present? – No, for they seem to think that what they are saying is controversial. What is going on?

Perhaps their meaning is clearer when they turn linguistic, and say that there is no determinate truth about the future. A modal realist who believed in genuine branching, in which his world overlaps with others by having initial segments in common, could agree with that. To have determinate truth about the future, it helps to have a future; but also, it helps to have only one future. If there are two futures, and both are equally mine with nothing to choose between them, and one holds a sea fight and the other doesn't, what could it mean for me to say that *the* future holds a sea fight? Not a rhetorical question: we have three options. (1) It is false that the future holds a sea fight; because 'the future' is a denotationless improper description. (2) It is true that the future holds a sea fight; because 'the future' denotes neither of the two partial futures but rather their disunited sum, which does hold a sea fight. (3) It is neither true nor false that the future holds a sea fight; because 'the future' has indeterminate denotation, and we get different truth values on different resolutions of the indeterminacy. Offhand, the third option – indeterminacy – seems best. (At least it lets us talk in the ordinary way about matters on which the futures do not differ; what has the same truth value on all resolutions is determinately true or false.) But whichever way we go, our customary thought about 'the' future is in bad trouble. Against the common sense idea that we have one single future, advocates of many may join forces with advocates of none; but the advocates of many have the better of it, for they have no cause to despair. I do not suggest that philosophers of the unreal or indeterminate future are, in fact, modal realists who accept branching. But modal realists can make good sense of much that they say. So whatever motivates these philosophers to deny that we have a single future might equally motivate a modal realist to accept branching.

Why not, given that the overlap is limited enough not to raise the problem of accidental intrinsics? Well, one man's reason is another man's *reductio*. The trouble with branching exactly is that it conflicts with our ordinary presupposition that we have a single future. If two futures are equally mine, one with a sea fight tomorrow and one without, it is nonsense to wonder which way it will be – it will be both ways – and yet

I do wonder. The theory of branching suits those who think this wondering *is* nonsense. Or those who think the wondering makes sense only if reconstrued: you have leave to wonder about the sea fight, provided that really you wonder not about what tomorrow will bring but about what today predetermines. But a modal realist who thinks in the ordinary way that it makes sense to wonder what *the* future will bring, and who distinguishes this from wondering what is already predetermined, will reject branching in favour of divergence. In divergence also there are many futures; that is, there are many later segments of worlds that begin by duplicating initial segments of our world. But in divergence, only one of these futures is truly ours. The rest belong not to us but to our other-worldly counterparts. Our future is the one that is part of the same world as ourselves. It alone is connected to us by the relations – the (strictly or analogically) spatiotemporal relations, or perhaps natural external relations generally – that unify a world. It alone is influenced causally by what we do and how we are in the present. We wonder which one is the future that has the special relation to ourselves. We care about it in a way that we do not care about all the other-worldly futures. Branching, and the limited overlap it requires, are to be rejected as making nonsense of the way we take ourselves to be related to our futures; and divergence without overlap is to be preferred.[7]

There is a less weighty argument against branching, and indeed against overlap generally. What unifies a world, I suggested, is that its parts stand in suitable external relations, preferably spatiotemporal. But if we have overlap, we have spatiotemporal relations between the parts of different worlds. For instance, let P be the common part – say, a shared initial segment – of two different worlds W_1 and W_2, let R_1 be the remainder of W_1, and let R_2 be the remainder of W_2. Then the appropriate unifying relations obtain between P and R_1, and also between P and R_2. But now the relations obtain between parts of two different worlds: between P, which is *inter alia* a part of the world W_1, and R_2, which is part of the different world W_2.

Of course it is also true that P and R_2 are parts of a single world W_2. So at least we can still say that whenever two things are appropriately related, there is some world they are both parts of, even if they may be parts of other worlds besides. Or can we say even that? In a sense, even R_1 and R_2 are related, in a stepwise back-and-forward way, via P. For instance, R_1 and R_2 might stand to one another in the complex temporal relation: successor-of-a-predecessor-of. Yet R_1 and R_2 are not both parts

---

[7]In his 'Theories of Actuality', Adams makes the same point; but while I use it in favour of modal realism without overlap, Adams uses it in favour of ersatzism.

of any one world. Thus overlap complicates what we must say in explaining how worlds are unified by spatiotemporal interrelation, and thereby differ from trans-world individuals composed of parts of several worlds. The complication is unwelcome, but I think it's nothing worse. Overlap spoils the easiest account of how worlds are unified by interrelation: namely, the mereological analogue of the definition of equivalence classes. But alternative accounts are available (as in the parallel problem about time discussed in my 'Survival and Identity'), so I presume that a modal realist who wished to accept overlap would not be in serious difficulty on this score. Still less is there any problem if the only overlap we accept is the sharing of universals; we need only say that a world is unified by the spatiotemporal (or whatever) interrelation of its *particular* parts.

If we stay with the simple account of how worlds are unified, we will conclude that where there is branching, there is one single world composed of all the branches. That would not be branching *of* worlds, but branching *within* worlds; and so the overlap of branches would not be overlap of worlds. Branching within worlds, I think, is to be accepted: it is possible that the spacetime of a world might have such a shape, and if that is a possible way for a world to be then it is a way that some world is. Some world; but there is no reason to think that such a world is ours. Respect for common sense gives us reason to reject any theory that says that we ourselves are involved in branching, or that if we are not, that can only be because (contrary to accepted theory) our world is governed by deterministic laws. But we needn't reject the very possibility that a world branches. The unfortunate inhabitants of such a world, if they think of 'the future' as we do, are of course sorely deceived, and their peculiar circumstances do make nonsense of how they ordinarily think. But that is their problem; not ours, as it would be if the worlds generally branched rather than diverging.

I noted that our special cases of trans-world identity, sharing of universals and sharing of initial segments in branching, avoid the problem of accidental intrinsics. They avoid another well-known problem as well. A friend of overlap might wish to say that trans-world identity follows lines of qualitative similarity. Or he might not; whether to say this is part of the topic of haecceitism, to be considered in section 4.4. But if he does, his problem is that identity is transitive, similarity in general is not. But it is *approximate* similarity that fails to be transitive; whereas the supposed sharing of universals, and likewise the supposed sharing of initial segments in branching, would follow lines of *exact* similarity. When we have the exact similarity in a respect between two instances of unit negative charge, or the perfect match when two worlds start out exactly alike in their history, there is no discrepancy of formal character to stop us from taking these as cases of trans-world identity.

4.3   *Against Trans-World Individuals*

The Hume Highway runs between the capital cities of two adjacent states. Thus it is present in one state and in the other. Call this a case of 'interstate identity' if you like: a highway that runs through one state is identical with a highway that runs through the other, there is one highway that runs through them both. But the states do not overlap thereby; they share no (particular) part in common. The highway consists of parts, one part in one state and another in the other. It is partly in each state. The parts are not identical; they don't even overlap. But the highway which includes the one part is identical with the highway which includes the other. More simply: there is a highway they are both parts of.

Likewise Hume (no relation) runs between 1711 and 1776. He is present in the early half of the century and in the later half. Call this a case of 'identity over time' if you like: a man who runs through the early years is identical with a man who runs through the later years, there is one man who lives both early and late. But the times do not overlap thereby; they share no (particular) part in common. Hume consists of parts, different parts in different times. He is partly in each of the times during his life. The parts of him are not identical; they don't even overlap. But the man which includes one part is identical with the man which includes the other. More simply: there is a man they are both parts of.

Or so say I. (And he.) Of course this account of Hume's perdurance through time is controversial; many would favour the view that he endures, wholly present at every time of his life, so that those times do overlap by having him as a shared part. That would be 'identity over time' in a truer sense. Such endurance may appeal to intuition, but – so I argued in the previous section – it creates a disastrous problem about Hume's temporary intrinsic properties. The enduring Hume, multiply located in time, turns out to be intrinsically shapeless; he bent-shapes one time, he straight-shapes another, but these relations are no part of the way he is, considered in himself. I call that a *reductio*. Likewise 'trans-world identity' in the truest sense – overlap of worlds – creates a disastrous problem about the accidental intrinsic properties of the alleged common parts. But when we therefore reject overlap of worlds, we need not reject trans-world identity in the lesser sense which corresponds to the interstate identity of the Hume Highway or to (what I take to be) the identity over time of Hume.

I shall argue that indeed there are things that enjoy trans-world identity in this sense. But then I shall argue that we ourselves, and other things that we ordinarily name, or classify under predicates, or quantify over, are not among them. So I oppose trans-world individuals not by denying their existence – not when I quantify without restriction – but rather by denying that they deserve our attention.

I do not deny the existence of trans-world individuals, and yet there is a sense in which I say that they cannot possibly exist. As should be expected, the sense in question involves restricted quantification. (See the discussion of restricting modifiers in section 1.2.) It is possible for something to exist iff it is possible for the whole of it to exist. That is, iff there is a world at which the whole of it exists. That is, iff there is a world such that, quantifying only over parts of that world, the whole of it exists. That is, iff the whole of it is among the parts of some world. That is, iff it is part of some world – and hence not a trans-world individual. Parts of worlds are *possible* individuals; trans-world individuals are therefore *impossible* individuals.

To call the trans-world individuals 'impossible' in this sense is not an argument for ignoring them – that comes later. It is only a terminological stipulation. If we thought they should not be ignored, perhaps because we thought that we ourselves were trans-world individuals, it would be appropriate and easy to give 'possible individual' a more inclusive sense. We could say that an individual exists at a world iff, quantifying only over parts of that world, *some part* of that individual exists – that way, the trans-world individuals would count as possible.[8]

I claim that mereological composition is unrestricted: any old class of things has a mereological sum. Whenever there are some things, no matter how disparate and unrelated, there is something composed of just those things. Even a class of things out of different worlds has a mereological sum. That sum is a trans-world individual. It overlaps each world that contributes a part of it, and so is partly in each of many worlds.

We are happy enough with mereological sums of things that contrast with their surroundings more than they do with one another; and that are adjacent, stick together, and act jointly. We are more reluctant to affirm the existence of mereological sums of things that are disparate and scattered and go their separate ways. A typical problem case is a fleet: the ships contrast with their surroundings more than with one another, they act jointly, but they are not adjacent nor do they stick together. A class of things from different worlds might do well on the first *desideratum*, but it will fail miserably on the other three. Far from being

---

[8]Indeed, I think that in this sense, there would be no impossible individuals. No individual is wholly distinct from all the worlds; so every individual is divisible into parts which are parts of worlds. What of an individual that stands in none of the external relations that unify worlds? – According to what I said in section 1.6, it cannot be a worldmate of anything else; but without worldmates it can still be a world all on its own. Or, if its parts are not suitably interrelated, it can divide into several individuals each of which is a world all on its own.

adjacent, these things will not be spatiotemporally related in any way; they can exert no cohesive forces whatever on one another, nor can they have any joint effects. (See section 1.6.) So if composition could be restricted in accordance with our intuitions about this-worldly cases, then doubtless trans-world composition would fall under the ban.

But composition cannot be restricted in accordance with our intuitions about this-worldly cases, as I shall shortly argue. Therefore a ban on trans-world composition, though unproblematic in itself, would be unmotivated and gratuitous. The simple principle of absolutely unrestricted composition should be accepted as true.[9]

The trouble with restricted composition is as follows. It is a vague matter whether a given class satisfies our intuitive *desiderata* for composition. Each *desideratum* taken by itself is vague, and we get still more vagueness by trading them off against each other. To restrict composition in accordance with our intuitions would require a vague restriction. It's not on to say that somewhere we get just enough contrast with the surroundings, just enough cohesion, . . . to cross a threshold and permit composition to take place, though if the candidate class had been just a little worse it would have remained sumless. But if composition obeys a vague restriction, then it must sometimes be a vague matter whether composition takes place or not. And that is impossible.

The only intelligible account of vagueness locates it in our thought and language. The reason it's vague where the outback begins is not that there's this thing, the outback, with imprecise borders; rather there are many things, with different borders, and nobody has been fool enough to try to enforce a choice of one of them as the official referent of the word 'outback'.[10] Vagueness is semantic indecision. But not all of language is vague. The truth-functional connectives aren't, for instance. Nor are the words for identity and difference, and for the partial identity of overlap. Nor are the idioms of quantification, so long as they are unrestricted. How could any of these be vague? What would be the alternatives between which we haven't chosen?

The question whether composition takes place in a given case, whether a given class does or does not have a mereological sum, can be stated in a part of language where nothing is vague. Therefore it cannot have a vague answer. There is such a thing as the sum, or there isn't. It cannot be said that, because the *desiderata* for composition are satisfied to a borderline degree, there sort of is and sort of isn't. What is this thing such

---

[9] I really do mean *absolutely* unrestricted – for instance, I see no bar to composition of sets with individuals, or particulars with universals, or cats with numbers. But here it will be enough to consider the composition of particular individuals.

[10] I realise that one can construct a so-called 'vague object' as a class of precise objects – that is, objects *simpliciter* – and then quantify over these classes. I take that project to be part of an analysis of vagueness in language, not an alternative to it.

that it sort of is so, and sort of isn't, that there is any such thing? No restriction on composition can be vague. But unless it is vague, it cannot fit the intuitive *desiderata*. So no restriction on composition can serve the intuitions that motivate it. So restriction would be gratuitous. Composition is unrestricted, and so there are trans-world individuals.

(To be sure, a ban against trans-world composition would not itself be a vague restriction, so it would not fall victim to the argument just given. But taken by itself it would be unmotivated. To motivate it, we have to subsume it under a broader restriction. Which can't be done, because a well-motivated broader restriction *would* be vague.)

Restrict quantifiers, not composition. Vague existence, speaking unrestrictedly, is unintelligible; vague existence, speaking restrictedly, is unproblematic. Is it so, ignoring things that don't measure up to certain standards of unification of their parts, that this class has a mereological sum? Definitely yes, if the sum definitely does measure up; definitely no, if it definitely doesn't; not definitely one way or the other, if the sum is a borderline case with respect to unification. There is a sum, unrestrictedly speaking, but it can perfectly well be a vague matter whether this sum falls within a vaguely restricted domain of quantification. Speaking restrictedly, of course we can have our intuitively motivated restrictions on composition. But not because composition ever fails to take place; rather, because we sometimes ignore some of all the things there really are.

We have no name for the mereological sum of the right half of my left shoe plus the Moon plus the sum of all Her Majesty's ear-rings, except for the long and clumsy name I just gave it; we have no predicates under which such entities fall, except for technical terms like 'physical object' (in a special sense known to some philosophers) or blanket terms like 'entity' and maybe 'thing'; we seldom admit it to our domains of restricted quantification. It is very sensible to ignore such a thing in our everyday thought and language. But ignoring it won't make it go away. And really making it go away without making too much else go away as well – that is, holding a theory according to which classes have mereological sums only when we intuitively want them to – turns out not to be feasible.

If unrestricted composition is granted, I can reformulate counterpart theory in terms of trans-world individuals. This will begin as an exercise in definition-mongering, nothing more. For the time being, I shall continue to suppose that ordinary individuals – we ourselves, and other things we have ordinary names and predicates and quantified variables for – never exist at more than one world. Of course an ordinary individual will exist *according to* other worlds, thanks to its other-worldly counterparts. Still, it is a part of one world only, and neither the whole nor any (particular) part of it is part of any other world. In short: my usual doctrines. Only the formulation will change.

(*Almost* my usual doctrines. For simplicity I shall impose one extra assumption: that the counterpart relation is symmetric. Also, I shall leave one assumption in force that I would sometimes be willing to drop: that nothing is a counterpart of anything else in its own world. I take both of these assumptions to be correct for some but not all reasonable candidate counterpart relations, so that imposing them amounts to somewhat narrowing down what the counterpart relation might be, and thus giving up a little of the built-in flexibility of counterpart theory.)

As suggested above, let us call an individual which is wholly part of one world a *possible* individual.[11] If a possible individual X is part of a trans-world individual Y, and X is not a proper part of any other possible individual that is part of Y, let us call X a *stage* of Y. The stages of a trans-world individual are its maximal possible parts; they are the intersections of it with the worlds which it overlaps. It has at most one stage per world, and it is the mereological sum of its stages. Sometimes one stage of a trans-world individual will be a counterpart of another. If all stages of a trans-world individual Y are counterparts of one another, let us call Y *counterpart-interrelated*. If Y is counterpart-interrelated, and not a proper part of any other counterpart-interrelated trans-world individual (that is, if Y is maximal counterpart-interrelated), then let us call Y a *∗-possible* individual.

Given any predicate that applies to possible individuals, we can define a corresponding starred predicate that applies to ∗-possible individuals relative to worlds. A ∗-possible individual is a ∗-*man* at W iff it has a stage at W that is a man; it ∗-*wins the presidency* at W iff it has a stage at W that wins the presidency; it is a ∗-*ordinary individual* at W iff it has a stage at W that is an ordinary individual. It ∗-*exists* at world W iff it has a stage at W that exists; likewise it ∗-*exists in its entirety* at world W iff it has a stage at W that exists its entirety, so – since any stage at any world does exist in its entirety – a ∗-possible individual ∗-exists in its entirety at any world where it ∗-exists at all. (Even though it does not exist in its entirety at any world.) It ∗-*is not a trans-world individual* at W iff it has a stage at W that is not a trans-world individual, so every ∗-possible individual (although it *is* a trans-world individual) also ∗-is not a trans-world individual at any world. It is a ∗-*possible individual* at W iff it has a stage at W that is a possible individual, so something is a ∗-possible individual *simpliciter* iff it is a ∗-possible individual at every world where it ∗-exists. Likewise for relations. One ∗-possible individual ∗-*kicks* another

[11]I avoid the convenient phrase 'world-bound individual' because it often seems to mean an individual that exists *according to* one world only, and I very much doubt that there are any such individuals.

at world W iff a stage at W of the first kicks a stage at W of the second; two *-possible individuals are *-*identical* at W iff a stage at W of the first is identical to a stage at W of the second; and so on.

Two further conventions for the starred language. I shall often omit 'at W' when the world in question is ours; and I shall use starred pronouns as variables over *-possible individuals, saying, as it might be, that if one *-man *-kicks *-another then the *-latter *-kicks *-him back.

To any name of a possible individual, there corresponds a predicate: 'Humphrey' and 'is Humphrey', or 'Socrates' and 'Socratises'. Our schema for defining starred predicates applies as much to these predicates as to any other. A *-possible individual *-*is Humphrey* at W iff it has a stage at W that is Humphrey. If 'Humphrey' names our Humphrey and not his other-worldly counterparts, this means that a *-possible individual *-is Humphrey iff Humphrey is its stage at the actual world. We could try defining names for *-possible individuals, saying for instance that *-*Humphrey* is the one that *-is Humphrey. The problem is that, since Humphrey has twin counterparts at some worlds, many different possible individuals *-are Humphrey, and so are equally candidates to bear the name '*-Humphrey'. We can say in the plural that all of them are *-Humphreys. As for the name in the singular, let us regard it as ambiguous: its different disambiguations make it name different *-Humphreys. But often its ambiguity will not matter. The *-Humphreys, though different, are all *-identical at this world. Therefore all or none of them are *-men at this world, all or none of them *-win the presidency at this world, and so on. The things we might say using the starred name in non-modal contexts will have the same truth value on all disambiguations. Such a sentence is true, or is false, for every way of disambiguating its starred names. (For short: *every way*.) For instance it is true, every way, that *-Humphrey is a *-man. It is false, every way, that *-Humphrey *-wins.

As for modal contexts, we should note that two possible individuals are counterparts iff there is some *-possible individual of which they both are stages. (Here I use the two simplifying assumptions I imposed on the counterpart relation.) Then Humphrey has some other-worldly stage as a counterpart iff, for some way of disambiguating the starred name (for short: *some way*) that stage belongs to *-Humphrey. I would ordinarily say that Humphrey might have won iff he has some counterpart who wins; and that he is essentially a man iff all his counterparts are men. Now I can say, equivalently, that Humphrey might have won iff, some way, there is a world where *-Humphrey *-wins; and he is essentially a man iff, every way, *-Humphrey is a *-man at every world where *-he *-exists.

But 'might have won' and 'is essentially a man' are predicates that apply to possible individuals. So we can star them: a *-possible individual *-*might*

have won at world W iff it has a stage at W that might have won; a
∗-possible individual is ∗-*essentially a man* at world W iff it has a stage
there that is essentially a man. Now we can say that ∗-Humphrey might
have won iff, some way, there is a world where ∗-Humphrey ∗-wins; and
∗-Humphrey is ∗-essentially a man iff, every way, ∗-Humphrey is a ∗-man
at every world where ∗-he ∗-exists.

We have very little remaining use for the unstarred predicates and names
and pronouns of ordinary things, since we can use the starred vocabulary
even when talking entirely about what goes on at this world.[12] At this
point somebody – as it might be, the long-suffering compositor – might
be heard to suggest a new convention for our language, at least when
it is used outside the philosophy room: leave off all the stars. Do it: then
here are some doctrines I take to be true.

> Humphrey is a possible individual; he is an ordinary individual; he is
> not a trans-world individual. He exists; he exists at many worlds; he
> exists in his entirety at any world where he exists at all. He is a man;
> he is essentially a man because, every way, he is a man at every world
> where he exists. He lost; but he might have won because, some way,
> there is a world where he wins. Every way, Humphrey is identical to
> Humphrey. But, some way, there are some worlds where Humphrey
> is not identical to Humphrey.

I dare say a fan of 'trans-world identity' might like this new theory better
than he liked counterpart theory. That would be a mistake. It *is*
counterpart theory.[13] New terminology is not a new theory. Saying that
a horse's tail is a leg does not make five-legged horses. Saying that
Humphrey exists in his entirety at many worlds does not make overlap
of worlds. I told you just what my words were meant to mean, and I'm
their master, so you needn't hope that really they mean something else.

---

[12]At this point, we have something resembling various systems of quantified modal
logic that quantify over individual concepts: functions from worlds to individuals. Carnap's
Meaning and Necessity system is of this kind; but there is more of a resemblance to later
systems that quantify only over certain selected individual concepts. See, for instance,
Kaplan, 'Transworld Heir Lines'; Thomason, 'Modal Logic and Metaphysics' (the system
Q3); Gibbard, 'Contingent Identity'; and many papers by Hintikka from the sixties and
seventies. If worlds never overlap, then there is a one-to-one correspondence between my
trans-world individuals and functions from worlds to parts of themselves. So if those
functions were the only individual concepts we wanted to quantify over, we might as well
replace set-theoretic construction by mereology. It is sometimes hard to tell how these
systems are meant to be understood – whether ordinary things are supposed to be the world-
to-individual functions or the values of those functions, whether the worlds or the
individuals or both are supposed to be ersatz.

[13]Plus unrestricted composition, plus two slightly restrictive assumptions on the
counterpart relation.

There's a question whether this fan of trans-world identity ought to like counterpart theory any better when he finds out how it can be restated. Probably not. Sometimes it can indeed enhance the plausibility of a theory to gain verbal agreement with what opponents want to say, even at the cost of a bit of gentle reinterpretation, but in the case at hand the reinterpretation is much too violent to buy any plausibility. Further, if what's wanted is trans-world identity, I have all along agreed to it in the uncontroversial sense: Humphrey – he himself, the whole of him – exists (in his entirety) *according to* many worlds. Many worlds represent *de re* of him that he exists. They do it by counterparts, but they do it. This is a less devious way to give the fan what he says he wants.

So far, counterpart theory reworded, first harmlessly and then deceptively. But now someone might say that I have made one mistake, as follows. When I worked my way around to the starless abbreviation of the starred language, I did *not* forge a deceptive imitation of our ordinary language. Rather, *that* was our ordinary language. I returned home and knew the place for the first time. We ourselves, and other things that we ordinarily name, or classify under predicates, or quantify over, *are* trans-world individuals unified by counterpart relations. It is quite wrong to ignore such things; we would be ignoring, *inter alia*, ourselves. If anything, it is the stages that we should ignore and leave out of our restricted quantifying.

The theory that ordinary things are trans-world individuals, unified by counterpart relations among their stages, really is a different theory from mine. But the difference is limited. There is no disagreement about what there is; there is no disagreement about the analysis of modality. Rather, there is extensive *semantic* disagreement. It is a disagreement about which of the things my opponent and I both believe in are rightly called persons, or sticks, or stones.

In his 'Worlds Away', Quine portrays a form of modal realism that treats ordinary things as trans-world individuals, perduring through non-overlapping worlds in just the way they perdure through time and space. It isn't that he advocates such a view; rather, he takes for granted that this is what modal realism would be.[14] The reason is that he takes the analogy of time and modality as his guide. In the case of time we do not think of ourselves as momentary stages, but rather as trans-time sums of stages. (I agree.) So we should say the same in the case of modality. (Why?) But it turns out that the analogy is not so very good after all;

---

[14]'Worlds Away' appears to be about genuine modal realism. There is no connection with the mathematical construction of ersatz worlds he had considered in 'Propositional Objects' (see section 3.2), unless it be a subterranean connection by way of Pythagorean reduction and ontological relativity.

the unification of the sums is much more problematic for modality than it is for time. (Again I agree.) So much the worse for modal realism. (No – so much the worse for following the analogy wherever it may lead.)

Grant me, what is controversial, that we perdure through time by having distinct temporal stages at different times; else Quine's analogy of time and modality doesn't even begin. (Then if in addition we are trans-world individuals, there is a double summation: we are composed of stages at different worlds, which stages in turn are composed of stages at different times within the same world. And of course those are composed in turn of spatial parts.) Even so, the unification of the sums would be more problematic for modality than it is for time, in three different ways.

(1) The temporal parts of an ordinary thing that perdures through time are united as much by relations of causal dependence as by qualitative similarity. In fact, both work together: the reason the thing changes only gradually, for the most part, is that the way it is at any time depends causally on the way it was at the time just before, and this dependence is by and large conservative. However, there can be no trans-world causation to unite counterparts. Their unification into a trans-world individual can only be by similarity.

(2) To the extent that unification by similarity does enter into perdurance through time, what matters is not so much the long-range similarity between separated stages, but rather the linkage of separated stages by many steps of short-range similarity between close stages in a one-dimensional ordering. Change is mostly gradual, but not much limited overall. There is no such one-dimensional ordering given in the modal case. So any path is as good as any other; and what's more, in logical space anything that can happen does. So linkage by a chain of short steps is too easy: it will take us more or less from anywhere to anywhere. Therefore it must be disregarded; the unification of trans-world individuals must be a matter of direct similarity between the stages. (Quine rests his objection on this point.)

(3) In the case of temporal perdurance, it is possible to get pathological cases: fission, fusion, and people who gradually turn into different people. These arise when the relation that unites the stages is intransitive, so that different perduring people overlap. Then what do we say when a stage shared between two (or more) people is present? Strictly speaking, two people are present there by way of that one stage, but the fact that there are two is extrinsic to the time in question. It seems for all the world that there is only one. We will have to say something counter-intuitive, but we get a choice of evils. We could say that there are two people; or that there is one, but really we're counting stages rather than people; or that there is one, and we're counting people, but we're not counting all the people who are present; or that there is one, and we're counting people, but we're not counting them by identity. (See my 'Survival and Identity'.)

It really isn't nice to have to say any of these things – but after all, we're talking about something that doesn't really ever happen to people except in science fiction stories and philosophy examples, so is it really so very bad that peculiar cases have to get described in peculiar ways? We get by because ordinary cases are not pathological. But modality is different: pathology is everywhere. Whenever something in this world has two counterparts that are not counterparts of each other, we get two different maximal counterpart-interrelated trans-world individuals which share a common stage at this world. That could happen because the this-worldly stage has twin counterparts at some world – and I'd like to know how *anything* could ever fail to have twin counterparts somewhere, except under some very restrictive notion about what eligible candidates for a counterpart relation there are. Or it could happen still more easily that something has two counterparts at different worlds that are not counterparts of each other. The counterpart relation is a matter of some sort of similarity, little differences add up to big differences, so of course there is intransitivity. So the modal case will always, or almost always, give us the same choice of evils about how to count that the temporal case gives us only in connection with far-fetched stories. If trans-world individuals are oddities we mostly ignore, no harm done if we have puzzles about how to count them from the standpoint of a world where they share stages. But if they are said to be ordinary things that we cannot ignore, then these puzzles are much more obnoxious.

These three considerations are general. They apply against the doctrine that we ourselves are trans-world individuals, and equally against the doctrine that sticks and stones are trans-world individuals. But in the case of ourselves, there is a fourth consideration. Consider the various desires of my various temporal stages in this world. They differ, of course; but there is plenty of common purpose to it. To some extent, stages want to fulfil the remembered desires of earlier stages: I strive for something today mainly because I wanted it yesterday. That is what it means not to be a quitter. To a greater extent, stages want to fulfil the foreseen desires of later stages: that is prudence. It isn't quite all for one and one for all, of course – how I envy my future self who is sending this manuscript away! – but it is so to a great extent. Even if it is in the first instance the momentary stages that do the desiring, still a person perduring through time is capable of collective self-interest. Not so across worlds. My this-worldly self has *no* tendency to make the purposes of its other-worldly counterparts its own. Far from wishing good fortune to all the counterparts alike, what it wants is that it should be one of the most fortunate among them. There is no common purpose. The supposed trans-world person, no matter how well unified by counterpart relations, is not the sort of integrated self that is capable of self-interest. How could it be, in view of the absolute lack of causal connection between its parts, and the non-contingency of its total allotment of good and ill fortune? It would be strange and pointless to think of the trans-world sums in the way we are accustomed to think of ourselves. That is further reason to set the trans-world individuals aside as oddities best ignored.

The final, and simplest, reason is that a modal realism which makes ordinary things out to be trans-world individuals disagrees gratuitously with common opinion. After all, not all of us are modal realists; and those who are not (even the ersatzers) couldn't possibly think of ordinary things as having parts in many worlds. Surely it is better for modal realists if they can think of people, sticks, and stones exactly as others do.

4.4   Against Haecceitism

David Kaplan introduced the term 'haecceitism' in the following famous passage.

> There seems to be some disagreement as to whether we can meaningfully ask whether a possible individual that exists in one possible world also exists in another without taking into account the attributes and behavior of the individuals that exist in the one world and making a comparison with the attributes and behavior of the individuals that exist in the other world. The doctrine that holds that it does make sense to ask – without reference to common attributes and behavior – whether *this* is the same individual in another possible world, that individuals can be extended in logical space (*i.e.* through possible worlds) in much the way we commonly regard them as being extended in physical space and time, and that a common 'thisness' may underlie extreme dissimilarity or distinct thisnesses may underlie great resemblance, I call *Haecceitism* . . . . The opposite view, *Anti-Haecceitism*, holds that for entities of distinct possible worlds there is no notion of transworld being. They may, of course, be linked by a common concept – as Eisenhower and Nixon are linked across two moments of time by the concept *the president of the United States* and distinguished, at the same pair of moments, by the concept *the most respected member of his party* – but there are, in general, many concepts linking any such pair and many distinguishing them. Each, in his own setting, may be clothed in attributes which cause them to resemble one another closely. But there is no metaphysical reality of sameness or difference which underlies the clothes. Our interests may cause us to *identify* individuals of distinct worlds, but then we are creating something – a transworld continuant – of a kind different fom anything given by the metaphysics. Although the Anti-Haecceitist may seem to assert that no possible individual exists in more than one possible world, that view is properly reserved for the Haecceitist who holds to an unusually rigid brand of metaphysical determinism. ('How to Russell a Frege-Church', pages 722–3; Loux, pages 216–17.)

I consider myself to be an anti-haecceitist in more or less the sense that Kaplan had in mind. I also think it is worth holding on to the term, which has gained some currency. But before we go on, it is necessary to pull out the main haecceitist doctrine from Kaplan's rather large bundle of views.

The main doctrine, I take it, is the denial of a supervenience thesis. All hands agree in distinguishing two ways that worlds – genuine or ersatz – might differ. (1) Worlds might differ in their qualitative character; or, for ersatz worlds, in the qualitative character they ascribe to the concrete world. That is to say, they might exhibit or represent different patterns of instantiation of the natural intrinsic properties and external relations, and might thus disagree about just what kinds of things there are or about how things of the various kinds are spatiotemporally arranged and causally related.[15] Suppose we had a mighty language that lacked for nothing in the way of qualitative predicates, and lacked for nothing in its resources for complex infinitary constructions, but was entirely devoid of proper names for things; then the qualitative differences would be those that could be captured by descriptions in this mighty language. (2) Also, worlds might differ in what they represent *de re* concerning various individuals: this-worldly individuals at least, and also other-worldly individuals if such there be. Thus, whatever account we might give of representation *de re* by genuine or ersatz worlds, it remains that there are some of them which represent *de re*, of Humphrey (the Humphrey of our world), that he wins the presidency and there are others that represent, of him, that he loses. What is the connection between these two ways for worlds to differ? Does representation *de re* supervene on qualitative character? Is it so that whenever two worlds differ in representation *de re*, that is because they differ qualitatively? Or are there sometimess differences in representation *de re* without benefit of any difference whatever in qualitative character? If two worlds differ in what they represent *de re* concerning some individual, but do not differ qualitatively in any way, I shall call that a *haecceitistic difference*. *Haecceitism*, as I propose to use the word, is the doctrine that there are at least some cases of haecceitistic difference between worlds. *Anti-haecceitism* is the doctrine that there are none.

If that's what the issue before us is, then there are many things that it is not. It will be instructive to distinguish some separable questions, lest we underestimate the range of alternative positions that are available to us.

---

[15]Here I count causal relationships as a matter of 'qualitative character'; it may or may not be that they supervene on qualitative character more narrowly defined, in particular on the point-by-point distribution of local qualitative character. I discuss this question in the Introduction to my *Philosophical Papers*, volume II.

(1) Haecceitism is not the doctrine of trans-world identity in the uncontroversial sense: the claim that sometimes many (genuine or ersatz) worlds represent *de re*, concerning one and the same individual, that it exists and it does this or that. That much would be so whether or not representation *de re* supervenes on qualitative character. Likewise, the 'unusually rigid brand of determinism', which would deny that the same thing ever exists according to many worlds, is not anti-haecceitism. (It isn't a form of haecceitism either, on my definition, unless it is conjoined with a claim that there are qualitatively indiscernible worlds.)

Still less is haecceitism a mere acknowledgement of representation *de re* as a legitimate notion, one that we are entitled to use without qualms when we classify worlds and stipulate which of them we want to consider. So when Kripke emphatically insists[16] that it is entirely legitimate and proper to specify worlds by making reference to individuals – call this *Kripkean specification* – he is not entering into any debate over (what I call) haecceitism, and no anti-haecceitist need hesitate to agree with him. Similarly, we can all agree that it is proper to specify one out of a pack of dogs as 'the ugly one' without thereby entering into any debate over whether aesthetic properties do or do not supervene on shape and colouration.

Anti-haecceitism does indeed imply that any Kripkean specification of worlds could in principle be replaced by a qualitative specification – but not that this replacement is something that the Kripkean specifier had in mind, or something it is feasible to discover, or even something that could be expressed in finitely many words. Even if anti-haecceitism is true, there are two different reasons why we should expect Kripkean specifications to remain indispensable in practice. One reason is just that supervenience falls short of finite definability, to say nothing of manageably concise definability. The other reason is that Kripkean specification, understood as an anti-haecceitist would understand it, makes implicit reference to the not-fully-known qualitative character of this-worldly things. An analogy: consider the class of men wealthier than the Shah of Iran ever was. I have succeeded in specifying a class of men; that same class could have been specified in terms of net worth in dollars; but since the exact wealth of the Shah was a well-kept secret, I cannot substitute the second specification for the first. The same will happen if I specify the class of men whose intrinsic and extrinsic qualitative character bears a certain relation to the not-fully-known actual qualitative character of Humphrey; or if I specify the class of worlds where such men win the presidency, which last is Kripkean specification understood in the anti-haecceitist way.

Kripkean specification is both legitimate and indispensable. No issue

---

[16]As in *Naming and Necessity*, pages 44–7.

there. But if anyone purports to distinguish qualitatively indistinguishable worlds by means of Kripkean specification, then and only then must the anti-haecceitist object. And even then, he needn't object to Kripkean specification *per se*. He can continue to tolerate it, as we shall see, and object rather to the presupposition that what gets specified must be a possible world.

(2) Haecceitism also is not the doctrine of trans-world identity in the controversial sense that we considered in section 4.2: overlap of worlds. One way to be a haecceitist would be to accept a plurality of overlapping worlds, and to give an account of haecceitistic differences in terms of the common parts of different worlds. But there are other ways. More likely, a haecceitist will be some sort of ersatzer. His ersatz worlds may differ haecceitistically in what they say about Humphrey, but Humphrey himself will not be a common part of the ersatz worlds that disagree about him. Or if he is, that will be only in the irrelevant way that one word might be common to many texts.

(3) We might state anti-haecceitism as the doctrine that representation *de re* is determined by qualitative character. But we shouldn't take that to mean that representation *de re* is *fully* determined by anything. The doctrine only says that insofar as there is determinacy at all, it is qualitative character that does the job; where determinacy in virtue of qualitative character gives out, there determinacy itself gives out. Haecceitism claims that some non-qualitative aspect of worlds makes at least some contribution to determining representation *de re*; anti-haecceitism denies it. That is one question. The extent of determinacy is another.

The point applies to supervenience theses generally. If as a materialist I say that mental facts are entirely determined by physical facts (if we set aside worlds endowed with properties alien to our world), I needn't insist that mental facts are entirely determined. I can admit that there's no right answer to the question whether fuddled Fred loves or hates his father. What would make it so that he loves or that he hates is that one or another eligible assignment of content would best fit the physical facts; but in Fred's case two systems fit equally well, and well enough, and better than their eligible competitors, and according to one he loves and according to the other he hates; so what the physical facts make true is not that he loves or that he hates, but rather that he is in a state of befuddlement and indeterminacy that cannot straightforwardly be called the one thing or the other. We have not settled what such a condition as Fred's ought to be called. So Fred's story, as told in the language of simplistic folk psychology, is riddled with truth-value gaps left by our semantic indecision. No worries for materialism: it remains that the whole mental truth, such of it as there is, supervenes on the physics. Something else supervenes on the physics too: the whole truth about what the range of indeterminacy is, about whether a given simplistic mental description does or does not fall in the class within which there is no uniquely right choice.

No matter how representation *de re* is determined, whether by qualitative character or by non-qualitative determinants or some of each, the question of determinancy is still with us. The questions are linked only to this extent. Among various alternative theories of the nature of (genuine or ersatz) worlds and of representation *de re*, it might turn out that the ones that permit haecceitistic differences also imply something (welcome or unwelcome) about the extent of determinacy; and likewise for the ones that rule out haecceitistic differences. We shall take up the question of determinacy in the next section.

(4) Anti-haecceitism does not imply any doctrine of identity of indiscernibles. We do have a converse implication: if we never have two worlds exactly alike in qualitative character, then *a fortiori* we never have two such worlds that differ in representation *de re*, so anti-haecceitism follows automatically. But anti-haecceitism is neutral about whether there are qualitatively indiscernible worlds: there can be any number of indiscernible worlds, so long as they are alike not only qualitatively but also in representation *de re*. If worlds are alike in both of these respects, perhaps they are altogether indiscernible – how else might they differ?

For all I know, there are many indiscernible worlds, so that the worlds are even more abundant than we would otherwise think. I see no theoretical benefits to be gained by supposing that there are or that there are not, so on this question I advise that we remain agnostic.[17]

If we consider not genuine but ersatz worlds, we must take care what we mean in saying that identity of indiscernibles implies anti-haecceitism. For remember that the relevant qualitative character of an ersatz world is not the qualitative character which that ersatz world itself *has*; rather, it is the qualitative character which that ersatz world ascribes, truly or falsely, to the concrete world. If all ersatz worlds alike are abstract simples with no qualitative character to speak of, they may yet differ qualitatively in the relevant sense if somehow they manage to represent the concrete world differently. Or if the ersatz worlds are linguistic constructions, two

---

[17]I am inclined to agree with Unger '(Minimizing Arbitrariness', page 47) that we have reason to reject hypotheses that involve gratuitous arbitrariness, and thereby suggest – unacceptably – that the geography of logical space is a contingent matter. For instance, we may reject the obnoxiously arbitrary hypothesis that each world has exactly seventeen, or exactly aleph-seventeen, indiscernible duplicates; or the hypothesis that nice worlds have more duplicates than nasty ones. But the hypothesis that there is no duplication at all is not obnoxiously arbitrary; and neither is the hypothesis that all worlds alike are infinitely reduplicated to the same extent, provided we do not specify some obnoxiously arbitary infinite cardinal. So the principle of rejecting arbitrariness does not tell us whether or not there are indiscernible worlds.

of them might differ in the order of their clauses, their choice between synonyms, or what have you,[18] and nevertheless might be entirely equivalent in what they say about the qualitative character of the concrete world. So the sort of identity of indiscernible ersatz worlds which would be sufficient but not necessary for anti-haecceitism would have little to do with issues of identity of indiscernibles as ordinarily understood.

(5) Despite its name, haecceitism is not the acceptance of *haecceities*: non-qualitative properties of 'thisness' which distinguish particular individuals.[19] One might indeed expound haecceitism in terms of haecceities, saying that when two worlds differ haecceitistically, they disagree about which haecceities are coinstantiated with which qualitative properties. But a haecceitist need not believe in non-qualitative properties. He might even be some kind of nominalist and reject properties altogether.

In the other direction, you don't have to be a haecceitist to believe in haecceities. I am no haecceitist; but I hold that (on one legitimate conception of properties among others – see section 1.5) there is a property for any set whatever of possible individuals. This property I identify with the set itself. So we get properties that are in no way qualitatively delineated, and some of these are haecceities of this- and other-worldly individuals. A unit set of an individual is one especially strict sort of haecceity. Also, for any individual and any counterpart relation, there is the set of that individual together with all its counterparts, and this is a less strict sort of haecceity.

(6) Anti-haecceitism, properly speaking does not imply anti-haecceitism for less-than-maximally-specific 'miniworlds'. For many limited purposes it is convenient and perfectly harmless to conflate possible worlds, ignoring some respects of difference between them. For genuine modal realism, the miniworlds thus abstracted might be bigger things than the worlds themselves: they might be equivalence classes consisting of worlds that differ only in the ignored respects. For linguistic ersatzism, the miniworlds might be smaller things: they might be abridged linguistic descriptions, as opposed to the complete descriptions which are the ersatz worlds themselves. (For pictorial ersatzism they would again be equivalence classes; for magical ersatzism they would be less-than-maximal elements of the algebra of abstract simples.) Kripke gives us an elementary example from school:

---

[18]Whether this could happen depends on details of the construction. The maximal consistency of ersatz worlds might or might not mean that each one says everything it has to say in all different ways that its language affords.

[19]See Adams, 'Primitive Thisness and Primitive Identity', for further discussion of the difference between these questions.

Two ordinary dice . . . are thrown, displaying two numbers face up. For each die, there are six possible results. Hence there are thirty-six possible states of the pair of dice, as far as the numbers shown face-up are concerned, though only one of these states corresponds to the way the dice actually will come out. We all learned in school how to compute the probabilities of various events (assuming equiprobability of the states). . . . Now in doing these school exercises in probability, we were in fact introduced at a tender age to a set of (miniature) 'possible worlds'. The thirty-six possible states of the dice are literally thirty-six 'possible worlds', as long as we (fictively) ignore everything about the world except the two dice and what they show. . . . Now in this elementary case, certain confusions can be avoided. . . . The thirty-six possibilities, the one that is actual included, are (abstract) *states* of the dice, not complex physical entities. Nor should any school pupil receive high marks for the question 'How do we know, in the state where die A is six and die B is five, whether it is die A or die B which is six? Don't we need a "criterion of transstate identity" to identify the die with a six – not the die with a five – with our die A?' The answer is, of course, that the state (die A, 6; die B, 5) is *given* as such (and distinguished from the state (die B, 6; die A, 5)). The demand for some further 'criterion of transstate identity' is so confused that no competent schoolchild would be so perversely philosophical as to make it. The 'possibilities' simply are not given qualitatively . . . . If they had been, there would have been just twenty-one distinct possibilities, not thirty-six. (Preface to *Naming and Necessity*, pages 16–17.)

I do not take issue with any of this (except that I would give the philosophical pupil high marks despite the error of his ways). I too could be an ersatzer for this simple case, since it is no problem to devise a worldmaking language with resources enough to distinguish these miniworlds and with a purely syntactic test for consistency. Its sentences might as well take the very form illustrated in the quotation: 'die A, 6; die B, 5' and so forth. I too would be happy to specify the thirty-six miniworlds in terms of what they represent *de re* concerning each of the two dice. By so doing, I too would gladly distinguish miniworlds without benefit of any qualitative difference – except, of course, for the countless respects of qualitative differences that we have agreed to ignore, such as differences having to do with the different origins and histories and locations and exact size and shape of the two dice.

But what has any of this to do with any controversy in metaphysics? If ignoring is our game, we can ignore what we will and attend to what we will. Nothing stands in the way of ignoring underlying differences while attending to other differences that supervene on them – in which case the supervenience of the latter will be part of what we are ignoring. The mental may supervene on the physical, in fact I am convinced that it does, yet sometimes I manage to attend to the mental lives of people while ignoring the physics of them. Representation *de re* may supervene on qualitative character, in fact I am sure that it does, yet that is no reason why we may not attend to the former, ignore the latter, conflate worlds that agree in representation *de re* but differ qualitatively, and specify these conflations in the appropriate non-qualitative terms. We may; and we do.

You may have been under the impression that Kripke and I are the arch-haecceitist versus the arch-anti-haecceitist. (I myself have sometimes been under that impression.) It isn't so. Kripke vigorously defends doctrines loosely associated with (what I call) haecceitism; but I accept those doctrines too, and if that is enough to make one a 'haecceitist' then we are all haecceitists together and a useful term needs to be scrapped and replaced. As for the main issue, haecceitistic differences between worlds, I reject them and Kripke does not accept them. He only rejects a reason to reject them. Apart from that, he is explicitly neutral.

> With respect to possible states of the entire world, I do not mean to assert categorically that, just as in the case of the dice, there are qualitatively identical but distinct (counterfactual) states. What I do assert is that *if* there is a philosophical argument excluding qualitatively identical but distinct worlds, it cannot be based simply on the supposition that worlds must be stipulated purely qualitatively. What I defend is the *propriety* of giving possible worlds in terms of certain particulars as well as qualitatively, whether or not there are in fact qualitatively identical worlds. (Preface to *Naming and Necessity*, page 18.)

I read this as a declaration of neutrality about haecceitism because I take Kripke to assume that the 'qualitatively identical but distinct worlds' in question would be worlds that differed haecceitistically, rather than distinct worlds that differed in no way at all. Given his insistence that the worlds are in some sense 'abstract', he has every reason to set the second case aside.

The principal thing to say in favour of haecceitism is just that we do seem to have some intuitively compelling cases of haecceitistic difference. Suppose, for instance, that ours is a world of one-way eternal recurrence with a first epoch but no last. One of the epochs is ours. Which epoch? – there seem to be many possibilities, one of which is the actual one. Perhaps our epoch is in fact the seventeenth; but we might instead have lived in the 137th epoch. So it seems that there is a possible world that is qualitatively just like ours – the same infinite sequence of epochs, all exactly alike, and exactly like the epochs of our world – but that represents *de re*, concerning us, that we live in the 137th epoch rather than the seventeenth. Then the difference between that world and ours is a haecceitistic difference. No matter that ours is perhaps not really a world

of eternal recurrence. For haecceitism concerns not our world alone
but all the worlds, wherefore it is not contingent on which world
is ours.

The principal thing to say against haecceitism is just that when we survey
the various forms of genuine or ersatz modal realism, we find that the
ones that are congenial to haecceitistic differences are the ones that we
have already seen to be in serious trouble on other grounds. What's more,
it turns out that there is a cheap substitute for haecceitism. We can give
the haecceitist differences very like the ones he wanted, but without getting
into trouble by taking them to be haecceitistic differences between worlds.
So we should reject haecceitism not for any very direct reason, but rather
because its intuitive advantage over the cheap substitute – if indeed it has
any advantage at all – costs us far more trouble than it's worth.

To begin. First, genuine modal realism with overlap of worlds is
congenial to haecceitistic differences. There is no reason why proponents
of this view – if there were any – should not accept haecceitism.
Haecceitistic differences can be explained in terms of the differing parts
of qualitatively indiscernible worlds. Just as two duplicate strings may
share a dot though one puts it in the middle and the other puts it at one end

. . . . .

.

.

.

.

so it might happen that two duplicate worlds share an individual though
one puts him in the seventeenth epoch and the other puts him in the 137th;
and thereby those two worlds could differ in what they represent *de re*
about which epoch is his. And just as our shared dot may be no part
of a third string

. . . . .

which duplicates the first two, so our shared individual might be no part
of a third world which duplicates the first two; and thereby that third
world represents *de re* of him that he does not exist at all. If representation
de re works by overlap, haecceitistic differences are not a problem. They
are only to be expected. You can have your haecceitism, but you have
to pay: wherever there seem to be contingent intrinsic properties of things,
you have to say that the seeming property is really a relation. The intrinsic
nature of the things that stand in these new-found relations is shrouded
in mystery. That was my main argument against overlap (in section 4.2)
and I think it is worse trouble than haecceitism is worth.

Next, consider modal realism without overlap of worlds. This is the theory I favour; I considered the drawbacks of overlap in section 4.2, and the drawbacks of various versions of ersatzism in chapter 3. But if it is preferred, then haecceitistic differences of worlds become utterly mysterious.[20]

I ask what the non-qualitative determinants of representation *de re* are, and how they do their work. A haecceitist who believed in overlap would have had a good answer, but if he gives up on overlap, he throws that answer away and he owes me another. Somehow, non-qualitative aspects of things and worlds are supposed to be relevant to what is represented *de re* concerning other things in other worlds. For instance, a winner is part of some world that does not overlap ours, and thereby it is represented *de re*, concerning Humphrey, that he might have won. *Ex hypothesi*, this trans-world relevance is not identity; because we have given up on overlap. It is a relation which relates distinct things in distinct worlds. *Ex hypothesi* it is not (or not entirely) a qualitative counterpart relation of the sort that I favour; because we want haecceitism. So what is it? Call it a *non-qualitative counterpart relation* – that label will do to be going on with, though really I regard it as a contradiction in terms.

The haecceitist might say that when two things are non-qualitative counterparts, that is because they stand in a certain relation. Or they share a certain property. Or they are both included as parts of a certain trans-world mereological sum. But *any* two things stand in infinitely many relations, share infinitely many properties, and are both included as parts of infinitely many sums. For any class of ordered pairs, however miscellaneous, there is the relation of being paired by a member of that class; for any class of things, however miscellaneous, there is the property of belonging to that class and there is the mereological sum of that class. Perhaps the haecceitist thinks that some of all these relations or properties or sums are somehow special, and he meant to speak only of the special ones. (Perhaps he also thinks that only the special ones exist.) Then he must tell me which of all the relations and properties and sums I believe in are the special ones. He cannot say that the special ones are the ones that carve along the qualitative joints; that I can understand,[21] but that does not meet his need to single out some of all the ones that *don't* carve along the joints. He must avoid circularity. I do not think he can answer me. If he cannot, he leaves it entirely mysterious what it could mean to say that things were non-qualitative counterparts.

---

[20]The next several pages are mostly adapted from my 'Individuation by Acquaintance and by Stipulation', pages 23–31, with the kind permission of the editors of *The Philosophical Review*.

[21]Though perhaps only by taking it as an inescapable primitive distinction; see section 1.5, and my 'New Work for a Theory of Universals'.

(I have another, but far less serious, objection to the idea of a non-qualitative counterpart relation. In section 1.6, I suggested that perhaps there are no natural external relations whatever between parts of different worlds; and that if so, we could bypass the idea of 'analogically spatiotemporal' relations and say simply that worlds are unified by external interrelatedness. A non-qualitative counterpart relation would presumably sink that hope.)

There is no way to make sense of a non-qualitative counterpart relation; so if we are to be modal realists and reject overlap, then we had better also reject haecceitism. But can we afford to? We still have the seeming cases of haecceitistic difference. It would be very implausible and damaging, I think, just to defy the intuitions. We must reject haecceitistic differences between worlds, and yet acknowledge genuine differences between possibilities.

This we can do. Our problem rests on the presupposition that differences between possibilities are differences between possible worlds. Abandon that presupposition, and our problem solves itself. We satisfy the haecceitist's intuitions on the cheap, giving him the distinctions between possibilities that he rightly demands without buying into any mysterious non-qualitative aspects of worlds.

Possibilities are not always possible worlds. There are possible worlds, sure enough, and there are possibilities, and possible worlds are some of the possibilities. But I say that *any* possible individual is a possibility, and not all possible individuals are possible worlds. Only the biggest ones are.

The world is the totality of things. It is the actual individual that includes every actual individual as a part. Likewise a possible world is a possible individual big enough to include every possible individual that is compossible with it (where compossibility, the relation that unites worldmates, is a matter of strictly or analogically spatiotemporal relatedness, or perhaps of external relatedness generally). It is a way that an entire world might possibly be. But lesser possible individuals, inhabitants of worlds, proper parts of worlds, are possibilities too. They are ways that something less than an entire world might possibly be. A possible person, for instance, is a way that a person might possibly be.

It is usual to think that the unit of possibility is the possible world. I divide this thesis, retain part and reject part. It is true, and important, that possibilities are invariably provided by whole possible worlds. There are no free-floating *possibilia*. Every possibility is part of a world – exactly one world – and thus comes surrounded by worldmates, and fully equipped with extrinsic properties in virtue of its relations to them. What is not true is that we should count distinct possibilities by counting the worlds that provide them. A single world may provide many possibilities, since many possible individuals inhabit it.

To illustrate, consider these two possibilities for me. I might have been one of a pair of twins. I might have been the first-born one, or the second-born one. These two possibilities involve no qualitative difference in the way the world is. Imagine them specified more fully: there is the possibility of being the first-born twin in a world of such-and-such maximally specific qualitative character. And there is the possibility of being the second-born twin in exactly such a world. The haecceitist says: two possibilities, two worlds. They *seem* just alike, but they must differ somehow. They differ in respect of 'cross-identification'; that is, they differ in what they represent, *de re*, concerning someone. Hence they must differ with respect to the determinants of representation *de re*; and these must be non-qualitative, since there are no qualitative differences to be had. I say: two possibilities, sure enough. And they do indeed differ in representation *de re*: according to one I am the first-born twin, according to the other I am the second-born. But they are not two worlds. They are two possibilities within a single world. The world in question contains twin counterparts of me, under a counterpart relation determined by intrinsic and extrinsic qualitative similarities (especially, match of origins). Each twin is a possible way for a person to be, and in fact is a possible way for me to be. I might have been one, or I might have been the other. There are two distinct possibilities for me. But they involve only one possibility for the world: it might have been the world inhabited by two such twins. The haecceitist was quite right when he thought that purely qualitative worlds gave us too narrow a range of distinct possibilities. He concluded that worlds must not be purely qualitative. He'd have done better to conclude that *worlds* gave us too narrow a range of possibilities. The parts of worlds also must be put to use.

For a second illustration, consider the thought that I might have been someone else. Here am I, there goes poor Fred; there but for the grace of God go I; how lucky I am to be me, not him. Where there is luck there must be contingency. I am contemplating the possibility of my being poor Fred, and rejoicing that it is unrealised. I am not contemplating a possibility that involves any qualitative difference in the world – not, for instance, a world where someone with origins just like mine suffers misfortunes just like Fred's. Rather, I am contemplating the possibility of being poor Fred in a world just like this one. The haecceitist will suggest that I have in mind a qualitative duplicate of this world where the non-qualitative determinants of representation *de re* somehow link me with the qualitative counterpart of Fred. But this distorts my thought: I thought not just that I might have lived Fred's life, but that I might have been Fred living Fred's life. Maybe I misunderstood my own thought – it's hard to be sure – but let's see if the haecceitist's amendment is really needed. I think not. I suggest that the possibility I have in mind is not a world that is like ours qualitatively but differs from ours haecceitistically. Instead it is a possible individual, in fact an actual individual, namely poor Fred himself. Like any other possible person, he is a possible way for a person to be. And in a sense he is even a possible way for me to be. He is my counterpart under an extraordinarily generous counterpart relation, one which demands nothing more of counterparts than that they be things of the same kind.[22] Any property that one of my counterparts does have is a property that I might have; being Fred – being literally identical with him – is such a property; and so there is a sense in which I might have been him. That is not to say that the world might have been such that I was Fred – it makes no sense to thank God for His gracious favouritism in making the world be as it is, rather than some different way such that I would have been poor Fred! The possibility in question is a possibility for me, not for the world. It is not some other world, differing haecceitistically from ours, which represents *de re* of me that I am Fred; it is Fred himself, situated as he is within our world.[23]

Likewise for the apparent haecceitistic differences that arise if we live in the seventeenth epoch of a world of eternal recurrence. The possibility which represents me *de re* as living instead in the 137th epoch is not some other world that differs haecceitistically from ours; it is my this-worldly duplicate in the 137th epoch. Insofar as he is my counterpart (that is, on those resolutions of vagueness that make him my counterpart despite the fact that we are worldmates) he is a possibility for me; that is all I need mean when I say that I might have been him.

Besides possible individuals, world-sized and smaller, there are still other possibilities: *joint possibilities* for sequences of more than one individual, taken in a given order. These joint possibilities are themselves sequences of appropriate length, with all their terms drawn from a single world. A suitable pair of individuals in a given order, for instance, (take this as a two-term sequence) is a way that a pair of individuals might possibly be. Imagine that we live in a spatially symmetric world. The entire history

[22]In 'Counterpart Theory and Quantified Modal Logic' I took it as axiomatic that nothing can have any counterpart besides itself in its own world. I would now consider that requirement appropriate under some but not all resolutions of the vagueness of the counterpart relation.

[23]Thomas Nagel discusses the thought that he might have been someone else. He writes 'my being TN (or whoever I in fact am) *seems* accidental . . . it seems as if I just *happen* to be the publicly identifiable person TN' ('The Objective Self', page 225). He insists that this thought should be respected at face value, and not converted into the more tractable thought that I might have lived a different life. I in turn insist that it should not be converted, as Nagel himself proposes, into the thought that really he is not TN after all, but rather he is a 'self' which happens to view the world through TN but might have viewed the world through someone else. (How would that help? Couldn't you work up a sense of contingency and luck about being one 'self' rather than another?) The treatment I suggest here is due, in essentials, to Hazen, 'Counterpart-theoretic Semantics for Modal Logic', page 331.

of one side is replicated on the other side. But it didn't have to be so. An alternative possibility for the world starts out symmetric, just as this world supposedly is; but tomorrow one side is destroyed by a catastrophe and the other side survives. I have my twin, J, on the other side. One joint possibility for me and my twin is that I am killed in the catastrophe and he survives. Another, which I prefer, is that he is killed and I survive. The haecceitist has his way of distinguishing the two possibilities. I have my cheaper way. The world of the catastrophe has its pair of twins, K who gets killed and L who lives. Therefore it provides two pairs of compossible individuals: ⟨K, L⟩ and ⟨L, K⟩. These are two different ways for a pair of individuals to be, differing only in order. In particular, they are two different ways for the pair ⟨I, J⟩ to be, two different joint possibilities for me and my twin. Both K and L are qualitative counterparts of both I and J; further, the relations between K and L are like the relations between I and J;[24] and so there is a natural sense in which both the pairs ⟨K, L⟩ and ⟨L, K⟩ are qualitative counterparts of the pair ⟨I, J⟩. Of these two joint possibilities for ⟨I, J⟩, ⟨L, K⟩ is the one I prefer. Still other joint possibilities are sequences with repetitions or gaps. There might have been a world with no duplication, but only one shared counterpart H of the twins I and J. One joint possibility for the pair ⟨I, J⟩ is that they might have both existed and been identical; this is the pair ⟨H, H⟩, a sequence with a repetition. Another is that I alone might have existed: this is the pair ⟨H, *⟩, a gappy sequence with the second term omitted. (I mark the gap by a star.) A third is that J alone might have existed: this is the pair ⟨*, H⟩, a gappy sequence with the first term omitted.[25] Once again, we have our desired difference of possibilities without any difference of worlds.[26]

[24]On the need to consider these similarities of relations, see Hazen, 'Counterpart-theoretic Semantics for Modal Logic', and my *Philosophical Papers*, volume I, pages 44–6.

[25]An n-place sequence consists of terms indexed by the numbers 1 through n; a gappy n-place sequence consists of terms indexed by some but not all of these numbers. When gaps are permitted, the same sequence can be written in different ways and will be a joint possibility for sequences of different lengths. Thus ⟨X, Y⟩, ⟨X, Y, *⟩, ⟨X, Y, *, *⟩, and so on are all the same thing; this thing may be an ungappy possibility for pairs and an increasingly gappy possibility for triples, quadruples, and so on.

[26]The problem of the symmetric world and its asymmetric alternative is given in Adams, 'Primitive Thisness and Primitive Identity'. The treatment I suggest for it is again due, in essentials, to Hazen, 'Counterpart-theoretic Semantics for Modal Logic' and is based on Hazen's treatment in *The Foundations of Modal Logic*. Hazen applies the treatment on a grander scale; we can reach his proposal in four steps. (1) We could take joint possibilities for infinite, indeed perhaps transfinite, sequences. (2) Instead of indexing by finite numbers or transfinite ordinals to make a sequence, we could use some other system of indexing; then a joint possibility for an indexed family of individuals is another family, indexed by the same indices (perhaps with gaps), of individuals from a single world. (3) A natural system would be to index every member of the original family by itself; then these same individuals will serve to index the other families that are joint possibilities

I noted an analogy in section 1.2. We often quantify restrictedly over worlds, limiting our attention to those that somehow resemble ours, and we call this a restriction to 'accessible' worlds. And we often quantify restrictedly over possible individuals, limiting our attention to those that somehow resemble some given this-worldly individual, and I call this a restriction to 'counterparts' of that individual. To underline the analogy, we might usefully borrow some terminology. In the broadest sense, all possible individuals without exception are possibilities for me. But some of them are *accessible* possibilities for me, in various ways, others are not. (Likewise for joint possibilities: in the broadest sense, all pairs of possible individuals are possibilities for any pair, but some are accessible possibilities in various ways that others are not.) My qualitative counterparts are *metaphysically accessible* possibilities for me; or better, each of many legitmate counterpart relations may be called a relation of metaphysical accessibility. My epistemic alternatives – those possible individuals who might, for all I know, be me – are *epistemically accessible* possibilities for me; my doxastic alternatives are *doxastically accessible*; and so on, whenever content may be given by a class of alternative possible individuals (see section 1.4). Metaphysical and (for instance) epistemic possibilities for me are not things of two different sorts. They are *possibilia* out of the same plurality of worlds. The difference is in the accessibility.

Note that when we talk of what is the case according to individual possibilities, we can in a sense assign content to the possibility regardless of questions of accessibility. Whether this other-worldly winner is a possibility according to which *Humphrey* wins depends on whether he is an accessible possibility for Humphrey; but be that as it may, he is in any case an individual possibility *of winning*.

Mind you, new terminology does not make a new theory. I'm still doing business at the same old stand – counterpart theory. Whether I call them individual possibilities or possible individuals, they still remain just what they always were: parts of this and other worlds. Whether I speak of counterpart relations or accessibility relations (metaphysical accessibility, as opposed to epistemic or doxastic or the like) I still mean some sort of relations of comparative similarity. It is Humphrey's winning counterparts who make it so that he might have won. Likewise when I speak of joint possibilities and their counterpart or accessibility relations – it's still similarity, though this time it's similarity of sequences so that similarity in relations between the terms of the sequence may play a role. The purpose

___

for the original family. (4) Finally, we might take our families to include all inhabitants of a given world. Then the joint possibilities for these most inclusive indexed families are what Hazen calls 'stipulational worlds'. These simulate worlds that differ haecceitistically; but I think it is best to insist that they are not worlds, and fall into place alongside their smaller siblings as part of the anti-haecceitist's way of explaining away the haecceitist's intuitions.

of the alternative terminology is only to help you see how to make the substitution I favour: differences between worldmate individuals in place of haecceitistic differences between worlds. That is my cheap substitute for haecceitism.

Is 'cheap' an understatement? Is there any cost at all? I think there is – simply the cost of making a break with established theory, on which all differences between possibilities are supposed to be differences between possible worlds. It is chaos if too many questions come open all at once, therefore theoretical conservatism is a good idea. There should be a presumption in favour of the incumbent theory, and against gratuitious substitutes. But if I was right that the theories congenial to haecceitism are in serious trouble on other grounds, and if we still want at least a simulation of haecceitistic difference, then I think my substitute is by no means gratuitous, and cheap at the price.

So I think it best, in general, to say that representation *de re* is done not by worlds, but by the appropriate individual (or joint) possibilities that are available within the various worlds. Still it remains true, for the most part, that one world will provide at most one accessible possibility for a given individual (or sequence). The exceptions come only if we get multiple counterparts within a world, either because we have an uncommonly repetitious world or because we use an uncommonly lax counterpart relation. Therefore, for the sake of familiarity, I shall mostly revert to speaking of representation *de re* by worlds, or of what is the case about an individual according to a world.

Continuing our survey of theories to see which ones are congenial to haecceitism, we turn next to the versions of ersatz modal realism introduced in chapter 3. Pictorial ersatzism presumably goes the same way as the genuine modal realism that it so closely imitates: there could be a version with overlap and a version without. The first would be congenial to haecceitism but would mystify us by the way it transformed properties into relations. The second would be uncongenial to haecceitism; would explain representation *de re* in terms of qualitative counterpart relations between 'abstract' ersatz individuals (or between those and actual concrete things); and would provide quasi-haecceitistic differences between possibilities for individuals, these being for the most part proper parts of ersatz worlds.

As for magical ersatzism, I have no idea how abstract simples could manage to do any representing at all, be it *de re* or be it qualitative, so still less do I have any idea whether they must do the one thing by doing the other. It's bad enough to be a magician, but I don't see why it's any worse to be a haecceitist as well.

Linguistic ersatzism, which for all its primitive modality and false conflations still seems the strongest rival to genuine modal realism, can easily go either way. To provide for haecceitistic differences, we need only make our ersatz worlds in a language equipped with proper names. These might be the ordinary proper names of everyday language; or they might be the subscripted letters that serve as individual constants in a typical formal language; or they might be the Lagadonian proper names of actual things, that is the things themselves; or whatever we please. Whatever the names are, they enable an ersatz world to say of an individual, by name, that it has so-and-so property. If representation *de re* works by naming, there is no reason for it to be governed by qualitative character. Let us suppose that we do not endow the names with descriptive content – or anyway not too much descriptive content – so that we preserve consistency if we make new ersatz worlds from old by some sort of substitution of names. That substitution will not change the qualitative character which the ersatz world ascribes to the concrete world. But it will normally make a difference to what is represented *de re* concerning the named individuals. Suppose again that ours is a world of one-way eternal recurrence; suppose that we have names – perhaps Lagadonian – for ourselves, and different names for our 137th-epoch counterparts; start with the actualised ersatz world, swap the names of the inhabitants of the seventeenth and the 137th epochs, and you get a new ersatz world that differs haecceitistically from the original. It falsely says of us by name, and thereby represents of us *de re*, that we live in the 137th epoch. On this version of linguistic ersatzism, haecceitistic differences are no problem. Again they are only to be expected, and the problem would be to avoid them.

At least, that is so if all we want are haecceitistic differences about actual individuals. If representation *de re* works by naming, then where names give out, representation *de re* and haecceitistic differences give out as well. We at least have Lagadonian names for all actual individuals, whether or not we have more ordinary names. But we have no Lagadonian names for unactualised other-worldly individuals because, if ersatzism is true, there are no such things. We can and do introduce descriptive terms that would denote things if, but only if, the world were suitably different; but this method of naming relies on qualitative character (and qualitative relations to already named things) and so cannot increase our stock of haecceitistic differences. It seems that linguistic ersatzism once again forces us to conflate possibilities because we cannot distinguish them in a this-worldly language. This time, instead of losing qualitative differences having to do with nameless alien properties, we lose *de re* differences having to do with nameless unactualised individuals. This time, I think the lost differences needn't be missed. We could be content to let them go, ending with a divided theory: haecceitism for possibilities having to do with actual individuals, anti-haecceitism for remoter possibilities having to do with unactualised individuals.[27]

If a linguistic ersatzer does not want haecceitistic differences, he isn't stuck with them. He has two alternative remedies.[28] (1) He might construct his ersatz worlds in two steps, first incorporating the haecceitistic differences he regards as artificial and afterward 'factoring out' those differences. He starts with sentences in a worldmaking language equipped with names. In the first step he takes (infinite) maximal consistent conjunctions of sentences. Some of these conjunctions will be *isomorphic*, differing only by a permutation of names. In the second step he takes (infinite) maximal disjunctions of mutually isomorphic conjunctions. This is like what Carnap does when he defines structure-descriptions – qualitative ersatz miniworlds saying how many individuals of each of several kinds there are – as disjunctions of isomorphic state-descriptions.[29] Or (2) he might leave out the proper names in the first place, limiting the resources of his worldmaking language to provide only for qualitative description. This would be like defining structure-descriptions as numerically quantified sentences: there are five round red things, six square blue ones, no square red ones, ...

Either way, our ersatzer needs a new account of representation *de re*: for his qualitative ersatz worlds either say nothing about individuals by name which distinguishes one from the rest, or else they decline to speak of individuals by name at all. But a new account is not far to seek: the ersatzer is welcome to borrow counterpart theory.[30] Recall that along with our linguistic ersatz worlds, we also get linguistic ersatz individuals. These are maximal consistent descriptions of individuals, sets of open sentences or of predicates, which are actualised if they are true of something and which may be actualised according to an ersatz world. They are as complete as the resources of the worldmaking language permit. If the worldmaking language is purely qualitative, or if we take

[27]The system of Skyrms's 'Tractarian Nominalism' requires this division, along with the Ramsification of alien properties of which I complained in section 3.2. See also McMichael, 'A Problem for Actualism about Possible Worlds'.

[28]How about a third remedy: keep the proper names, but endow them with so much descriptive content that a substitution of names would invariably destroy consistency? For instance, he could deem it not just false but inconsistent to say of me, by name, that I inhabit any but the seventeenth epoch. The trouble is that if this world contains indiscernibles, for instance if it exhibits two-way eternal recurrence rather than the one-way recurrence just considered, then our naming cannot be entirely descriptive. No matter how much descriptive loading we give the names, at least the names of indiscernibles can still be swapped without destroying consistency, and that still gives us some haecceitistic differences.

[29]'On Inductive Logic', page 79; note that for the finite case, Carnap takes state-descriptions as conjunctions rather than sets.

[30]McMichael is an anti-haecceitist ersatzer who has proposed exactly that, though it may be that his ersatzism is not the purely linguistic version here considered but rather a linguistic-magical hybrid.

disjunctions to factor out the non-qualitative part of what is said, then these ersatz individuals will be maximally specific qualitative descriptions. We have Humphrey; he is part of the 'concrete' world; he has a complete and correct qualitative description which we may call 'ersatz Humphrey'. Ersatz Humphrey is a purely qualitative ersatz individual, actualised according to the actualised ersatz world. There are no other concrete worlds, says ersatzism, and there are no other-worldly concrete Humphreys to be counterparts of ours. But there are other ersatz worlds; and there are other linguistic ersatz Humphreys, actualised according to various linguistic ersatz worlds but not actually actualised. These unactualised ersatz Humphreys may be so-called because they are, so to speak, counterparts of the actualised ersatz Humphrey, the one that correctly describes Humphrey himself.

The ersatz counterpart relation between ersatz individuals is a stranger thing than it might seem. We would think it was a matter of (intrinsic and extrinsic) qualitative similarity, on a par with relations of qualitative similarity between actual 'concrete' individuals. Not so: after all, ersatz individuals are descriptions, chunks of language, and their similarity *qua* chunks of language may have little to do with the similarity of individuals they would correctly describe. *I* can say that two ersatz individuals are counterparts, in a derivative sense, just when both of them describe genuine individuals that are counterparts in my original sense (which is indeed a matter of qualitative similarity). But an ersatzer cannot agree, because he does not believe in genuine individuals described by unactualised ersatz individuals. Might we say, modally, that two ersatz individuals are counterparts iff, necessarily, if they were both actualised, then they would describe genuine individuals which would be counterparts in the primary sense? No; because of the way ersatz individuals mirror their worlds, it will normally be impossible for two counterpart ersatz individuals both to be actualised, so the conditional will collapse into vacuity. Maybe the ersatzer had better acknowledge his ersatz counterpart relation as part of his primitive apparatus – and a modal primitive to boot. Maybe he won't mind, having already resigned himself to primitive modality.

The anti-haecceitist ersatzer faces the intuitively compelling cases of haecceitistic difference. For the most part he may borrow my way of dealing with them, *mutatis mutandis*, as follows. Not all possibilities are ersatz worlds; ersatz individuals also are possibilities for individuals. (And pairs of them are joint possibilities for pairs of individuals, and so on.) One ersatz individual is a possibility for another – and for the genuine individual, if any, which the second describes – if the first is an ersatz counterpart of the second. One ersatz world may afford many different possibilities for the same (genuine or ersatz) individual; and when the haecceitist thinks we have haecceitistic differences between ersatz worlds, what we really have are different individual possibilities provided by the same ersatz world. But there is one limitation. It reflects one of the lesser shortcomings of linguistic ersatzism: there is no way to get indiscernible ersatz individuals. I might have been one of twins, either the first-born one or the second-born one – no worries so far, two different ersatz twins are actualised according to the same purely qualitative ersatz world, and each one is an individual possibility for me. But also I might have been one, or I might have been the other, of two *qualitatively indiscernible* twins – and this time the anti-haecceitist ersatzer is forced to disagree, because one ersatz individual must do duty for both of the two indiscernible individual possibilities that I claim to distinguish. I think that what he says is intuitively wrong, but also I think that what we want to say about the case is uncertain and negotiable.

If haecceitistic differences are accepted at all, a question arises about their extent. We can distinguish more and less extreme versions of haecceitism. The most moderate version would say that qualitative character does most of the job of determining representation *de re*, and haecceitistic differences only arise when there are ties to be broken. The most extreme version says that qualitative character does nothing at all to constrain representation *de re*: anything could have any qualitative character, for instance there is a (genuine or ersatz) world according to which you are a poached egg. And of course there is a spectrum of intermediate positions.

As an anti-haecceitist, I might be expected to say that the fewer haecceitistic differences the better – best is abstinence, second best is moderation. Not so. A fairly extreme haecceitism is more defensible than it may seem. Further, it has the obvious advantage over moderation: the less we believe in qualitative limits to haecceitistic difference, the less we need an account of how those limits are imposed.[31]

'If someone says I could have been a poached egg, I refute him thus: I could *not* have been a poached egg! Extreme haecceitism flies in the face of common opinion about what's possible, and that's all there is to it.' – Not so. When you insist, no matter how forcefully, that you could not have been a poached egg, the extreme haecceitist can agree. Not quite unequivocally, of course. After all, he *does* believe in worlds according to which you are a poached egg. So if he speaks absolutely without restriction, ignoring none of all the possibilities he thinks there are, then he has to say you could have been a poached egg. But he doesn't have

---

[31]It was Pavel Tichý who persuaded me that extreme haecceitism was a theory worthy of serious attention, and in the discussion to follow I am much indebted to him. But I cannot remember our conversations in any detail; therefore I cannot tell how much of the position I shall present comes from Tichý and how much is a figment of my own imagination. I do not say that Tichý holds, or ever did hold, any part of the position discussed; I do not claim any part of it as my own work.

to speak without restriction. All hands agree that very often our modalities are quantifications restricted to 'accessible' worlds – we tacitly ignore worlds where the past differs, where the actual laws of nature are violated, where there are alien natural properties, or what have you. The extreme haecceitist need only say that this tacit restricting goes further than we usually think: even when all the other restrictions come off, still we persist in ignoring far-out worlds where things differ too much in qualitative character from the way they actually are. Almost always, apart from philosophical discussions that can scarcely be put in evidence as samples of 'linguistic intuition', at least these far-out worlds are left aside as inaccessible. Leaving them aside, indeed you could not have been a poached egg – which is just what you said.

Or is it? You probably thought you *were* speaking unrestrictedly. You had two opinions:

(1) that you meant something true when you said you could not have been a poached egg, and

(2) that in saying so, you did not mean to be quantifying over less than all the possibilities there are.

The extreme haecceitist has a way to agree with (1), but at the cost of disagreeing with (2). He is 'speaking with the vulgar' – that is, he is granting the truth of what you said, but disputing your understanding of what you meant.

Two opposite views are taken of such manoeuvres. Some say that speaking with the vulgar is a worthless trick: we know perfectly well what we mean, and if it isn't what the trickster means, then his merely verbal agreement with us is no agreement at all. It does nothing fair to enhance the plausibility of his doctrines. On this view, to speak with the vulgar by agreeing with (1) while disputing (2) is just a dishonest way of covering up genuine and serious disagreement. Others say there is theory and there is evidence; evidence may not be tampered with, theory must be made to fit evidence, but otherwise theory is up for grabs. If it fits the evidence and is duly systematic, what more could you ask? The evidence is naive linguistic intuition, such as (1), and evidence is sacrosanct. But (2) is just a piece of semantic theory – ill-considered unsystematic folk theory at that – and must compete on equal terms with rival theories. On this second view, success in speaking with the vulgar is a perfect defence.

I take a middle view. There is no sharp line between sacrosanct intuition and freewheeling theory. As theorists, we start where we are – where else? – with a stock of initial opinions, and we try to rework them into something better, guided partly by conservatism and partly by the pursuit of theoretical unity. Any revision of previous opinions counts as some cost.

But some of our opinions are firmer and less negotiable than others. And some are more naive and less theoretical than others. And there seems to be some tendency for the more theoretical ones to be more negotiable. If the extreme haecceitist can agree with (1) at the cost of disputing (2), that is still a cost. He has not escaped scot-free. But the cost that way is much less than if he had been unable to agree with (1) at all. His speaking with the vulgar does something for him, if not everything. Perhaps it does enough. That depends on what he stands to gain.

He stands to avoid a burdensome debt. A moderate haecceitist says that there are qualitative constraints on haecceitistic difference; there is no world at all, however inaccessible, where you are a poached egg. Why not? He owes us some sort of answer, and it may be no easy thing to find a good one. Once you start it's hard to stop – those theories that allow haecceitistic differences at all do not provide any very good way to limit them. The extreme haecceitist needn't explain the limits – because he says there aren't any.

Being a haecceitist involves a choice of evils. Perhaps the least bad way is to make linguistic ersatz worlds in a language equipped with proper names – state-descriptions, or something of that sort. That way, the haecceitist is stuck with primitive modality and with a conflation of some seemingly different possibilities – or so I've argued in section 3.2 – but maybe he doubts this, or maybe he tolerates these drawbacks more willingly than he could tolerate a blanket denial of all haecceitistic differences. Now consider a set of sentences, otherwise a suitable candidate to be an ersatz world, which says of you, by name, that you are a poached egg. If this set is consistent, it is an ersatz world according to which you are a poached egg. The burden of moderation, therefore, is to say what makes this set inconsistent. It isn't inconsistent in a narrowly logical sense. It isn't inconsistent in virtue of axioms concerning the incompatibility of a few fundamental properties and relations of simple things, like the axiom saying that no particle is both positively and negatively charged. And it isn't inconsistent in virtue of axioms relating local to global descriptions, like the axiom saying that if particles are arranged in such-and-such way there is a talking donkey. (The candidate ersatz world says what it should about your particles: they are arranged in the way that's right, according to the local–global axioms, for a poached egg.) *Any* linguistic ersatzer needs axioms of these two kinds; and he needs primitive modality – so I've argued – in order to say which sentences of the proper form are to be his axioms. But the extreme haecceitist, and the anti-haecceitist as well, can stop there. The moderate haecceitist needs further axioms of quite a different kind: axioms in which proper names occur essentially, such as an axiom which says of you, by name, that you are not a poached egg. And once more, the only way to tell which sentences of the appropriate form are the axioms is to say that the axioms are the ones that are necessarily true.

Is that so bad? If you're stuck with primitive modality, why not enjoy it? Anybody can say: my axioms are all the sentences, of *whatever* form, that are necessarily true. Or, bypassing the axioms altogether: a set of sentences is consistent iff it is possible for all its sentences to be true. That will do as well for the moderate as for the extremist. But it doesn't do very well for anybody. What would be more informative – more of a theory – would be to list, if not the axioms themselves, at least the kinds of necessary axioms that suffice for a minimum basis. If so, it seems that the moderate haecceitist requires three fundamentally different kinds, while his rivals at both extremes get by with two. Primitive modality is bad news, and more kinds are worse than fewer. Here the extreme haecceitist is better off than the moderate.

Now suppose that the would-be haecceitist prefers his worlds genuine, rather than ersatz. If so, he'd better accept overlap. (The alternative of a non-qualitative counterpart relation seems more of a mystery still.) Then he has to say – or so I've argued in section 4.2 – that things have no accidental intrinsic properties. Something must have the same intrinsic nature at all worlds that it is part of – all worlds whatever, not ignoring inaccessible worlds. Most of what we usually take to be your intrinsic nature – your shape, size, mass, composition, and so on – is contingent (at least if we drop all accessibility restrictions) and therefore cannot be intrinsic after all. Rather, it consists of external relations which you bear to some but not others of the worlds that share you as a common part. The only intrinsic nature you have left is the part that could not possibly have been otherwise. ('Not possibly' in the most unrestricted sense.) And perhaps not even the whole of that. Suppose you have your exact size accidentally but your approximate size essentially. Might your approximate size, at least, be genuinely intrinsic? – No, because it is a disjunction of exact sizes and those, being accidental, must be relations. Stripped of your shape and size and all, and considered apart from your unexpectedly rich pattern of relationships, you haven't much character to call your own. Small comfort that what's left is yours essentially. You are, if not quite a bare particular, at least pretty scantily clad.

I can't really imagine what it would be like to believe this story – of course those who sing the praises of 'trans-world identity' never have *this* in mind – so I haven't much idea what else someone might be ready to swallow after having gone this far. I can only say that if some haecceitist wants to explain why you could not possibly have been a poached egg, it seems quite a handicap to have begun by turning so many of the differences between you and a poached egg into mere external relations rather than matters of intrinsic nature. External relations are so called because they *don't* supervene on the intrinsic natures of their *relata*, so how can your intrinsic nature stop you from poached-egging some one of the worlds you're part of? I would rather not be required to answer that question. Whatever remnant is left of your intrinsic nature will automatically be essential, but beyond that there seems to be no intelligible way to impose any limit on qualitative variation. In this case too, a fairly extreme haecceitism seems preferable to moderation.

Up to a point, extreme haecceitism runs in parallel with my own anti-haecceitist theory of 'individual possibilities'. Both theories are prepared to distinguish possibilities without qualitative difference of worlds, though for me these possibilities are not different worlds but different possible individuals within the same world. Both begin by acknowledging quite a wide range of possibilities, and afterward cut down the range by accessibility restrictions. Thus I don't deny that poached eggs are genuine possibilities – it's just that they're inaccessible for the likes of us, in other words they're not among our counterparts. Both theories base their accessibility restrictions on qualitative similarity; that makes for inconstancy and indeterminacy, so that in some very special context poached-egghood might count as an accessible possibility for you after all. (See section 4.5.) But the parallels are superficial. The underlying difference of principle remains: my worlds differ qualitatively or not at all.

I have been supposing that haecceitism would be supported by producing intuitive examples of haecceitistic difference. But there is another line of argument in support of haecceitism: Chisholm's Paradox, as it is called by those of us who dislike its conclusion. In a nutshell, it runs as follows. Surely the qualitative essences of things allow at least a little bit of leeway – something which is a certain way could have been at least a little bit different – and yet chains of little differences can add up to big differences, so qualitative essences must allow not just a little leeway but a lot. In that case, they cannot stand in the way of haecceitistic differences.

Chisholm presents the problem as follows. Suppose for the sake of the argument that Adam and Noah can be said to exist and have various properties not only in this world, W^1, but in other worlds as well. (Despite Chisholm's caution in supposing this, I take it to be trans-world identity in the uncontroversial sense – his 'exist in' is my 'exist according to', and it is left wide open what it would mean for Adam and Noah to exist in a world.) The essences of Adam and Noah allow at least a little bit of leeway. So we have a world W^2 where Adam and Noah are just a little bit different – Adam revised just a little bit toward the way Noah is in this world, Noah revised just a little bit toward the way Adam is in this world. But now from the standpoint of W^2 it is still true that the essences allow at least a little bit of leeway. So we have a world W^3 where Adam is revised just a little bit more toward the way Noah is in this world, and Noah just a little bit more toward the way Adam is in this world. But now from the standpoint of W^3 . . . 'Proceeding in this way, we arrive finally at a possible world W^n which would seem to be exactly like our present world W^1, except for the fact that the Adam of W^n may be traced back to the Noah of W^1 and the Noah of W^n may be traced back to the Adam of W^1.' (Chisholm, 'Identity through Possible Worlds', page 3; Loux, page 82.) If so, that is a haecceitistic difference between the worlds W^1 and W^n. So we have a paradox for anti-haecceitists.

In addition, we have been forced to conclude that Adam's and Noah's essences tolerate more revision than we might have thought. And there is worse to come: couldn't we trace a very long chain of very small revisions leading from you to a poached egg? So we have a paradox for essentialists, including moderate haecceitists, who think that the essences of things are somewhat tolerant but not extremely tolerant.

Chisholm's paradox has recently been discussed especially as a problem for essentialism of origins. (See, for instance, Chandler and Salmon.) We have a lot of planks, enough to build two ships to the same plans. (Let's confine our attention to worlds exactly alike up to the start of the ship-building, so that we needn't fuss about the identities of the planks.) Here at this world, W^1, we build the good ship *Adam* from half the planks and the good ship *Noah* from the other half. We think it essential to *Adam* and *Noah*, respectively, to originate from more or less the planks they actually did originate from. More or less – but surely it would be extravagant to deny that *just one pair* of planks could have been swapped! So we have a world W^2 . . . . And in the end we have a world W^n where *Adam* is built from the planks used in W^1 to build *Noah*, and *vice versa*. That may offend against anti-haeccetism, if we arrange the details to make W^1 and W^n come out qualitatively indiscernible. But whether or not it offends against anti-haecceitism, and whether or not we care, certainly it offends against essentialism of origins. Further, the offence begins long before we get all the way to W^n. It's bad enough to have *Adam* and *Noah* each built with a mixture of many right planks and many wrong planks. If our limit of tolerance was three wrong planks, world W^4 is already paradoxical.[32]

I don't distinguish this paradox about origins from Chisholm's original paradox. Nobody ever said that qualitative similarity had to be entirely, or

---

[32]It is, of course, wrong to suppose a determinate and precise limit; Chisholm's paradox is, among other things, a *sorites*. But it would be best if we can separate questions about the proper treatment of vagueness from questions about the metaphysics of modality. I think we can. I regard vagueness as semantic indecision: where we speak vaguely, we have not troubled to settle which of some range of precise meanings our words are meant to express. I believe the vagueness of *de re* modality can be understood in just this way (see section 4.5) and if so, it will do no harm to pretend we have settled on some or other precise limit of tolerance.

even mostly, intrinsic. Match of origins, exact or approximate, or in this case similarity in respect of the previous history of one's planks, will do as one extrinsic respect of qualitative similarity. If we want to place great stress on similarity of origins – I would say, if we speak so as to evoke that sort of counterpart relation – we may.

The paradox is safest if we take many small steps, but simplest if we take few. The simplest version involves only two qualitatively different kinds of worlds, and four maximally specific qualitative roles for individuals – men or ships – in those worlds. Our world, let us suppose, is an Adam–Noah world; the Adam role and the Noah role are occupied in it by the individuals we call Adam and Noah. The Noam role and the Adah role are two compossible roles, each halfway between the Noah role and the Adam role, and as different from one another as the Adam role and the Noah role are. A Noam–Adah world is one where those two roles are occupied. Because the four roles are maximally specific, all worlds where the Adam role and the Noah role are occupied are exactly alike; likewise for all worlds where the Noam role and the Adah role are occupied. Please grant me that essences tolerate enough revision so that, necessarily, an occupant of the Adam role could have occupied the Noam role, and an occupant of the Noam role could have occupied the Noah role. No point denying it – if you do, I will just increase the number and decrease the difference of intermediate roles until the denial becomes absurd, thereby cluttering the example to no good purpose. Consider Adam. His essence tolerates enough revision to let him occupy the Noam role. If he had, his essence would then have tolerated enough more revision to let him occupy the Noah role. So Adam could have been such that he could have occupied the Noah role. *So Adam could have occupied the Noah role.* Here is the fatal move, disastrous for anti-haecceitists and essentialists alike: it leads both to a haecceitistic difference between our Adam–Noah world and another one, and to the conclusion that Adam's essence must be twice as tolerant as we had initially assumed.[33]

Counterpart theory defends against the fatal move by denying that the counterpart relation is transitive. Adam could have occupied the Noam role, because he has a counterpart who does. That counterpart could have

---

[33]Given what we have already assumed, it would be reasonable to assume also that Noah's essence tolerates enough revision to let him occupy the Noam role. If so, we seem to have a second haeccetistic difference. There is the Noam–Adah world where Adam occupies the Noam role, and there is the Noam–Adah world where Noah occupies it. This resembles Salmon's Four Worlds Paradox; except that I get by with three worlds, since I use one world – ours – twice over to provide both Adam and Noah. I reply that the very same Noam–Adah world, and indeed the very same individual possibility in it, represents *de re*, concerning Adam, and that he occupies the Noam role, and also represents *de re*, concerning Noah, that he occupies it. That can happen, I say, if Adam and Noah share a common counterpart.

occupied the Noah role, because he has a counterpart who does. Adam could have been such that he could have occupied the Noah role because he has a counterpart of a counterpart who does. (This counterpart of a counterpart is, in fact, none other than Noah himself.) But a counterpart of a counterpart is not necessarily a counterpart. The counterpart relation works by similarity. Little differences add up to big differences. Noah is enough like someone who is enough like Adam to be his counterpart to be his counterpart, but that doesn't mean that Noah is enough like Adam to be his counterpart.[34]

There is supposed to be a different defence available. Instead of relying on intransitivity of the counterpart relation to block the fatal move – indeed, without assuming counterpart theory at all – we could instead rely on inaccessibility of worlds.[35] It goes as follows. We have three worlds: our world W^1, an Adam–Noah world where Adam occupies the Adam role; W^2, a Noam–Adah world where Adam occupies the Noam role; and W^3, another Adam–Noah world where Adam occupies the Noah role. So there *are* two worlds that differ haecceitistically. And there *is* a world according to which Adam occupies the Noah role. But accessibility is intransitive: W^3 is accessible from W^2 which is accessible from W^1, however W^3 is not accessible from W^1. So from the standpoint of W^1, W^3 doesn't really count – no worries! It is not so, *if* we ignore worlds inaccessible from ours, that we have a case of haecceitistic difference. It is not so, *if* we ignore worlds inaccessible from ours, that we have a world where Adam is revised enough to occupy the Noah role.

Say I: this is no defence, this is capitulation. In these questions of haecceitism and essence, by what right do we ignore worlds that are deemed inaccessible? Accessible or not, they're still worlds. We still believe in them. Why don't they count?

Why are we anti-haecceitists or essentialists in the first place? Did linguistic intuition declare *ex cathedra*: 'Adam could not have occupied the Noah role'? Is our situation that we know this must mean something true though we haven't much notion what? Is our task just to discover some sort of semantic machinery that will make the deliverances of intuition come true, never mind how? Then indeed the machinery of accessibility might serve as well as anything.

Our real situation is not like that at all. If naive intuition claims to decide such a recondite matter, we ought to tell it to hold its tongue. What

---

[34]Again I waive the requirement that nothing can have any counterpart in its own world except itself; I take that to be a feature of some reasonable counterpart relations but not of others. Noah can be disqualified as Adam's counterpart simply on grounds of dissimilarity.

[35]The inaccessibility defence is due to Chandler; it has recently been championed by Salmon against Forbes, who favours a counterpart-theoretic defence.

we want is theory. We need an explanation of how representation *de re* works. One hypothesis says that it works by (genuine or ersatz) qualitative counterpart relations. Other hypotheses say that it works in other ways: by non-qualitative counterpart relations, or by trans-world identity (in the sense of overlap), or by naming, or by magic. One way or another, all these other hypotheses are in bad trouble. Only the qualitative hypothesis is left standing. But that hypothesis gives us no way for any world to represent *de re*, of Adam, that he occupies the Noah role. That's the right reason to believe that he could not have done so. But it's a reason to believe more: that there are no worlds where Adam occupies the Noah role – no worlds *at all*, accessible or not.

Either the non-qualitative hypotheses are all kaput, or else not. If they are, we have no idea how even an *in*accessible world could represent Adam as occupying the Noah role. If not, we have no reason to oppose haecceitism. One way, the inaccessibility defence doesn't work. The other way, we have nothing that needs defending. The 'defence' gives away the point of anti-haecceitism in order to defend the *words* 'Adam could not have occupied the Noah role'. Who needs that?

Someone does need it: the extreme haecceitist. Not that he needs it as a defence against the argument of Chisholm's paradox – on the contrary, he *accepts* the argument! Presumably he thinks the non-qualitative hypotheses are not all kaput. He's already given away the point of anti-haecceitism. But he can use a defence of the words. More urgently, he can use a defence of the words 'Adam could not have occupied a poached-egg role' which squares with his doctrine that there are worlds where Adam does exactly that. Faced with our naive insistence that Adam could not have been a poached egg, he'd better find a way to agree, even if at the cost of making the words mean something a bit different from what we might have thought. As we've already seen, he may speak with the vulgar by positing accessibility restrictions: ignoring far-out worlds where things differ too much from the way they actually are, there are no worlds where Adam has the qualitative character of a poached egg. Indeed the accessibility of the not-too-far-out worlds is intransitive, and indeed the intransitivities are such as to block the argument of Chisholm's paradox in just the way that Chandler proposes. But none of this helps the cause of anti-haecceitism or essentialism. What it helps is the extreme haecceitist's plan of speaking with the vulgar.

Chandler said from the start that the violations of essence were still there, even if consigned to ignored worlds. He writes 'under this hypothesis, "it is not possible that this bicycle should have come into existence made up of entirely different parts" cannot be interpreted to mean that there are no worlds of any sort in which the bicycle came into existence made up of entirely different parts. It can only be taken to mean that worlds in which this occurs, if there are any, are not possible relative to the *actual* world'. ('Plantinga and the Contingently Possible', page 108.) But we look in vain, in Chandler's paper and many other places, for an account of what it means to deny that some world is 'relatively possible'. I think it is like saying: there are things such that, ignoring them, there are no such things. Ignoring all the worlds where such-and-such obnoxious things happen, it is impossible that such things happen. Yes. Small comfort.

I said earlier that, up to a point, the extreme haecceitist's theory parallels my own. In particular, his way and mine of dealing with Chisholm's paradox – his intransitive accessibility of worlds, my intransitive counterpart relation – are much alike. In fact, I too might say that I deal with Chisholm's paradox by calling some possibilities inaccessible. And I too say that accessibility is intransitive because it's a matter of similarity. But when *I* say it, I'm talking about accessibility between individual possibilities; and that's just another terminology for counterpart theory. When Adam occupies the Adam role in our world, and could have been such that he could have occupied the Noah role, what's two steps away is not an inaccessible world; it's an inaccessible individual possibility. We need no haecceitistic differences of worlds. In fact the inaccessible possibility in question isn't other-worldly at all, it's just our very own Noah. And he isn't inaccessible once and for all; there are ever so many counterpart relations, some tighter and some looser, and we can truly say that Noah is a possibility for Adam or that he isn't, so long as we don't say both in quite the same breath. To this inconstancy I now turn.

4.5   Against Constancy

The Great Western Railway ought to have absorbed two other railways early on: the Bristol and Gloucester, and the Birmingham and Gloucester. But it tried to drive too hard a bargain. In 1845 the line from Bristol to Gloucester to Birmingham fell into rival hands. Therefore, after the grouping of railways in 1923, the post-grouping Great Western lacked a part that it might have had. What we know as the Great Western, without the missing line, was the whole of the Great Western; not, as it so easily might have been, a part of a still Greater Western.

This is an instance of a much-discussed paradox.[36] Most versions involve what I would take to be temporal parts, or temporal parts of spatial parts, that something might have had or might have lacked. Such versions

---

[36]See Wiggins, 'On Being in the Same Place at the Same Time'; my 'Counterparts of Persons and Their Bodies'; Gibbard, 'Contingent Identity', Geach, *Reference and Generality* (third edition), pages 215–18; van Inwagen, 'The Doctrine of Arbitrary Undetached Parts'; and Robinson, *The Metaphysics of Material Constitution.*

are all very well for me, since I believe in arbitrary spatiotemporal parts; but to bring home the problem to those who do not believe in temporal parts, I have preferred a purely spatial example. The missing line was at no time a part of the post-grouping Great Western; whereas with better luck in 1845, the line would have been part of it for the entire quarter-century of its existence.[37]

Here is the paradox. Let GWR − be the Great Western as it actually was without the missing line. Let GWR be the Great Western. Let GWR + be the sum of GWR − and the missing line. Here is GWR, in other words GWR − ; they are identical. But the plural is a nonsense of grammar: 'they' are one thing, and *it* is self-identical. What might have happened to *it*? It is GWR; so it would have been greater, in fact it would have been identical to GWR + . It is GWR − ; so it would have been only a part of GWR, not the whole, and hence not identical to GWR, which would instead have been identical to GWR + . Most certainly it, that is GWR − , would not have been identical to GWR + . We contradict ourselves about what would have become of this one thing which we can refer to in two ways: as GWR or as GWR − .

It is incredible to say, under the circumstances, that GWR and GWR − are, after all, two different things: that they are really not identical or that they are only 'relatively identical'. ('Relative identity' is not identity, as may be seen from the fact that it sometimes holds between things which differ in their other relative identities.) We have one thing. What we have two of, besides names for it, are ways of representing. There is some kind of equivocation built into representation *de re*, and the equivocation shows up when we get conflicting answers. We have a suitable (genuine or ersatz) world according to which the Bristol–Gloucester–Birmingham line was absorbed, and we have the actual thing that is called GWR and also called GWR − . That one world manages to represent that one thing as including the line, and also manages to represent that one thing as excluding the line. Evidently the way the representing works is not constant. One name evokes one way of representing, and the other another. At least in this way the difference of names matters, though they differ not at all in what they name.

[37]To dodge strife about temporal parts, it is important that the post-grouping Great Western should have been in some sense a new and different railway from the pre-grouping Great Western. On this I take the word of O. S. Nock; 'It is sometimes lightly remarked that the Great Western was hardly affected at all. This is very far from the case, and it was a new Great Western Railway that came into being from 1923 onwards. The old company did not absorb the local lines in Wales. Although the old Great Western Railway Company was not wound up the leading Welsh lines came into the new organisation as *constituents*, not absorbed companies or subsidiaries'. (*History of the Great Western Railway*, volume III, pages 1–2.)

You might think that what is going on is simpler than I have made out: the names are non-rigid, they amount to abbreviated definite descriptions, they differ in what they would have named if history had been different in the way supposed. (I mean that they differ in what they would have named under their actual interpretation – it is irrelevant what different interpretation they might have been given in the different history.) You might think we're not dealing with representation *de re* at all, still less with a peculiarly equivocal form of it, but merely with a difference in what would have been named by names with different non-rigid senses. This might be partly right. Perhaps my introduction of the names did give them different non-rigid senses, so that the names would not have named the same thing if history had been different. Perhaps I also failed in my attempt to word the crucial sentences so as to favour *de re* readings. That hypothesis solves our original problem. But that doesn't get us far. For I can restate the problem so that the difference-between-non-rigid-names solution will not apply.

I ask you: think of this thing we've been talking about under two names – now, what would have happened to *it* if the line had been absorbed? Now you're stuck. I haven't used either name. You know well enough what thing is in question, and you know well enough what sort of (genuine or ersatz) world is in question, you know that I'm asking *de re* what happens to that thing according to such a world – and you have no unequivocally right answer. Your trouble, I think, is that two ways of representing have been evoked just previously, and now I'm giving you no guidance to help you choose between them. The fact (if it is a fact) that the two ways were evoked by two non-rigid names is irrelevant.

Here is another way to recover our problem, blocking the difference-of-non-rigid-names solution. Let's introduce new names which definitely are abbreviated descriptions:

GWR/Jupiter $=^{df}$ that which is GWR if the line was not absorbed, otherwise the planet Jupiter;

GWR $-$ /Jupiter $=^{df}$ that which is GWR $-$ if the line was not absorbed, otherwise the planet Jupiter.

These contrived names are non-rigid for sure; but in a way that blocks the solution. Had the line been absorbed, they would not have differed in what they named; because then they would both have named (a counterpart of) Jupiter. And in actuality also they do not differ in what they name; because the line was not absorbed, so they both name the same thing, namely the thing we have called sometimes GWR and sometimes GWR $-$. So consider this thing. What might have happened to *it*? *It* is GWR/Jupiter, namely by being GWR; so if the line had been absorbed, *it* would have included the line, *it* would have been GWR $+$.

It is GWR – /Jupiter, namely by being GWR – ; so if the line had been absorbed, *it* would not have included the line, *it* would still have been GWR – . In no case would *it* have been the planet Jupiter, right? – If you agree with that, you must agree that my wording with the stressed pronouns succeeded in setting up a *de re* reading and making it irrelevant what our non-rigid names would have named. (This may not be a firm matter; if my life depended on it I could probably manage to hear the question in the other way and give an honest answer 'It would have been Jupiter'. Perhaps some people could hear it that way more easily than I. It is enough that the reading I have described is possible, it needn't be inevitable.) So we have back our inconstancy in representation *de re*. And the difference between the contrived names which makes them evoke different ways of representing is not a difference in what they would have named if the line had been absorbed, because there is no such difference. Instead, our contrived names borrowed the evocative powers of the original names 'GWR' and 'GWR – ' that appeared so conspicuously within them and within their definitions. I admit I helped them along when I reminded you that GWR/Jupiter was GWR, and that GWR – /Jupiter was GWR – . But as those identities are true, I do not see how it can have been unfair to say so.

I think there is a great range of cases in which there is no determinate right answer to questions about representation *de re*, and therefore no right answer to questions about modality or counterfactuals *de re*.[38] Could Hubert Humphrey have been an angel? A human born to different parents? A human born to different parents in ancient Egypt? A robot? A clever donkey that talks? An ordinary donkey? A poached egg? Given some contextual guidance, these questions should have sensible answers. There are ways of representing whereby some worlds represent him as an angel, there are ways of representing whereby none do. Your problem is that the right way of representing is determined, or perhaps underdetermined, by context – and I supplied no context.

You could do worse than plunge for the first answer to come into your head, and defend that strenuously. If you did, your answer would be right. For your answer itself would create a context, and the context would select a way of representing, and the way of representing would be such as to make your answer true. (If at all possible. Perhaps not if you gave an especially silly answer, such as that Humphrey could have been a poached egg, yet he could not have been a human born to different parents.) That is how it is in general with dependence on complex features of context. There is a rule of accommodation: what you say makes itself true, if at all possible, by creating a context that selects the relevant features so as to make it true. Say that France is hexagonal, and you thereby set

[38]However, attitudes *de re* are a very different story. There is still indeterminacy, but it arises in other ways. See the final section of my 'Attitudes *De Dicto* and *De Se*'.

the standards of precision low, and you speak the truth; say that France is not hexagonal (preferably on some other occasion) and you set the standards high, and again you speak the truth.[39] In parallel fashion, I suggest that those philosophers who preach that origins are essential are absolutely right – in the context of their own preaching. They make themselves right: their preaching constitutes a context in which *de re* modality is governed by a way of representing (as I think, by a counterpart relation) that requires match of origins. But if I ask how things would be if Saul Kripke had come from no sperm and egg but had been brought by a stork, that makes equally good sense. I create a context that makes my question make sense, and to do so it has to be a context that makes origins not be essential.

Attend to the variety of what we say about modality and counterfactuals *de re*, and I think you will find abundant evidence that we do not have settled answers, fixed once and for all, about what is true concerning a certain individual according to a certain (genuine or ersatz) world. The way of representing is not at all constant. Different answers are often right in different contexts, as witness the comfort with which we adhere to, or presuppose, opposed answers. '*It* would have included the Bristol–Gloucester–Birmingham line.' '*It* would have been only part of a still Greater Western.' – Can you really take this as a dispute? It can very well happen that no answer is determinately right, for lack of the contextual guidance that normally does the determining.

Even within a single context, we can find opposed answers that are right together. That could happen in the case of the Great Western and the missing line. But it happens more prominently in familiar puzzles about how a bit of stuff constitutes the thing that is made of it. To dodge strife about temporal parts, it will be best to begin with a case where the stuff constitutes the thing for all the time that either the stuff or the thing exists: the plastic is synthesised right in the mold, so it no sooner exists at all than it constitutes the dishpan; and the dishpan is destroyed just when the plastic is incinerated. But suppose the factory had received its order for plastic dishpans a day later. The same bit of plastic would have been made; for the raw materials were already divided into portions just right to fill one mold. But it would have been made in another mold, and it would have constituted a wastebasket. The dishpan would have been made the next day out of different plastic. It reeks of double counting to say that here we have a dishpan, and we also have a dishpan-shaped bit of plastic that is just where the dishpan is, weighs just what the dishpan weighs (why don't the two together weigh twice as much?), and so on. This multiplication of entities is absurd on its face; and it only obfuscates the matter if we say that the plastic and the dishpan are

---

[39]See my 'Scorekeeping in a Language Game'.

'relatively identical' while implying that they are absolutely *not* identical.

But if the plastic and the dishpan are identical, what would have happened to 'them', or rather to *it*, if the plastic had been made in the form of a wastebasket, and the dishpan had been made the next day out of different plastic? *It* would have been a wastebasket; *it* would have been a dishpan made the next day – those answers, I submit, are both correct. The (genuine or ersatz) world in question represents the one thing twice over, in two different ways, once as a bit of plastic in the form of a wastebasket, and once as another bit of plastic in the form of a dishpan made the next day. Both ways of representing work together in one context to make good sense of the statement that the plastic does constitute the dishpan but it might not have done; in fact, it *is* the dishpan ('is' of identity) but it might not have been. It and the dishpan – it and itself – might have coexisted without being identical! This sounds outrageous. It sounds like doublethink – I concede the identity of the plastic and the dishpan, yet when it suits me I still distinguish them. Not so. I only distinguish what everyone must distinguish: two different references, in different words, to the one thing. And I say that these different references tend to evoke two different ways of representing, whereby one world can make conflicting representations *de re* concerning that one thing. You can double up the ways of representing, here within one context, for one world, concerning one plastic dishpan. Or else you can double up entities, somehow distinguishing the dishpan from its plastic after all. I submit that the first doubling is more credible than the second.

I think the more common case of temporary constitution is no different. This time, make a statue of wax. The wax exists before and after the statue does, but for a time – for all the time the statue exists – the wax constitutes it. The statue and a temporal part of the wax are identical. Under other circumstances it would have been a statue made of different wax; and it would have been formed into a nondescript lump sitting next to the statue. A certain world represents it twice over in different ways, once as the statue and once as the lump. Likewise for the still more temporary constitution of a wave by ever-changing water, or a flame by ever-changing gas.

Notice the one thing I can't say: I can't pull out the subject and conjoin the predicates, saying in the first case 'it would have been both a wastebasket and a dishpan made the next day' or in the second case 'it would have been both a statue made of different wax and formed into a nondescript lump'. For whatever the world represents *de re*, in the two different ways, it does not represent that anything satisfies the conjoined predicates.

I do not see how the resources of quantified modal logic can draw the distinction we need. Let A specify the circumstances in question; let F and G be the two predicates not to be conjoined. We have two formulas:

necessarily, if A then F(X), and necessarily, if A then G(X);

necessarily, if A then both F(X) and G(X).

But they will be equivalent, under any standard treatment. So we cannot say that the first is true and the second false if the A-worlds represent X in one way as satisfying F and in another way as satisfying G. But if the resources of quantified modal logic, unless improved in some non-standard way, do not know how to draw the distinction we need, the more fools they. *We* know how to draw it.

The inconstancy of *de re* representation can easily be explained in counterpart theory. We have many and varied relations of comparative similarity. Some differ from others because they put different weights or priorities on different respects of (intrinsic or extrinsic) qualitative similarity; and even if they are alike in the respects of comparison they stress, they can still differ because one is more stringent than another. Any of these relations is a candidate to be expressed by the word 'counterpart'. Likewise many different relations, some more stringent and some less, some stressing some respects of comparison and others stressing others, have a claim to be called 'similarity'. The exact meaning of 'counterpart' or 'similar' is neither constant nor determinate. These words equivocally express a range of different semantic values, and the limits of the range are subject to pressures of context. Two things may be counterparts in one context, but not in another; or it may be indeterminate whether two things are counterparts. Inconstancy in representation *de re* is exactly what we should expect under the hypothesis that it works by comparative overall similarity of complex things. What would be hard to understand, had it been found, would be constancy.

   (If counterpart theory is right, the language of *de re* modality is governed by relations of similarity. And of course the language in which we say explicitly that things are similar or different also is governed by relations of similarity. Suppose we mix the two; then the mixed language will be governed by similarity twice over. Then it is vulnerable twice over to indeterminacy, and subject twice over to contextual pressures that push the resolution of indeterminacy one way or another. Should we expect uniform resolution, so that the *de re* modality is governed by exactly the same relations of similarity that govern explicit predications of similarity or difference? Or should we expect a messier situation, in which one sort of similarity gets played off against another? If we had uniform resolution then, as Feldman and others have observed, it would be contradictory to say such things as that I might have been very different from the way I actually am. (Worse yet: I might have been very different from the way I actually am while at the same time someone else was very similar to the way I actually am.) That certainly does not *sound* contradictory. It sounds true. And what makes it true, I suggest, is a counterpart of mine who is very similar to me under one similarity relation that governs the *de re* modality, but very dissimilar to me under another similarity relation that governs the explicit predications. For instance, someone might be my counterpart in virtue of close match of origins, but differ very much from me in later life. (I don't mean to suggest that either similarity relation is fully determinate; or that one sort of similarity relation is assigned permanently to one job and another to the other.) We have the messy situation, with different similarity relations playing off against each other in a single context. And that should be no surprise: the same thing happens even when all talk of similarity is explicit and *de re* modality is out of the picture. I can say that Ted and Fred are very much alike, yet very different. Uniform resolutions would make that a contradiction – so much the worse for them! The fundamental principle of contextual resolution of indeterminacy is that what makes a resolution right is that it makes good sense of what has been said. It is no good making what has been said come out flagrantly contradictory, so any uniform resolution gets disqualified at once. As for the narrowing down of non-uniform resolutions, most likely that must wait on what gets said next.)

A world where the Bristol–Gloucester–Birmingham line was absorbed provides two rivals to serve as counterparts of the this-worldly Great Western Railway. The larger candidate is better in one way: like the this-worldly Great Western Railway, it is the whole of a railway. The smaller candidate is better in other ways: it matches the geographical extent of the this-worldly Great Western, and also its parts can be put into correspondence with the parts of the this-worldly Great Western in such a way that corresponding parts are excellent counterparts of one another. Stress the respects of comparison in which the first candidate has the advantage, and we get a counterpart relation whereby the world in question represents the Great Western as including the line. Stress the respects in which the second has the advantage, and we get a counterpart relation whereby the world in question represents the Great Western as being no more extensive than it actually is, and as being less than the whole of a railway. It is understandable that the first counterpart relation should be evoked by the name 'GWR' for the this-worldly Great Western, and that the second should be evoked by the alternative name 'GWR – ' for the very same thing. Likewise it is understandable that the contrived names 'GWR/Jupiter' and 'GWR – /Jupiter' also should evoke the first and second counterpart relations respectively, thanks to the appearance within them of the original names. If the contrived names are less decisively evocative, that too is only to be expected.[40]

When discussing the case in a more neutral setting, I dodged the question whether the names 'GWR' and 'GWR – ' were rigid. In the setting of counterpart theory, I can return to that question. Rigidity in the strict sense means naming the same thing at all worlds, or at least all worlds where that thing exists. That's all very well for numerals and the like, but without overlap of worlds we wouldn't expect an ordinary proper name of a person or a thing – of a railway, say – to be strictly rigid. However, an ordinary proper name might well be *quasi-rigid*: that is, it might name at another world the counterpart there of what it names here.

(Complications. (1) What if there is no counterpart at the other world? – Then let the name be denotationless there. (2) What if there are two? – Then let the name be indeterminate in denotation between the two. (3) What if, despite all that wording and context may do to help, it remains indeterminate which inhabitant of the other world is the counterpart of the thing named here? – Then again let the name be indeterminate in denotation. (4) So far, I have been saying what it means for a name to be quasi-rigid with respect to this world; but it can likewise be quasi-rigid with respect to other worlds, and quasi-rigid *simpliciter* iff it is so with respect to every world where it names anything.)

Given inconstancy of counterpart relations, we may have to say that a name is quasi-rigid under some counterpart relations but not under others. For instance, a name may be quasi-rigid under the counterpart relation it tends to evoke, but not under the counterpart relation that another name of the same thing tends to evoke. I think that is the case for the names 'GWR' and 'GWR – ', given the way I introduced them. (However the contrived names 'GWR/Jupiter' and 'GWR/Jupiter' are not quasi-rigid under any reasonable counterpart relation.) When a name is quasi-rigid under the counterpart relation it tends to evoke, then it doesn't matter whether or not we take its occurrence in a modalised predication as *de re*. We might ask whether the this-worldly denotation of 'GWR' is such that its other-worldly counterpart, under the relation evoked by 'GWR', is the whole of a railway. Or we might ask whether the other-worldly denotation of 'GWR', which is to be the counterpart

---

[40]I claim that in this case and many others, different names of the same thing tend to evoke different counterpart relations, thereby reducing the semantic indeterminacy of modal idioms governed by counterpart relations. But I do not claim (1) that evocative names eliminate all indeterminacy, or (2) that an evocative name favouring one sort of counterpart relation always outweighs other contextual pressures favouring another, or (3) that every name without exception – still less, every referring expression – tends to evoke some counterpart relations rather than others, or (4) that the semantic indeterminacy of modal idioms governed by counterpart relations is so severe as to render those idioms meaningless except when something – as it might be, an evocative name – is present to reduce the indeterminacy. Compare Gibbard's treatment of contingent identity, which resembles mine but does make these claims; thus it seems to me fundamentally right, but exaggerated.

of the this-worldly denotation under the relation evoked by 'GWR', is the whole of a railway. It's the same question either way. There are three ways for the choice of a name to make a difference to the proposition expressed by a sentence: (1) by a difference in this-worldly denotation, (2) by a difference in other-worldly denotation, and (3) by a difference in what counterpart relations tends to be evoked. If a name is quasi-rigid under the counterpart relation it tends to evoke, then (2) and (3) merge. To isolate the effect of (3) – and thereby see the need for inconstancy of counterpart relations – we must blank out (2), as I did in introducing the contrived names 'GWR/Jupiter' and 'GWR – /Jupiter'.

A parallel treatment applies to our case of a thing and the matter that constitutes it. Here at this world we have the plastic made in the form of a dishpan out of a certain portion of raw materials; and at another world, the plastic made out of the counterpart of that portion of raw materials was made in the form of a wastebasket, and a dishpan was made the next day out of different plastic. Let us suppose that counterparthood for the portion of raw materials is unproblematic: perhaps the raw materials already were divided into separate portions before there was any divergence between the alternative world and ours. We have two candidates to be the counterpart of the plastic which is the dishpan. If we stress match of origins, the other-worldly wastebasket is the better candidate. So we have a counterpart relation – that is, a way of representing – whereby the world in question represents the plastic, that is the dishpan, as being made in the form of a wastebasket instead. But if we stress similarity of form, and perhaps also such matters as the order it fills and the place to which it goes, the other-worldly dishpan is the better candidate. So we have another counterpart relation – another way of representing – whereby the world in question represents the dishpan, that is the plastic, as being made a day later out of different raw materials. Here at this world (the only world it is part of) the dishpan just is the plastic; but different ways of referring to this single thing tend to evoke different counterpart relations.

Likewise for our case of temporary constitution: the statue is a temporal part of the wax; but under one counterpart relation a certain world represents it as a nondescript lump, whereas under another counterpart relation that same world represents it as a statue made of different wax. Calling it the wax evokes the first counterpart relation, calling it the statue evokes the second.[41]

I distinguish two different ways that something might have multiple counterparts in another world. The first way is that there are different

---

[41]See Robinson for a general discussion of constitution in terms of inconstancy of counterparts; and my 'Counterparts of Persons and Their Bodies' for discussion of a special case, the permanent or temporary constitution of a person by his body.

counterpart relations, differing in the comparative weights or priorities they give to different respects of comparison, which favour different candidates. This is the inconstancy of counterparts that we have been considering. The second way is that there might be a single counterpart relation, given by a single system of weights or priorities, which on occasion is one–many: it delivers multiple counterparts because of ties – say, the tie between a pair of twins. It is not that one system of weights and priorities favours one twin, and another favours the other. (Indeed that might be so, but take a case where it is not.) Rather, any reasonable system results in a tie. It was this second way of having multiple counterparts that forced us to acknowledge different individual possibilities within a single world, lest we be tempted to demand haecceitistic differences between the worlds themselves. But we need to allow for both ways of having multiple counterparts. The first cannot take the place of the second, because sometimes the candidates will be tied under any reasonable standards. The second cannot take the place of the first, because it does not provide a way for influence of context to tilt the decision one way or the other.

So far I have simplified the discussion of inconstancy by ignoring my previous proposal that accessible individual possibilities, not worlds, are what represent *de re*. But now we should merge the two topics, to acknowledge that inconstancy and ties might occur together. Take first the case of the Great Western and the missing line. We have the this-worldly individual, excluding the line, which we call GWR or GWR – . A world where the line was absorbed gives us two individuals, that is, two individual possibilities: the one that includes the line and the one that doesn't. It is not at all equivocal what these two possibilities, if accessible, would represent *de re* concerning the this-worldly individual. The first would represent it as including the line; whereas the second would represent it as excluding the line and being less than the whole of a railway. What *is* in question is which one is accessible. This question is the same as the question which individual is the counterpart. Translating what I said before: there are two accessibility relations for individual possibilities, both based on comparative similarity. The name 'GWR' (or 'GWR/Jupiter') for the this-worldly individual tends to evoke the accessibility relation that stresses similarity in respect of being the whole of a railway. The name 'GWR – ' (or 'GWR – /Jupiter'), though it names the same thing, tends to evoke the accessibility relation that stresses similarity in geographical extent and correspondence of parts. If nothing is said that decisively evokes one rather than the other, we might fall into indecision. Or perhaps by default we get an accessibility relation that makes *both* individual possibilities accessible. In that case – as in the cases of twin counterparts that tempt us into haecceitism – one world gives us two different individual possibilities for the same thing. But there is another way to get multiple individual possibilities: suppose that every epoch of a world of eternal recurrence contains a Great Western that succeeds in absorbing the line. This world provides two rival infinite classes of counterparts – that is, of individual possibilities – for the this-worldly Great Western. Stress one respect of similarity, and it provides infinitely many accessible individual possibilities of including the line; stress another, and it provides infinitely many accessible individual possibilities of excluding the line and being less than the whole of a railway; do nothing to evoke one stress or the other, and either it becomes indeterminate which kind of individual possibilities that world affords or else it affords a mixture of both kinds.

Along with individual possibilities, we had joint possibilities for sequences; for instance, pairs. These include identity pairs and non-identity pairs; and so we get, if not exactly a sense in which one thing might have been two (or *vice versa*), at least a sense in which an identity pair might have been a non-identity pair (or *vice versa*). I don't know whether it is wise to call this 'contingent identity'. Perhaps so; or perhaps that phrase should be reserved either for the unproblematic phenomenon of contingent co-referentiality of descriptions, or else for the absurd notion that one thing has an individual possibility of not being self-identical. At any rate, call the phenomenon what you will, we have the this-worldly identity pair of GWR and GWR – , that is of one thing twice over; and we have the other-worldly non-identity pair of GWR and GWR – , two different things. The second pair, if it were an accessible joint possibility for the first pair, would provide the identity pair with a possibility of being non-identical. But to give the requisite accessibility of pairs, we need to stress different respects of similarity for the first terms of the pairs and for the second; and besides, we have to play down the respect of similarity in which identity pairs are *ipso facto* alike and non-identity pairs are *ipso facto* alike. That may seem an implausibly complicated way for accessibility of pairs to work. Yet unless this sort of accessibility relation is available, what accounts for our inclination to say that one thing might have been two? I suppose the relation is available; and it is evoked when it must be, that is when it is required if what has been said is to be true.

It is well for my preferred theory – genuine modal realism, without overlap, and with qualitative counterpart relations – that it has no trouble making representation *de re* come out inconstant. But I cannot claim this as an advantage of my approach over its leading rivals, because they too – with one partial exception – can provide for inconstancy with equal ease.

Suppose we preferred the haecceitistic sort of counterpart theory: genuine modal realism, no overlap between worlds, representation *de re* by means of non-qualitative counterpart relations. As noted in the previous section, a non-qualitative counterpart relation would be a very mysterious thing to have to take as primitive. But I don't see that many of them would be significantly more mysterious than one, and if we had many counterpart relations of whatever sort, we would have the resources for inconstancy. (Or perhaps we could have mixed counterpart relations, conjoining one fixed non-qualitative relation with various different qualitative similarity relations. The non-qualitative part provides the desired haecceitistic differences, the qualitative part provides the inconstancy.) The mysteries of this theory are severe, but provision for inconstancy does nothing to make them worse.

Suppose next that we preferred linguistic ersatzism in an anti-haecceitistic version: we have maximal consistent descriptions in qualitative terms – qualitative ersatz individuals – and an ersatz world represents *de re* by means of ersatz counterpart relationships among these ersatz individuals. For instance, we have one ersatz individual that describes Humphrey as he actually is, we have a second that is a counterpart of the first but differs by including the description 'wins the presidency', we have an ersatz world according to which that second ersatz individual is actualised; and thereby that ersatz world represents Humphrey *de re* as winning. (Or we might prefer to say that it is the counterpart ersatz individual itself – an accessible individual possibility – that does the representing *de re*.) If so, it is as easy as ever to have many respects of comparison. For instance, we have one ersatz individual that describes the Great Western as it actually is, without the Bristol–Gloucester–Birmingham line; and we have two others, both actualised according to a certain ersatz world, which are rival candidates to be counterparts of the first. One of them purports to describe a Greater Western that includes the line; whereas the other purports to describe something that is less than the whole of a railway and that excludes the line. Which candidate is favoured depends on how much weight we give to different respects of comparison; and that is how one ersatz world represents the Great Western in two conflicting ways (alternatively, that is how one ersatz world affords two conflicting individual possibilities for it).

Suppose next that we preferred linguistic ersatzism in its haecceitistic version, in which representation *de re* works by naming. A linguistic ersatz world represents *de re*, concerning the Great Western, that it does or doesn't include the line, by containing or implying a sentence which says of the Great Western, by name, that it does or doesn't include the line. But then we can have inconstancy if our worldmaking language includes two different names for the Great Western: 'GWR' and 'GWR – ', for instance. An ersatz world can represent the Great Western under one name as more inclusive, under the other name as being less than the whole of a railway. In order to make sure that when the names go their separate ways, the difference between them will be in the right direction, the names must have some descriptive content; axioms that distinguish the names will have to figure in the definitions of consistency and thence of ersatz worlds.

As we might expect, the one theory that has some trouble providing for inconstancy is genuine modal realism with overlap, in which representation *de re* works by trans-world identity. It was easy to see how we could have many rival candidates to be the counterpart relation, differing both in stringency and in the stress given to various respects of comparison. Not so for identity. There is only one candidate to be the relation of (numerical) identity: it can only be the relation that everything bears to itself and nothing bears to anything else. There is no room for different contexts to go different ways about which relation is to be called identity; and there is no room for indeterminacy caused by indecision between rival candidates.

(The truth value of an identity *sentence* may indeed depend on context, or remain indeterminate. But when that happens, the fault lies not with identity but elsewhere. If the singular terms that flank the identity sign have inconstant or indeterminate denotation, that is apt to make the truth value of the sentence inconstant or indeterminate. But that is not a case of inconstant or indeterminate identity between two different things denoted by those terms; nor yet is it a case of inconstant or indeterminate self-identity. The relevant things are one and all thoroughly self-identical, and none of them is at all identical to anything except itself. What's left murky is the question which exactly are the relevant things.)

Then to the extent that representation *de re* works by trans-world identity, understood as overlap, there is no room for it to be inconstant or indeterminate whether a given world represents a given thing as existing; or, if it does, which part of that world it is whose properties are those that the given thing has according to that world. And that makes it difficult for matters of *de re* modality to be inconstant or indeterminate. Suppose we ask whether Humphrey might have been exactly spherical in shape. Suppose we stipulate that we have in mind the broadest sort of possibility, without any accessibility restrictions. Suppose, *per impossibile*, that spherical shape is not the intrinsic property it seems to be, but rather is a relation that things sometimes bear to worlds of which they are parts – so really we are asking whether Humphrey spheres any of the worlds he lives in. And yet suppose that 'exactly spherical' remains as precise and unequivocal as we are accustomed to think. Now *all* openings for inconstancy and indeterminacy are gone. Our question has to have a right answer, constant and determinate.

But that is only so long as the question concerns absolutely unrestricted possibility. I've argued that modal realism with overlap is congenial to extreme haecceitism, and uncongenial to essentialist constraints. If so, then we could be content to agree that, speaking absolutely unrestrictedly, Humphrey could indeed have been exactly spherical in shape. That is quite definitely so – no inconstancy, no indeterminacy. And he could have been stranger things than that! But on an extreme haecceitist overlap theory, absolutely unrestricted modality loses much of its interest. To capture more commonplace modal opinions, we bring on the accessibility restrictions – and these *are* matters of the qualitative character of things, therefore they are ideally suited to go inconstant and indeterminate. It may be absolutely settled that a world represents Humphrey as spherical – but it may be completely unsettled whether that world is a not-too-far-out world where things are not too different from the way they actually are, and therefore completely unsettled whether that world is one that we should ignore as inaccessible when we say what might have happened to Humphrey.

Counterpart theory treats the question whether Humphrey might have been spherical as follows. Some other-worldly spheres are rather distant counterparts of Humphrey, none are very close counterparts of him, and how close the closest of them are depends on which respects of comparison you stress. So the question whether Humphrey might have been spherical, that is whether any sphere is his counterpart, takes the form: how close is close enough? An extreme haecceitist overlap theory treats the same question as follows. Some other worlds where Humphrey is a sphere are rather distantly accessible from our world, none are very closely accessible, and how close the closest of them are depends on which respect of comparison you stress. So the question whether Humphrey might have been spherical, that is whether any world where he is spherical is accessible from ours, takes the form: how close is close enough? In the unclear cases as in the clear ones, this theory runs parallel to counterpart theory. Restricted modality *de re* can be as inconstant and indeterminate as we please.

Our initial example of inconstancy turns not on stringency but on different respects of comparison. Here again, *mutatis mutandis*, an extreme haecceitist overlap theory runs parallel to counterpart theory. We have the individual GWR, in other words GWR − ; under the overlap theory, it is absolutely settled which worlds do and do not represent that individual as including the missing line; but it is not settled whether that individual might have included the missing line until it is settled which are the worlds we ought not to ignore. And that is a matter of how we weigh similarity in respect of being a whole railway versus similarity in respect of geographical extent and correspondence of parts. There context matters, and different names might evoke different accessibility relations. And that is how GWR and GWR − are identical, yet we want to say, speaking *de re* (since the Jupiter trick would block the alternative solution), that GWR would have included the line and GWR − would have been less than the whole of a railway.

So far, so good. But there is one thing that I think we want to say that cannot be provided in the overlap theory, and that is one more reason why some other view should be preferred. Take the case of the plastic that constitutes the dishpan for the whole of the time that either one exists. (The case of GWR and GWR – would do as well.) I say that the plastic and the dishpan are identical. I also say they might not have been, namely if the plastic had been made in the shape of a wastebasket and the dishpan had been made the next day from different plastic. What I mean is not the uncontroversial truth that 'the plastic' and 'the dishpan' (used exactly as I use them, say by an other-worldly duplicate of me) might not have referred to the same thing. And what I mean is not the absurd falsehood that something, namely the plastic which is the dishpan, has a *de re* possibility of failing to be self-identical. What I mean is that an identity pair has the *de re* possibility of being a non-identity pair. Is there a way to make sense of this? Counterpart theory obliges, once we provide for pairs to be counterparts of pairs. But the overlap theory will not oblige, and that is a point against it.

To oblige, the overlap theory would have to say that the very same pair is an identity pair at one world and a non-identity pair at another world. This is not a difference in how the pair is represented, as an ersatzer would say. It is not a difference between counterpart pairs, as I would say. Only one alternative remains: it must be a difference in the relations that the one pair bears to different worlds. But how could that be true? Being an identity pair is an intrinsic matter. That is just the way the pair is in itself, not an external relation of the pair to this world. It is hard enough to understand the idea that intrinsically shapeless things are differently shape-related to different worlds (or times) but it is harder still to understand how something could bear a being-an-identity-pair relation to some worlds and not to others. This just cannot be so. If the pair is wholly present in many worlds, then if it's an identity pair anywhere then it's an identity pair everywhere. At no world is it anything else. Then it is determinately and unrestrictedly necessary that it be an identity pair. That is inescapable: nothing we might do with inconstant accessibility restrictions can undo it.

'Contingent identity' is a tricky business. It isn't clear what should be meant by the phrase: some things it might mean are uncontroversial, some are absurd. But one thing to mean by it which seems neither trivial nor absurd is that an identity pair has the *de re* possibility of being a non-identity pair. Some theories, for instance counterpart theory, can make good enough sense of that. But the overlap theory, to its discredit, cannot.

Works Cited

Adams, Robert M. 'Theories of Actuality', *Noûs*, 8 (1974), pp. 211–31; reprinted in Loux, *The Possible and the Actual.*

— 'Primitive Thisness and Primitive Identity', *Journal of Philosophy*, 76 (1979), pp. 5–26.

— 'Actualism and Thisness', *Synthese*, 49 (1981), pp. 3–42.

Anderson, John. 'The Knower and the Known', *Proceedings of the Aristotelian Society*, 27 (1927), pp. 61–84.

Anscombe, G. E. M. *Intention*. Blackwell, 1957.

Armstrong, D. M. *Universals and Scientific Realism* (two volumes). Cambridge University Press, 1978.

— 'Identity Through Time', in *Time and Cause: Essays Presented to Richard Taylor*, ed. by Peter van Inwagen, Reidel, 1980.

Bealer, George. *Quality and Concept*. Clarendon, 1982.

Benacerraf, Paul. 'Mathematical Truth', *Journal of Philosophy*, 70 (1973), pp. 661–79.

Bennett, Jonathan. 'Killing and Letting Die' (first of three lectures on 'Morality and Consequences'), in *The Tanner Lectures on Human Values*, volume II, ed. by Sterling W. McMurrin, Cambridge University Press, 1981.

Bigelow, John. 'Possible Worlds Foundations for Probability', *Journal of Philosophical Logic*, 5 (1976), pp. 299–320.

— 'Believing in Semantics', *Linguistics and Philosophy*, 2 (1978), pp. 101–44.

Black, Max. 'The Elusiveness of Sets', *Review of Metaphysics*, 24 (1971), pp. 614–36.

Boolos, George. 'To Be is to Be a Value of a Variable (or to Be Some Values of Some Variables)', *Journal of Philosophy*, 81 (1984), pp. 430–49.

Bricker, Phillip. *Worlds and Propositions: The Structure of Logical Space*. Ph.D. dissertation, Princeton University, 1983.

Burge, Tyler. 'Individualism and the Mental', *Midwest Studies in Philosophy*, 4 (1979), pp. 73–121.

Campbell, Keith K. 'The Metaphysic of Abstract Particulars', *Midwest Studies in Philosophy*, 6 (1981), pp. 477–88.

— 'Abstract Particulars and the Philosophy of Mind', *Australasian Journal of Philosophy*, 61 (1983), pp. 129–41.

Carnap, Rudolf. 'On Inductive Logic', *Philosophy of Science*, 12 (1945), pp. 72–97.

— *Meaning and Necessity*. University of Chicago Press, 1947.

— 'A Basic System of Inductive Logic', Part I, in *Studies in Inductive Logic and Probability*, volume I, ed. by Rudolf Carnap and Richard C. Jeffrey, University of California Press, 1971; part II, in *Studies in Inductive Logic and Probability*, volume II, ed. by Richard C. Jeffrey, University of California Press, 1980.

Chandler, Hugh. 'Plantinga and the Contingently Possible', *Analysis*, 36 (1976), pp. 106–9.

Chisholm, Roderick. 'Identity through Possible Worlds: Some Questions', *Noûs*, 1 (1967), pp. 1–8; reprinted in Loux, *The Possible and the Actual*.

— *The First Person: An Essay on Reference and Intentionality*. Harvester Press, 1981.

Cresswell, M. J. 'The World is Everything that is the Case', *Australasian Journal of Philosophy*, 50 (1972), pp. 1–13; reprinted in Loux, *The Possible and the Actual*.

— *Logics and Languages*. Methuen, 1973.

— 'Hyperintensional Logic', *Studia Logica*, 34 (1975), pp. 25–38.

— and von Stechow, Arnim. '*De Re* Belief Generalized', *Linguistics and Philosophy*, 5 (1982), pp. 505–36.

Davies, Martin. *Meaning, Quantification, Necessity: Themes in Philosophical Logic*. Routledge and Kegan Paul, 1981.

Dummett, Michael. *Frege: Philosophy of Language*. Duckworth, 1973.

Ellis, Brian. *Rational Belief Systems*. Blackwell, 1979.

Escher, M. C. *The Graphic Work of M. C. Escher*. Duell, Sloan and Pearce, 1961.

Etchemendy, John. *Tarski, Model Theory, and Logical Truth*. Ph.D. dissertation, Stanford University, 1982.

Feldman, Fred. 'Counterparts', *Journal of Philosophy*, 68 (1971), pp. 406–9.

Field, Hartry. *Science Without Numbers*. Princeton University Press, 1980.

Forbes, Graeme. 'Canonical Counterpart Theory', *Analysis*, 42 (1982), pp. 33–7.

— 'Two Solutions to Chisholm's Paradox', *Philosophical Studies*, 46 (1984), 171–87.

Forrest, Peter. 'Occam's Razor and Possible Worlds', *Monist*, 65 (1982), pp. 456–64.

— 'Ways Worlds Could Be', *Australasian Journal of Philosophy*, 64 (1986).

— and Armstrong, D. M. 'An Argument Against David Lewis' Theory of Possible Worlds', *Australasian Journal of Philosophy*, 62 (1984), pp. 164–8.

Gale, George. 'The Anthropic Principle', *Scientific American*, 245 (1981), No. 6, pp. 154–71.

Geach, Peter. *Reference and Generality*, third edition. Cornell University Press, 1980.

Gibbard, Allan. 'Contingent Identity', *Journal of Philosophical Logic*, 4 (1975), pp. 187–222.

Glymour, Clark. 'On Some Patterns of Reduction', *Philosophy of Science*, 37 (1970), pp. 340–53.

Goodman, Nelson. *The Structure of Appearance*. Harvard University Press, 1951.

Grandy, Richard. 'Reference, Meaning and Belief', *Journal of Philosophy*, 70 (1973), pp. 439-52.

Haack, Susan. 'Lewis' Ontological Slum', *Review of Metaphysics*, 33 (1977), pp. 415-29.

Hazen, Allen. 'Expressive Completeness in Modal Languages', *Journal of Philosophical Logic*, 5 (1976), pp. 25-46.

— *The Foundations of Modal Logic*. Ph.D. dissertation, University of Pittsburgh, 1977.

— 'Counterpart-Theoretic Semantics for Modal Logic', *Journal of Philosophy*, 76 (1979), pp. 319-38.

— 'One of the Truths about Actuality', *Analysis*, 39 (1977), pp. 1-3.

Hilbert, David. Über das Unendliche', *Mathematische Annalen*, 95 (1926), pp. 161-90: translated in *Philosophy of Mathematics: Selected Readings*, second edition, ed. by Paul Benacerraf and Hilary Putnam, Cambridge University Press, 1983.

Hilpinen, Risto. 'Approximate Truth and Truthlikeness', in *Formal Methods in the Philosophy of the Empirical Sciences*, ed. by M. Przełecki, Reidel, 1976.

Hintikka, Jaakko. 'Quantifiers in Deontic Logic', *Societas Scientiarum Fennica, Commenationes Humanarum Litterarum*, 23 (1957), No. 4.

— *Knowledge and Belief*. Cornell University Press, 1962.

— *Models for Modalities: Selected Essays*. Reidel, 1969.

— *The Intentions of Intentionality and Other New Models for Modalities*. Reidel, 1975.

Hunter, Graeme, and Seager, William, 'The Discreet Charm of Counterpart Theory', *Analysis*, 41 (1983), pp. 73-6.

Jackson, Frank, 'A Causal Theory of Counterfactuals', *Australasian Journal of Philosophy*, 55 (1977), pp. 3-21.

Jeffrey, Richard C. *The Logic of Decision*. McGraw-Hill, 1965; second edition, University of Chicago Press, 1983.

Johnston, Mark. *Particulars and Persistence*. Ph.D. dissertation, Princeton University, 1983.

Kanger, Stig. *Provability in Logic*. Almqvist and Wiksell, 1957.

Kaplan, David. 'How to Russell a Frege-Church', *Journal of Philosophy*, 72 (1975), pp. 716-29; reprinted in Loux, *The Possible and the Actual*.

— 'Transworld Heir Lines', in Loux, *The Possible and the Actual*.

Kim, Jaegwon. 'Psychophysical Supervenience', *Philosophical Studies*, 41 (1982), pp. 51-70.

Kratzer, Angelika. 'What "Must" and "Can" Must and Can Mean', *Linguistics and Philosophy*, 1 (1977), pp. 337-55.

Kripke, Saul. 'A Completeness Theorem in Modal Logic', *Journal of Symbolic Logic*, 24 (1959), pp. 1-14.

— 'Semantical Considerations on Modal Logic', *Acta Philosophica Fennica*, 16 (1963), pp. 83-94; reprinted in *Reference and Modality*, ed. by Leonard Linsky, Oxford University Press, 1971.

— 'A Puzzle about Belief', in *Meaning and Use*, ed. by Avishai Margalit, Reidel, 1979.

— *Naming and Necessity.* Harvard University Press (1980); previously printed (except for the preface) in *Semantics for Natural Language*, ed. by Donald Davidson and Gilbert Harman, Reidel, 1972.

Leonard, Henry S., and Goodman, Nelson. 'The Calculus of Individuals and Its Uses', *Journal of Symbolic Logic*, 5 (1940), pp. 45–55.

Leslie, John. 'Observership in Cosmology: the Anthropic Principle', *Mind*, 92 (1983), pp. 573–9.

Lewis, C. I. 'The Modes of Meaning', *Philosophy and Phenomenological Research*, 4 (1944), pp. 236–49.

Lewis, C. S. *Studies in Words.* Cambridge University Press, 1960.

Lewis, David. 'An Argument for the Identity Theory', *Journal of Philosophy*, 63 (1966), pp. 17–25; reprinted in Lewis, *Philosophical Papers*, volume I.

— 'Counterpart Theory and Quantified Modal Logic', *Journal of Philosophy*, 65 (1968), pp. 113–26; reprinted in Loux, *The Possible and the Actual* and, with added postscripts, in Lewis, *Philosophical Papers*, volume I.

— 'Anselm and Actuality', *Noûs* 4 (1970), pp. 175–88; reprinted, with added postscripts, in Lewis, *Philosophical Papers*, volume I.

— 'General Semantics', *Synthese*, 22 (1970), pp. 18–67; reprinted, with added postscripts, in Lewis, *Philosophical Papers*, volume I.

— 'Counterparts of Persons and Their Bodies', *Journal of Philosophy*, 68 (1971), pp. 203–11; reprinted in Lewis, *Philosophical Papers*, volume I.

— *Counterfactuals.* Blackwell, 1973.

— 'Survival and Identity', in *The Identities of Persons*, ed. by Amélie O. Rorty, University of California Press, 1976; reprinted, with added postscripts, in Lewis, *Philosophical Papers*, volume I.

— 'Scorekeeping in a Language Game', *Journal of Philosophical Logic*, 8 (1979), pp. 339–59; reprinted in Lewis, *Philosophical Papers*, volume I.

— 'Attitudes *De Dicto* and *De Se*', *Philosophical Review*, 88 (1979), pp. 513–43; reprinted, with added postscripts, in Lewis, *Philosophical Papers*, volume I.

— 'Index, Context, and Content', in *Philosophy and Grammar*, ed. by Stig Kanger and Sven Öhman, Reidel, 1981.

— 'Ordering Semantics and Premise Semantics for Counterfactuals', *Journal of Philosophical Logic*, 10 (1981), pp. 217–34.

— 'Logic for Equivocators', *Noûs*, 16 (1982), pp. 431–41.

— *Philosophical Papers*, (two volumes). Oxford University Press, 1983 and 1986.

— 'New Work for a Theory of Universals', *Australasian Journal of Philosophy*, 61 (1983), pp. 343–77.

— 'Extrinsic Properties', *Philosophical Studies*, 44 (1983), pp. 197–200.

— 'Individuation by Acquaintance and by Stipulation', *Philosophical Review*, 92 (1983), pp. 3–32.

— 'Putnam's Paradox', *Australasian Journal of Philosophy*, 62 (1984), pp. 221–36.

— 'Against Structural Universals', *Australasian Journal of Philosophy*, 64 (1986).

— 'Causal Explanation', in Lewis, *Philosophical Papers*, volume II.

— 'Events', in Lewis, *Philosophical Papers*, volume II.

Loux, Michael. *The Possible and the Actual: Readings in the Metaphysics of Modality.* Cornell University Press, 1979.

Lycan, William. 'The Trouble with Possible Worlds', in Loux, *The Possible and the Actual.*

McGinn, Colin. 'Modal Reality', in *Reduction, Time and Reality*, ed. by Richard Healy, Cambridge University Press, 1981.

McMichael, Alan. 'A Problem for Actualism about Possible Worlds', *Philosophical Review*, 92 (1983), pp. 49–66.

— 'A New Actualist Modal Semantics', *Journal of Philosophical Logic*, 12 (1983), pp. 73–99.

Meinong, Alexius. Über Gegenstandstheorie', translated in *Realism and the Background of Phenomenology*, ed. by Roderick M. Chisholm, Free Press, 1960.

Miller, David. 'Popper's Qualitative Theory of Verisimilitude', *British Journal for the Philosophy of Science*, 25 (1974), pp. 166–77.

Mondadori, Fabrizio. 'Counterpartese, Counterpartese*, Counterpartese$_D$' *Histoire, Epistémologie, Langage*, 5 (1983), pp. 69–94.

Montague, Richard. 'Logical Necessity, Physical Necessity, Ethics, and Quantifiers', *Inquiry*, 3 (1960), pp. 259–69; reprinted in Montague, *Formal Philosophy.*

— *Formal Philosophy: Selected Papers of Richard Montague.* Yale University Press, 1974.

Nagel, Thomas. 'The Objective Self', in *Mind and Knowledge: Essays in Honor of Norman Malcolm*, ed. by Carl Ginet and Sydney Shoemaker, Oxford University Press, 1983.

Nerlich, Graham. *The Shape of Space.* Cambridge University Press, 1976.

Niven, Larry. 'All the Myriad Ways', *Galaxy* (1968); reprinted in Niven, *All the Myriad Ways*, Ballantine Books, 1971.

Nock, O. S. *History of the Great Western Railway*, volume III. Ian Allan, 1967.

Perry, John. 'Can the Self Divide?' *Journal of Philosophy*, 69 (1972), pp. 463–88.

Plantinga, Alvin. 'Transworld Identity or Worldbound Individuals?' in *Logic and Ontology*, ed. by Milton Munitz, New York University Press (1973); reprinted in Loux, *The Possible and the Actual.*

— *The Nature of Necessity.* Oxford University Press, 1974.

— 'Actualism and Possible Worlds', *Theoria*, 42 (1976), pp. 139–60; reprinted in Loux, *The Possible and the Actual.*

Popper, Karl. 'Truth, Rationality, and the Growth of Scientific Knowledge', in Popper, *Conjectures and Refutations*, Routledge and Kegan Paul, 1963.

Prior, Arthur N. *Past, Present and Future.* Clarendon, 1967.

— *Objects of Thought.* Clarendon, 1971.

— and Fine, Kit. *Worlds, Times, and Selves.* Duckworth, 1977.

Quine, Willard Van Orman. 'Propositional Objects' in Quine, *Ontological Relativity and Other Essays*, Columbia University Press, 1969.

— 'Worlds Away', *Journal of Philosophy*, 73 (1976), pp. 859–63; reprinted in Quine, *Theories and Things*, Harvard University Press, 1981.

Ramsey, Frank P. 'Theories', in Ramsey, *The Foundations of Mathematics*, Routledge and Kegan Paul, 1931; and in Ramsey, *Foundations*, Routledge and Kegan Paul, 1978.

Richards, Tom. 'The Worlds of David Lewis', *Australasian Journal of Philosophy*, 53 (1975), pp. 105–18.

Robinson, Denis. *The Metaphysics of Material Constitution*. Ph.D. dissertation, Monash University, 1982.

Roper, Andrew. 'Toward an Eliminative Reduction of Possible Worlds', *The Philosophical Quarterly*, 32 (1982), pp. 45–59.

Salmon, Nathan. *Reference and Essence*. Princeton University Press, 1981.

Schlesinger, George N. 'Possible Worlds and the Mystery of Existence', *Ratio*, 26 (1984), pp. 1–17.

Sciama, Dennis W. 'Issues in Cosmology', in *Some Strangeness in the Proportion: A Centennial Symposium to Celebrate the Achievements of Albert Einstein*, ed. by Harry Woolf, Addison-Wesley, 1980.

Scriven, Michael. 'The Key Property of Physical Laws – Inaccuracy', in *Current Issues in the Philosophy of Science*, ed. by Herbert Feigl and Grover Maxwell, Holt, Rinehart and Winston, 1961.

Shoemaker, Sydney. 'Causality and Properties', in *Time and Cause: Essays presented to Richard Taylor*, ed. by Peter van Inwagen, Reidel, 1980.

Skyrms, Brian. 'Possible Worlds, Physics and Metaphysics', *Philosophical Studies*, 30 (1976), pp. 323–32.

— 'Tractarian Nominalism', *Philosophical Studies*, 40 (1981), pp. 199–206.

Slote, Michael. *Metaphysics and Essence*. Blackwell, 1975.

Smart, J. J. C. *Ethics, Persuasion and Truth*. Routledge and Kegan Paul, 1984.

Stalnaker, Robert. 'A Theory of Conditionals', in *Studies in Logical Theory*, ed. by Nicholas Rescher, Blackwell, 1968.

— 'Possible Worlds', *Noûs*, 10 (1976), pp. 65–75; reprinted in Loux, *The Possible and the Actual*.

— *Inquiry*. MIT Press, 1984.

Stenius, Eric. 'Sets', *Synthese*, 27 (1974), pp. 161–88.

Stout, G. F. 'Are the Characteristics of Particular Things Universal or Particular?' *Proceedings of the Aristotelian Society*, supplementary volume 3 (1923), pp. 114–22.

Swoyer, Chris. 'The Nature of Natural Laws', *Australasian Journal of Philosophy*, 60 (1982), pp. 203–23.

Teller, Paul. 'A Poor Man's Guide to Supervenience and Determination', *Southern Journal of Philosophy*, supplement to volume 22 (1984), pp. 137–62.

Thomason, Richmond. 'Modal Logic and Metaphysics', in *The Logical Way of Doing Things*, ed. by Karel Lambert, Yale University Press, 1969.

Tichý, Pavel. 'On Popper's Definitions of Verisimilitude', *British Journal for the Philosophy of Science*, 25 (1974), pp. 155–60.

Unger, Peter. 'Minimizing Arbitrariness: Toward a Metaphysics of Infinitely Many Isolated Concrete Worlds', *Midwest Studies in Philosophy*, 9 (1984), pp. 29–51.

van Fraassen, Bas C. 'The Only Necessity is Verbal Necessity', *Journal of Philosophy*, 74 (1977), pp. 71–85.

van Inwagen, Peter. 'Indexicality and Actuality', *Philosophical Review*, 89 (1980), pp. 403–26.

— 'The Doctrine of Arbitrary Undetached Parts', *Pacific Philosophical Quarterly*, 62 (1981), pp. 123–37.

— *An Essay on Free Will*. Clarendon, 1983.

— 'Plantinga on Trans-World Identity', in *Alvin Plantinga: A Profile*, ed. by James Tomberlin and Peter van Inwagen, Reidel, 1985.

Wiggins, David. 'On Being in the Same Place at the Same Time', *Philosophical Review*, 77 (1968), pp. 90–5.

Williams, Donald C. 'On the Elements of Being', *Review of Metaphysics*, 7 (1953), pp. 3–18 and 171–92; reprinted in Williams, *Principles of Empirical Realism*, Charles Thomas, 1966.

— 'Dispensing with Existence', *Journal of Philosophy*, 59 (1962), pp. 748–63.

— 'Necessary Facts', *Review of Metaphysics*, 16 (1963), pp. 601–26.

Index

Printed and bound by CPI Group (UK) Ltd, Croydon, CR0 4YY

22/02/2023

03194221-0001